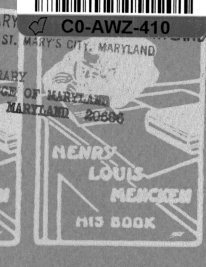

HENRY
LOUIS
MENCKEN
HIS BOOK

HENRY
LOUIS
MENCKEN
HIS BOOK

HENRY
LOUIS
MENCKEN
HIS BOOK

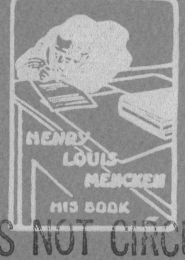

HENRY
LOUIS
MENCKEN
HIS BOOK

HENRY
LOUIS
MENCKEN
HIS BOOK

HENRY
LOUIS
MENCKEN
HIS BOOK

HENRY
LOUIS
MENCKEN
HIS BOOK

HENRY
LOUIS
MENCKEN
HIS BOOK

HENRY
LOUIS
MENCKEN
HIS BOOK

H. L. M.

H. L. M.

THE MENCKEN
BIBLIOGRAPHY

Compiled by
BETTY ADLER

with the assistance of
JANE WILHELM

Published for The Enoch Pratt Free Library
on the occasion of its 75th Anniversary

THE JOHNS HOPKINS PRESS, BALTIMORE

Library of Congress Catalog Card Number 61 - 15699

THIS BOOK HAS BEEN BROUGHT TO PUBLICATION WITH THE
ASSISTANCE OF A GRANT FROM THE FORD FOUNDATION.

FOREWORD

Since the death of Henry L. Mencken in 1956 interest in his work, among scholars and the reading public, has been growing from year to year. Three volumes of hitherto uncollected articles have appeared; there have been new paperback editions of earlier works, a volume of his letters, and a selection from his notebooks, entitled *Minority Report*. The work of recent years, critical and biographical, listed in this bibliography offers conclusive evidence of the permanence of his reputation.

It is fitting that this volume should appear as a seventy-fifth anniversary publication of the Enoch Pratt Library. Mencken was a life-long resident of Baltimore and a loyal friend and user of its public library. More than a decade before his death he expressed his intention of giving the Pratt Library the greater part of his books and manuscripts. Frequent additions to his initial gifts were received during his lifetime, and further additions of books and documents have been made by his brother, August Mencken. The chief features of the collection at present are: practically all of H. L. Mencken's typed manuscripts; his published works in all their editions and translations; more than a hundred volumes of his personal clipping books; family documents, portraits, and memorabilia; and several thousand of the most valuable and interesting volumes from his library. The bulk of his vast literary and professional correspondence was bequeathed to the New York Public Library.

The Pratt Mencken collection is housed in an attractive room on the third floor of the Central Library. By the terms of the bequest it may be used only by authors and scholars doing advanced research. The large collection of Menckeniana in the Library's subject departments is quite adequate to fill the requests of students and readers.

FOREWORD

The cataloging of the large and varied collection of manuscripts, books, pamphlets, and periodicals gathered in the Mencken Room was made possible by the generous contributions of friends of Mencken, of the Deiches Funds, and of August Mencken. The continuing support of the Mencken family has also provided for special custodians to supervise the use of the room.

With these rich resources it is not surprising that the Pratt Library has become a center of Mencken studies. The room has been visited since its opening, April 17, 1956, by scores of journalists, authors, and scholars, from this country and abroad. An even greater number have requested specific information or help in research through correspondence.

Research activities and countless queries of a more ephemeral nature have underlined the need for an exhaustive bibliography of works by and about H. L. Mencken. August Mencken initiated the project and generously offered to sponsor it. Preliminary work had been done by H. L. Mencken's former secretary, Mrs. Rosalind C. Lohrfinck, who listed the contents of the many bound volumes of Mencken's manuscripts, newspaper work, and magazine articles —also the almost incredible record of his thousands of book reviews.

The compilation of the *The Mencken Bibliography* was entrusted to Miss Betty Adler, an experienced librarian and free-lance writer. Her work on a catalog of the Mencken Room and her long-time interest in the subject have admirably fitted her for the task. Miss Jane Wilhelm, who compiled the section on Mencken's newspaper work, assisted for several years in the arrangement and research use of the collection, as a member of the staff of the Library's Literature Department. Using the Mencken collection, the general collections of the Pratt Library, plus the resources of many other large public, college, and university libraries, the compilers have worked for three years on the task of running to earth every item worth recording concerned with the man Mencken and his work as author, critic, newspaperman, philologist, or editor. The Library is grateful to Miss Mary N. Barton, distinguished reference librarian and bibliographer, for her advice and her painstaking review of the manuscript from the viewpoint of bibliographic form.

FOREWORD

No matter how prolonged or conscientious the effort, a bibliography of the scope of this one is never finally completed nor entirely accurate. The compilers and the Library will welcome additions and corrections. The study of H. L. Mencken and his world will never be a closed book.

July, 1961

Richard Hart, Head
Literature and Language Department
Enoch Pratt Free Library

PREFACE

This bibliography attempts to present a detailed picture of H. L. Mencken's work as author, journalist and editor. The first part, devoted to his own writings, is inclusive; the second part, devoted to opinions about his work and personality, is selective. The selection was based on importance and length of material, never on partiality towards the subject. A man who spent his life fighting for freedom of expression, denouncing censorship and who could enjoy publishing a *Schimpflexikon* would have been the first to object to exclusion on the basis of unfavorable criticism. We have, however, excluded anthologies. Mencken's books are available in most libraries, and the essays, chapters or sections reprinted in standard anthologies are readily located in the *Essay and General Literature Index*. We have frequently indicated in the annotation where a specific article is reprinted.

H. L. Mencken's foresight in gathering most of what he wrote and what was written about him, greatly facilitated the work and added to its inclusiveness. He had this material bound into elegant blue morocco scrapbooks, and furnished most of them with a typed preface. Whenever possible, this unpublished material has been used in the explanatory notes. No other manuscript material is listed.

I wish to publicly express my thanks to Mr. August Mencken, whose generosity made this work possible; to Mr. Richard Hart for reading the manuscript; to Miss Mary N. Barton, who was always willing to advise, counsel and guide, generously sharing her bibliographic knowledge; to the Maryland Department and the entire staff of the Reference Department of the Enoch Pratt Free Library, who did not simply answer questions, but eagerly and joyously offered to "dig" for the seemingly unfindable; to Mr. A. Aubrey Bodine, who, in memory of his friend, donated the

PREFACE

use of the photograph of HLM in his study on Hollins Street; to Mr. Leo Martin, head of the Library's Print Shop, for the line drawing of Mencken's press badge that appears at the beginning of "Newspaper Work"; and to dozens of librarians who answered requests for bibliographic citations of their organization's periodicals.

I hope future students, for whom this work is primarily intended, will enjoy using the bibliography as much as I have enjoyed compiling it.

Betty Adler

TABLE OF CONTENTS

H. L. M.

BIBLIOGRAPHIES

1920

HENDERSON, F. C., *pseud*. Bibliography. *In* H. L. Mencken: Fanfare, by Burton Rascoe; The American Critic, by Vincent O'Sullivan; Bibliography, by F. C. Henderson. New York, Knopf, 1920. p. 21–32.

HLM compiled the first published bibliography of his work. "F. C. Henderson was the falseface of H.L.M. As I recall it, someone else was to have done that brief bibliography. He failed, at the last moment, so I had to spit on my own lily-white hands and tackle the job." HLM (*See* Swan, p. 108–109, below, 1950.)

1923

MOSS, DAVID, *comp*. American First Editions . . . a series of Bibliographic Checklists, no. 31. H. L. (Henry Lewis [*sic*]) Mencken. Publisher's Weekly 102: 1327–1328, April 28, 1923.

1924

FREY, CARROLL. A Bibliography of the Writings of H. L. Mencken, with a foreword by H. L. Mencken. Philadelphia, The Centaur Bookshop, 1924. 70 p. front. (port. by Willem Wirtz), ports., facsims.

One of the series of Centaur Bibliographies of American Writers, compiled especially for the collector.

1927

KENNEDY, ARTHUR GARFIELD. A Bibliography of Writings on the English Language from the Beginning of Printing to the End of 1922. Cambridge, Mass., Harvard University Press; New Haven, Yale University Press, 1927.

Nos. 11583 and 11617 list philological articles in the Baltimore *Evening Sun* and New York *Evening Mail*; 11627 and 11637 list reviews of first and second editions of *The American Language*.

BIBLIOGRAPHIES

1929

MANLY, JOHN MATTHEWS and EDITH RICKERT, *eds.* Contemporary American Literature, Bibliographies and Study Outlines. Introduction and revision by Fred B. Millett. New York, Harcourt [1929]. p. 236–239.

Classified listing of HLM's books, as well as books and magazine articles about him.

1939

BURKE, WILLIAM JEREMIAH. The Literature of Slang. New York, The New York Public Library, 1939.

Annotated list of HLM's philological articles and books, and reviews about them. *See* index for various references.

1940

MILLETT, FRED BENJAMIN. Contemporary American Authors, a Critical Survey and 219 Bio-Bibliographies. New York, Harcourt, 1940. p. 480-486.

The section of HLM's books repeats the material in Manly and Rickert (*See* above, 1929) and brings it up to date. "Studies and Articles" about HLM includes mainly material after 1929. Appraisal of the *American Mercury's* influence and scope is given in the "Critical Survey," p. 191–192.

1942

BLANCK, JACOB NATHANIEL. Merle Johnson's American First Editions. 4th ed. rev. and enl. New York, Bowker, 1942. p. 358–361.

Listing of HLM's books.

1947

WEST, HERBERT FAULKNER. The Mind on the Wing; A Book for Readers and Collectors. New York, Coward-McCann, 1947. p. 177–203.

"This check list has been mainly compiled from the Richard H. Mandel Collection in the Dartmouth Library."

1950

SWAN, BRADFORD F. Making a Mencken Collection. Yale University Gazette. 24: 101-113, Jan., 1950.

Article on the collection given to Yale by one of HLM's earliest collectors. Contains many personal observations.

BIBLIOGRAPHIES

1954

LEARY, LEWIS GASTON. Articles on American Literature, 1900-1950. Durham, Duke University Press, 1954. p. 211-213.

Alphabetical author list of magazine articles about HLM.

1957

PORTER, BERNARD H. H. L. Mencken, a Bibliography. [Pasadena, Calif. Geddes Press] 1957. 24 p.

Based on West, *see* above, 1947. Reprinted, minus annotations and comments, in *Twentieth Century Literature* 4: 100-107, Oct., 1958.

1960

INDEX TO ARTICLES ON AMERICAN LITERATURE, 1951–1959, prepared in the Reference Department, University of Pennsylvania Library. Boston, G. K. Hall, 1960. p. 245–246.

Alphabetical list by author of magazine articles about HLM; a continuation of the Leary bibliography; *see* above, 1954.

MODERN LANGUAGE ASSOCIATION OF AMERICA. AMERICAN LITERATURE GROUP. COMMITTEE ON MANUSCRIPT HOLDINGS. American Literary Manuscripts; a Checklist of Holdings in Academic, Historical, and Public Libraries in the United States. Austin, University of Texas Press [1960] p. 252-253.

List of holdings of manuscripts, letters and other primary source material in fifty-three libraries.

WORKS by H. L. MENCKEN

HLM's own words are used as explanatory notes when available. Many are quoted from his typed introductory remarks to his bound volumes of typescripts, and have never been previously published. Their source is indicated as EPFL, followed by the Enoch Pratt Free Library's Mencken Room catalog number for the typescript. Volumes HLM presented to friends, who later gave them to the Library, have the donor's name indicated: Knopf (for Alfred A. Knopf, publisher) or Katz (for Joseph Katz, Baltimore advertising executive).

BOOKS AND PAMPHLETS

1902

LOUDON PARK CEMETERY COMPANY, 1853-1902. [Baltimore, Williams and Wilkins] 15 p. col. front., illus.

"I also, at various times, did jobs for advertisers. I remember very well composing a pamphlet . . . setting forth the comforts of eternal life in its cemetery with great eloquence." HLM, 1925 (EPFL—A29, p. 100)

STIEFF (CHARLES M.), INC. Echoes from the Hub. [Baltimore, 1902] 40 p. illus.

STIEFF (CHARLES M.), INC. A Record of Three Score Years, 1842–1902. [Baltimore, R. S. Read & Son, 1902] 24 p. illus. ports.

STIEFF (CHARLES M.), INC. Stieff Pianos. [Baltimore, 1902] 15 p. illus.

These three advertising pamphlets are all unsigned. The first is sometimes referred to by its Preface "A Word at the Start," p. 1–2.

1903

VENTURES INTO VERSE, Being Various Ballads, Ballades, Rondeaux, Triolets, Songs, Quatrains, Odes and Roundels, All Rescued from the Potters' Field of the Old Files and Here Given Decent Burial (Peace to their Ashes) by Henry Louis Mencken, with illustrations & other things by Charles S. Gordon & John Siegel. Baltimore, Marshall, Beck & Gordon, 1903. 40 p. illus.

Forty poems most of which were written between 1896 and 1900, reprinted from the *Bookman, Leslie's Weekly, Life, The New England Magazine, The National Magazine* and the Baltimore *Herald* (Oct. 28, Nov. 8, 11, 18, Dec. 9, 16, 30, 1900, and Jan. 20, Feb. 10, 1901). "My first book was the product of the desire of the printers to display their craftsmanship. At the time, 1903, I was no longer writing verse. . . . My newspaper work was so heavy and I began to be so much more interested in prose that I abandoned versifying before I was twenty-three years old." HLM (EPFL—A29, p. 123–125). One hundred copies issued. A facsimile edition of 250 copies was issued by Smith's Book Store, Baltimore, 1960.

1905

GEORGE BERNARD SHAW: HIS PLAYS. Boston, Luce, 1905. 107 p.

"Brentano had just begun to print Shaw's plays in America and I was immediately interested in them. I therefore proposed to Brentano that he let me write a book upon them somewhat like Shaw's 'Quintessence of Ibsen'; when he declined the offer, I turned to John W. Luce & Company of Boston, who had just printed Shaw's 'On Going to Church.' . . . I delivered the manuscript to Schaff on April 11, 1905, and the book was published the following Autumn. It was the first book on Shaw ever printed. . . . The book was printed from type, and when it got out of print no further printing was possible." HLM (EPFL—A29, p. 125, 137)

1908

THE PHILOSOPHY OF FRIEDRICH NIETZSCHE. Boston, Luce, 1908. xiii, 325 p. front. (port.)

"Schaff suggested that I do a volume on Nietzsche, who was then beginning to be talked about in America though still vaguely. This I think was in 1906. At the time I knew next to nothing about Nietzsche myself, but the project interested me, and I immediately began to seek light. In the Enoch Pratt Free Library in Baltimore I found a complete set of Nietzsche's works in German and also a copy of the biography of him by his sister. I undertook the formidable job of reading all this stuff. . . . It took me a year to write it." HLM (EPFL—A29, p. 125–126)

Reissued in London in 1908 by Fisher Unwin, from the American plates, with "Books and Articles about Nietzsche" omitted, although not deleted from the Table of Contents, (xiii, 321 p. port.).

The second edition was actually a reprinting. The third edition (Boston, Luce, 1913. xiii, 304 p.) included a new "Preface to the Third Edition" and changes in the section "Nietzsche, the Prophet."

1912

THE ARTIST, A DRAMA WITHOUT WORDS. Boston, Luce, 1912. 33 p.

Reprinted from *The Bohemian Magazine* 17: 805–808, Dec., 1909 (Bo-
hemiana). Later reprinted in *Smart Set* 49: 79–84, Aug., 1916; in *A Book of
Burlesques,* 1916 and thereafter; and translated into Spanish by Gonzalo G.
de Mello as "El Virtuoso, Drama Mudo" in *Social* (Habana) 11: 51, 92, Oct.,
1926.

Other editions: *The Artist, a Satire in One Act* (New York, Lane, 1917. 12
p.) an acting version; *The Artist, a Drama Without Words* (New York,
French, 1920. 14 p.) "reprinted from *A Book of Burlesques,* c. 1916, 1920 . . ."

1914

THE OLD *Sun* AIN'T WHAT SHE USED TO BE. [2] p.

Reprinted from the Baltimore *Sun,* Oct. 13, 1914.

1915

THE SMART SET. A Note to Authors. 1915. 7 p.

A policy statement, indicating aims, interests and needs of the magazine for
those submitting novelettes, short stories, plays and poetry.

THE SMART SET. [Rejection Notice] 1915. [4] p.

Pamphlet used as rejection slip, listing twelve items of "Don't Send Us,"
and eight of "What We Want."

THE SMART SET. Suggestions to Our Visitors. [Baltimore, 1915?]
[4] p.

Twenty-six policy statements "issued as a jocosity by Nathan and me.
We thought so little of it that we hesitated to saddle the *Smart Set* with
the cost of it; I had it printed in Baltimore and shared the expense. I
wrote nearly all of it." HLM (EPFL—A29, p. 142). Reprinted in *The
Theatre of George Jean Nathan,* by Isaac Goldberg (New York, Simon, 1926.
p. 71–73).

1916

A BOOK OF BURLESQUES (Opus 12). New York, Lane, 1916. 253 p.

"These pieces cover 3 or 4 years and are chiefly reprinted, though with
many changes, from the *Smart Set,* the *Bohemian,* and the Baltimore *Evening
Sun.* 'The Artist' is included by arrangement with Messrs. John W. Luce
& Co., of Boston, who published it separately."—Prefatory note.

Other editions: New York, Knopf, 1920. 237 p. "Includes some epigrams
from *A Little Book in C Major.* . . . To make room for them several
of the smaller sketches in the first edition have been omitted."—(Chaps. xi,
xii,xiv,xv). "Nearly the whole contents of the book appeared originally in
the *Smart Set.*"—Preface. New rev. ed. Second printing, April, 1920. "The
printing of this Third Edition offers a chance to include several things
omitted from two earlier editions. But in general it is identical with the

second edition."—Preface. Third printing, (again revised) August, 1920. Contains a slightly different "Preface to the Third Edition." Fourth printing again revised) December, 1921. 239 p. Contains slight textual changes, and a new "Preface to the Fourth Edition." English edition issued by Jonathan Cape, 1923. 239 p. Reprinted from the American plates of the fourth printing, 1921. Fifth printing (again revised) November, 1924. Identical text as fourth printing, but Preface omitted. Knopf also issued it as a Borzoi Pocket Book.

THE CREED OF A NOVELIST. New York, 1916. 16 p.

Reprinted from the *Smart Set* 50: 138–143, Oct., 1916. HLM's review of Dreiser's *A Hoosier Holiday* issued by John Lane Co. to advertise the book. The pamphlet is enclosed in a replica of the book jacket.

A LITTLE BOOK IN C MAJOR (Opus 11). New York, Lane, 1916. 79 p.

"Nearly all the epigrams (226) in this little volume were first printed in the *Smart Set*. For some reason I don't recall 'Opus 10' was changed to 'Opus 11' on the title page of the book. It was published by the American branch of the John Lane Company in 1916, and had only a small sale. . . . The musical quotation following the title page—it is the first phrase of the German soldiers' song, 'Ich hatt' einen Kameraden': 'I had a comrade'—is the nearest thing to a dedication that I have ever printed in any of my books. It was addressed to Theodor Hemberger, a German friend in Baltimore, who taught me a great deal about music, and with whom I was in constant association during the difficult days of the World War." HLM, 1937 (EPFL—A97)

1917

A BOOK OF PREFACES (OPUS 13). New York, Knopf, 1917. 283 p.

Contents: Joseph Conrad; Theodore Dreiser; James Huneker; Puritanism as a Literary Force.

Other editions: Second (revised) edition, 1918. 288 p. Slight textual changes, original Preface replaced by "Preface to Second Edition," index added. In 1919, a four page publicity announcement consisting mainly of excerpts from review in *Mercure de France*, Jan. 16, 1919, was issued. [Third edition, 1920] Same as second (revised) edition but with a new "Preface to Third Edition." Fourth printing, January, 1922. 236 p. Minor changes, and a new "Preface to Fourth Printing." It was used by Jonathan Cape, London, for the English edition of 288 p. All subsequent printings are the same. Issued in 1928 by Knopf as a Borzoi Pocket Book, reprint of the fifth printing, February, 1924.

IRELAND: HER BOOKS. New York, Lane, 1917. 8 p.

Reprinted from the Baltimore *Evening Sun*, Nov. 10, 1916. HLM's review of Ernest A. Boyd's *Ireland's Literary Renaissance* was issued by the John Lane Co. as advertisement for the book.

VIRTUOSI OF VIRTUE. 1917. [8] p.

Reprint from the *Chicago Sunday Tribune*, Dec. 2, 1917.

1918

DAMN! A BOOK OF CALUMNY. New York, Philip Goodman, 1918.
103 p.

"Goodman was an advertising man who had a hankering for the publishing business. At the same time [as *In Defense of Women*] he brought out a little book of mine . . . also made up largely of reprints from the *Smart Set*. His publishing venture failed and he turned to theatrical producing, at which, after a few successes, he also failed." HLM, 1937 (EPFL—A89). The book was twice reprinted, though called editions, without change. The fourth edition consists of ix, 139 p. with slight changes in text and a preface added. "Opus 14" appears only on the slip cover. Alfred A. Knopf, when he became HLM's publisher, persuaded him to drop the Opus numbering. He issued it under title *A Book of Calumny* in 1918, using the text as fourth edition, but with Preface omitted.

IN DEFENSE OF WOMEN. New York, Ppilip [*sic*] Goodman, 1918.
218 p.

" . . . this little book was begun on February 4, 1918, and finished later, on March 15. It made such rapid progress mainly because substantial parts of it had been printed previously in the *Smart Set*, of which I had become co-editor since 1914. Aside from my light work for the magazine, I had little to do during 1918, for the United States was engaged in the World War at the time, and the censorship prevented me doing any considerable writing for newspapers. I was unable to print my views of Wilson and his warlocks, which was a very low one, and I refused to engage in patriotic whooping. Thus I had to devote myself to neutral matters. After finishing *In Defense of Women*, I began work on *The American Language*, giving most of the Spring and Summer of 1918 to it. Toward the end of the year I made my translation of Nietzsche's *Der Antichrist*." HLM, 1937 (EPFL—A89)

A second edition, actually another printing, was issued with the publisher's name correctly spelled, and "Opus 15" printed on title page. "His sales of *In Defense of Women* were very small—as I recall them, under 1000. In 1919 [*sic*] the book was taken over by Alfred A. Knopf, who first bound up and published Goodman's unused sheets and then reset the book. I revised it in 1922. . . . It began to sell steadily after that, and by June, 1928, it had reached its eleventh printing." HLM, *ibid*.

Various editions: New York, Knopf, 1918. 218 p., *see* annotation above; in 1922 Knopf issued it as v. 6 of the Free Lance Books (xviii, 219 p.) and all subsequent editions contain this Introduction, though with minor changes. In the same year it was issued as A Star Book (Garden City Publishing Company, 1922. xvi, 210 p.).

The first English edition of *In Defence of Women*, with the English spelling of "defence" in title, appeared in 1923 (London, Cape. 233 p.) In the same year there was also a German edition, *Verteidigung der Frau*, Übertragen von Franz Blei (München, Müller, 1923. 360 p. Die Bücherei der Abtei Thelem; begründet von Otto Julius Bierbaum).

Knopf issued a "Revised, reset, and republished . . . Ninth printing, March 1927" (xvi, 210 p.) which omitted p. xvi-xviii of prior Introduction. In London, Cape reissued in 1927 their 1923 publication, but made it part of

BOOKS AND PAMPHLETS

The Travellers' Library series. It was issued in Leipzig by Tauchnitz in English (*In Defence of Women*. Copyright edition. 255 p. Collection of British Authors. Tauchnitz edition, v. 4782).

The following year it appeared in Hungarian: *A Nők Védelmében!* Forditotta Dr. Fekete Oszkar, bevezette Dr. Juhász Andor (Budapest, Révai Kiadás, 1928. 230 p. Világ Könyvtár). Finally, the most translated of all of HLM's works appeared in French, *Défense des Femmes* (*In Defence of Women*). Préface de Paul Morand. Traduit de l'anglais par Jean Jardin. (Paris, Gallimard, 1934. 204 p.)

MR. CABELL OF VIRGINIA. New York, McBride [1918] 1 *l.* folded as 8 p.

Reprinted from the New York *Evening Mail*, July 3, 1918. Issued as advertisement for James Branch Cabell's books by Robert McBride & Co.

1919

THE AMERICAN LANGUAGE; a Preliminary Inquiry into the Development of English in the United States. New York, Knopf, 1919. x, 374 p.

"It was probably written in 1915 or 1916. Part of it was picked up from . . . 'The American: his language,' published in the Smart Set [40: 89–96, Aug., 1913]. The opening became the opening of the first edition. . . . Knopf and I were in fear that there would only be a small public waiting for such a book, so the first edition was limited to 1500 copies. It sold out at once, and brought a great many letters from readers. I proceeded at once to a revision of the book." HLM (EPFL—A2)

Other editions and supplements:

Second edition, rev. and enl., 1921. xvii, 492 p. "Nearly every page shows changes . . . Especially in the first chapter and chapters on Tendencies in American, American and English Today, American Spelling, and Proper Names in American there are summaries of much new matter. The discussion of foreign languages in the United States . . . is new, as well as Preface to the Revised Edition."—Preface. This revised edition was published in England by Cape in 1922.

Third edition, rev. and enl., 1923. ix, 489 p. " . . . extensively revised. I have added new material to nearly every chapter, and all of them have been diligently scrutinized for errors."—Preface to Third Edition. Previous prefaces to first and second editions are omitted. A German translation was based on this edition: *Die Amerikanische Sprache* (*das Englisch der Vereinigten Staaten*). Deutsch bearbeitet von Heinrich Spies (Leipzig, Teubner, 1927. viii, 176 p. port.).

Fourth edition corrected, enl. and rewritten, 1936. xi, 767, xxix p. " . . . a complete reworking, following to some extent outlines of the earlier editions, but with many additions and a number of emendations and shortenings . . . also modifies the thesis they set forth . . ."—Preface to the Fourth Edition. It was published in England by Kegan, Paul, Trench, Trubner. A Braille edition in fourteen volumes is available in the Library of Congress, Division for the Blind.

WORKS BY H. L. M.

Supplement I. 1945. xv, 739, xxxv p. " . . . not a new edition . . . and repeats only a small and inconsiderable amount of the matter in the fourth edition . . . [Supplements] *The American Language,* fourth edition, through Chapter VI."—Preface. Knopf received the fourth Carey-Thomas Award, Jan. 24, 1946, for the book's "handling and publishing."

Supplement II. 1948. xiii, 890, xliii p. Follows plan of *Supplement I* for chapter VII–XIII.

The entire set is published by Routledge, London, and McClelland, Toronto.

PREJUDICES: FIRST SERIES. New York, Knopf, 1919. 254 p.

Contents: Criticism of Criticism of Criticism; The Late Mr. Wells; Arnold Bennett; The Dean; Professor Veblen; The New Poetry Movement; The Heir of Mark Twain; Hermann Sudermann; George Ade; The Butte Bashkirtseff; Six Members of the Institute; The Genealogy of Etiquette; The American Magazine; The Ulster Polonius; An Unheeded Law-Giver; The Blushful Mystery; George Jean Nathan; Portrait of an Immortal Soul; Jack London; Among the Avatars; Three American Immortals.

"My 'Prejudices' books were largely made up of reprints from magazines and newspapers—mainly the *Smart Set* (later the *American Mercury*) and the Baltimore *Evening Sun.* But there was always a great deal of expansion and rewriting . . . The first draft of the one on H. G. Wells got lost and I had to rewrite it—a dreadful job." HLM (EPFL—A162)

Issued in London by Cape in 1921, and by Knopf in 1923 in the Borzoi Pocket Book Series. For the 1924 Christmas gift giving season, Knopf issued first four volumes of *Prejudices* bound in Borzoi style.

1920

THE LITERARY CAPITAL OF THE UNITED STATES. Chicago, 1920. 6 p.

"This essay was first published in the *Nation* of London, April 17, 1920, and reprinted by permission of the Wednesday Book Page of the Chicago *Daily News,* May 12, 1920."

PREJUDICES: SECOND SERIES. New York, Knopf, 1920. 254 p.

Contents: The National Letters; Roosevelt: an Autopsy; The Sahara of the Bozart; The Divine Afflatus; Exeunt Omnes; Scientific Examination of a Popular Virtue; The Allied Arts; The Cult of Hope; The Dry Millenium; Appendix on a Tender Theme.

Issued in London by Cape in 1921. In 1925, Dr. W. H. Bates of New York City printed p. 14–16, "The National Letters: 2. The Answering Fact," as a pamphlet to use as eye exercises to relieve eye strain.

1921

THE SMART SET. A Personal Word. [1921] 14 p.

Description of editorial and business organization of the magazine. It was an attempt to boost circulation, but only resulted in bringing in twenty new ones.

SPIRITUAL AUTOPSIES; an Article on Gamaliel Bradford. New York, Houghton, 1921. 4 p.

Reprinted from the Literary Review of the New York *Evening Post,* HLM's review of Bradford's *American Portraits: 1875–1901* issued by Houghton Mifflin Co. as advertisement for the book.

1922

PREJUDICES: THIRD SERIES. New York, Knopf, 1922. 328 p.

Contents: On Being an American; Huneker: a Memory; Footnote on Criticism; Das Kapital; Ad Imaginem Dei Creavit Illum; Star-Spangled Men; The Poet and his Art; Five Men at Random; The Nature of Liberty; The Novel; The Forward-Looker; Memorial Service; Education; Types of Men; The Dismal Science; Matters of State; Reflections on the Drama; Advice to Young Men; Suite Americaine.

Published in London by Cape in 1923, 329 p.

1923

THE SMART SET. [Announcement of the Relinquishing of the Editorship . . . and Founding The American Mercury.] New York, Oct. 10, 1923. 1 *l.*

1924

PREJUDICES: FOURTH SERIES. New York, Knopf, 1924. 305 p.

Contents: The American Tradition; The Husbandman; High and Ghostly Matters; Justice under Democracy; Reflections on Human Monogamy; The Politician; From a Critic's Notebook; Totentanz; Meditations in the Methodist Desert; Essay in Constructive Criticism; On the Nature of Man; Bugaboo; On Government; Toward a Realistic Aesthetic; Contributions to the Study of Vulgar Psychology; The American Novel; People and Things.

Errata sheet attached to fly leaf. Issued in London by Cape in 1925.

A REVIEW OF "AMERICANISM." 1924. 8 p.

Reprint of HLM's review of W. T. Colyer's *Americanism, a World Menace,* from *Smart Set* 70: 138–140, April, 1924.

1925

H. L. MENCKEN ON *The Nation.* Baltimore, 1925. 2 p.

Opinions on the magazine *The Nation,* reprinted from the Baltimore *Evening Sun,* July 6, 1925.

MY DEAR WALPOLE, an Open Letter from H. L. Mencken. New York, Doran, 1925. [2] p.

Reprinted from *The Bookman* 62: 438–439, Dec., 1925, in answer to Walpole's "My dear Mencken," 62: 246–248, Nov., 1925.

WORKS BY H. L. M.

PREJUDICES. London, Cape, 1925. 256 p. (paperback)

"These essays were all taken from the first four volumes of my *Prejudices*.
. . . In the text itself changes are still few . . . but in the main this book
is a selection, not a revision."—Note. Reissued in hard cover as *Selected
Prejudices* (London, Cape, 1926. 255 p. The Travellers' Library). *Selected
Prejudices: Second Series,* consisting of pieces "first published in various
volumes 1922–1927" was issued the following year (London, Cape, 1927. 223 p.
The Travellers' Library).

THE REWARDS OF VIRTUE. Baltimore, 1925. 6 p.

Reprinted from the Baltimore *Evening Sun,* May 31, 1925.

1926

THE FRIENDS OF THE SALOON. Preliminary Announcement. Bull.
no. 1 (Confidential) n.p. Jan., 1926. 1 *l.*

There was no further publication.

HATRACK CASE. Statement. 1926. 1 *l.* mimeo.

"Private. This statement is not for publication, but it is offered in the
thought that you are interested personally."

NOTES ON DEMOCRACY. New York, Knopf, 1926. v, 212 p.

"I began making notes for it in 1910 or thereabout. The actual writing
began in 1923. But it logged. I resumed it in November, 1925, and finished
it June 3, 1926." HLM, Sept. 12, 1936 (EPFL—A161.1, Knopf). "The text
included some matter picked up from the *Smart Set,* the *American Mercury*
and the Baltimore *Evening Sun,* but most of it was new, and the picked-up
parts were all rewritten.

"Most of the notices of the book were furiously hostile. There was a second
edition [i.e. printing] in November 1926, but after that sales fell off. Knopf
brought out two luxurious forms of the first edition for the collectors who
flourished in those days. One, consisting of 200 copies was bound in figured
paper with a green cloth back and a paper label. The other, consisting of 35
copies, of which only 30 were for sale, was printed on Japan vellum and bound
in vellum." HLM, 1937 (EPFL—A161). Issued in London by Cape, 1927.
224 p.

A German translation *Demokratenspiegel; Übersetzung von Dora S[ophie]
Kellner, mit Lithographien von A. Paul Weber* was issued in Berlin, by
Widerstands Verlag in 1930 (xl, 141 p. front., illus.). "The translator was the
daughter of Professor Leon Kellner of Vienna. She sent a copy of her version
to the former German Kaiser at Doorn, and he was so much pleased with it
that he sent me two photographs of himself, with complimentary inscriptions."
HLM, *ibid.*

PREJUDICES: FIFTH SERIES. New York, Knopf, 1926. 307 p.

Contents: Four Moral Causes; Four Makers of Tales; In Memoriam: W.J.B.;
The Hills of Zion; Beethoven; Rondo on An Ancient Theme; Protestantism
in the Republic; From the Files of a Book Reviewer; The Fringes of Lovely

Letters; Essay in Pedagogy; On Living in Baltimore; The Last New Englander; The Nation; Officers and Gentlemen; Golden Age; Edgar Saltus; Miscellaneous Notes; Catechism.

Issued in London by Cape, 1927. 307 p.

To Friends of the American Mercury, a Statement by the Editor. New York, 1926. 6 p.

An injunction against the Postmaster General, restoring the April issue to the mails, was issued by Judge Mack in the Federal District Court at New York, May 11, 1926. With this is bound: "Commonwealth vs. Mencken, opinion of Justice P. Parmenter," and "The American Mercury *v.* J. Frank Chase *et al.*" 3 p.

1927

Chiropractic. Chicago, 1927. 4 p.

Reprinted from the *Chicago Tribune,* Feb. 13, 1927.

Editorial. New York, April 1927. 3 p.

Reprinted from the *American Mercury* 10: 415-417, April, 1927, and enclosed in replica of magazine cover.

James Branch Cabell. New York, McBride, 1927. 32 p. front. (port.) , facsim.

In 1928 this pamphlet was reissued in hard cover, with slight textual changes and illustrations omitted. 31 p.

Prejudices: Sixth Series. New York, Knopf, 1927. 317 p.

Contents: Journalism in America; From the Memoirs of a Subject of the United States; The Human Mind; Clarion Call to Poets; Souvenirs of a Book Reviewer; Five Little Excursions; Hymn to the Truth; The Pedagogy of Sex; Metropolis; Dives into Quackery; Life under Bureaucracy; In the Rolling Mills; Ambrose Bierce; The Executive Secretary; Invitation to the Dance; Aubade; Appendix from Moronia.

Issued in London by Cape, 1928. 317 p.

Saturnalia. Cleveland, William Feather, 1927.

Reprinted from the Baltimore *Evening Sun,* July 18, 1927.

Selected Prejudices. New York, Knopf, 1927. 166 p.

"These essays are all taken from the first five volumes of my series of *Prejudices* . . . I have made a few changes, but they are of no importance; the collection is a selection, not a revision. A similar selection bearing the same title but in two volumes, is published in England in the Travellers' Library of Mr. Jonathan Cape, my English publisher. But the English and American Collections are not identical."—Note. Reprinted by Modern Library, New York, 1930.

STERLING. San Francisco, Printed by John Henry Nash, 1927. [2] *l.*

A broadside of HLM's tribute to George Sterling, written at the request of J. H. Nash.

1928

EDITORIAL. With This Issue The American Mercury Completes Its Fifth Year. 1928. [8] p.

Reprint of editorial, *American Mercury* 15: 407–410, Dec., 1928.

WHAT MENCKEN THINKS OF EL PASO AND JUAREZ. 1928. [4] p.

Reprint from *El Paso Times,* Oct. 27, 1928.

1929

H. L. MENCKEN'S ESSAYS, selected with notes by Gen Sakuma. Tokyo, Keibundo [1929] 139 p.

Mainly selections from *Prejudices,* chap. IX extracted from *The American Language.*

MR. MENCKEN TO THE BOOK PUBLISHERS. New York, The American Mercury, 1929. 4 p.

"Mr. Mencken's message . . . was in its original state a speech . . . spoken into a recording machine from which a single gramophone record was made."— Preface.

PRÉJUGÉS. Traduction et notes de Régis Michaud. Paris, Boivin, 1929. xix, 296 p. front. (port.) (Écrivains et Penseurs Américains)

Mainly selections from *Prejudices,* with a few selections from *Notes on Democracy, A Book of Prefaces* and *In Defense of Women.*

1930

ANGOFF, CHARLES. A Literary History of the American People. New York, Knopf, 1930. [4] p.

Prepublication announcement and order for the first two volumes.

LO, THE POOR BOOKSELLER. Hollywood, Calif. [Distributed by Stanley Rose, Ltd.] for The Picador Press. 9 p.

Reprint of editorial from the *American Mercury* 21: 151-155, Oct., 1930.

SAMLADE FÖRDOMAR, artiklar och essayer. Urval och översättningar Anna Lenah Elgström och Cid Erik Tallqvist. Förstal av Anna Lenah Elgström. Stockholm, Bonniers, 1930. 273 p.

Selections from *Prejudices.* Introduction describes HLM's place in the cultural development of the United States.

BOOKS AND PAMPHLETS

TREATISE ON THE GODS. New York, London, Knopf, 1930. ix, 363, xii p.

"I recall that I finished it on Thanksgiving night, 1929 . . . The book did very well, and its sales went beyond 13,000 before the end of 1930. It was published in March, and there were two printings before publication. Two more printings followed in March, and there was a fifth in April. A sixth followed in June, and a seventh in October. In March, 1932, Knopf let out the plates to the publishers of the Blue Ribbon series of dollar reprints. They printed, as I recall it, 20,000 copies. This cheap reprint damaged the sales of the regular edition, though Knopf reprinted it again in May, 1932, and yet again in February, 1933. Knopf, in those days, had a branch of his publishing house in London. He published the book there in April, 1930." HLM, 1937 (EPFL—A176). The English edition has place of publication on title page reversed, to read London, New York.

Other editions and printings:

Eighth printing issued as Blue Ribbon Book, 1932. *See* annotation above.

Second edition, corrected and rewritten. New York, Knopf, 1946. ix, 302, xvii p. "In the first four sections I found no need of more than a few small changes, so they remain substantially as written. But Section V had to be reworked rather elaborately . . . The Bibliographical note . . . asked for but little revision."—Preface. This edition was reprinted in London by G. Allen.

1932

MAKING A PRESIDENT; a Footnote to the Saga of Democracy. New York, Knopf, 1932. 185 p.

"Mainly . . . my reports of the two national conventions of 1932, for the Baltimore *Evening Sun*."—Note. *See* Newspaper Work for detailed listing.

1933

PROJECT FOR A LICENSING ACT FOR BALTIMORE CITY. Baltimore, 1933. 22 p.

"The proposals herein contained were printed in the Baltimore *Evening Sun* of January 23, 24 and 25, 1933."

1934

TREATISE ON RIGHT AND WRONG. New York, Knopf, 1934. viii, 331, xix p.

"The writing was begun early in 1931, but there were many interruptions, and it was not until late in 1933, after I had got rid of the editorship of the *American Mercury*, that I was able to give my steady attention to it. My notes for it had been accumulating for many years. It seemed to follow naturally after 'Treatise on the Gods' . . . [but] had a smaller sale . . . 'Treatise on the Gods' was brought out at a dollar . . . This killed its sale in the standard edition and taught me a lesson. I refused to let Knopf let out 'Treatise on Right and Wrong' to any of the dollar-book publishers." HLM (EPFL—A175)

Issued same year in London by Kegan Paul, Trench, Trubner (ix, 277 p.). Subsequently issued by Routledge as no. 1 of their New World series. The Ryerson Press (Toronto) issued the Canadian edition.

WORKS BY H. L. M.

1935

THE ANATOMY OF QUACKERY. Cleveland, William Feather, 1935.

Reprinted from the Baltimore *Evening Sun,* Dec. 12, 1935.

EREZ ISRAEL. New York, Priv. print. [by B. P. Safran at The New School] 1935. 15 p.

Twenty-five copies issued, some with title page in Hebrew. "Reprinted by courtesy of the *Evening Sun,* Baltimore, from 'Notes on the Holy Land,' April 2, 1934, and 'Erez Israel,' April 9, 1934."

1936

THE INCOMPARABLE PHYSICIAN. [San Francisco, T. W. McDonald] 1936. 41 p.

"Copies of this reprint of a Mencken burlesque were made for members of the senior class of the School of Medicine of the University of California." Reprinted from *Smart Set* 47: 214-242, Nov., 1915, "In violation of the old *Smart Set* copyright—but I have forgiven him." HLM (EPFL—D Pam— Knopf). Reissued in 1940 as *The Eminent Physician* [Berkeley, Calif., The Gillick Press 7 p.]. "529 copies have been printed by T. W. McD. and Charles Gregory for Dorothy McDonald, M.D."

1937

THE JOHNS HOPKINS HOSPITAL. [Baltimore, The Hospital, 1937] 48 p. mimeo.

Reprinted from a series of twenty articles in the Baltimore *Sun,* July 6-28, 1939.

1939

NOTES ON A MORAL WAR. Boston, Porter Sargent, 1939. 1 *l.* (Sargent Bull. #10)

"Reprinted from a Baltimore *Sun* editorial, Oct. 8, 1939."

1940

AN AMERICAN EDITOR SPEAKS. Four Editorials on "Fake" Neutrality . . . from "The Sun" of Baltimore, Maryland. [Mt. Vernon, Wash. (state), The Concord Press, 1940] 8 p.

Reprinted from the *Sun,* Sept. 10, 24, Oct. 8 and 15, 1939.

"GENERALLY POLITICAL." New York, Columbia University, 1940. 13 p.

Written for the Institute of Arts and Sciences at Columbia University.

HAPPY DAYS, 1880-1892. New York, Knopf, 1940. xi, 313 p. front. (port.)

"Some of these chapters have appeared, either wholly or in part, in the *New Yorker.*" Note on verso of title page. *See* Magazine Articles, 1936-39, for detailed listing. It was published in London by Kegan Paul, Trench, Trubner (later Routledge), and in Toronto by the Ryerson Press.

QUICKSTEPS TO WAR. Boston, Porter Sargent, 1940. 1 *l.* (Sargent Bull. #74)

"Reprinted from editorials in the Baltimore *Sun*, Aug. 4 and July 28, 1940," issued on Aug. 7. Reprinted in *Getting US into War*, by Porter Edward Sargent (Boston, The Author, c. 1941. p. 405-407).

TRIUMPH OF DEMOCRACY. Boston, Porter Sargent, 1940. 1 *l.* (Sargent Bull. #70)

"Culled from . . . editorials in the Baltimore *Sun*, July 21 and 7, 1940." Issued on July 26.

1941

NEWSPAPER DAYS, 1899-1906. New York, Knopf, 1941. xi, 313 p. front. (port.)

"Some of these chapters have appeared, either wholly or in part, in the *New Yorker.*"—Note. "They are from the series Days of Innocence . . . sometimes with the titles changed and nearly always in an extended form." HLM (EPFL—A48). *See* Magazine Articles, 1941, for detailed listing. Issued in London in 1942 by Kegan Paul, Trench, Trubner (later Routledge) and in Toronto by the Ryerson Press.

1943

BEETHOVEN. From Prejudices: Fifth Series. [Baltimore, 1943] 7 p. ports., illus. (music)

"Made for H. L. Mencken by R. J. Buchholz, July 1943."

HEATHEN DAYS, 1890-1936. New York, Knopf, 1943. x, 299 p. front. (port.)

"Some of these chapters have appeared either wholly or in part, in the *New Yorker,* and one, 'Downfall of a Revolutionary,' was first published in *Esquire.*"—Note. *See* Magazine Articles, 1941, for detailed listing. Published in Toronto by the Ryerson Press. Armed Services edition. New York, Council on Books in Wartime, Inc., 1943. 254 p. (Armed Forces edition A–13)

1946

CHRISTMAS STORY, illustrated by Bill Crawford. New York, Knopf, 1946. 31 p. illus. (pt. col.)

Reprint of "Stare Decisis," *New Yorker* 20: 17-21, Dec. 30, 1944. Published in Toronto by the Ryerson Press.

1947

THE DAYS OF H. L. MENCKEN: Happy Days. Newspaper Days, Heathen Days. New York, Knopf, 1947. 313, 313, 299 p. ports.

Each part has special title page and is paged separately.

VACHEL LINDSAY. [Washington, D. C., John S. Mayfield, 1947] 3 p.

"This tribute to the poet—written shortly after his death—is printed here for the first time."

1948

HENRY L. MENCKEN INTERVIEWED by Donald Howe Kirkley, Sr. [Washington, D. C.] U. S. Library of Congress, Recording Laboratory, PL18–PL19. 1948. 4 sides. 12 in. 33⅓ rpm. microgroove.

Recorded in Studio B, June 30, 1948. Also issued by Caedmon Records, as "H. L. Mencken Speaks," TC–1082. Excerpts in "Voice from the Past," *Time* 68: 89-90, Nov. 5, 1956.

1949

A MENCKEN CHRESTOMATHY, edited and annotated by the author. New York, Knopf, 1949. xvi, 627 p.

"The aim of this volume is simply to present a selection of my out-of-print writings. . . . They come mostly from books, but others are magazine and newspaper pieces that never got between covers, and a few of them are notes never previously published at all. . . . The books levied on here are the six of the 'Prejudices' series, 'A Book of Burlesques,' 'Damn: a Book of Calumny,' 'In Defense of Women,' 'Making a President,' 'Notes on Democracy' and 'Treatise on Right and Wrong.' . . . In general, I have made few changes in the original texts. . . . But when it seemed to make for clarity I have not hesitated to change the present tense into the past, and to omit repetitive and otherwise unnecessary passages."—Preface. Abridgement in *Omnibook* 12: 59-77, June, 1950. port.

"Menckeniana: a selection from H. L. Mencken's *A Mencken Chrestomathy*." With a forenote by George Jean Nathan. New York, Knopf, 1949. 16 p.

1955

THE VINTAGE MENCKEN, gathered by Alistair Cooke. New York, Vintage Books, 1955. xiv, 240 p. (Vintage Books K 25)

"I followed his sensible instinct [in *A Mencken Chrestomathy*] here only in reprinting almost nothing of his youthful work and very little of his political musings later than 1933. But I wanted to do something that was beyond the purpose of the *Chrestomathy*, namely to give the new Mencken reader a running account of his life as he wrote and lived it."—Introduction.

BOOKS AND PAMPHLETS

1956

A CARNIVAL OF BUNCOMBE, edited by Malcolm Moos. Baltimore, The Johns Hopkins Press; London, Oxford University Press, 1956. xix, 370 p.

Sixty-nine political articles from the Baltimore *Evening Sun*, Monday Articles, Feb., 1920—Nov. 9, 1936. "I have quoted other articles . . . covering specific campaigns and other political subjects that do not appear in this collection."—Acknowledgements. Published in Toronto by Burns and McEachern. Selections from the Introduction and text, were published in *The Johns Hopkins Magazine* 8: 6-7, 29-31, Nov., 1956. port.

Reissued in 1960 with title *H. L. Mencken On Politics, a Carnival of Buncombe* (Edited with an introduction and glossary by Malcolm Moos. New York, Vintage Books. xviii, 365, xi p. A Vintage Book K 101)

MINORITY REPORT: H. L. Mencken's Notebooks. New York, Knopf, 1956. vi, 293 p.

"This is not a book, but a notebook. It is made up of selections chosen more or less at random from the memoranda of long years devoted to the pursuit, anatomizing and embalming of ideas."—Preface. Excerpts in The Baltimore *Sun,* May 22, 1956, with caricatures; and in *Life* 40: 75-76, 78, Feb. 20, 1956.

1958

A BATHTUB HOAX AND OTHER BLASTS & BRAVOS FROM THE CHICAGO TRIBUNE, by H. L. Mencken, edited, with an introduction and notes by Robert McHugh. New York, Knopf, 1958. 286 p.

Reprint of fifty-four columns from the *Chicago Tribune,* 1924–1927.

PREJUDICES, a Selection Made by James T. Farrell, and with an Introduction by Him. New York, Vintage Books, 1958. xx, 258 p. (Vintage Books K 58)

Thirty-five selections from 1st—6th series.

1961

H. L. MENCKEN ON MUSIC, a Selection by Louis Cheslock. New York, Knopf 1961. xvi, 222, iv p. ports., facsims. (music)

Selections of criticism, reminiscences and commentary on music reprinted from the *Evening Sun, Smart Set,* the *American Mercury* and the *Chicago Tribune.* Mr. Cheslock's "Prelude" is a biography of HLM in music; a "Postlude" gives the history of the Saturday Night Club.

CONTRIBUTIONS TO
BOOKS AND PAMPHLETS

Works co-authored or compiled by HLM are entered by title; those he edited, selected, translated, the single one he ghosted, and those for which he provided an introduction are listed under their author's names, according to standard library practice. HLM's own words are chosen as notes whenever available.

1899

OLD COURTHOUSES OF MARYLAND. *In* A Monograph of the New Baltimore Court House. One of the Greatest Examples of American Architecture, and the Foremost Court House of the United States, including a Historical Sketch of the Early Courts of Maryland. [Baltimore, Frank D. Thomas, 1899] p. [8-27]

"This book was brought out by Frank D. Thomas, son of the contractor who built the courthouse. He asked Max Ways, the city editor of the Baltimore *Herald,* to find him someone to write the part here headed 'Old Court Houses of Maryland,' and Max recommended me. I was then a young reporter on the *Herald.* Frank paid me $25 for the job—a princely honorarium in those days." HLM, Jan. 24, 1936 (EPFL—D160—Katz)

1905

HENRY LOUIS MENCKEN. *In* The Vagabonds. Autobiographies and Sketch of the Vagabonds. Baltimore, Hotel Caswell, 1905, p. 16.

Unsigned autobiographical sketch attributed to HLM. Pamphlet prepared for this dinner club's annual reunion on New York's Eve, 1905, and contains a "who's who" of each member and an account of the year's activities. HLM gave a talk on Shaw.

1908

SUMMER IN JAMAICA. *In* By Rail or by Water, Facts of Interest to

CONTRIBUTIONS

Travelers and Importers, edited by Arthur W. Robson. Baltimore, 1908. p. 125–126.

1909

IBSEN, HENRIK. A Doll's House. Newly translated from the definitive Dano-Norwegian text; edited, with an introduction and notes by Henry L. Mencken. Boston, Luce, 1909. xxvii, 150 p. (The Players' Ibsen)

Introduction p. v-xxiv: "When I joined the staff of the Baltimore *Sun* in the Summer of 1906, I was given the task, among other things, of writing its principal theatrical review each week. I had had three years' experience in the theatre on the Baltimore *Herald,* and was greatly interested in the emerging drama of the time. In particular, I was interested in Ibsen and his influence. In 1904 or thereabout I had begun to collect Ibseniana, and I kept on assembling it long after I had shut up my shutters as a dramatic critic and ceased to go to the theatre. . . . I gave the collection to the library of the University of Leipzig in 1928.

"While I was working as a dramatic critic I naturally met some of the actors and actresses who were playing Ibsen, then enjoying a considerable popularity in the American theatre. They told me that the William Archer translations of his plays were all very stiff, and that they had to make frequent changes in the texts for acting purposes. This gave me the notion that a more idiomatic translation might be useful, and I interested an old friend, Holger A. Koppel, Danish consul at Baltimore, in the project. A bit later I discussed it with Harrison Hale Schaff, head of the Boston publishing firm of John W. Luce & Company (which had published my Shaw and Nietzsche books), and he suggested that we do the plays for him as single volumes, each with a somewhat elaborated introduction and notes.

"We began with 'A Doll's House,' and then proceeded to 'Little Eyolf.' Koppel, who of course knew Dano-Norwegian perfectly, called off a rough but literal translation of each speech, and I compared it with two or three good German translations and we thus perfected the text. Sometimes we simply corrected the Archer version; at other times we had to rewrite it completely. The final text was then compared with a French translation (Koppel also knew French), and I gave it a thorough editing, trying to avoid all 'literary' phrases . . .

" 'A Doll's House' and 'Little Eyolf' . . . got fairly good notices, but the sales were very small. Schaff, as I recall it, asked $1 a volume for the little books—and in the Archer edition, published by Scribner, a reader could get three plays for $1.50. . . . We never got any royalties. Schaff seldom paid them, and in this case they were hardly earned." HLM (EPFL—A87) "Soon after . . . [they were published] I began a revision of the texts. The two little books were failures, and in consequence the revisions were never put into type." HLM (EPFL—A88)

IBSEN, HENRIK. Little Eyolf. Newly translated from the definitive Dano-Norwegian text. Edited, with introduction and notes by

Henry L. Mencken. Boston, Luce, 1909. xxv, 125 p. (The Players' Ibsen)

Introduction p. v-xxi. *See* annotation above.

JOURNALISM AS A TRADE. *In* How a Press Club Can Aid Its City. Issued by The Journalist Club of Baltimore for the Week of July 26, 1909. p. [5-6]

SMITH, LANGDON. Evolution, a Fantasy. Boston, Luce, 1909. 51 p.

1 p. on Nietzsche, opposite p. xiv.

1910

HIRSHBERG, LEONARD KEENE. What You Ought To Know About Your Baby. New York, The Butterick Pub. Co., 1910. 97 p.

"There was in those days a demand among magazines for medical articles and one day Ellery Sedgwick asked me to find a man at the Johns Hopkins who would be willing to write them for *Leslie's Weekly.* I discovered such a man in Dr. Leonard K. Hirshberg. . . . He put down the facts and I wrote the articles. The combination turned out to be very successful and pretty soon we were deluged with orders. Among the magazines we worked for was the *Delineator,* then edited by Dreiser. Dreiser ordered a whole series of articles on the feeding and care of children. . . . The series was afterward published as a book." HLM (EPFL—A29, p. 109–110). "I wrote the whole text (save the questions and answers), Hirshberg supplied the facts." HLM (EPFL—D278, Katz)

NIETZSCHE, FRIEDRICH WILHELM. The Gist of Nietzsche, arranged by Henry L. Mencken. Boston, Luce, 1910. 60 p.

[Harrison Hale] "Schaff, head of John W. Luce & Co., proposed to me that I do a small volume of selections from Nietzsche. I put together five or six thousand words and then tired of the job. Schaff himself contributed some other stuff. Unfortunately, he knew no German and thus could not judge the value of the translations he selected; many of them were terribly bad. Worse, the book when it came out turned out to be full of idiotic typographical errors . . . For these reasons, I lost all interest in the volume and was delighted several years ago to hear that it was out of print." HLM (EPFL—A29, p. 130)

MEN VERSUS THE MAN, a Correspondence between Rives La Monte, Socialist, and H. L. Mencken, Individualist. New York, Holt, 1910. 252 p.

Six letters by La Monte and six replies by HLM. "In 1909 certain articles I had written attracted the attention of Robert Rives Lamonte [*sic*], a Socialist intellectual then employed on the Baltimore *News.* Lamonte was one of the editors of the *International Socialist Review.* . . . We fell into a correspondence and the result was a formidable series of letters. Finally Lamonte suggested that we polish them a bit and try to publish them as a book. I gave him full charge of the affair and the first publisher he approached, Henry Holt, accepted the book. . . . It was a complete failure commercially and was soon remaindered. . . . The book seems somewhat archaic today but it at least shows one thing clearly, that my politics were firmly formulated so early as 1909. I'd change the essential doctrine very little if I had it to rewrite today." HLM (EPFL—A29, p. 127–128)

1911

IN JACKSON'S DAY. *In* Announcements of Awards in the Prize Contest for Reviews of The Prodigal Judge by Vaughn Kester [given by] the Bobbs-Merrill Co. p. [7-8]

HLM's review appeared in the Baltimore *Evening Sun*, March 14, 1911, p. 6, and was awarded third prize of $100.00 in the Bobbs-Merrill contest.

1913

BRIEUX, EUGÈNE. Blanchette and The Escape, Two Plays by Brieux, with Preface by H. L. Mencken, translated from the French by Frederick Eisemann. Boston, Luce, 1913. xxxvi, 240 p.

Preface p. i-xxxvi.

SILVIN, EDWARD, *ed.* Why I Am Opposed to Socialism; Original Papers by Leading Men and Women. Sacramento, Calif., The Author, 1913. 53 p.

HLM's opinion, p. 6-7.

1914

EUROPE AFTER 8:15, by H. L. Mencken, George Jean Nathan, Willard Huntington Wright. With decorations by Thomas H[art] Benton. New York, Lane; Toronto, Bell & Cockburn, 1914. 222 p. front., illus.

HLM wrote the Preface, "Munich," and first and last parts of "London," the latter combined with a piece by Wright. "In 1913, while Willard H. Wright was editor of the *Smart Set,* he proposed that he, Nathan and I do a series of articles for the magazine on the great cities of Europe and especially on those noted for their gaiety. I had recently returned from a trip abroad and so proceeded to do two articles at once, one on Munich, printed in the *Smart Set* for April, 1913 [39: 103-111], and one on London [40: 99-107, June, 1913]. The latter, for some reason that I don't remember, was signed George Weems Peregoy . . . . Due to the fact that it was published in 1914, just before the war, the book was a complete failure and was soon remaindered." HLM (EPFL—A29, p. 131)

1916

Program annotations for the concerts of the Baltimore Symphony were written by HLM for the first concert, Friday

Feb. 11, 1916, and for two years thereafter. These notes were reprinted on the editorial page of the [Baltimore] Evening Sun.

STRANGE, FAR-OFF PLACES. *In* Facts of Interest to Travelers and Importers by Rail and Water, edited by Arthur W. Robson. Baltimore, 1916. p. 25-28.

1917

PISTOLS FOR TWO, by Owen Arthur James Hatteras, 1862-1923 [pseud]. New York, Knopf, 1917. 42 p.

HLM wrote the introductory and closing remarks, p. 1–5, 39–42, and the biographical sketch of Nathan, p. 5–21; Nathan wrote the sketch about HLM, p. 21–39. "The plan of it was my idea . . . Nathan and I contributed $300 toward the cost of printing it. At the start, Knopf distributed it gratis, but the demand for it soon became so great that he began to sell it at, first for fifty cents and then for a dollar." HLM (EPFL—A29, p. 136)

1918

HOWE, EDGAR WATSON. The Blessing of Business. Topeka, Kansas, Crane, 1918. 76 p.

Quotation from HLM as Preface.

IBSEN, HENRIK. The Master Builder. Pillars of Society. Hedda Gabler. Introduction by H. L. Mencken. New York, Boni, 1918. xii, 305 p. front. (port.) (The Modern Library)

Introduction p. v-xii. HLM had made a transcript of *Hedda Gabler* in 1909, "but it was never published, and that is as far as it went." HLM (EPFL—A87)

WILDE, OSCAR. Ben Kutcher's Illustrated Edition of A House of Pomegranates, and The Story of the Nightingale and the Rose; with an introduction by H. L. Mencken. New York, Moffat, 1918. viii, 180 p. front., illus.

Preface p. i-viii. The same Preface by HLM is included, p. v-xii, in a later edition, *A House of Pomegranates*, with an introduction by H. L. Mencken, illustrated by Ben Kutcher (New York, Dodd, 1925. xii, 180 p. front., illus.)

1919

DREISER, THEODORE. Twelve Men. New York, Boni, 1919. 17 p.

HLM's review, p. 4–8, is reprinted from the New York *Sun*, April 13, 1919, in this booklet of collected reviews issued by Boni, Liverwright Co. as an advertisement.

HOWE, EDGAR WATSON. Ventures into Common Sense. New York,

Knopf, 1919. 273 p. (The Free Lance Books II; edited with introduction by H. L. Mencken)

Introduction p. 7–29. "The 'Free Lance' books were suggested by Knopf, though I selected the name for them, taking it from the title of my old column in the Baltimore *Evening Sun*. The series was a failure and was abandoned after six volumes had been published." HLM (EPFL—A29, p. 136)

Reissued in Pocket Book series, 1924.

1920

THE AMERICAN CREDO. A Contribution toward the Interpretation of the National Mind, by George Jean Nathan and H. L. Mencken. New York, Knopf, 1920. 191 p.

HLM wrote the Preface, p. 7–103; Nathan, the Credo. A German translation of HLM's Preface, by Tony Noah appeared as "Das Amerikanische Credo" *in Die Grenzboten*, 81: 141-144, 166-171, 203-206, 232-235, 266-270, 294-297, 331-333, 362-365, Jan. 28—March 18, 1922.

In 1921 "At Christmas, we got out, for the amusement of friends, a four page compendium [p. 193-196, articles 499-526 of *Credo*] containing articles that could not be printed in the book itself." HLM (EPFL—A29, p. 136). HLM's Preface in the 1922 rev. and enl. ed. of *The American Credo* (266 p. 869 paragraphs) was unchanged.

BAROJA Y NESSI, Pío. Youth and Egolatry, by Pío Baroja, translated from the Spanish by Jacob S. Fassett, Jr., and Frances L. Phillips. New York, Knopf, 1920. 265 p. (The Free Lance Books, I; edited with introduction by H. L. Mencken)

Introduction p. 11–20.

EMERGENCY COMMITTEE ORGANIZED TO PROTEST AGAINST THE SUPPRESSION OF JAMES BRANCH CABELL's *Jurgen*. Jurgen and the Censor, Report. New York, Priv. print. for the Committee, 1920. 77 p.

HLM note, p. 53–54.

H. L. MENCKEN: FANFARE. *See* Books and Pamphlets about HLM, 1920.

HELIOGABALUS, A BUFFOONERY IN THREE ACTS, by H. L. Mencken and George Jean Nathan. New York, Knopf, 1920. 183 p.

" 'Heliogabalus' was begun as a sort of joke. One night in 1919, sitting in Roger's saloon on 6th avenue and 45th street in New York, Nathan and I fell into talk about the trade of writing plays. I argued that writing one was probably the easiest of all literary enterprises, and Nathan was disposed to agree. Finally, I suggested that we do one together—to prove it. The idea for 'Heliogabalus' occurred to me immediately. It had two halves. The first half was that the hero should be a man universally disreputable, and the second was that there should be nothing in the play save time-honored theatrical buncombe. Every sort of novelty in the plot was to be barred, and the so-called psychology was to be as transparent as possible.

"I returned to Baltimore, and set to work on the first draft. Despite a heavy pressure of other work I finished it in four or five weeks. Nathan found some holes in the dramatic action, and contributed a number of details, but the play was mainly mine—in fact, at least nine-tenths mine.

"When we finished the MS. we had a prompt copy made, bearing the *nom de plume* of C. Farley Anderson. The managers of the time shied away from it as in fear of the Comstocks, and we decided to publish it. Knopf brought it out in a limited edition of 2000 copies, along with a subsidiary *de luxe* edition of 60 copies. Both were sold out in a week or two. The notices the piece got attracted the managers who had been afraid of it before, and we received several offers for the American stage rights. The late Will A. Page offered us $10,000 down, in addition to the usual royalties. But we announced grandly that the United States was too little civilized to see such a play, and that only the foreign stage rights were for sale. This brought in Charles A. Feleky, a Hungarian connected with the theatre. He wanted the German rights, and we gave them to him, for he was an intelligent and honest man. He had the German translation made and published at his own expense. Various German managers nibbled at it, but the deflation of 1920 made it impossible, for any of them to reproduce a piece requiring new scenery. Thus nothing came of Feleky's friendly offices.

"Some years later William Gillette proposed to present the play in New York, but for some reason that I forget his project blew up. Other American actors showed interest in it from time to time. So late as 1936 we received overtures from an agent representing John Barrymore. But we always held somewhat aloof. Bit by bit the play had been pirated by musical comedy and burlesque writers. The big bed, which was my invention, was often seen on Broadway. It was surely obvious enough." HLM, 1937 (EPFL—A86). An Acting Edition of two hundred copies, none for sale, was also issued in 1920.

A German translation, *Heliogabel, ein Schwank in Drei Akten* aus dem Amerikanischen von H. L. Mencken & George Jean Nathan, Deutsch von Peter Perpentikel, was published in Berlin by Theatralia Verlag in 1920 (79 p. At head of title: Unverkäufliches Manuskript.) It was unbound, and in the usual form of German plays intended for use of theatres.

MUIR, EDWIN. We Moderns: Enigmas and Guesses. New York, Knopf, 1920. 244 p. (The Free Lance Books, IV; edited with introduction by H. L. Mencken)

Introduction p. 7–21.

NIETZSCHE, FRIEDRICH WILHELM. The Antichrist. Translated from the German with an introduction by H. L. Mencken. New York, Knopf, 1920. 182 p. (The Free Lance Books, III; edited by H. L. Mencken)

CONTRIBUTIONS

Introduction p. 7–38, used without changes in all subsequent editions. In 1923 it was issued as a Borzoi Pocket Book (Introduction p. 7–36). A new edition, Sept., 1931, was actually a reprint.

WILLA CATHER. *In* The Borzoi 1920, Being a Sort of Record of Five Years' Publishing. New York, Knopf, 1920. p. 28–31.

1921

CABELL, JAMES BRANCH. The Line of Love; Dizain des Mariages. With an introduction by H. L. Mencken. New York, McBride, 1921. xv, 261 p.
Introduction p. vii-xiii.

MORRISON, ARTHUR. Tales of Mean Streets. Preface by H. L. Mencken. New York, Boni, 1921. xxvii, 251 p. (The Modern Library)
Preface p. i-xxv.

NIETZSCHE, FRIEDRICH WILHELM. The Nietzsche-Wagner Correspondence, edited by Elizabeth Foerster-Nietzsche, translated by Caroline V. Kerr, introduction by H. L. Mencken. New York, Boni, 1921. xvii, 312 p.
Introduction p. xi-xvii.

WOOD, JAMES NELSON. Democracy and the Will to Power, with an introduction by H. L. Mencken. New York, Knopf, 1921. 244 p. (The Free Lance Books, V; edited with introduction by H. L. Mencken)
Introduction p. 7–17.

1922

POLITICS. *In* Civilization in the United States, edited by Harold Edmund Stearns. New York, Harcourt, 1922. p. 21–34, 532. Published in London by Cape.

1924

FREY, CARROLL. A Bibliography of the Writings of H. L. Mencken. *See* Bibliographies, 1924.
Foreword by HLM, p. 3-6.

THE STYLE OF CABELL. *In* A Round Table in Poictesme, a Symposium; edited by Don Marshall Bregenzer and Samuel Loveman.

Cleveland, Priv. print. for Members of The Colophon Club, 1924. p. 115–117.

1925

AMERICANA, 1925; edited by H. L. Mencken. New York, Knopf, 1925. x, 311 p.

"This collection is the work of hundreds of readers of *The American Mercury*—so many, indeed, that it would be impracticable to acknowledge individually the editor's debt to them."—Preface. Issued in London by Hopkinson. x, 309 p. *The American Mercury* in 1926 issued a reprint of Knopf's second printing, Nov., 1925.

Americana, 1926. New York, Knopf, 1926. xi, 279 p. "This collection, like its predecessor, 'Americana: 1925,' is in part the work of thousands of readers of *The American Mercury.* . . . I have added to the present volume an appendix from Foreign Parts."—Preface. Issued in London by Hopkinson.

MEMORANDUM. *In* The Borzoi 1925, Being a Sort of Record of Ten Years of Publishing. New York, Knopf, 1925. p. 138–141.

A vignette of Alfred A. Knopf by HLM. Reprinted in *The Borzoi Reader,* edited with an introduction and notes by Carl Van Doren (New York, Knopf, 1936, p. 652–655).

MR. MENCKEN REFLECTS ON JOURNALISM. *In* Three Important Opinions About Newspapers and Newspaper Men, issued by the Department of Journalism of the University of Colorado. Boulder, 1925. p. 1-3, reprinted from the New York *World.*

SWIFT, JONATHAN. Gulliver's Travels, with an introduction by H. L. Mencken. New York, Knopf, 1925. xxii, 363 p.

Introduction p. v-vii.

ULMANN, DORIS, *comp.* A Portrait Gallery of American Editors, Being a Group of XLIII Likenesses; with critical essays by the editors and an introduction by Louis Evan Shipman. New York, Rudge, 1925.

HLM's autobiographical sketch, p. 108–111 (chap. 27) with portrait by Ulmann.

1926

AMERICANISM. *In* The Encyclopaedia Britannica, 13th ed. 1926. 29: 104–105.

Reprinted in *Seven Famous Reprints from the New Thirteenth Edition of The Encyclopaedia Britannica,* with Biographies of the Authors, (London, The

Encyclopaedia Britannica Co., 1927. p. 75–80, biog. p. 74.) Slightly revised and word list added for the fourteenth edition of 1929, 1: 773–776. Thereafter the article remained unchanged until the 1957 edition.

CRANE, STEPHEN. Major Conflicts: George's Mother. The Blue Hotel. Maggie. Introduction by H. L. Mencken. New York, Knopf, 1926. xiii, 218 p. (The Work of Stephen Crane, edited by Wilson Follett. v. X)

Introduction p. ix-xiii.

1927

THE AMERICAN MERCURY. Three Years, 1924 to 1927. The Story of a New Idea and Its Successful Adaptation, with a postscript by H. L. Mencken. New York, The American Mercury, 1927. 45 p.

Postscript, p. 33-36.

THE JOURNAL OF A VOYAGE TO HOBOKEN, N.J. *In* Morrow's Almanack for the Year of Our Lord 1928, Being Bissextile or Leap Year & Makes Since the Creation by the Account of Certain Fundamentalists 5932 Years & By the Account of Certain Evolutionists x Years. Burton Rascoe, Philom. New York, Morrow, 1927. p. 89.

1928

MENCKENIANA: A SCHIMPFLEXIKON. Expurgated edition. New York, Knopf, 1928. 132 p.

"Some salient specimens of the anti-Mencken invective."—Note. The material was collected by Sara Powell Haardt and edited by HLM. There was no "unexpurgated ed." The book is frequently referred to by its subtitle.

1929

AMERICANISMS. *In* The Encyclopedia Americana. 1929. 1: 567–569.

Appears in all subsequent editions and printings to date.

HUNEKER, JAMES GIBBON. Essays, selected with an introduction by H. L. Mencken. New York, Scribner, 1929. xxiii, 492 p.

Introduction p. ix-xxiii. Issued in London by Laurie.

POSSELT, ERICH, *ed.* On Parade, Contributions by Prominent Authors, Caricatures by Eva Herrmann. New York, Coward McCann, 1929. x, 179 p.

HLM's contribution, p. 106, caricature p. 107, brief bibliography p. 109.

1930

BOOKS-BALTIMORE. The 10,000 Best American Books in Print. Catalogue no. 1, 1930–1931. Baltimore, Md. [An Associate of Warwick and York, Inc.] 1930. 91 p.

"HLM and Heinrich E. Buchholz of Warwick and York, Inc. of Baltimore, selected and edited this list. As it was not a financial success, the project was dropped." HLM (EPFL—D Pam.)

HELDER, JACOB. Greatest Thoughts on Immortality. New York, Smith, 1930. p. 112–114.

HLM's letter included in part 2 of "Negative and Agnostic."

PIERCY, JOSEPHINE KETCHUM, ed. Modern Writers at Work. New York, Macmillan, 1930. p. 84–85.

Letter about his writing habits in answer to editor's inquiry, precedes reprint of "Bach to Bach" from *Prejudices: Sixth Series.*

1931

COOPER, JAMES FENIMORE. The American Democrat, with an introduction by H. L. Mencken. New York, Knopf, 1931. xx, 184 p. (Americana Deserta)

Introduction p. xi-xx. The same introduction by HLM is included, p. v-xiv, in a later edition, *The American Democrat, or Hints on the Social and Civic Relations of the United States of America* (With an introduction by H. L. Mencken and an introductory note by Robert E. Spiller. New York, Knopf, 1956. xxviii, 190 p. A Vintage Book K 26).

LIVING PHILOSOPHIES, by Albert Einstein, John Dewey . . . H. L. Mencken [and others] New York, Simon, 1931. p. 179–193 port.

HLM's contribution was first published in the *Forum* series entitled "What I Believe" 84: 133-139, Sept., 1930. Asked to contribute to the new edition, entitled *I Believe, the Personal Philosophies of Certain Eminent Men and Women of Our Time* (edited, with introduction and biographical notes, by Clifton Fadiman. New York, Simon, 1939. p. 389–391) HLM stated "Rereading it today, I see no reason for altering a single item of it. If I were formulating it again, I'd formulate it in almost precisely the same terms." p. 389.

1932

DURANT, WILL. On the Meaning of Life. New York, Ray Long and Richard R. Smith, 1932. p. 30-36.

Letter from HLM and Durant's evaluation. Reprinted in: *Current Prose, a College Reader,* edited by R. J. Geist and Thomas A. Bledsoe (New York and Toronto, Rinehart, 1953. p. 252–255) and in *A Treasury of the World's Great Letters from Ancient Days to Our Own Time,* edited by Max Lincoln Schuster (New York, Simon and Schuster, 1940. p. 507–510).

CONTRIBUTIONS

Lewis, Sinclair. Elmer Gantry, roman traduit de l'anglais par Régis Michaud. Paris, Fayard, 1932. 593 p. (Univers)

Préface par HLM, p. 7–12.

Tobey, James Alner. Cancer, What Everyone Should Know About It. With introductions by Joseph Colt Bloodgood and H. L. Mencken. New York, Knopf, 1932. xxix, 313 p. front. (port.) illus., ports., maps, facsims.

Introduction p. xix-xx.

1935

Johnson, Merle. You Know These Lines, a Bibliography of the Most Quoted Verses in American Poetry. Foreword by H. L. Mencken. New York, Baker, 1935. xviii, 195 p.

Foreword p. ix-xi.

United Daughters of the Confederacy. A Brief Addressed to the Electors of the Hall of Fame, New York University, in Behalf of Sidney Lanier, Poet and Musician. Macon, Ga., April, 1935. p. 26.

Brief tribute by HLM written Sept. 30, 1932.

1936

Haardt, Sara Powell. Southern Album, edited, with a preface by H. L. Mencken. Garden City, N.Y., Doubleday, 1936. xxviii, 289 p.

Preface p. vii-xxiii, includes biographical sketch of his wife, as memorial tribute.

Schreiber, Georges. Portraits and Self-Portraits, collected and illustrated by Georges Schreiber. Boston, Houghton, 1936. p. 103-107. port.

Autobiographical sketch by HLM.

1937

Janvier, Meredith. Baltimore Yesterdays. Baltimore, H. G. Roebuck, 1937. xviii, 161 p. front., illus., ports.

Preface by HLM, p. vii-xiv.

Mencke, Johann Burkhard. The Charlatanry of the Learned. Translated from the German [i.e. Latin] by Francis E. Litz, with notes and an introduction by H. L. Mencken. New York, Knopf, 1937. 178 p. fronts. (facsims.) ports.

Editor's Preface, p. 3–45, is a history of the celebrated eighteenth-century blast at fake erudition, plus a brief genealogy of the Mencken family.

THE SUNPAPERS OF BALTIMORE, 1837-1937 [by] Gerald W. Johnson, Frank R. Kent, H. L. Mencken, Hamilton Owens. New York, Knopf, 1937. xii, 430, xvi, xvi p. illus., ports.

"Mr. Mencken wrote chapters XI to XVIII (p. 205–365) inclusive . . . [and] served as general editor."—Preface.

1938

SQUIRE, MARIAN, comp. The Stag at Ease; a Cookbook. Caldwell, Idaho, Caxton Printers, 1938. p. 98-99.

HLM's recipe for Deviled Crabs among "the culinary preferences of a number of distinguished male citizens of the world."— (Subtitle)

1939

WEAVER, JOHN V. A. In American, the Collected Poems of . . ., with a foreword by H. L. Mencken. New York and London, Knopf, 1939. xvii, 316 p. front. (port.)

Foreword p. v-xi. Issued in Toronto by the Ryerson Press.

1940

THE COMPETENT MAN. In Alfred A. Knopf, Quarter Century. [Norwood, Mass., The Plimpton Press, 1940] p. 17-21.

Reprinted in Alfred A. Knopf at 60. (New York, Priv. print., 1952. p. 55–59). "This piece was originally written for Alfred A. Knopf, Quarter Century in 1940. Because no book honoring AAK would be complete without Mencken, it is here reprinted."—Forenote to article.

SUMNER, WILLIAM GRAHAM. Sumner Today, Selected Essays of William Sumner, with Comments by American Leaders, edited by Maurice R. Davie. New Haven, Yale University Press; London, Oxford University Press, 1940. p. 113-114.

Comment by HLM on Sumner's essay "The Absurd Effort to Make the World Over."

1942

MENCKEN, AUGUST, ed. By the Neck, a Book of Hangings. Selected from contemporary accounts and edited with an introduction by August Mencken. Foreword by H. L. Mencken. New York, Hastings House, 1942. xx, 264 p. illus.

Foreword p. v-viii.

A New Dictionary of Quotations on Historical Principles from Ancient and Modern Sources, selected and edited by H. L. Mencken. New York, Knopf, 1942. xiii, 1347 p.

"This book is based upon a collection of quotations begun in 1918 or thereabout for my own use. Its purpose was to keep track of sayings that, for one reason or another interested me and seemed worth remembering, but that, also for one reason or another, were not in the existing quotation-books. The collection grew steadily, helped by the contributions of friends who knew of it, and there arose inevitably the notion that it might be worth printing. To that end, of course, it would be necessary to conduct a more systematic search for material than I had ever undertaken, and to admit some of the common stock of other such works. In March, 1933, I suggested to Charles Angoff, then my assistant at the *American Mercury*, that he join me in this enterprise, and for a couple of years thereafter the two of us proceeded with it. But in 1935 Mr. Angoff found himself unable to give it the time it needed, and so withdrew. Thereafter I continued it on my own, and have since dealt with it unaided."—Preface.

1943

Notes on American Given Names. *In* Bookmen's Holiday, Notes and Studies Written and Gathered in Tribute on Harry Miller Lydenberg. New York, The New York Public Library, 1943. p. 70–80.

1944

The Sun, Baltimore. Stylebook: The Sunpapers of Baltimore. [Baltimore, A. S. Abell Co., 1944] 95 p.

This project was inspired by HLM, who wrote and revised most of the book. It has been subsequently used as a model by many U. S. newspapers.

1945

Why I Am Not a Book Collector. *In* For Loving a Book, Further News Adventures Among Bins and Bibliophiles, by Charles Honce. With an overture by H. L. Mencken. Mt. Vernon, N.Y., The Golden Eagle Press, 1945.

"Overture: Mr. Mencken lifts his baton," p. [xv.]

1946

Dreiser, Theodore. An American Tragedy. Introduction by H. L. Mencken. Memorial edition. Cleveland, World Pub. Co., 1946. xvi, 409 p.

Introduction p. ix-xvi. In 1948, another edition, illustrated by Grant Reynard, 874 p., included the identical introduction, p. 7–12.

SLANG. *In* The Encyclopaedia Britannica. 14th ed. 1946. 20: 773–776.

> HLM helped write this article which appeared from 1946-1954 and entirely wrote the lists of American slang included in this article. From 1955 to the present edition, he helped write the section of American slang included in the article "Slang."

1948

THE AMERICAN LANGUAGE. *In* Literary History of the United States, edited by Robert E. Spiller. New York, Macmillan, 1948. 2: 663–675 (chap. 40)

> In 1953 a revised edition in one volume, included this chapter, identical paging.

JOHNSON, BURGES. The Lost Art of Profanity. Foreword by H. L. Mencken; drawings by Orson Lowell. Indianapolis, Bobbs-Merrill, 1948. 223 p. illus.

> Foreword p. [9-11] and also dedicated to HLM.

KROLL, HARRY HARRISON. Looking Backward, a Successful Author Reviews His Past To Help Beginners on Their Upward Climb. With a foreword by H. L. Mencken. [Denver, Colo., 1948] 7 p.

> "This report is reprinted with the addition of a Foreword [p. 2] by H. L. Mencken, from the Nov. 5, 1947 issue of *The Author & Journalist.*"

1949

THE BIRTH OF NEW VERBS. *In* Philologica: The Malone Anniversary Studies, edited by Thomas A. Kirby and Henry Bosley Wolf. Baltimore, The Johns Hopkins Press, 1949. p. 313–319.

NEWSPAPER WORK

"Their general tendency from the start was towards the annihilation of frauds of all sorts." HLM (EPFL—A29)

H. L. Mencken was a newspaperman. From 1899 to 1948, excepting two breaks during the two World Wars, when, realizing that his outspoken objections to U.S. participation were an embarrassment to his paper and he voluntarily resigned, HLM was a working journalist.

Newspapers are probably the most ephemeral of man's written works and therefore are not included in bibliographies. However, since the advent of microfilm, journalism has become archival. A bibliography of the works of H. L. Mencken would not be complete without his contributions to newspapers.

Having no precedent to follow, the content and methods of procedure of this section of the bibliography have evolved during the process of compilation.

This is an inclusive listing of HLM's major, signed contributions to the Baltimore *Herald,* the Baltimore *Sunpapers,* the New York *Evening Mail,* the *Chicago Sunday Tribune,* and the New York *American.*

Unsigned news items, editorials and theatre reviews written for the Baltimore *Herald* and the Baltimore *Sunpapers* from 1899 to 1910 have been indicated only by the inclusive dates for the periods HLM wrote them.

A listing of miscellaneous articles appearing in other papers has been included, but is not inclusive. Miscellaneous articles, which have been impossible to trace, have been omitted.

Articles written for foreign newspapers, since they are few in number, relatively unimportant, and the papers largely unobtainable, have been omitted altogether.

The major newspapers for which HLM wrote are listed chronologically by the date of HLM's first association with them. Under the heading for each individual newspaper HLM's contributions are listed chronologically by the date of individual articles or the date of the first article of a series or column. Miscellaneous articles are gathered together at the end of the newspaper section.

Inclusive entries are given for columns. Individual titles, dates and explanatory notes, where necessary, are given for series of articles. When a column or series has a distinctive title it is so listed, as "THE FREE LANCE"; in other cases the entry is under HLM's official title, as "Reporter"; or under an inclusive heading, as "[Articles]."

The form used for newspaper articles is: author (this for interviews only, all others are by HLM and author's name has been omitted); title or headline of article, column or series; title of newspaper; date; page; edition (this for news stories only); title of column and author's name (this only if the article appeared in another author's column, and occurs only in Miscellaneous Articles and Interviews). In the listings of individual articles of a series, when an explanatory phrase is given, other than in a note, it follows the date and page in parentheses.

All newspapers cited are from the collections of the Enoch Pratt Free Library of Baltimore, the Library of Congress or the New York Public Library. Most newspaper files, either bound or on microfilm, contain only one edition for each date. Editorial page articles, and articles of a general nature are not affected by changes of editions. News articles, however, may change or be omitted altogether in succeeding editions of one day's paper. Therefore, for news articles, the edition has been noted.

Articles which have been syndicated, are listed under the heading of the paper for which they were written. Other papers which carried the articles have been listed, when known, but no attempt has been made to trace the papers which printed single articles, or which printed a series either in whole or in part.

The miscellaneous articles written by HLM for the Associated Press and for various newspapers were often carried by the national press. A single article printed in ten different papers could carry ten different titles or headlines. However, only one newspaper citation has been given for each article, and each has been listed by its title or headline in that paper.

The final listing in the Newspaper Section is Interviews. Interviews have been listed as such because they are neither by HLM, i.e. in his prose style, nor about him, i.e. in the third person; the interviews are largely quotations of HLM's spoken words with introductory and transitional remarks by the interviewer.

NEWSPAPER WORK—TABLE OF CONTENTS

THE BALTIMORE HERALD

It was on the *Herald*, while making his spectacular rise from unpaid reporter at nineteen to Secretary and Editor at twenty-six, that HLM launched the by-line that was to shake the country —*H. L. Mencken.*

Reporter. Baltimore Morning Herald February 23, 1899—October 1901.

HLM's first news stories, the theft of a horse and buggy near Kingsville and the showing of a cineograph at the Otterbein Memorial U.B. Church in Hampden, appeared on Friday, February 24, 1899, but his position on the *Herald* staff was that of unpaid volunteer, taking him to the outer suburbs and unpopular city assignments, until the following August. He was then put on the payroll and moved rapidly through the reportorial circuit to the eminence of City Hall: Southern Police District, August 1899—Spring, 1900; Northwest and Western Police Districts, Spring 1900—July 1900; Central Police District, July 1900—February 1901; City Hall, February 1901—September 1901. In September of 1901 Mencken was taken off City Hall and made Dramatic Editor for the *Morning Herald,* but in October he was promoted to Sunday Editor, so held the title for less than a month.

" . . . a newspaper reporter, in those remote days, had a grand and gaudy time of it, and no call to envy any man. . . . I believed then, and still believe today [1940], that it was the maddest, gladdest, damnest existence ever enjoyed by mortal youth. . . . I was at large in a wicked seaport of half a million people, with a front seat at every public show, as free of the night as of the day, and getting earfuls and eyefuls of instruction in a hundred giddy arcana, none of them taught in schools. . . . I was laying in all the worldly wisdom of a police lieutenant, a bartender, a shyster lawyer, or a midwife." *Newspaper Days* p. vi–ix.

[Articles]. Baltimore Sunday Herald 1900–1901.

At the Edge of the Spanish Main. August 26, 1900, p. 22 (Jamaica.)
Where Orchids Are Called Weeds. September 2, 1900, p. 22 (Jamaica.)
Seen on the Streets of Kingston. September 9, 1900, p. 22 (Jamaica.)
The Boy and the Man (A Christmas Ballad). December 23, 1900, p. 35.
To Kruger [Stephanus J. P., Boer statesman], Edmond Rostand's Latest Poem, with an English Translation in Verse Made Especially for the Sunday Herald, December 30, 1900, p. 1.
Theatrical Alphabet. March 17—April 14, 1901, comic section, unsigned.
Train Glimpses of the South. May 26, 1901, editorial page.

During the summer of 1900, while still a reporter, Mencken began selling articles to Sunday papers which the *Herald* received free for setting them up in galleys. Those that were used by the *Sunday Herald* are unsigned and Mencken kept no clippings of them, therefore they are not listed here.

WORKS BY H. L. M.

RHYME AND REASON. Baltimore Sunday Herald October 28—November 11, 1900, editorial page. Poetry.

KNOCKS AND JOLLIES. Baltimore Sunday Herald November 18, 1900 —February 24, 1901, editorial page. Poetry.

TERSE AND TERRIBLE TEXTS. Baltimore Morning Herald December 3, 1900—May 13, 1901, editorial page. Prose.

"I had a drawer full of verse . . . . My column ran on until my reserves of prosody began to be depleted. I then diluted it with more and more prose, and finally it became prose altogether." HLM refers here to all three columns.

"Terse and Terrible Texts" was often unsigned, sometimes appeared with another by-line, and was irregular; in all there were nineteen. The poetic contributions to the poetry columns made up the bulk of the contents of *Ventures Into Verse* and as such the better verses were reprinted extensively in other newspapers when the book was reviewed.

[Dispatches]. Baltimore Morning Herald and Baltimore Sunday Herald May 9–14, 1901, p. 1.

Mencken received his first big out-of-town assignment when he was sent to Jacksonville, Florida, to cover the fire damage of May 3rd and the arrival of the *Herald's* relief train. The articles praised, and undoubtedly pleased, the citizens of Baltimore; but HLM, who claimed this experience as the birth of his theory of the Gospel of Service, gives a much more diverting account in *Newspaper Days,* "The Gospel of Service," p. 94.

UNTOLD TALES. Baltimore Sunday Herald July 7, 1901—February 2, 1902, editorial page.

While covering City Hall Mencken developed a gleeful and disrespectful fascination with politics and politicians. The tales were laid in ancient Rome and dealt with local politics in broad farce. The first of these appeared in the last "Knocks and Jollies" Column on February 14, 1901; the second in the *Morning Herald* on Monday June 17, 1901; the remainder appeared under a large boxed head, signed and numbered consecutively. There were thirty-three in all.

" . . . a series of buffooneries. . . . In more than half of them the heroes were hanged in the last paragraph."

Reprinted in: Goldberg, Isaac. *The Man Mencken,* A Biographical and Critical Survey. (N.Y., Simon, 1925) p. 342-370, "Specimens of the *Untold Tales* Baltimore Herald, 1901."

BALTIMORE AND THE REST OF THE WORLD. Baltimore Morning Herald May 20—September 23, 1901, editorial page.

This column started humorously but "it gradually lost its humorous character and became a sort of private, individual column." The column was unsigned and usually appeared on Mondays, Wednesdays, and Fridays but there are irregularities. This heading turns up again on the editorial page of the *Sunday Herald* for February 9, 16, and 23, 1902.

PLAYS AND PLAYERS. **Baltimore Morning Herald September 1901—October 1903, daily Monday through Friday, editorial page.**

In September of 1901 Mencken was made Dramatic Editor of the *Morning Herald* and he took over the daily theatre column. The column is never signed and the exact dates on which Mencken took over in 1901 and left off in 1903 are not known.

Sunday Editor. Baltimore Sunday Herald October 1901—October 1903.

While Sunday Editor Mencken wrote editorials, edited the theatre page, and wrote a few articles for the paper. He continued to do the daily theatre column for the *Morning Herald* and it was during this period that he became well known, among Eastern journalists, as a foremost newspaper dramatic critic.

[Articles]. Baltimore Sunday Herald 1902–1903.

Impressions of One of the Prince's Staff [German Prince Henry]. March 2 and 8, 1902, editorial page, unsigned.

With the Cranks at the Mayor's Office. June 8, 1902, editorial page.

Gen. Kitchener, War Machine. June 15, 1902, p. 25.

The Island War: A Tale of a Monarchy [signed George W. Allison, believed to be HLM]. December 28, 1902, p. 19.

A Pilgrimage to Old Mt. Vernon. August 9, 1903, magazine section p. 1.

City Editor. Baltimore Morning Herald October 1903—August 31, 1904.

Mencken continued to do some theatrical reviews and to write occasional articles for the *Sunday Herald*; but the rigors of the job of City Editor left him little time for writing, and less liking for administrative posts.

The climax of HLM's career on the *Herald* came with the great Baltimore Fire of February 7, 1904. Mencken was called in at 11:30 A.M. on Sunday February 7th and did not return home until Sunday February 14th. Two extra editions of the paper were printed on Sunday in the *Herald* building; the Monday morning edition was printed in the *Post* building in Washington; the Tuesday morning edition was printed at the, far from adequate, offices of the old *World* in Baltimore; the Wednesday morning edition was again printed in Washington; the Thursday morning edition was printed in Philadelphia and rushed to Baltimore via a special B & O train. This last arrangement lasted for five weeks before the *Herald* was able to return to Baltimore.

"I was pulled out of bed at eleven o'clock on a Sunday morning and went to the office to get out an extra. The fire at that time was confined to a single block and seemed likely to be put out before the end of the afternoon. But at nine o'clock that night, after the *Herald* had printed two extras, one of them illustrated with fire views, I received notice that the building was to be dynamited and so it had to be abandoned. I left with my overcoat pockets stuffed with copy and a package of cuts in my hands. [Lynn R.] Meekins [chief editor] at once suggested that we proceed to Washington and try to get out next morning's paper with the plant of the Washington *Post*. He rushed for the train at once, and I followed an hour later. When I got to Washington with two or three reporters and the foreman of our composing room, I found that Meekins had already come to an arrangement with Scott C. Bone, then Managing Editor of the *Post,* and that everything was ready for us. We printed a four-page paper in Washington that night and brought it to Baltimore early the next morning." HLM (EPFL—A29)

"During the week following the outbreak of the fire the *Herald* was printed in three different cities, and I was present at all of its accouchements, herding dispersed and bewildered reporters at long distance and cavorting gloriously in strange composing-rooms. My opening burst of work without a stop ran to sixty-four and a half hours, and then I got only six hours of nightmare sleep, and resumed on a working schedule of from twelve to fourteen hours a day, with no days off and no time for meals until work was over. It was brain-fagging and back-breaking, but it was grand beyond compare—an adventure of the first chop, a razzle-dazzle superb and elegant, a circus in forty rings. When I came out of it at last I was a settled and indeed almost a middle-aged man, spavined by responsibility and aching in every sinew, but I went into it a boy, and it was the hot gas of youth that kept me going." *Newspaper Days* p. 277–278.

[Dispatches] Republican National Convention, Chicago. Baltimore Morning and Sunday Herald June 19–24, 1904.

Senator Fairbanks [Charles Warren Fairbanks U.S. Senator, R. Ind.] Will Accept the Second Place on the Ticket. June 19, p. 1.

Maryland in Van of National Convention. June 20, p. 1.

Convention Crowds Resemble a Durbar. June 21, p. 1.

Virginia Delegation Had a Lively Fight. June 21, p. 2.

Senator Depew [Chauncey Mitchell Depew, U.S. Senator, R. New York] Causes First Enthusiasm. June 21, p. 2.

Harry S[ythe] Cummings [Negro Politician] Much in Demand. June 21, p. 2.

Listless Delegates and Many Empty Seats Marked Opening of Republican Convention; Applause Broke Out at Wide Intervals, But Enthusiasm Was Lacking and Cheers and Hand Clapping Were Feeble. June 22, p. 1.

"Uncle" Joe Cannon [Joseph Gurney Cannon, U.S. Representative, leader of reactionary Republicans] Worked the Convention of Republicans to a High Pitch of Enthusiasm; Characteristic Speech and Gestures by Permanent Chairman of the Chicago Assembly Carried Delegates and Spectators Off Their Feet, June 23, p. 1.

Theodore Roosevelt Named for President; Charles W. Fairbanks for Vice-President; Republicans Roused From Their Lethargy of First Session and Pandemonium Reigned When the Presidential Nomination Was Made. June 24, p. 1.

[Dispatches] Democratic National Convention, St. Louis. Baltimore Morning and Sunday Herald July 5–11, 1904.

Enthusiasm Lacking in Democratic Hosts. July 5, p. 2.

Maryland Delegates Penned in Hotel. July 5, p. 2.

Painful Indifference Prevails at St. Louis. July 6, p. 1.

Maryland Delegates Visit World's Fair. July 6, p. 2.

Enthusiastic Cheers for Mr. [Stephen Grover] Cleveland Mark Opening of Big Democratic Convention, but the Opposition to [Alton Brooks] Parker [Chief Justice, Court of Appeals] is Waning; Mention of Sage of Princeton's Name [Woodrow Wilson] by Temporary Chairman John Sharp Williams Signals for Wild Outburst of Applause. July 7, p. 1.

William J. Bryan, Once Powerful, Goes Down to Defeat Before the Forces that Will Nominate Chief Judge Parker; Amid Cheers of His Friends in the Galleries the Eloquent Nebraskan is Vanquished by Votes of His Well Organized Opponents. July 8, p. 1.

Hinges of St. Louis Lid Are Broken. July 8, p. 1.

Marylanders Prepare to Return Home. July 8, p. 1.

Parker's Name Placed Before the Democratic Convention Accompanied by Demonstration of Greatest Enthusiasm. Hearst and Others are Brought Before the Delegates; For Half an Hour Delegates from Many States Paraded, Shouted and Shrieked to Show Their Intentions at the Call of the Roll. July 9, p. 1.

Marylanders Start for Home Today. July 9, p. 2.

Hon. Henry G. Davis for Vice-President. Judge Alton B. Parker's Stand for Gold Indorsed by the Democratic Convention; Crowds Held on Throughout the Night to Witness William Jennings Bryan's Gallant Fight Against the Power He Downed Eight Years Ago. July 10, p. 1.

Wornout Democratic Delegates Depart from Scenes of the Strenuous Struggle Which Ended in Declaration for Gold. July 11, p. 1.

Weary Marylanders Are Returning Home. July 11, p. 2.

Mencken attended his first pair of conventions as legman for Al Goodman who taught him the ropes and the rules of what was to become one of his favorite, never to be missed, shows. It is interesting to note that in 1904 Mencken used the adjective gallant to describe W. J. Bryan's fight against the opposing forces at the Democratic Convention.

City Editor. Baltimore Evening Herald August 25, 1904–1905.

On Thursday August 25th the first issue of the *Evening Herald* appeared. After one staff struggled with two papers for a week the *Morning Herald* was dropped, the last issue appearing on Wednesday August 31, 1904. Mencken continued as City Editor for the *Evening Herald*.

THE PASSING OF "THE HILL." Baltimore Evening Herald March 15, 1905, p. 7.

Apparently the only signed article HLM wrote while City Editor.

NOTES IN THE MARGIN. Baltimore Sunday Herald October 9, 1904 —February 5, 1905, editorial page. Literary-Dramatic.

Managing Editor. Baltimore Evening Herald 1905—January 20, 1906.

MERE OPINION. Baltimore Sunday Herald November 19, 1905— March 11, 1906, theatre page.

[Theatrical Articles]. Baltimore Sunday Herald December 10-31, 1905, page opposite theatre page.

Secretary and Editor. The [Baltimore] Herald January 20—June 17, 1906.

> The paper was in heavy difficulties and HLM's time was occupied with its death throes. On Sunday June 17, 1906 the announcement appeared that there would be "no further publication of the *Sunday Herald,* the *Evening Herald,* or the *Weekly Herald.*"

THE BALTIMORE EVENING NEWS

News Editor. [Baltimore] Evening News June–July, 1906.

"By this time [1906] I was pretty well known in journalistic circles, and when the *Herald* blew up all of the other Baltimore papers instantly offered me jobs. I chose the post of news editor on the Baltimore *Evening News*, offered to me by Charles H. Grasty, who was then publisher of that paper. The *News*, after long lean years, was now a great success. In fact, it was fast going ahead of the Baltimore *Sun* which had been the leading paper of Maryland for two generations. I wrote editorials on the *News* under Dr. Fabian Franklin, who was then editor, and also made up the paper. Grasty was a charming fellow and, at that time, an excellent newspaper man. Unfortunately, his notions of the compensation suitable to journalists were not unlike those of Colonel Cunningham [chief editor of the *Herald* in 1899]; he paid me, as I recall it, about $30 a week. Accordingly, when the *Sun* offered me $43 to take charge of its Sunday edition recently acquired, I accepted. Thus my term of service on the *News* was not much more than a month." HLM (EPFL—A29)

THE BALTIMORE SUNPAPERS
1906-1917

Editor. [Baltimore] Sun July 30, 1906—April 18, 1910.

"The new Sunday edition was a paltry thing of twelve pages and I was allowed but $100 a week to buy stuff for it. . . . Soon I was put to writing editorials and later on became dramatic critic of the paper. . . . On the *Sun* I had a free hand and soon began a vigorous assault upon the frauds prevailing in the theatre of that day. . . . It grossly offended the local managers and they began to complain. . . . [Walter W.] Abell [publisher] stood by me very gallantly, but in the end I concluded that the managers were right—that it was a bit unjust after all for me to treat them so hardly. They had to take whatever plays the theatrical syndicate sent them. . . . So I resigned as dramatic critic and have avoided the job ever since. That was in 1909." HLM (EPFL—A29)

Editor. [Baltimore] Evening Sun April 18, 1910—December 1916.

"In April, 1910, [Charles H. Grasty owner and publisher] started an evening edition and transferred me to it as an editor without title and with few definite duties. The responsible editor was J[ohn] H[aslup] Adams. I wrote two editorials a day for Adams and also contributed a column special article to the editorial page. In addition, I had a thumb in various other jobs about the office. The result was that I was kept busy and that I enjoyed life immensely." HLM (EPFL—A29)

[Articles]. [Baltimore] Evening Sun April 18, 1910—May 6, 1911, editorial page.

1910

Good Old Baltimore. April 18.
Socialism Today. April 20.
Wars Upon Alcohol. April 22.
William Shakespeare. April 23.
Joseph Conrad. April 26.
The One Hundred Best Plays. April 27.
A Great Norwegian. April 28.
Psychotherapy. April 29.
On Whiskers. May 2.
The Indian. May 3.
The Charity Bill. May 4.
The Literary Life. May 6.
A Negro State? May 7.
"The Winter's Tale." May 10.
A Drama of Ideas. May 12.
Thoughts on Eating. May 13.
The Wedding Season. May 16.
The Pestiferous Fly. May 18.

Victuals: a Reverie. May 19.
More Psychotherapy. May 21.
The Theatrical Year. May 23.
A New Nation Arises. May 24.
Notes in the Margin. May 26.
A Plea for Comedy. May 28.
In the Vestry Room. May 30.
Sousa, Et Cetera. May 31.
First Editions. June 1.
An Eternal Mystery. June 2.
Mr. Taft at Work. June 3.
Hidden Treasures. June 4.
On Jurisprudence. June 6.
The Play Record. June 9.
Marginal Notes. June 10.
Marginal Notes. June 11.
Summer Novels. June 13.
China's New Senate. June 18.
Marion Harland. June 20.

Marginal Notes. June 21.
The Pimlico Road. June 22.
Marginal Notes. June 23.
On Medical Fees. June 24.
Lower California. June 25.
Chiefly Musical. June 27.
"East Lynne" Wins. June 30.
A Wild German. July 2.
Notes on Morals. July 7.
At Back River. July 12.
In the Rosin Dust. July 13.
French Marriages. July 14.
Europe Since 1815. July 15.
A Tale of 1904. July 18.
The New Thought. July 20.
An Old-Time Actor. July 22.
Back to Torture! July 23.
On Cigarettes. July 25.
Marginal Notes. July 26.
The Actor. July 27.
World Languages. July 28.
The Profane Art. August 5.
Curbing the Cops. August 6.
Neurasthenia. August 8.
Trouble Ahead. August 10.
Exit the Maxims. August 11.
In Germany. August 12.
Exit G. B. Shaw. August 13.
The American. August 15.
Genius vs. Cash. August 16.
The Happy Life. August 17.
A Russian Critic. September 19.
On Tobacco. October 4.
About Best-Sellers. October 5.
Cholera Again. October 6.
The Two Englishes. October 10.
Jim the Penman. October 11.
The Expurgators. October 13.
England's English. October 14.
American Cooking. October 15.
Spoken American. October 19.
More American. October 20.
The Book. October 21.
William V. Moody. October 22.
American Pronouns. October 25.

Empty Pessimism. October 27.
William Gillette. October 28.
A Call for Help. October 29.
An Examination. November 1.
Sunday Theatres. November 2.
Nietzscheana. November 3.
French Melodrama. November 5.
Poor Old Ibsen. November 7.
A New Court? November 8.
Percy MacKaye. November 9.
The Pension Grab. November 10.
Good for the Reds! November 11.
The Printed Play. November 15.
Henri Bataille. November 16.
A Hall of Fame. November 17.
The Moral Mind. November 18.
Jerome K. Jerome. November 23.
On Hanging. November 25.
The Tzs-Cheng Yuan. November 26.
A Notable Novel. November 28.
The Mikado. November 30.
The Dramatic Critic. December 1.
At the Pole. December 2.
Mental Vibrations. December 3.
Avery Hopwood. December 6.
Eating, An Elegy. December 7.
England's Crisis. December 8.
An English Issue. December 9.
Tolstoiana. December 10.
The Death Rate. December 12.
A Maker of Tunes. December 13.
August Strindberg. December 14.
On "Life-Waste." December 16.
Various Matters. December 17.
The Lords Spiritual. December 19.
Christmas Books. December 20.
Christmas Books II. December 21.
Direct Elections. December 22.
Various Matters. December 23.
Christmas Sermon. December 24.
The Fitch Plays. December 27.
Wm. Clyde Fitch. December 28.
In Liberia. December 29.
Various Matters. December 30.

1911

Lizette Reese. January 2.
Lizette Reese II. January 3.
Lizette Reese III. January 4.
On Old Books. January 5.
Concerning 'The Lily.' January 6.
The Balalaika. January 9.

Jones at the Bat. January 11.
Do We Go Ahead? January 13.
Various Matters. January 16.
The 16th Amendment. January 18.
Rupert Hughes. January 19.
Various Matters. January 20.

What is Truth? January 23.
James Forbes. January 24.
Literary Vandals. January 25.
The Baconians. January 26.
An Idol Smashed. January 27.
On "Macbeth." January 30.
"Der Rosenkavalier." January 31.
England's Paupers. February 1.
On Autographs. February 2.
"La Samaritaine." February 3.
Health Laws. February 8.
The Lowden Bill. February 9.
Pinero's Latest. February 10.
On Being Fat. February 11.
A Notable Novel. February 14.
Everywoman. February 15.
The Trial of Joan. February 16.
Home Rule! February 17.
Russian Fiction. February 20.
Mrs. Fiske's Roles. February 21.
The New Peers. February 22.
Eugene Walters. February 23.
On Quotations. February 24.
An Irish Genius. February 27.
Round One! February 28.
The Oregon Plan, I-VII. March 1–8.
About "The Faun." March 9.
Legalized Murder. March 10.
Ambitious Bards. March 13.
In Jackson's Day. March 14.
The Child-Actor. March 16.
Uncle Sam's Money. March 17.

The Varieties. March 18.
Mental Healing. March 21.
The Novel Today. March 22.
More Poetry! March 23.
The Literary Life. March 24.
On Free Speech. March 25.
Mr. Shakespeare. March 27.
Stage Censors. March 28.
The Bard Again. March 29.
The Open Road. March 30.
Slaying the Bard. March 31.
Up the Valley. April 1.
In Re Shakespeare. April 3.
At the Theatres. April 4.
The Last Round. April 6.
"The White Ship." April 8.
Italian Bands. April 13.
The Vernal Bards. April 14.
Daniel Frohman. April 17.
On Dreams. April 18.
The Pied Piper. April 19.
The New Theatre. April 20.
Fortunata. April 21.
The Party System. April 22.
Flying by Night. April 24.
A Woman's Plays. April 25.
A Symphony. April 27.
"The Honorable." April 28.
The Ueberbrettl'. April 29.
On Bartenders. May 1.
The Minstrel Men. May 2.
Vaudeville Songs. May 3.
On Alcohol. May 6.

These articles were signed M. or H.L.M. Mencken may well have written additional ones that were not so designated. It was the articles signed H.L.M. that interested Harry C. Black, a young stockholder. Black liked the articles so well that he suggested to Grasty that, who ever H.L.M. was, he be given a column of his own and be permitted to sign it. The result was "The Free Lance."

THEODORE ROOSEVELT: A Study of the Man. [Baltimore] Evening Sun Friday June 17, 1910, p. 7. Full page single article.

THE FREE LANCE. [Baltimore] Evening Sun May 8, 1911— October 23, 1915, editorial page, daily.

"The Free Lance" first appeared on Monday, May 8, under the two column head "The World in Review." "The Free Lance" head was first used on May 9, and on the 9th, 10th and 11th appeared with a two column head. From May 12 until the end, the series appeared under a one column head, with an occasional use of two columns. There were some irregularities, the column did not appear on the following dates: July 3, August 2, 5, 7, 9, 10, 14, 16, 19, 22, 29, 31,

NEWSPAPER WORK

September 2, 12, 15, 19, 22, 1911; April 18–June 1 (HLM in Munich) 1912; September 17–29, (HLM on vacation) 1913; April 13–May 28, (HLM on vacation) 1914; January 5–30, (HLM in Germany) May 20, 21, 22, June 17, 18, July 20, 21, 22, August 18–30, September 1, 2, 3, 8, 13–18, 20, 22–25, 27, 1915.

"My work for the *Sun* between 1910 and 1915 greatly facilitated the organization of my ideas. I conducted a column that was highly controversial and every statement I made in it was instantly attacked. This pressure forced me to examine my notions very carefully. I emerged from the experience very tough-minded and with considerable skill at controversy.

"Its success in Baltimore was extraordinary. Nothing of the sort had ever been heard of there before. In substance 'The Free Lance' was a private editorial column devoted wholly to my personal opinions and prejudices. At the start, my ribaldries and contumacies greatly worried Grasty, and at one time he made me pledge him my word as an old friend that I would never attack any Church or any clergyman, as such, in the column. I got out of this pledge in a few weeks through the fact that the Methodist ministers of the town called a public meeting and attacked me. Grasty instantly agreed that as the party attacked I had a moral right to reply. That reply ran serially for five years thereafter . . . . I carried on endless wars against the Anti-Saloon League, the vice crusaders, the town boomers, and other such frauds. I also devoted a great deal of space to politics, particularly to local politics.

"I lost all my battles. I can't recall one that ended in victory. Nevertheless, the net effect of 'The Free Lance' column was probably beneficial, though I certainly had no intention of making it so, for I believe I am almost completely devoid of public spirit. What it did was to accustom Baltimoreans to the freest imaginable of free discussion. . . . The *Sun,* especially the *Evening Sun,* guards this right of free speech very jealously and attacks every attempt to invade it with the utmost ferocity. Inasmuch as no such policy was ever heard of in the *Sun* office before I set up 'The Free Lance,' I incline to think that I had something to do with establishing it.

" . . . , it was the rule of the paper that any denunciation of me in turn, however extravagant, should be printed. I had one column. Beside it were two columns, mainly devoted to such denunciations. I controlled that space myself, and saw to it that all the worst attacks were printed. This was partly mere bombast and braggadocia, but also partly genuine belief in free speech." HLM (EPFL—A29)

"An Answer to Mencken from the Trenches in Flanders," Letter to the Editor, from A. D. Smith, Jr., No. 66237, Somewhere in Belgium with the Canadian Expeditionary Force, November 28, [1915]. Appeared in The [Baltimore] Evening Sun December 18, 1915, editorial page, answering various "Free Lance" articles and published by *The Sun* in the column space.

11 FEARFUL HOURS OF DEMOCRACY'S CANDIDATE-MAKING. [Baltimore] Evening Sun Friday June 28, 1912, p. 3.

Democratic National Convention, Baltimore. Full page article.

THE FREE LANCE IN WASHINGTON. [Baltimore] Evening Sun Monday March 3, 1913, p. 1. (Suffragette Parade.)

WEEK OF WORLD—BETTERING AND HIGH ENDEAVOR. [Baltimore] Sun November 2, 1913, part 3, p. 1.

The cartoon by McKee Barclay was used for the first time with this article and carried the line, "photo by Bachrach." This cartoon was used occasionally with articles by HLM in the Sunday *Sun*.

MENCKEN THROWS LIFE TO HON. ANDERSON. [Baltimore] Sun November 9, 1913, part 3, p. 3. (Local Anti-Saloon League leader.)

[Articles]. [Baltimore] Sun October 18—December 20, 1914, Section 2.

The Week in Review. October 18, p. 1.
London So Like Baltimore. October 25, p. 1.
How Germans Smashed Namur. November 1, p. 1.
Is This Way Germans Face a Hostile World. November 8, p. 1.
Married Men Braver Than Bachelors? No! November 15, p. 1.
Do You Speak English or American? November 22, p. 1.
Where "American" Differs from the Old English Language. November 29, p. 3.
National Characteristics Are Shown in the Use of Words. December 6, p. 2.
They Differ Widely in the Spelling of Words. December 13, p. 1.
Schools Don't Attempt to Teach the Language Americans Speak. December 20, p. 2.

[Articles]. [Baltimore] Evening Sun October 25, 1915—December 6, 1916, editorial page.

1915

Notes for a Proposed Treatise upon the Origin and Nature of Puritanism. October 25.
More Notes for a Work upon the Origin and Nature of Puritanism. November 2.
The War in Its Last Phase. November 8.
Are the Germans Immoral? Of Course! November 11.
The Hunting of the Snark. November 16. (U.S. bogus neutrality.)
More Proofs of German Immorality. November 22.
An Antidote to the Drama League. November 29.
On Preparedness. December 1.
Hoch France! December 3.
Hypenophobia. December 9. (Pro-British vs. pro-German.)
The Report of the Vice Commission. December 28.
The Report of the Vice Commission (Second Article). December 30.

1916

The Report of the Vice Commission (Third Article). January 1.
The Traffic in Babies in Baltimore. January 11. (Death rate among foundlings.)
In Defense of College Women. January 25.
Mobilizing the Mountebanks. January 31. (Preparedness campaign.)
The Curtain Rings Down on the Vice Report. February 2.
Eine Kleine Sinfonie In F Dur. February 9. (Beethoven's Eighth Symphony.)
Rattling the Hyphen. February 12. (The arts.)
The Bozart. February 15. (The arts.)
The Impending Orgy. February 17. (Billy Sunday.)

NEWSPAPER WORK

Schubert. February 22.
The Pious Meditations of an American-German. February 24.
Flights of Fancy. February 29.
Doctor Seraphidus et Ecstaticus. March 14. (Billy Sunday.)
Preparedness at the Bat. March 16.
The Calliope of Zion. March 27. (Billy Sunday.)

"Mencken Not a Rival to 'The Man We All Adore,'" by Solomon T. Shandy. "A comment or two upon the several recent screeds denouncing our incomparable Homme de Lettres because, for sooth, he makes to shine the somewhat satirical light of reason upon the Knockneed creed and the obfuscated theology of the 'Calliope of Zion' . . . " Appeared in the [Baltimore] Evening Sun May 13, 1916, editorial page.

Theological Soarings. March 31.
James Huneker. April 7.
Pious Meditations. April 10.
O Fruehling, Wie Bist Du So Schoen. April 12. (Schumann.)
Music and Other Vices. April 24.
The Tumult Dies. May 2. (Billy Sunday.)
The American Best-Seller, in Four Parts. Part I. May 9.
Variations in G Minor. May 11.
The American Best-Seller, in Four Parts. Part II. May 15.
Apologia Pro Vita Sua. May 17.
The American Best-Seller, in Four Parts. Part III. May 25.
The American Best-Seller, in Four Parts. Part IV. May 30.
The Paradise of the Third-Rate. June 1. (United States.)
Answers to Correspondents. June 13.
On With the Dance! June 14. (Politics and the war.)
Joseph Conrad, in Four Parts. Part I. June 20.
Joseph Conrad, in Four Parts. Part II. June 26.
Notes on the Drama. June 28.
Prose Libre. July 6.
Joseph Conrad, in Four Parts. Part III. July 10.
Joseph Conrad, in Four Parts. Part IV. July 12.
More Notes for a Work Upon the Origin and Nature of Puritanism. July 14.
More Notes for a Work Upon the Origin and Nature of Puritanism. July 19.
Various Platitudes. July 20.
Theodore Dreiser. July 26.
More Dreiseriana. August 1.
Two Dreiser Novels. August 4.
More Platitudes. August 11.
The Free Lance (Retired). September 1.
Notes on the American Language. September 7.
Here at Home. September 15. (Baltimore.)
Notes from a Day-Book. September 21.
Pious Reflections. September 25.
Oh, Henry, How You Talk! October 5. (Hay fever.)
Manias and Malaises. October 16.
An American Symphony. October 19. (Dvorak and The New World Symphony.)
On Christian Science. October 23.
At Last! At Last! October 31. (Dr. Tom Hare's prohibitionists parade.)
Contribution to a Catalogue Raissoné of Things That Might be Improved. November 8.

Ireland: Her Books. November 10. (Ernest A. Boyd's *Ireland's Literary Renaissance*.) Reprinted as a pamphlet.

The Coming Rough-House. November 15. (The Uplift.)

Franz Joseph Haydn. November 23.

A Busted Bugaboo. November 29. (Puritanism.)

If You Have Tears to Shed—! December 6. (Tschaikowsky.)

[Dispatches]. [Baltimore] Sun and Evening Sun January 28—March 21, 1917.

Germany United, Mencken:—Germans to Go on Fighting. Sunday January 28, p. 1.

Mencken and Hapgood Describe the Situation in Germany and in England-Germans Determined. Sunday February 4, p. 4.

Berlin Calm, But Earnest, in Face of Action of U.S. Morning, February 6, p. 2.

Mencken Says Americans in Berlin Are Absolutely Safe But They Feel Anxiety. Evening, February 9, p. 1.

Notes of a War-Time Journey. Evening, February 12, editorial page.

Mencken at Kirkwall, Sees Searching of Ships-Notes of a War-Time Voyage—II. Morning, February 14, p. 1.

War Booms Norway-Mencken; Automobiles, Champagne and Diamonds Result of High Prices, But Picture Also Has a Dark Side. Sunday February 18, p. 1.

Henry Mencken Cables Story of "Ticklish Moments" in Berlin. Morning, March 6, p. 1.

Mencken Gives Glimpses of Trench Warfare as Seen on Eastern Front. Evening, March 12, p. 1.

Berlin in War Time. Evening, March 12, editorial page.

Life at the Front Seen by a Visitor Who Found Remarkable Food Supply. Evening, March 14, p. 2.

A Russian Town Under German Rule Proves to be Quiet with Guns Near. Evening, March 15, p. 2.

On the Eastern Front. Evening, March 19, editorial page.

The Land of Hindenburg. Evening, March 21, editorial page.

THE DIARY OF A RETREAT. [Baltimore] Sun March 10–22, 1917.

Berlin At Time of Break. March 10, p. 1.

Berlin on Its Doubtful Day. II. March 11, p. 1.

Americans Near Panic. III. March 12, p. 2.

Berlin Calm at Crisis. IV. March 13, p. 3.

Dark Days for Americans. V. March 14, p. 3.

German Public Stirred Up. VI. March 15, p. 3.

Americans Leave Berlin. VII. March 16, p. 7.

Out of Germany At Last. VIII. March 17, p. 3.

Across French Border. IX. March 18, p. 5.

Headed for Sunny Spain. X. March 19, p. 3.

In Sunny Spain At Last. XI. March 20, p. 3.

Steaming Towards Home. XII. March 21, p. 3.

Brought to Conclusion. XIII. March 22, p. 9.

"In [December] 1916 I went to Germany as correspondent for the Baltimore Sun. . . . In February, 1917, when the United States broke off relations with Germany, I was with the German Army on the Eastern Front, near Dvinsk. . . . I thereupon returned to Berlin, and found that, under the German military regulations, no correspondent could leave the country until six weeks after his return from the front. I settled down to spend the six weeks in Berlin. Meanwhile, Ambassador Gerard and his staff were preparing to go home, and a number of American correspondents were planning to go with them. The latter were known to be excessively anti-German. Certain other correspondents, who proposed to remain in Germany, thought it would be a good idea to get me out, so that I might counteract the efforts of the German-eaters. They accordingly made representations to Ludendorff . . . , and orders that I should be permitted to go at once reached Berlin a few hours before Gerard's special train was scheduled to depart. The General Staff gave me a place on it, and so I left with Gerard, but not as a member of his party.

"After a few days in Berne, I proceeded to Paris. All sailings from Northern European ports had been suspended on account of the U-boat proclamation, but it was reported in Paris that Spanish liners were still running. No one had apparently ever heard of a Spanish liner before. . . . I quietly departed for Madrid, and there, by the aid of the American Embassy, got a room on a Spanish liner sailing from La Corunna five or six days later. I thus beat Gerard and the other correspondents home by a week. I wrote my stuff on the ship—50,000 words in 10 days—and filed it when I reached Havana. It was printed serially over a period of two weeks. But it did no good. The war was already on by the time I got to Havana. In fact, some of my stuff had to be killed; no American newspaper, at that time, would print it. Nevertheless, it was the truth." HLM (EPFL—A29)

The John H. Wheeler, Inc., Newspaper Features handled Mencken's articles from Germany and offered them for sale to newspapers in the United States, exclusive of Baltimore. Mencken, of course, had his own arrangements with the *Sunpapers.* Wheeler Inc. handled the news articles as well as "The Diary of a Retreat" series and they were carried in whole or in part by the following papers: the [Chicago] *Examiner,* the [Minneapolis] *Journal,* the [New York] *Evening Mail,* the [New York] *World,* the [Philadelphia] *North American,* the [Rochester] *Herald,* the [Seattle] *Times.*

[Dispatches]. [Baltimore] Sun March 12–15, 1917.

Intervention Issue in Cuba (Havana). I. March 12, p. 1.
Blow Dealt Cuban Rebels. II. March 13, p. 1.
Cuban Liberals Hope to Force U.S. to Act. III. March 14, p. 1.
Cuban Revolt Blows Up. IV. March 15, p. 2.

[Dispatches]. [Baltimore] Evening Sun March 14–29, 1917, editorial page.

San Cristobal de la Habana. March 14.
The Fight at Cajigal, The Tannenberg of Cuba. March 16.
A Cuban Revolution. March 26.
Notes of a Revolution. March 29.

Mencken returned to the United States from Germany aboard a Spanish ship bound for Cuba. A Cuban revolution had just broken out and the *Sun* cabled him to stop in Havana and get the news. He arrived in Havana on March 5 and returned to his home on March 14.

"A day out of Havana I received a wireless from the Baltimore *Sun* saying that a revolution was on in Cuba, and that there was a heavy censorship, and the American press was getting only government canned-goods and the even less reliable press-matter of the revolutionary junta in New York. I was ordered to stop off in Havana and find out the truth. I had a friend there, Captain Asmus Leonhard, of the Munson Line. I sent him a wireless, and his launch met the ship when we reached port. A few hours later he had introduced me to all the chief government officials, from President Menocal down. Meanwhile, I had met Dr. Hermann M. Biggs, formerly Health Commissioner of New York, on the ship. Biggs, it so happened, had many acquaintances in Cuba, and among them were some of the leaders of the revolution. He gave me access to them. (They were leading very secluded lives in Havana). Thus I got at both sides, and soon had all the facts. I sent my stuff to Key West by passengers on the daily ferry-boat, and there it was filed, and so reached the *Sun*. In this business the New York *World* joined the *Sun*." HLM (EPFL—A29)

"On my return [from Germany and Cuba] the United States entered the war and it was impossible for me to do any newspaper work of the kind I was accustomed to." HLM (EPFL—A29)

"At the time these pieces were written for the New York *Evening Mail* Dr. Edward A. Rumely was its publisher, and John E. Cullen . . . , its managing editor. I wrote, as I recall it, two articles a week, but sometimes one of them was published in two installments. It was war time, and inasmuch as Rumely was known to be pro-German (as I was) he had hard sledding. By my arrangement with him and Cullen I was not to discuss the war, but now and then a reference to it slipped in, and more than one of my articles had to be suppressed. In the end Rumely was railroaded to Sing Sing, his paper was seized, and I lost my job." HLM EPFL—A115) *See* account in William Manchester's Life of Mencken, *Disturber of the Peace,* p. 104–105.

"When the paper was suppressed by the Government in 1918, I stopped writing and believed that I was done with newspaper work forever." HLM (EPFL—A29)

[Articles]. [New York] Evening Mail June 18, 1917—July 8, 1918.

1917

Beer and Light Wines Urged as Necessity to Fight Drunkenness. June 18, p. 7. (Their use by Allied armies as sedative.)

George Ade, American. July 7, book page.

James Gibbons Huneker. July 21, book page.

"Sister Carrie's" History. August 4, book page.

Anti-Saloon League Lobby Has Congress Badly Scared. August 21, back page.

Prohibition Hypocrisy Due to Job-Chasing "Statesmen." August 27, back page. (Anti-Saloon League control of small but active bloc.)

Minority of Church Members Backs Anti-Saloon League's Fight. September 5, back page.

Heroes of Forensic Battles Royal Make "Congress Record" Cheapest Book in World. September 14, p. 3. (And most amusing.)

"Reformers" Oppose Sanitary Measures Against Disease. September 18, p. 7. (Prefer "moral zones" around camps.)

Negro Spokesman Arises to Voice His Race's Wrongs. September 19, back page. (Kelly Miller, Dean of College of Arts and Sciences, Howard University, writes to President Wilson.)

Nothing Dead About Language U.S. Boys Take to the Trenches. September 28, back page.

Bold Seer of West Strips American Life of Hypocrisy. October 2. (E. W. Howe.) Page missing, article probably appeared on this date. Unverified.

Suffragist-Suffragette. October 9, back page.

$1 a Day War Tax on Bachelors. October 10, p. 8. (Its advantages.)

Time Will Mold Our Speech. October 15, p. 7.

Civilized Chicago. October 23, p. 10.

How They Say It "Over There." October 25, back page.

Lopsided "Scientific" Evidence Against the Demon Rum. October 30, back page. (Dr. Eugene Fisk's book, *Alcohol*.)

Mark Twain's Americanism. November 1, p. 9.

Have Men Rights? November 2, p. 9. (Now that women have so many.)

The Good Worst-Sellers. November 3, p. 9.

The Hoe-Down Begins to Soar. November 7, p. 9. (Negro music.)

Authors Held to Blame. November 8, back page. (For unpublished manuscripts.)

The Sahara of the Bozart. November 13, p. 6. (The South.)
    Mistakenly attributed by Mencken to *The Evening Sun* in *The Sunpapers of Baltimore*, p. 378.

Penology: a Sick Science. November 14, back page.

Meditations on the Fair. November 15, p. 8. (On women.)

The Divine Afflatus. November 16, p. 5. (The creative artist and inspiration.)

Meditations on the Fair. November 16, p. 13. (On women.)

Virtuosi of Virtue. November 20, p. 6. (The professional uplifters.)

Some Secrets of Beauty. November 23, p. 13. (Physical attributes of beauty.)

Marriage: an Elegy. November 26, p. 11.

On Swearing. November 28, p. 5.

On Swearing, Article II. November 30, p. 15.

Let Us Forget It for Awhile. December 3, p. 9. (Sex education for romance.)

The Carrel-Dakin Treatment. December 6, back page.

From A Day-Book, Part I. Dcember 11, p. 6.

From A Day-Book, Part II. December 13, p. 9.

What Americans Die Of, Part I. December 17, p. 5. (Census Bureau's annual report.)

What Americans Die Of, Part II. December 18, p. 10.

Under the Campus Pump, Part I. December 26, p. 9. (Are professors really free?)

Under the Campus Pump, Part II. December 27, p. 9.

A Neglected Anniversary. December 28, p. 9. (History of the bathtub.)

"On December 28, 1917, I printed in the New York *Evening Mail* . . . , an article purporting to give the history of the bathtub. This article, I may say at once, was a tissue of absurdities, all of them deliberate and most of them obvious. . . . This article . . . , was planned as a piece of spoofing to relieve the strain of war days and I confess that I regarded it, when it came out, with considerable satisfaction. It was reprinted by various great organs of the enlightenment, and after a while the usual letters began to reach me from readers. Then, suddenly, my satisfaction turned to consternation. For those readers, it appeared, all took my idle jocosities with complete seriousness. Some of them, of antiquarian tastes, asked for further light on this or that phase of the subject. Others actually offered me corroboration. But the worse was yet to come. Pretty soon I began to encounter my perposterous 'facts' in the writings of other men. . . . They got into learned journals. They were alluded to on the floor of Congress. They crossed the ocean, and were discussed solemnly in England and on the continent. Finally, I began to find them in standard works of reference. Today, I believe, they are accepted as gospel everywhere on earth. To question them becomes as hazardous as to question the Norman Invasion." "Melancholy Reflections," *Chicago Sunday Tribune*, May 23, 1926, Drama Section.

NEWSPAPER WORK

Reprinted in: "The Fable That Caused a Furore," *Chicago Sunday Tribune,* August 22, 1926, Drama Section p. 2; *The Bathtub Hoax and Other Blasts and Bravos from the Chicago Tribune by H. L. Mencken,* edited, with an introduction and notes, by Robert McHugh. (N.Y. Knopf, 1958) "A Neglected Anniversary," p. 4-10; *A Mencken Chrestomathy,* p. 592-597.

1918

The Morals of Congress, Part I. January 2, p. 9.
The Morals of Congress, Part II. January 3, p. 5.
Grand, Lovely, Enviable Creatures, Part I. January 4, p. 6. (Superior male should be protected by law from women.)
Grand, Lovely, Enviable Creatures, Part II. January 7, p. 5.
The Forgotten Man. January 10, p. 8. (Prohibition.)
The Big, Big D, Part I. January 14, p. 7 (Swearing.)
The Big, Big D, Part II. January 15, p. 9.
The "Dry" Code of Ethics. January 19, p. 4.
Heathen Reflections, Part I. January 21, p. 7.
Heathen Reflections, Part II. January 22, p. 9.
A Glance at Pedagogics. January 23, p. 11. (Teaching methods.)
The Sunday School, Part I. January 24, p. 9.
The Sunday School, Part II. January 25, p. 7.
Who Is Honorable? January 26, p. 9. (Use of the term Hon.)
The Critical Vocabulary. January 31, p. 9. (English must borrow it.)
Variations on the Wedding March, Part I. February 1, p. 9.
Zoos. February 2, p. 9. (Why zoos?)
Prohibition Statistics. February 4, p. 6.
The Secret of Life. February 4, p. 8. (Biological and scientific discoveries.)
Reform Walks the Plank. February 5, p. 9. (Professional reformers.)
Variations on the Wedding March, Part II. February 6, p. 10.
Notes from a Diary. February 11, p. 6.
Meditations on the Fair. February 13, p. 11.
On Publishers. February 16, p. 9.
The Intelligence of Women. February 20, p. 13.
The Tone Art. February 22, p. 9.
The Literary Life. February 25, p. 9.
Literature from the East Side. February 28, p. 11.
The Drama of Ideas. March 2, p. 10. (Drama should be entertaining.)
Thoughts on Monogamy. March 11, p. 9.
The Sea Change. March 15, p. 11. (Critical opinion of books in alien countries.)
Apologia Pro Sua Vita. March 18, p. 16. (On women.)
Prohibition and the Mails. March 20, p. 11.
Opportunities for Millionaires. March 22, p. 12. (To give money away.)
Pious Meditations. March 25, p. 7.
The American Novel. March 27, p. 11.
The Woman Voter. March 29, p. 11.
Poetry and Other Vices. April 1, p. 9.
Thoughts on Eating. April 5, p. 9.
Raising the Wind. April 9, p. 9. (Tips on sources of revenue for the government.)
The Curse of Spelling. April 11, p. 6.
In Praise of the Fair. April 13, p. 5.
Collars and Other Gauds. April 16, p. 6.

WORKS BY H. L. M.

The National Letters. April 19, p. 7.
American Victualry. April 25.
    Page missing, article probably appeared on this date. Unverified.
Notes from a Book of Phrases. April 29, p. 9.
The Woman of Tomorrow. May 2, p. 9.
The American. May 3, p. 9. (Not money hunger but social aspiration that moves him.)
Platitudes of To-morrow. May 7, p. 9.
George Tries to Do It. May 13, p. 7. (Differences between English and American speech.)
Dithyrambs on Alcohol. May 15, p. 12.
Variations in G Minor. May 17, p. 6. (Criticism and critics.)
The Decay of Victualry. May 20.
    Page missing, article probably appeared on this date. Unverified.
The New Doomesday Book. May 22, p. 11. (Anglicizing of names.)
Exit Typhoid. May 24, p. 7. (By sanitation and vaccine.)
Fifteen Hundred Words. May 27, p. 5.
The Poetry Question. May 29, p. 5.
How to Get a Husband. May 31, p. 13.
Callinectes Hastatus. June 3, p. 7. (Crabs.)
Meditations on a Day in June. June 5, p. 5.
The Uplift and Other Imbecilities. June 7, p. 10.
Literary Gabble. June 10, p. 5.
Elements of Victualry. June 12, p. 5.
Gratitude? Go To! June 17, p. 7. (Emotion of and demand for gratitude.)
The Puritan Complex. June 19, p. 7.
Authors and Other Fauna. June 21, p. 8.
The Duel of Sex. June 24, p. 6.
Sweating to Save Us. June 25, p. 8. (Anti-Saloon League.)
Notes and Queries. June 26, p. 6.
The Forward Looker. June 28, p. 9.
Prohibition and Other Malaises. June 29, p. 6.
Critics and Their Ways. July 1, p. 6.
    This article became famous under the title, "Criticism of Criticism of Criticism." Reprinted in: *Prejudices: First Series*, p. 9–21; *Criticism in America*, Its Function and Status. (N.Y., Harcourt, 1924), p. 176–190. The article which appeared in *The Smart Set*, April, 1917, "Criticism of Criticism of Criticism," is not the same article although it contains the same material.
Mr. Cabell of Virginia. July 3.
    Page missing, article probably appeared on this date. Unverified. Reprinted as a pamphlet.
Moral Reflections. July 5, p. 5.
    Part of this article was reprinted in: *The Vintage Mencken*, gathered by Alistair Cooke. (N.Y., Vintage Books, 1955), p. 69-73, "The Art Eternal."
Speaking Hay-Feverishly. July 8.
    Page missing, article probably appeared on this date. Unverified.

The *Evening Mail* for Tuesday July 9 carried notices of Dr. Rumely's arrest and change of control of the paper.

The *Evening Mail* articles were offered to the press in general. "Two or three papers nibbled at them but none printed them for more than a few weeks." HLM (EPFL—A29. The *Chicago Tribune* did reprint several, notably: "Civilized Chicago," "Virtuosi of Virtue," and "Critics and Their Ways." HLM reprinted many of the articles in his *Prejudices* Series, usually at least partially rewritten and with a change of title. "Curiously, much of his most enduring prose was written for the *Mail*. . . . In the Twenties, turning with his scissors and paste pot in search of *Prejudices* articles, he repeatedly came back to the *Mail* material, and when, thirty years later, he essayed to select his best out-of-print writing, the *Mail* was represented far out of proportion to the number of pieces printed." Manchester, *Disturber of the Peace.* p. 105.

THE BALTIMORE SUNPAPERS
1920—1948

"At the beginning of 1920, Paul Patterson, with whom I had been intimately acquainted on the Baltimore *Sun*, became publisher of the paper and urged me to rejoin its staff. Since then I have contributed an article a week to the *Evening Sun*, and have in addition covered the National Conventions . . . and done one or two other odd jobs. I am a member of the editorial counsel of the *Evening Sun* and am paid an annual retainer for sitting with it. I have no definite duties. The theory is that it is a useful thing to have at call a man familiar with the workings of the paper and yet removed from its policies. My relations to the staff of the *Evening Sun* are very intimate and cordial. I take great interest in the paper and have a hand in many of its enterprises. It is in many ways the most intelligent newspaper in America. Its policies are independent, it is an ardent and unwearied advocate of the vanishing liberties of the American people, and it is very enterprising in news-gathering." HLM (EPFL—A29)

Monday Articles

"The stuff I wrote for the *Evening Sun* between 1910 and 1935 included some of my best, and yet most of it is buried in their files. To be sure, I occasionally dredged out extracts from it for my Prejudices books, but they were few in number and of relatively little importance." HLM (EPFL—A30)

"In the columns of the *Evening Sun* I can say anything I please. I tackle subjects there that are never mentioned in other newspapers." HLM (EPFL—A29)

The following articles form a continuous series of HLM's contributions to the editorial page of *The Evening Sun*. There are articles in the series which appear on days other than Mondays; there are gaps in the series which occur when HLM was working on other assignments or was on vacation. In the main an article appeared each Monday and HLM gave to the series the inclusive title of "Monday Articles."

Many of the "Monday Articles" were commented upon, quoted and discussed in the national press. Some raised a storm of protest and brought forth a flood of articles in reply: editorials, news items, letters to the editor; some few in agreement, some in disagreement with HLM's thesis but in tribute to him as an invigorating force, the majority in disagreement in a range from angry to frenzied denunciation. A few of the more outstanding examples are: "Famine," which appeared on January 19, 1931, and dealt with Arkansas, and which led the Arkansas legislature to attempt to have HLM deported; the articles concerning the lynchings on the Eastern Shore of Maryland, which appeared in December of 1931 and October of 1933, and which led to an attempt by the Shoremen to boycott all Baltimore business houses; and the articles on the relative cultural standing of the forty-eight States, based on statistics compiled by HLM and Charles Angoff, which appeared on June 25 and July 16, 1934 and January 13, 1936, and which not a single state allowed to pass without copious comment.

A few citations to articles written in answer to HLM, which are of particular interest, or typical of attacks on HLM, or which HLM in turn answered in a Monday Article, have been included. Most of these appeared in the column space on the editorial page.

MONDAY ARTICLES. [Baltimore] Evening Sun February 9, 1920—January 31, 1938, editorial page.

1920

A Carnival of Buncombe. February 9. (The presidential aspirants.)
  Reprinted in: *H. L. Mencken, A Carnival of Buncombe,* edited by Malcolm Moos. (Baltimore, The Johns Hopkins Press, 1956) p. 5–10.
Literary Note. February 23. (Lizette Woodworth Reese.)
The Millennium Dawns. March 8. (The Volstead Act.)
The Intelligentsia. March 16. (The opinion weeklies.)
Notice to Neglected Geniuses. April 23. (Unpublished writers.)
The Clowns in the Ring. May 12. (The presidential aspirants.)
  Reprinted in: Moos. *A Carnival of Buncombe.* p. 11–14.
The Clash of Booms. May 17. (Herbert Hoover.)
Vive Le France! May 21. (Senator Joseph I. France of Maryland.)
A Glance Ahead. May 25. (Pressure groups vs. the ballot.)
The Armenian Buncombe. May 28.
  "Mr. Mencken and the Armenian Massacres," by Arthur O. Lovejoy. An answer to HLM's article. Appeared in the [Baltimore] Evening Sun May 31, 1920, editorial page.
Lodge. June 15. (Henry Cabot Lodge.)
  Reprinted in: *The Vintage Mencken,* gathered by Alistair Cooke. (New York, Vintage Books, 1955) p. 80–83.

WORKS BY H. L. M.

Einstein. June 24. (An example of the ebb and flow of fads in the U.S.)
San Francisco: A Memory. July 21.
Bayard vs. Lionheart. July 26. (Warren G. Harding and James M. Cox.)
    Reprinted in: Moos. *A Carnival of Buncombe.* p. 15-19.
Notes on the Drought. August 5. (Prohibition.)
Preliminary Report on the State of Literary Talent in the Republic. August 20.
Political Notes. August 25.
God Help Us All! August 30. (Big business monopolies.)
Another Millennium Dawns. September 6. (The vote.)
Campaign Notes. September 13.
    Reprinted in: Moos. *A Carnival of Buncombe.* p. 19–22.
The Bonus Banshee. September 20. (The veteran's bonus.)
Government by Blackleg. September 27. (A. M. Palmer's system of espionage.)
The Last Round. October 4. (The choice between candidates.)
    Reprinted in: Moos. *A Carnival of Buncombe.* p. 22–27.
On Being an American. October 11.
In Praise of Gamaliel. October 18. (Warren G. Harding.)
    Reprinted in: Moos. *A Carnival of Buncombe.* p. 27–31.
On American Letters. October 25.
The Last Gasp. November 1. (On voting and the issues on the local ballot.)
    Reprinted in: Moos. *A Carnival of Buncombe.* p. 32–35.
The Party System. November 8.
Free Speech—Truth—Justice—Idealism. November 15. (The objects of dis-
    cussion.)
Optimistic Note. November 22. (The political climate in the U.S.)
    Reprinted in: Moos. *A Carnival of Buncombe,* p. 35-38.
Let Us Be Happy! November 29. (On government profiteers.)
More Optimism. December 6. (Capitalism.)
The Blue-Nose At the Bat Again. December 13. (Blue laws.)
The New Taxes. December 20. (Income taxes.)
An American Troubadour. December 27. (Paul Dresser.)

1921

Peasant and Cockney. January 3. (Best sellers not based on excellence.)
Mr. Well's History. January 10. (H. G. Wells, *The Outline of History*.)
Liberty Emerges From the Sewers. January 17. (Duplex Printing Co. Case.)
The Millennium. January 24. (The effects of prohibition.)
The Asses' Carnival. January 31. (U.S. House of Representatives.)
Zechariah Chaffee, Jr. February 7. (The oppression of the citizen during World
    War I.)
James Huneker. February 14.
On the Art of Cussing. February 21.
Overture in C Major. February 28. (The problems that face Harding.)
Gamalielese. March 7. (Harding's inaugural address.)
    Reprinted in: Moos. *A Carnival of Buncombe,* p. 38–42.
General Sawyer. March 14. (On Sawyer's appointment to Brigadier-General of
    the Army Medical Corps.)
Southern Letters. March 21. (*The Reviewer,* the *Double-Dealer* and *All's Well*.)
Lansing. March 28. (Dr. Robert Lansing and the League of Nations.)
On a Favorite Spook. April 11. (The imminent destruction of civilization.)
The Free Lance. April 18. (Revived for one day on its 11th anniversary.)
The New Moses. April 20. (John Philip Hill, Maryland Congressman.)
A Great Moral Sport. April 25. (Capital punishment.)

Servants of Righteousness. May 2. (Prohibition enforcement officers.)
Gamalielese Again. May 9. (Harding's speeches.)
  Reprinted in: Moos. *A Carnival of Buncombe.* p. 42–46.
Confederate Strivings. May 16. (Southern letters.)
The Supreme Court. May 23.
Movies. May 30.
On Censorship. June 7.
Maryland. June 13.
Needless Alarms. June 20. (Pessimism over loss of men in World War I.)
The Millennium Again Postponed. June 27. (The American workingman.)
How Legends Are Made. July 5. (Dempsey-Carpentier Fight.)
The Futility of Censorship. July 11.
The Next Round. July 18. (Japanese-American relations.)
The Human Mind. July 25.
Political Notes. August 1.
Various Notes. August 8.
Optimism Looks Up. August 15. (The proposed Disarmament Conference.)
The American Tory. August 22.
The Lady Politicians. August 29.
Reflections on War. September 8. The Disarmament Conference to be held on
  November 12, 1921.)
The Ku Klux Buffoonery. September 12.
Slaying the Dragon. October 3. (Ku Klux Klan.)
The Arbuckle Case. October 10. (M. Arbuckle of Hollywood.)
The Impending Buffoonery. October 17. (Disarmament Conference.)
An Appeal to TNT. October 24. (Sacco-Vanzetti type cases.)
The Cancer Problem. October 31.
Essay in American. November 7. (Translation of the Declaration of Indepen-
  dence into American.)
Doctor Evangelicus. November 9. (Dr. Howard A. Kelly.)
The Show Begins. November 14. (Disarmament Conference held in Washington,
  D.C. November 12, 1921—February, 1922.)
II Andante Affettuoso. November 16. (Disarmament Conference.)
The Disarmament Follies. November 21.
Conference Notes. November 24. (Disarmament Conference.)
Notes on the Buffoonery. November 28. (Disarmament Conference.)
  "In Re the Case Mencken Vs. Harding Et Al," by Strickland Gillian. Comment
  on HLM's articles on the Disarmament Conference. Appeared in the [Balti-
  more] Evening Sun December 2, 1921, editorial page.
The Blue-Nose Utopia. December 5. (The effects of prohibition.)
So Far, So Good. December 12. (Disarmament Conference.)
  "The Downfall of Mencken," by Henry M. Hyde. On HLM's coverage of
  the Disarmament Conference by the Sun's political reporter. Appeared in the
  [Baltimore] Evening Sun December 14, editorial page.
Hosanna! December 19. (Disarmament Conference.)
Who's Loony Now? December 27. (Concerning the commutation of Eugene Debs'
  prison sentence.)
  Reprinted in: Moos. *A Carnival of Buncombe,* p. 47–51.

1922

The Human Mind: A Fragment. January 3.
A Boon to Bores. January 9. (The telephone.)
The Curtain Falls. January 16. (Disarmament Conference.)

WORKS BY H. L. M.

The National Letters. January 23. (Rise and fall of American Puritanism.)
Chiefly Political. January 30.
On Grammarians. February 6.
Notes on Labor. February 13.
The Boob Dictionary. February 15. (To be compiled by HLM, EAB, and AFL.)
The New Freedom. February 20. (The citizen's protection against injustice.)
Well, Gents, Here Is Your Liberty! February 27. (U.S. Government.)
The Black Art. March 6. (Spiritualism.)
The Blue-Nose Paradise. March 13.
Das Kapital. March 20. (Capitalism.)
Das Kapital: Canto II. March 27. (Capitalism.)
Footnote on Journalism. April 3.
Glouglou Patriotique. April 10. (America vs. Western Europe.)
What Ails the Republic. April 17. (Democracy is government by the inferior.)
Beethoven. April 24.
A Gang of Pecksniffs. May 2. (American Newspaper Publisher's Association.)
Art and the Mob. May 8.
Violets in the Sahara. May 15. (Southern letters.)
Utopia No. 3, 753, 231. May 22. (Gifford Pinchot, Governor of Pa.)
Streets and Their Names. May 29. (Baltimore.)
The Pratt Library. June 5.
Notes for an Honest Autobiography. June 12.
A Glance at California. June 19. (Mooney Case, Thomas J. Mooney, American
labor agitator.)
The Fourth of July. June 26. (Man's elementary rights have been invaded.)
Da Capo. July 3. (Vice crusades.)
Why Not Tell the Truth? July 10. (The Ku Klux Klan and religion.)
    "Why Not Tell the Truth?" by The Rev. Hugh Pendleton McCormick. An
    answer to HLM's article. Appeared in the [Baltimore] Evening Sun July 14,
    1922, editorial page.
    HLM's article was reprinted. [Baltimore] Evening Sun November 29, 1922,
    editorial page, by request after the Rev. Oscar Haywood of New York made
    the statement that he was undertaking to form a branch of the Ku Klux Klan
    among the Protestant clergymen of that city.
For Better, For Worse. July 17. (Marriage.)
    "What's the Matter With Mencken?" by A Psychoanalyst. "The writer of this
    article, a prominent New York authority on Freudian psychology, attempts to
    explain Mr. Mencken's attitude to society, conventional morality, etc., on the
    basis of Mr. Mencken's essay on marriage . . . " Appeared in the [Baltimore]
    Evening Sun August 7, 1922, editorial page.
Statesmen. July 24.
Moral Endeavor. July 31. (Prohibition.)
Notes From a Lonely Shore. October 23. (Den Helder, North Holland.)
Amsterdam. October 30.
Bugaboos. November 6. (Senator France of Maryland.)
The Air Grows Damp. November 13. (Prohibition and the chances for repeal.)
The Turks. November 20. (The cause of oil.)
The Ideal Commonwealth. November 27. (General Pershing's plan for com-
plete mobilization in time of war.)
The Invisible Empire. December 4. (Ku Klux Klan.)
The Boozeart. December 11. (On liquor and drinking.)
Political Progress. December 18. (On dealing justice to politicians.)
Confederate Notes. December 26. (Southern letters.)

NEWSPAPER WORK

1923

The Pink Bloc. January 2. (Politics and disarmament.)

Birth Control. January 9.

The Cause of Liberty. January 15. (European policies.)

Respect for the Law. January 22. (Prohibition.)

International Peace. January 29.

Chasing the Devil. February 5. (Moral crusades.)

Democratic Reflections. February 12.

The Joboisis. February 19. (The government jobholders.)

Respect for the Law. February 26. (Absurd laws.)

More Democratic Reflections. March 5.

Bearers of the Torch. March 12. (The teachers.)

Forty Years of Baltimore. March 19.

> "Takes Issue With Mencken on Freedom of Boy Today, Sigmund Levin Thinks He Has Crude Conception of Modern Youngster, Alfred J. O'Ferrall Gives His Recollections." Appeared in the [Baltimore] Evening Sun March 20, 1923, p. 34.

The Land of the Free. March 26. (Absurd laws.)

Making Ready for 1924. April 2. (Harding.)

> Reprinted in: Moos. *A Carnival of Buncombe*. p. 51–55.

Saviors of Civilization. April 9. (The French.)

> "Saviors of Civilization," A reply to H. L. Mencken by S. E. Mooers. Appeared in the [Baltimore] Evening Sun April 12, 1923, editorial page.

Educational Rolling Mills. April 16. (Overcrowded schools.)

> The May issue of *Scribner's* contained an article by Dr. Henry S. Pritchett, distinguished educator, entitled "Are Our Universities Overpopulated?" The reasoning and conclusion of Dr. Pritchett's article was so similar to Mencken's that the editor thought that a comparison of the more pertinent parts of both articles would be interesting and so reprinted parts of both under the title, "Educational Rolling Mills." Appeared in the [Baltimore] Evening Sun May 16, 1923, editorial page.

The National Letters. April 23.

Advice to Boomers. April 30. (Suggestions for attracting tourists.)

The Uplift in the Library. May 7. (Censorship.)

Hobgoblins. May 14. (Political bosses.)

Men in Cages. May 21. (Prison systems.)

Bach at Bethlehem. May 30. (Bethlehem Bach Choir Festival.)

The Siege of Genesis. June 4. (Genesis and Darwin in the schools.)

Next Year's Struggle. June 11.

> Reprinted in: Moos. *A Carnival of Buncombe*. p. 56–60.

Below the Potomac. June 18. (Labor, politics and the Klan.)

> "The South Hits Back." Reprints from Southern newspapers answering HLM's article. Appeared in the [Baltimore] Evening Sun July 18, 1923, editorial page.

> "Mr. Mencken and the South," by George F. Milton, Jr., Managing Editor of the *Chattanooga* [Tenn.] *News*. Appeared in the [Baltimore] Evening Sun August 15, 1923, editorial page.

The Yearning to Serve. June 25. (The moral reformers.)

The Vernacular. July 2.

Bogus Martyrs. July 9. (Pedagogs.)

The Nordic Blond Renaissance. July 16. (Anglo-Saxon bosh.)

> Reprinted in: *The Vintage Mencken*, gathered by Alistair Cooke. (New York,

Vintage Books, 1955) p. 127–137, "The Anglo-Saxon"; reprinted as a pamphlet, one sheet.

The Higher Learning in Maryland. July 23. (Johns Hopkins University and University of Maryland.)

Here in Maryland. July 31. (Liberty is still respectable in Maryland.)

Optimist Vs. Optimist. August 6. (Prohibition, enforced or repealed.)

Messiah No. 3,572. August 13. (Magnus Johnson and the farmer.)

Liberalism as a Falseface. August 20.

The American Novel. August 27.

Calvinism (Secular). September 3.
  Reprinted in: Moos. *A Carnival of Buncombe.* p. 65–69.

Notes of a Baltimorean. September 10.

On Victuals. September 17.

On Labor Leaders. September 24.

On Government. October 1.

Victims of the Uplift. October 8. (Federal judiciary.)

Respect for the Law. October 15.
  "A Lawyer Upholds Jury Trial Against Use of Injunction," by T. F. Cadwalader. In support of HLM's article. Appeared in the [Baltimore] Evening Sun October 19, 1923, editorial page.

The Impending Plebiscite. October 22.
  Reprinted in: Moos. *A Carnival of Buncombe.* p. 69–73.

Psychological Note. October 29. (The distinction between those who enjoy their work and those who suffer it as a necessary evil.)

On Education. November 5.

Post-Mortem. November 12. (Albert C. Ritchie, Gov. of Md. and the election.)

The Supreme Court. November 19.

The Police Magistrates. November 26.

More Crocodile Tears. December 3. (Free speech is not upheld by the courts.)

The Economy Chimera. December 10. (Taxes.)

Altruism as a Trade. December 17. (Ideal of service vs. the spoils system.)

On Art Galleries. December 24. (On the proposed Baltimore art gallery.)

The Christian Battle Royal. December 31. (Religion.)
  "A Letter From the Devil Regarding the Virgin Birth Controversy," reported by The Rev. Harry Foster Burns. In reply to HLM's article. Appeared in the [Baltimore] Evening Sun January 2, 1924, editorial page.

1924

What is a Christian. January 7.

Endowed Fatherhood. January 14. (Tax exemptions.)

The Progress of Moral Endeavor. January 21.

Crime and Punishment. January 28.

Teapot Dome. February 4.

Cal Rides the Storm. February 11. (Calvin Coolidge and the Teapot Dome scandal.)

On Journalism. February 18.

Moral Reflections. February 25.

A Government of Laws. March 3.

The Wages of Sin. March 10. (William Cabell Bruce.)

The Fount of Justice. March 17. (Department of Justice.)

The Immigration Problem. March 24.

Morals and the Moron. March 31. (Public morals and censorship.)

The Return to Normalcy. April 7. (Coolidge and the Teapot Dome scandal.)

Literary Meditations. April 14. (The artist is always a rebel.)
  Reprinted in: *The Vintage Mencken,* gathered by Alistair Cooke. (New York,
  Vintage Books, 1955) p. 146-147, "The Artist," an extract.
Literary Geography. April 21.
Murphy. April 28. (Charles Francis Murphy, Tammany Hall leader.)
Goose-Step Day. May 5. (Disarmament.)
On Getting a Living. May 12. (Students and the professions.)
Law and Order. May 19.
New York. May 26.
  "Going the Whole Hog," by Henry Edward Warner. On HLM's article. Ap-
  peared in the [Baltimore] Evening Sun May 29, 1924, editorial page.
The Clowns March In. June 2. (Republican Convention.)
  Reprinted in: Moos. *A Carnival of Buncombe.* p. 74–78.
Machiavelli Groans. July 10. (John W. Davis and the Convention.)
Post-Mortem. July 14. (Democratic Convention.)
  Reprinted in: Moos. *A Carnival of Buncombe.* p. 78–82.
On Art Galleries. July 28. (Concerning the loan for a Baltimore museum.)
Breathing Space. August 4. (The presidential candidates.)
  Reprinted in: Moos. *A Carnival of Buncombe.* p. 82–87.
Labor in Politics. August 11.
  Reprinted in: Moos. *A Carnival of Buncombe.* p. 87–91.
The New Woodrow. August 18. (Davis' acceptance speech.)
  Reprinted in: Moos. *A Carnival of Buncombe.* p. 92–96.
Meditations on the Campaign. August 25.
  Reprinted in: Moos. *A Carnival of Buncombe.* p. 96–100.
One Lustrum. September 1. (Prohibition.)
Goose-Step Day. September 8. (Pacifist and disarmament.)
Notes on the Struggle. September 15. (Presidential campaign.)
  Reprinted in: Moos. *A Carnival of Buncombe.* p. 101–105.
The Side Show. September 22. (Local politics.)
Preachers of the Word. September 29. (Religion.)
The Coolidge Buncombe. October 6.
  Reprinted in: Moos. *A Carnival of Buncombe.* p. 105–109.
Mr. Davis' Campaign. October 13.
  Reprinted in: Moos. *A Carnival of Buncombe.* p. 110–114.
Beneath the Magnolias. October 20. (*Journal of Social Forces.*)
The Supreme Court. October 27.
The Voter's Dilemma. November 3.
  Reprinted in: Moos. *A Carnival of Buncombe.* p. 114–118.
Autopsy. November 10. (On the election.)
  Reprinted in: Moos. *A Carnival of Buncombe,* p. 118–123.
Education Week. November 17.
On Government. November 24. (English government vs. American.)
The Show Begins. December 1. (Final convening of the 68th Congress.)
Chiropractic. December 8. (On man's right to choose a quack if he wants one.)
  Reprinted in: *The Vintage Mencken,* gathered by Alistair Cooke. (New York,
  Vintage Books, 1955) p. 148–153.
The Circus Complex. December 15. (Public shows.)
Manna from Heaven. December 22. (Misuse of laws in the U.S.)
Reflections on Journalism. December 29.

1925

Moral Progress. January 5.

The Land of the Free. January 12. (On the government suppression of the liberal paper, *Il Martello*.)

Old Days. January 19. (Baltimore in the 1880's.)

Oh, Long May It Wave! January 26. (On the unjust suspension of a school teacher in Baltimore in 1918–19.)

The Pratt Library. February 2.

The Golden Age. February 9. (Babbittry in the U.S.)

On Living in Baltimore. February 16.

On Capital Punishment. February 23.

The Uplift as a Trade. March 2.

The Judiciary. March 9.

The Johns Hopkins. March 16.

Traffic. March 23. (In Baltimore.)

> "Traffic (Second Series)," by "The Expert in Psychology." Refuting HLM's article. Appeared in the [Baltimore] Evening Sun March 25, 1925, editorial page.

The Coolidge Debacle. March 30.

On Law. April 6.

Elegy. April 13. (On the liberals.)

The Democrats Try It Again. April 20. (Efforts to reunite the party.)

Government by Jackass. April 27. (Concerning the new postal rates.)

Thomas Henry Huxley 1825–1925. May 4.

More "Law Enforcement." May 11. (Boyd case in Baltimore.)

The Battle Joins. May 18. (On the civilized minority.)

Wind Music. May 25. (Leopold Stokowski and his brass band.)

The Millennium Fades. June 1. (Sin is still with us.)

The Rewards of Virtue. June 8. (Burton Kendall Wheeler case.)

> Reprinted as a pamphlet.

The Tennesse Circus. June 15. (Scopes Trial.)

The Fruits of Go-Getting. June 22. (Population increase in Baltimore.)

Homo Neandertalensis. June 29. (Scopes Trial.)

The Nation. July 6.

> Reprinted as a pamphlet.

Tennessee In the Frying-Pan. July 20. (Scopes Trial.)

Bryan. July 27. (Obituary. William Jennings Bryan.)

> Reprinted in: *A Little Treasury of American Prose,* The Major Writers from Colonial Times to the Present Day, edited with an introduction by George Mayberry. (N.Y., Scribner, 1949) p. 800–807; *Modern American Prose,* edited by Carl Van Doren. (N.Y., The Literary Guild, 1934), p. 596–602; *Star Reporters and 34 of Their Stories,* collected, with notes and an introduction by Ward Greene. (N.Y., Random House, 1948), p. 252–255; *The Vintage Mencken,* gathered by Alistair Cooke. (N.Y., Vintage Books, 1955), p. 161–167," In Memoriam: W. J. B." "In Memoriam: W.J.B." which appeared in *The American Mercury* is not a reprint but a greatly expanded article which incorporates only a few paragraphs and phrases from the original article which appeared in the *Evening Sun.*

Young Bob. August 3. (Robert M. La Follette, Jr.)

Round Two. August 10. (Bryan and the circumstances of his death.)

Happy Days. August 17. (The enormous comedy of life in America.)

More Idealism. August 24. (England.)

American: Old Style. August 31. (Dr. Henry Wood, Johns Hopkins, obituary.)

Off the Grand Banks. September 7. (HLM at 45, on himself.)

Aftermath. September 14. (Scopes Trial.)

The Democratic Dilemma. September 21.
Da Capo. September 28. (Prohibition.)
Democratic Hopes. October 5. (Alfred E. Smith, Gov. of N.Y.)
States' Rights. October 12.
Notes of a Baltimorean. October 19. (Local merchants.)
Bunkophagia. October 26. (Coolidge.)
The Free City. November 2. (The big cities and reform.)
The Wesleyan Millennium. November 9. (Prohibition.)
See-Saw. November 16. (American laboring class.)
A Glance Ahead. November 23. (Coolidge and the next election.)
The Uplifters Try It Again. November 30. (On the sale of revolvers.)
On Religion in Politics. December 7.
On Babbitts. December 21.
Dreams of Peace. December 28.

1926

Carnival. January 4. (Christmas Eve Carnival in Baltimore.)
The New Depotism. January 11. (In the U.S.)
A Lesson for Pastors. January 18.
Innocent Bystanders. January 25. (Federal inspectors.)
The Age of Horses. February 1. (HLM's Baltimore boyhood.)
Liberty With Reservations. February 8. (In U.S.)
Baltimoriana. February 15. (Thomas Gordon Hayes, Mayor of Baltimore, and Richard M. Venable, Boss of the City Council.)
The Natural History of Service. February 22. (The public psychology.)
Hard Times. March 1. (Prohibition.)
The Tune Changes. March 8. (Ku Klux Klan.)
Officers and Gentlemen. March 15.
Sub-Potomac Agonies. March 22. (The South.)
The Next War to End War. March 29.
On Crime and Punishment. April 5. (Capital punishment.)
Spring in These Parts. April 12. (Maryland.)
The Accolade. April 19. (The taste of the White House becomes the taste of the nation.)
Dog Fall. April 26. (Law enforcement and prohibition.)
The Free State Spokesman. May 3. (Governor Albert C. Ritchie.)
The Pulitzer Prizes. May 10.
The State Campaign. May 17. (Maryland.)
The Turn of the Tide. May 24. (Senator James A. Reed of Missouri and prohibition.)
Farm Relief. May 31.
The Dominant Issue. June 7. (Prohibition.)
The Burning Deck. June 14. (The collapse of the Coolidge myth.)
Free Cities. June 21. (States' rights vs. cities' rights.)
The Nightshirt Passes. June 28. (Ku Klux Klan.)
Variations Upon a Popular Tune. July 5. (Law enforcement.)
Criminology. July 12.
The Shoe Changes Feet. July 19. (The consequences of prohibition repeal.)
New York. July 26.
Brahms. August 2.
Midsummer Reflections. August 9.
Finale of the Rogues' March. August 16. (Capital punishment in Maryland.)
Democratic Prospects. August 23. (For 1928.)

Valentino. August 30.
  Reprinted in: *The Vintage Mencken,* gathered by Alistair Cooke. (New York,
  Vintage Books, 1955), p. 170–174.
Grannan. September 6. (Eugene Grannan, Baltimore police magistrate.)
On Pullman Cars. September 13.
The Escape From Zion. September 20. (*Up From Methodism,* by Herbert Asbury.)
Miami. September 27. (Press handling of the hurricane.)
Del-Mar-Va. October 4. (Suggests it be made a separate state.)
  "Eastern Shoremen Criticize Printing Mencken Article," Letter to the Editor,
  by William H. Hayward. Appeared in the [Baltimore] Evening Sun October
  18, 1926, editorial page.
Forty Years of Baltimore. October 11.
Alcohol. October 18. (The study of alcohol and longevity by Raymond Pearl,
  Hopkins biologist.)
The Maryland Spokesman. December 6. (Governor Ritchie and his chances for
  the presidential nomination in 1928.)
Sister Aimee. December 13. (Aimee McPherson.)
The Library of Congress. December 20.
Liberty and the Wowser. December 27. (Dr. Howard A. Kelly.)
The Human Mind. December 30.

1927

Blue Laws. January 3.
On Railroad Travel. January 5.
Reminiscence. January 10. (On HLM's early days with the *Herald*.)
The Wowsers State Their Case. January 17. (The history of HLM vs. the clergy.)
The Chaplin Case. January 24. (Charles S. Chaplin.)
A Chance for Idealists. January 31. (On the Eastern Shore of Maryland.)
  "Seeks Mencken as Arbiter of Eastern Shore Elegance." Caroline County
  Delegate, William H. Alduson, replying to HLM's article in the House of
  Delegates, suggests that when bridge is built HLM may cross Bay and take
  job as social mentor. Appeared in the [Baltimore] Evening Sun February 3,
  1927, p. 2.
Aesthetic Diatribe. February 7. (On Baltimore.)
McAdoo. February 14. (William Gibbs McAdoo.)
Notes on the Free State. February 21. (Maryland.)
A Free State Measure. February 28. (Maryland and religion.)
On Free Speech. March 7.
Sidewalks. March 14. (On Baltimore.)
Lewis and His Novel. March 21. (*Elmer Gantry*.)
Poor Technique. March 28. (Prohibition, marriage and murder.)
The Missionaries. April 4. (China.)
  "Mencken's Dicta On Missionaries Flatly Denied." "Minister interested in
  Christianizing China takes sharp issue with statements in a recent article which
  he calls canards." Appeared in the [Baltimore] Evening Sun April 7, 1927,
  editorial page.
On Movies. April 11.
Sacco and Vanzetti. April 18.
Boston's Predicament. April 25. (On politics.)
Metropolis. May 2. (The cities vs. the counties in politics.)
On Happiness. May 9. (Religion.)
Across the Rio Grande. May 16.
The Mississippi Flood. May 23.

The Red Bugaboo. May 30.
The Golden Age of Pedagogy. June 6. (Higher education in America.)
The Home of the Crab. June 13. (Baltimore cuisine.)
New England. June 20.
West Baltimore. June 27.
Al Smith and His Chances. July 5.
> Reprinted in: Moos. *A Carnival of Buncombe.* p. 141–145.
Saturnalia. July 18. (Harding.)
Biology for Fundamentalists. July 25. (Rev. Morris Morris, *Man Created During Descent.*)
Call to the Sanctified. August 1.
Appalachis. August 8. (North Carolina.)
Notes on a Celebrated Case. August 15. (Sacco-Vanzetti Case.)
A Chance for an Idealist. August 22. (The communists and Sacco-Vanzetti.)
The Brahmin Takes the Count. August 29. (Sacco-Vanzetti.)
Old Days in West Baltimore. September 5.
The Campaign Against Blue Laws. September 12.
Laws. September 19. (Governor Ritchie's commission to investigate the public laws of Maryland.)
The Jobholder as Czar. September 26. (Government ownership.)
Baltimore in Transition. October 3. (Building laws.)
The Tumult Dies. October 10. (Prohibition.)
Twilight. October 17. (Coolidge.)
> Reprinted in: Moos. *A Carnival of Buncombe.* p. 123–127.
The Banks and Their Customers. October 24.
Vote as You Drink! October 31. (Mayor John W. Smith of Detroit.)
Baltimore's Wild West. November 7. (West Baltimore.)
Note on Censorship. November 14.
Big Bill. November 21. (William H. Thompson, Mayor of Chicago.)
Murderers. November 28. (Capital punishment.)
The Struggle Ahead. December 5. (The 1928 campaigns.)
> Reprinted in: Moos. *A Carnival of Buncombe.* p. 145–149.
Meditations at Vespers. December 12. (HLM and the clergy.)
On Common Decency. December 19. (Prohibition and the Ku Klux Klan.)
The Avalanche of Books. December 26.

1928

The End of a Good Man. January 2. (Snyder Case and Henry Judd Gray.)
The Scene of Carnage. January 16. (The coming conventions.)
The Goosegreasers at Work. January 23. (Havana Conference.)
The Spanish Main. January 30. (Havana.)
Baltimore Homes. February 13.
The Clowns Go Home. February 21. (Havana Conference.)
The Campaign Opens. February 27. (Senator Reed of Missouri.)
A New Union Station. March 5. (Pennsylvania R.R. in Baltimore.)
The School for Cynics. March 19. (American politics and morals.)
Catspaw. April 9. (Senator Thomas J. Walsh, of Montana.)
Note for Eugenists. April 16. (The Daughters of the American Revolution.)
Al. April 23. (Alfred E. Smith and his chances for the presidency.)
> Reprinted in: Moos. *A Carnival of Buncombe.* p. 150–154.
The New England Kaiserstadt. April 30. (Boston.)
Smoke. May 7. (In Baltimore.)
Barnyard Government. May 14. (Unequal distribution of representation.)

Bach at Bethlehem. May 21. (Bethlehem, Pa. and prohibition.)
The Impending Combat. May 28. (The campaigns.)
  Reprinted in: Moos. *A Carnival of Buncombe.* p. 154–158.
The Show Begins. June 4. (The conventions.)
The Issue Is Joined. July 3. (Prohibition.)
The Sun Do Move. July 9. (Prohibition.)
Justice in California. July 16. (Mooney Case.)
Real Issues At Last. July 23. (Unequal distribution of representation.)
  Reprinted in: Moos. *A Carnival of Buncombe.* p. 159–163.
Civil War in the Confederacy. July 30. (The campaign.)
  Reprinted in: Moos. *A Carnival of Buncombe.* p. 163–167.
Al and the Pastors. August 6. (Alfred E. Smith.)
  Reprinted in: Moos. *A Carnival of Buncombe.* p. 168–172.
The Hoover Manifesto. August 13.
  Reprinted in: Moos. *A Carnival of Buncombe.* p. 172–177.
The Riddle of Crime. August 20. (Crime and punishment.)
Onward, Christian Soldiers! August 24. (Religion and Al Smith in the South.)
  Reprinted in: Moos. *A Carnival of Buncombe.* p. 177-183.
The Campaign Opens. August 27. (Al Smith.)
  Reprinted in: Moos. *A Carnival of Buncombe.* p. 183–187.
The Show Begins. September 3. (The campaign.)
  Reprinted in: Moos. *A Carnival of Buncombe.* p. 187–192.
Der Wille Zur Macht. September 10. (The South and the clergy.)
  Reprinted in: Moos. *A Carnival of Buncombe.* p. 192–196.
Prophetical Musings. September 17. (The South.)
  Reprinted in: Moos. *A Carnival of Buncombe.* p. 196–200.
The Penitentiary Again. September 24. (In Baltimore.)
Turning Worms. October 1. (The clergy and the Ku Klux Klan.)
Travail. October 8. (School.)
  Reprinted in: *The Vintage Mencken,* gathered by Alistair Cooke. (New York, Vintage Book, 1955) p. 182–185.
Episode. October 15. (Al Smith Campaign Tour.)
Al in the Free State. October 29.
  Reprinted in: Moos. *A Carnival of Buncombe.* p. 200–205.
The Eve of Armageddon. November 5. (The campaign.)
  Reprinted in: Moos. *A Carnival of Buncombe.* p. 205–209.
Autopsy. November 12. (The election.)
  Reprinted in: Moos. *A Carnival of Buncombe.* p. 209–213.
Schubert. November 19.
The Circus is Coming. November 26. (Hoover administration.)
Crowded Streets. December 3. (In Baltimore.)
Gaudy Times. December 10. (The reformers.)
Changing Baltimore. December 17.
Cal as Literatus. December 24. (Coolidge's letter to Pulitzer.)
  Reprinted in: Moos. *A Carnival of Buncombe.* p. 127–131.
The War Upon Intelligence. December 31. (The public schools.)

1929

Politics As a Career. January 7.
A Treatise on the Americano. January 14. (*Middletown* by Robert and Helen Lynd.)
Notes of a Baltimorean. January 21. (Baltimore and businessmen.)
Overture to a Melodrama. January 28. (Church and state.)

NEWSPAPER WORK

The War Upon Intelligence. February 4.

Happy Days. February 11. (Prohibition.)

War Clouds. February 18. (England.)

Notes of a Baltimorean. February 25. (The Baltimore art museum and other public buildings.)

Exit. March 4. (Coolidge.)

Note on Law Enforcement. March 11. (Victor Krause case, etc.)

Doctor Illuminatus et Sublimis. March 18. (Bishop James Cannon, Jr.)

The Dignity of the Courts. March 25. (Harry B. Wolf case.)

Sunday Afternoon. April 1. (A commotion in the square on Hollins Street.)

Moral Notes. April 8.

Manifest Destiny. April 15. (South America.)

Uproars in Zion. April 22. (Labor in the South.)

On Respect for the Law. April 29. (Hoover and law enforcement.)

The Sinclair Case. May 6. (Harry F. Sinclair.)

Breaking the Strike. May 13. (The mill strike in N.C. and S.C.)

Bach at Bethlehem. May 20. (Bach Choir Festival at Bethlehem.)

The Laborious Hind. May 27. (The American farmer.)

Fact-Finding. June 3. (Hoover's law enforcement commission.)

The Johns Hopkins. June 10.

"Engineer's Club Rushes to Defend The Johns Hopkins," by C. G. Chevalier, Secretary of the Engineers Club of Baltimore. Appeared in the [Baltimore] Evening Sun June 19, 1929, editorial page.

Mooney and the Unions. June 17.

The Woes of a Holy Man. June 24. (Bishop Cannon and Wall Street.)

Another Millennium Dawns. July 1. (English Labor Government.)

Wesleyan Notes. July 15. (The clergy and the stock market.)

Days of Change. July 22. (In Baltimore.)

A Martyr Faces the Pyre. July 29. (Bishop Cannon.)

The Rebellion of the Damned. August 5. (Prisons and prisoners.)

A Glance Ahead. August 12.

The Police. August 19. (In Baltimore.)

Pole-Sitters. August 26.

Let There Be Light. September 2. (Bishop Cannon and his apologia.)

Metropolis. September 9. (New York and prohibition.)

The Ordeal of North Carolina. September 16.

Putting Down Wicked Thoughts. September 23. (Section 305 of the new tariff act.)

Witch Hunt. September 30. (William B. Shearer case.)

On Government. October 7.

The Trend of American Ethics. October 14.

Two Views of Justice. October 21.

More Law Enforcement. October 28. (Fox case.)

Hot Dogs. November 4.

The Origin and Nature of Law. November 11. (The new institute of law at Johns Hopkins.)

Leaves From a Note-Book. November 18.

Reprinted in: *The Vintage Mencken,* gathered by Alistair Cooke. (New York, Vintage Books, 1955) p. 188, "The Comedian," an excerpt.

The Charity Racket. November 25.

Notes on a Cuff. December 9.

The Lid Lifts Again. December 16. (The Christian Scientists.)

Georgia Twilight. December 30. (Julian Harris and the Columbus *Enquirer-Sun.*)

1930

Report From the Western Front. February 10. (Primarily on German beer.)

The Naval Conference. February 21.

England Revisited. February 24.

Queen of the Seas. February 28. (S. S. Bremen.)

Christian Science Technique. March 3. (Censorship.)

A Year of Hoover. March 10.

Sermon for the Young. March 17. (On drinking.)

Moral Discourses: II. March 24. (On drinking.)

The Naval Conference. March 31.

Notes on Victuals. April 7. (In France and England.)

Purifying the Movies. April 14. (Hudson Bill for movie censorship.)
 "Canon Chase Defends the Movie Censorship Bill," Letter to the Editor, by William Sheafe Chase. In answer to HLM's article. Appeared in the [Baltimore] Evening Sun May 27, 1930, editorial page.

Twenty Years. April 21. (Anniversary of *The Evening Sun.*)

The Beatitudes: American Model. April 28. (Dr. Peter Ainslie and the Army chaplains.)

News From Gomorrah. May 5. (New York and bootlegging.)

Peace Dreams. May 12.

The Men Who Rule Us. May 19. (Hoover administration.)
 Reprinted in: Moos. *A Carnival of Buncombe.* p. 214–218.

Hospitals. May 26. (Woman's Hospital in Baltimore.)

The Movie Censorship. June 2. (The Hudson Bill and Rev. Chase.)

Pontifex Maximus. June 9. (Bishop Cannon.)

The Way Out. June 16. (Prohibition and the Volstead Act.)

Notes on the New Tarriff. June 23.

Another Martyr to Service. June 30. (The Bill of Rights and the Volstead Act.)

The Book Trade. July 7. (Bookstores.)

Communism. July 14.

800,000. July 21. (Baltimore.)

The Comforts of Life. July 28.

The Bovine School of Ethics. August 4. (City vs. county.)

The Song of the Dove. August 11. (Law enforcement.)

The Public Service. August 18.

Notes of a Baltimorean. August 25. (On Baltimore.)

The Presidency. September 1.

Reconnaissance to Northward. September 8. (Pilsner in Montreal.)

The Maritimes. September 15. (Halifax.)

Over the Border. September 22. (Saint John.)

The Issue Is Joined. September 29. (Local politics.)

Sporting Gossip. October 6. (Bishop Cannon.)

Pole Sitter on a Hot Pole. October 13. (William Broening, Baltimore politician.)

Observations on the Campaign. October 20. (Local politics and Broening.)

Guardians of the Constitution. October 27. (Local politics.)

The Long Pull. November 3. (Politics.)

It Is Still the Free State. November 10. (National and local elections.)

Heroes and Gentlemen. November 17. (American Legion.)

Mass Production Salvation. November 24. (In Baltimore.)

Malt Liquor. December 1.

Looking Ahead. December 8. (To the 1932 conventions.)
 Reprinted in: Moos. *A Carnival of Buncombe.* p. 223–227.

Rumblings in England. December 15. (English politics.)

Troubled Days in Zion. December 22. (Prohibition.)
Little Red Ridinghood. December 29. (Hoover and his associates.)
  Reprinted in: Moos. *A Carnival of Buncombe.* p. 227–232.

1931

The Free State Chasm. January 5. (The proposed Chesapeake Bay bridge.)
Address to Ritchie Men. January 12.
Famine. January 19. (Arkansas.)
  "H. L. Mencken 'Condemned' by Arkansas Legislature: Article in *Evening Sun*
  Calls Forth Resolution that Critic Has Made State "Butt of Coarse Ribaldry'—
  Merit as Writer Granted, However," by the Associated Press. Appeared in the
  [Baltimore] Evening Sun February 6, 1931, p. 1.
  "A Reply From Arkansas," "An article on conditions in Arkansas entitled
  'Famine' by H. L. Mencken, was published in the *Evening Sun* several weeks
  ago. It has since aroused considerable comment in Arkansas, and recently the
  Legislature of the state passed a resolution condemning both the article and
  its author. The following communication, which is signed by Charles H.
  Brough, Governor of Arkansas during the War, and Dallas T. Herndon, the
  State Historian, is a reply to Mr. Mencken." Appeared in the [Baltimore]
  Evening Sun February 10, 1931, editorial page.
The Beginning of the End. January 23. (Wickersham Report on prohibition.)
What Is Ahead? January 26. (Hoover and prohibition.)
Leaves from a Notebook. February 2.
The Ways of Censors. February 9.
The Case of Arkansas. February 16. (An answer to Brough.)
  "Former Governor of Arkansas Replies to Mencken Article," by Charles H.
  Brough. Appeared in the [Baltimore] Evening Sun March 3, 1931, editorial
  page.
On Getting Rid of Blue Laws. February 23.
The Bonus. March 2. (The veterans bonus.)
How To Improve Arkansas. March 9. (An answer to Brough.)
Automobiles. March 16.
Hard Times. March 23. (Why are there hard times in the U.S.?)
Targets of Calumny. March 30. (Bootleggers.)
Leaves from a Waste-Basket. April 6.
The Law-Making Racket. April 13. (Maryland legislature.)
Agonies Under the Ermine. April 20. (The Supreme Court judges.)
Dr. France's Platform. April 27. (Dr. Joseph I. France.)
The Issues of the Hour. May 4. (Local politics.)
Baltimore Twilight. May 11.
The Hoover Bust. May 18.
  Reprinted in: Moos. *A Carnival of Buncombe.* p. 232–236.
Two Days of Bach. May 25. (Bach Choir Festival of Bethlehem.)
Wet Ruminations. June 1. (Prohibition.)
Graft. June 8. (On government.)
Wowsers at Bay. June 15. (Blue Laws.)
The White House Oracle. June 22. (Hoover.)
Radio Programs. June 29.
On Religious Liberty. July 6.
The Green Mountains. July 13. (Vermont.)
Wowsers on the Loose. July 20. (Blue Laws.)
Hoover in 1932. July 27.
  Reprinted in: Moos. *A Carnival of Buncombe.* p. 237–241.

Notes and Queries. August 3.
Believe It If You Can. August 10. (Al Capone and law enforcement.)
Imperial Purple. August 17. (The presidency.)
  Reprinted in: Moos. *A Carnival of Buncombe.* p. 241–246.
Katzenjammer. August 24. (Taxes and teachers.)
Minor Considerations. August 31.
Who Is To Blame? September 7. (On the downfall of various people.)
The End of an Era. September 14. (In the U.S.)
How to Feed the Poor. September 21.
Chickens Come Home to Roost. September 28. (Baltimore and the United Railways.)
The Men Who Rule Us. October 5. (On government.)
  Reprinted in: Moos. *A Carnival of Buncombe.* p. 246–251.
The Bishop Loquitur. October 12. (Bishop James Cannon, Jr.)
Politics in England. October 26.
A Great Democratic Triumph. November 2. (Politics in England.)
The Ritchie Campaign. November 9. (Governor Ritchie and the Presidency.)
Variations Upon a Favorite Theme. November 16. (Prohibition.)
The Freedom of the Air. November 23. (Radio campaigns.)
The Old Peruna Bottle. November 30. (League of Nations.)
The Eastern Shore Kultur. December 7. (The Salisbury lynching.)
  "Some Comments on a Mencken Article." Appeared in the [Baltimore] Evening Sun December 10, 1931, editorial page.
Sound and Fury. December 14. (Eastern Shore.)
  "The Shore and Mencken," by E. Clarke Fontaine. Appeared in the [Baltimore] Evening Sun December 22, 1931, editorial page.
  "Mobs Un-American, Says Rev. Caraker: Mencken's Article on Shore Termed 'Unfair,' 'Unjust' and 'Cause of Reaction.'" Appeared in the [Baltimore] Sun February 1, 1932, p. 18.
The Free State Pays the Price. December 21. (The Salisbury lynching.)
Blind Leaders of the Blind. December 28. (Communists.)

1932

The State of the Nation. January 4.
A Third of a Century. January 11. (HLM in middle life.)
The Moscow Nietzsches. January 18. (Capitalism and communism.)
West Indian Notes. January 25. (The Caribbean.)
Havana Revisited. February 1.
The Japanese Bugaboo. February 8. (The Japanese at Shanghai.)
Retreats and Advances. February 15. (On Baltimore.)
The Suffering Ether. February 22. (Radio Programs.)
Blood Upon the Moon. February 29. (The possibility of war with Japan.)
The Struggle to Make us Holy. March 7. (Blue laws.)
Tough Days for Pacifists. March 14.
On Sunday Laws. March 21. (The Lord's Day Alliance.)
The Lynching Psychosis. March 28. (The Salisbury lynching.)
The Taxpayer's Groans. April 4.
The Old Subject. April 11. (Prohibition.)
Where the Money Goes. April 18. (The cost of government.)
Sad Days for Wowsers. April 25. (The Blue laws and prohibition losing ground.)
The Impending Carnage. May 2. (The conventions.)
  Reprinted in: Moos. *A Carnival of Buncombe.* p. 251–256.
The Battle Joins. May 9. (The Democratic National Convention.)

On Hospitals. May 16.
Beware of Greeks! May 23. (Prohibition.)
Tough Babies. May 30. (The reformers.)
The Present Discontent. June 6. (The state of the nation.)
Aftermath. June 20. (The Republican National Convention.)
Where Are We At? July 5. (Roosevelt.)
    Reprinted in: Moos. *A Carnival of Buncombe*. p. 256–260.
The End of Prohibition. July 11.
Paying the Bill. July 18. (The cost of government.)
The Paramount Issue. July 25. (Prohibition.)
The Battle of Washington. August 1. (The campaign.)
The Fruits of Demagogy. August 8. (Local politics.)
Law Enforcement Blows Up. August 15. (Prohibition.)
More Bumps for the Taxpayer. August 22. (Proposed improvement schemes for
    Baltimore.)
Bauernkrieg. August 29. (Iowa farmers.)
The Paramount Issue. September 5. (Prohibition.)
Panem et Circenses. September 12. (The cost of government.)
On Advertising Baltimore. September 19.
The Duker Case. September 26. (Herman Webb Duker.)
Not Yet, and Maybe Not Even Soon. October 3. (Prohibition and Volstead Act
    repeal.)
The Hoover Bust. October 10.
    Reprinted in: Moos. *A Carnival of Buncombe*. p. 260–265.
Chickens Come Home. October 17. (Taxes.)
Pre-Mortem. October 24. (Hoover.)
    Reprinted in: Moos. *A Carnival of Buncombe*. p. 265–270.
They Call It Economy. October 31. (Local politics and taxation.)
The Young Voter. November 7.
Remarks At a Wake. November 14. (Prohibition.)
The End of a Happy Life. November 21. (Albert Hildebrandt.)
The Budget Is Balanced. November 28. (Baltimore's budget.)
The Triumph of the Rattan. December 5. (Taxes and the public schools.)
Hot Spot. December 12. (Local politics and Mayor Howard W. Jackson.)
What'll It Be Gents? December 19. (The Beer Bill.)
The Cost of Glory. December 26. (The veterans' bonus.)

1933

The Men Who Rule Us. January 2.
Notes from an Imaginary Diary. January 9.
Project for a Licensing Act for Baltimore City I–III. January 23–25.
    (A comprehensive statue to meet the need when the 18th Amendment is
    repealed.) Reprinted as a pamphlet.
The Coolidge Mystery. January 30.
    Reprinted in: Moos. *A Carnival of Buncombe*. p. 132–136; *The Vintage
    Mencken,* gathered by Alistair Cooke. (New York, Vintage Books, 1955), p.
    219–223, "Coolidge."
Economy: 1933 Model. February 6. (Taxation.)
Katzenjammer. February 13. (The public supported schools.)
The Dilemma of Statecraft. February 20. (Politics and taxes.)
Psychopathic Personalities. February 27. (Criminology.)
A Time to Be Wary. March 13. (Roosevelt's inauguration speech.)
    Reprinted in: Moos. *A Carnival of Buncombe*. p. 270–275.

Thirteen Years. March 20. (The end of prohibition and the Beer Act.)
The Tune Changes. March 27. (On government.)
 Reprinted in: Moos. *A Carnival of Buncombe.* p. 275–279.
The Legislative Arm. April 3. (Local government.)
After the Deluge. April 10. (Beer and the repeal of the 18th Amendment.)
The Twilight of the Idols. April 17. (Banks and bankers.)
Whoopla! April 24. (The abandonment of the gold standard.)
Vive Le Roi! May 1. (Roosevelt and Congress.)
 Reprinted in: Moos. *A Carnival of Buncombe.* p. 280–284.
Some Objections to Monarchy. May 8. (Roosevelt and Congress.)
Notes on Inflation. May 15.
The Red Glare Fades. May 22. (The communists.)
The Morgan Circus. May 29. (Judge Louderback and the House of Morgan.)
Something for Nothing. June 5. (U.S. Bonds.)
The Returns from Armageddon. June 12. (Prohibition repeal.)
A Day of Reckoning. June 19. (Government spending.)
Saving the World. June 26. (The World Economic Conference in London.)
The Governorship. July 3. (Phillips Lee Goldsborough.)
Armageddon. July 10. (The South.)
Goat. July 17. (Raymond Moley.)
The Utopia of Rogues. July 24. (Penology.)
Beery Reflections. July 31.
Pedagogy Comes Back. August 7.
Crime As a Trade. August 14. (Penology.)
New Liquor Laws. September 4.
Obsequies. September 11. (Prohibition.)
Jack Hart and Company. September 18. (Penology.)
Bootstrap Economics. September 25.
Leaves from a Notebook. October 2.
Battle Royal. October 9. (New York mayoralty campaign.)
The Euel Lee Case. October 16. (Eastern Shore lynching.)
Revels in Transchoptankia. October 23. (Lynching and the Eastern Shore.)
 "The Spirit of the Eastern Shore," by J. R. Barnes. (1933). Pamphlet. In
 answer to HLM's articles in the *Evening Sun* on the Eastern Shore.
Plans to Put Down Lynching. October 30.
The Morning After. November 6. (The National Recovery Act and General
 Hugh S. Johnson.)
Castles in the Air. November 13. (A Chesapeake Bay bridge.)
The Booze Bill. November 20. (Bill proposed by Governor Ritchie.)
Whoopee! Whoopla! November 27. (The Buy Now campaign.)
Victory! December 4. (Eastern Shore.)
Now That It Is Back. December 11. (Governor Ritchie's booze law.)
Down With the "Rich!" December 18. (Income taxes.)
The Patient Sits Up. December 26. (U.S. recovery from the depression.)

1934

Roosevelt. January 2.
 Reprinted in: Moos. *A Carnival of Buncombe.* p. 284–289.
Bad News for Mendicants. January 8. (Economics and government.)
The Costigan-Wagner Bill. January 15. (On lynching.)
Good and Evil in Utopia. January 22. (Blaisdell Case.)
Sold Down the River. January 29. (The American communists.)
A Planned Economy. February 5. (The New Deal.)

NEWSPAPER WORK

Where Your Money Goes. February 12. (The farmers subsidy.)
Baltimore in Transition. February 19.
On Wine-Bibbing. February 26.
New Morals for Old. March 5. (Attempts to amend the Ten Commandments.)
Maderia. March 12.
The Land of Moors. March 19. (Morocco.)
The Ruins of Carthage. March 26. (Carthage.)
Notes on the Holy Land. April 2. (Jerusalem.)
Erez Israel. April 9. (Israel.)
> Reprinted: *Erez Israel,* by H. L. Mencken. (N.Y., B. P. Safran at The New School, 1935.) "Notes on the Holy Land," April 2, 1934 and "Erez Israel," printed as one article.
The Piper Passes His Hat. April 16. (Government spending.)
Metamorphosis. April 23. (Naples.)
Daniel in the Lion's Den. April 30. (Bishop James Cannon, Jr.)
Honor to Whom Honor Is Due. May 7. (Roosevelt's Brain Trust.)
The Anti-Lynching Bill. May 14.
New Deal Psychology. May 21.
Trial by Hullabaloo. May 28. (U.S. trial system.)
Happy Days for Cynics. June 4. (Darrow Report on the NRA.)
On Life in Baltimore. June 11.
On Crimes of Violence. June 18. (Penology.)
The Locus of Hope. June 25. (New Deal popularity.)
The Red Menace. July 2. (Communism and the Brain Trust.)
A Beautiful Worm Turns. July 9. (The schoolma'ams vs. the pedagogical padrones.)
Friends of the New Deal. July 16.
Liquor and the Politicians. July 23.
Exit No. 1. July 30. (Capital punishment and penology.)
The Weather. August 6. (Government plans to change it.)
Plague. August 13. (Syphilis.)
Utopia Eat Utopia. August 20. (New Deal.)
Revolution by Pedagogy. August 27.
Night Club. September 3.
Forty Acres and a Mule. September 10. (Upton Sinclair's plan for California.)
Election Returns. September 17. (Local politics.)
The New Dispensation. September 24. (The New Deal.)
Taps for a General. October 1. (General Hugh S. Johnson.)
Happy Days. October 8. (The New Deal.)
Leaves from a Diary. October 15.
Right, Left, Right, Left. October 22. (The New Deal.)
Ups and Downs. October 29. (The New Deal.)
Notes on a Sample Ballot. November 5. (HLM's choices for the local election.)
Coroner's Inquest. November 12. (Governor Harry W. Nice.)
Opportunity. November 19. (The presidency of Johns Hopkins offered to Ritchie.)
Mathematical Exercises. November 26. (The Report of the National Survey of Potential Product Capacity.)
More and Better Psychopaths. December 3. (Capital punishment and penology.)
New Deal Realities. December 10.
Men in Cages. December 17. (Prisoners.)
105,000,000,000. December 24. (The New Deal and the Brain Trust.)
Historical Note. December 31. (The planned economy and the Brain Trust.)

WORKS BY H. L. M.

1935

Hail But Not Farewell. January 7. (Governor Ritchie.)

Premature Obsequies. January 14. (Capitalism.)

Huey. January 21. (Huey Long and his program for Louisiana.)

Storm Damage in Utopia. January 28. (Upton Sinclair.)

Etude Upon the Red Keys. February 4. (Government spending.)

Beery Ponderings. February 11.

Farley. February 18. (Jim Farley and Huey P. Long.)

Fallen Among Thieves. February 25. (Government spending.)

Götzendämmerung. March 4. (The New Deal.)

Meditations For March 15. March 11. (The Brain Trust and the economy.)

Huey and His Foes. March 18.

Chasing the Reds. March 25. (The anti-red bills.)

The Day Before the Primary. April 1. (Local politics.)

The New Deal: Canto II. April 8.

Twenty-Five Years. April 15. (Anniversary of the *Evening Sun.*)

The Johns Hopkins Hospital. April 22.

The Municipal Elections. April 29.

Getting Rid of the Money. May 6. (Government spending.)

Twilight of a God. May 13. (Robert E. Lee.)

The Red Bugaboo. May 20.

Wizards. May 27. (Harry L. Hopkins and the Civil Works Administration.)

English Notes. July 15. (London in July.)

New Deal: English Model. July 22.

Insulating the Army and Navy. (Senator Millard E. Tydings and the McCormack Bill.)

The Orgies of 1936. August 5. (Governor Nice's plans to have the Republican Convention in Baltimore.)

(Laughter). August 12. (The New Deal.)

The Constitution. August 19.

1936. August 26. (Roosevelt.)
> Reprinted in: Moos. *A Carnival of Buncombe.* p. 295–299.

The Lion of Judah. September 2. (Mussolini and Abyssinia.)

Wizards at Work. September 9. (Social Security.)

Storm Damage in Utopia. September 16. (Anti-Saloon League.)

The Murray Case. September 23. (Donald Gaines Murray, colored, and the University of Maryland Law School.)

Where the Money Goes. September 30. (The planned economy.)

What Goes Up – – –. October 7. (Huey Long and Roosevelt.)

The Pratt Library. October 14.

The Bills Come In. October 21. (The economy.)

The Taxpayer Pays All. October 28. (Ickes' housing and resettlement administrations.)

The Curse of Mankind. November 4. (Government.)

The War Against War. November 11. (Pacifist organizations.)
> "One Fresh from College Reports That Mr. Mencken Is Misinformed on Student Psychology," Letter to the Editor, by Richard P. Chambers. Appeared in the [Baltimore] Evening Sun November 13, 1935, editorial page.

The Next War. November 18. (A reply to Mr. Chambers.)

Leaves from a Day-Book. November 25.

Blue Monday in Utopia. December 2. (Communism in America.)

Wall Street Redivivus. December 9.

The Anatomy of Quackery. December 16. (The New Deal.)

NEWSPAPER WORK

Preliminaries. December 23. (On the conventions.)
The Utopia of Rogues. December 30. (U.S. and British judicial systems.)

1936

Overture in a Minor Key. January 6. (On the 1936 campaign.)
Citadels of Idealism. January 13. (New Deal popularity.)
Nine Old Men. January 20. (The Supreme Court.)
Why Not a King? January 27. (English politics.)
Rough Stuff Ahead. February 3. (The national conventions.)
An Army of Locusts. February 10. (Bureaucrats.)
Men of Vision. February 17. (Baltimore Trust Co.)
The Springs of Demagogy. February 24. (The voter and the vote.)
Ritchie. March 2. (Albert C. Ritchie.)
The Show Begins. March 9. (The national conventions.)
    Reprinted in: Moos. *A Carnival of Buncombe*. p. 299–304.
The Cold Grey Dawn. March 16. (The New Deal.)
The Fourth Amendment. March 23.
New Deal Demonology. March 30. (Roosevelt and the farmers.)
The Legislative Arm. April 6. (Local politics.)
The Pathology of Radicalism. April 13.
The More Abundant Dialectic. April 20. (Roosevelt's speech in Baltimore on
    April 13.)
    Reprinted in: Moos. *A Carnival of Buncombe*. p. 304–309.
The Woes of Arcadia. April 27. (Dr. Odum of the University of North Carolina.)
Turning On the Heat. May 4. (The primaries and the conventions.)
Moronia Felix. May 11. (Life in America.)
Pensions for Assassins. May 18. (Capital punishment and penology.)
    "Father Ayd Replies to Mencken's Piece on Criminal Justice," Letter to the
    Editor, by The Rev. Joseph J. Ayd, S. J., Loyola College. Appeared in the
    [Baltimore] Evening Sun May 22, 1936, editorial page.
The Rocky Road to Utopia. May 25. (The politicians and the Constitution.)
Policing the Judiciary. June 1.
The Black Legion. June 15.
On Banks. June 22.
The Combat Joins. July 6. (Parties and platforms.)
    Reprinted in: Moos. *A Carnival of Buncombe*. p. 309–313.
One Vote; One Dole. July 13. (The New Deal and the farmer.)
On Radical Professors. July 20. (The young and their elders.)
The Townsend Circus. July 27. (Francis E. Townsend.)
Succoring the Unsuccorable. August 3. (The farmers.)
The Next General American War. August 10. (Labor and industry.)
Burying the Dead Horse. August 17. (Roosevelt and his administration.)
    Reprinted in: Moos. *A Carnival of Buncombe*. p. 314–318.
The Radio Priest. August 24. (Father Coughlin and the Encyclical of May 15,
    1931.)
The Challenger. August 31. (Alfred M. Landon's speech at Buffalo.)
Why Not Gerald? September 7. (The campaign needs some first rate rabble-
    rousers.)
Stumping Tour. September 21. (Campaign tours.)
After the New Deal. September 28. (Roosevelt and Hearst.)
    Reprinted in: Moos. *A Carnival of Buncombe*. p. 318–322.
Windfall. October 5. (Earl Browder and the communists' cause in America.)
Hay Foot, Straw Foot. October 12. (Spain and the communists.)

WORKS BY H. L. M.

More and Easier Money. October 19. (Roosevelt and the farmer.)
Sham Battle. October 26. (The campaign.)
   Reprinted in: Moos. *A Carnival of Buncombe.* p. 323–327.
The Choice Tomorrow. November 2. (The election.)
   Reprinted in: Moos. *A Carnival of Buncombe.* p. 327–331.
Coroner's Inquest. November 9. (The election.)
   Reprinted in: Moos. *A Carnival of Buncombe.* p. 331–336.
Democratic Twilight. November 16. (The New Deal.)
Gone But Not Forgotten. November 23. (The Brain Trust.)
   "Mr. Mencken's Views on TVA's Paradise Are Held Erroneous," Letter to the
   Editor, by Warren Ogden. Appeared in the [Baltimore] Evening Sun December
   9, 1936, p. 29.
Decay and Rejuvenation. November 30. (Baltimore.)
The Income Tax. December 7.
The Public Prints. December 14. (Newspapers and politics.)
The Exile of Enzesfeld. December 21. (Edward VIII.)

1937

And On Earth Peace. January 4. (World politics.)
The Bill of Rights. January 11. (The DeJonge Case and the Smith Case.)
Doctor Fundamentalis. January 18. (The Rev. J. Greshan Machen and the
   fundamentalists.)
Sand and Sun. January 25. (Trip to Florida.)
Bull-Fight. February 1. (Labor vs. management.)
Auto-Da-Fe In Utopia. February 8. (The purge in Russia.)
The Cup and the Lip. February 15. (Reform and its results.)
Government by Stooge. February 22. (The New Deal and the courts.)
Victory. March 1. (Labor and management.)
The Dim Hereafter. March 8. (World politics and war.)
The Whole Hog. March 15. (Roosevelt and the Supreme Court.)
Juggernaut. March 22. (The automobile.)
The Mourners' Bench. March 29. (The treason trials in Russia.)
Sit Down. April 5. (Labor and management.)
Balance Sheet. April 12. (The Wallace report on the net gain to American labor
   of the New Deal.)
More and More Taxes. April 19.
Down With Boils. April 26. (Roosevelt and the New Deal.)
On Making Laws. May 3. (Maryland legislature.)
A Note on News. May 10. (Journalism.)
Man's Greatest Failure. May 17 (Government.)
The Art of Swearing. May 24.
A Tough Baby. May 31. (Capitalism.)
Taxes and Tax-Dodgers. June 7.
The Road to Salvation. June 14. (Roosevelt and government.)
Reminiscence. June 21. (Trip to Germany and Spain in 1917.)
Bullets for Ballots. June 28. (Labor and law.)
I See By the Papers. July 12. (Communism and labor.)
Semper Fidelis. July 26. (Joe Robinson.)
Santa Claus Is Safe. August 2. (Roosevelt and the farmer.)
Report from Moronia. August 9. (On the progeny of morons.)
The Wicked Wops. August 16. (Mussolini.)
Nightshirt Into Ermine. August 23. (Hugo L. Black and his appointment to the
   Supreme Court.)

The Right to Privacy. August 30.
The Pains of Disillusion. Sept. 6. (Roosevelt, Black and the Supreme Court.)
Third Term. September 13. (Roosevelt.)
Days of Change. September 20. (Democracy.)
The Future in Moronia. September 27. (Population.)
Fiends in Human Form. October 4. (Japan.)
Last Words on Hugo. October 11. (Hugo L. Black.)
Forty Acres for a Vote. October 18. (Roosevelt farm policy.)
The Housing Investigation. October 25. (The Duke of Windsor.)
The Mediterranean Beelzebub. November 1. (International politics.)
Doped. November 8. (The South and the New Deal.)
Duel in a Morgue. November 15. (Hoover and Landon.)
The Line-Up. November 22. (Russia.)
The Campaign in the Free State. November 29. (Maryland.)
Every Man His Own Radio. December 6. (Professor J. B. Rhine and Extra-Sensory Perception.)
The Best-Laid Plans. December 13. (The planned economy.)
The Common Enemy. December 20. (Governments.)
Labor Rows. December 27. (The AFL and the CIO.)

1938

Chiggers in Utopia. January 3. (Communism in America.)
Wizards With Headaches. January 10. (The New Deal and the depression of '38.)
The Next Miracle. January 17. (Government housing.)
The Drums Begin to Roll. January 24. (The looming threat of war.)
Third Term. January 31. (Roosevelt.)

National Conventions
Campaign Tours and Speeches
1920 1924 1928 1932 1936 1940 1948

"The news of the day does not spring into the world well formed and neatly labeled; it is, instead, a very ragged and imperfect thing in its native state, and it issues from the space-time continuum in most irregular spurts. The dispatch [listed here as, "Farley Surrender on Rules Leaves 4 Bitter Battles." June 28, 1932] is the final text of a series which began at 9 A.M. of June 28 and ran until 3 P.M. During that time four different forms of it got into as many editions of the *Evening Sun* and some of those forms were made up of four or five different sections, dispatched at different times and even from different places. . . .

"The purely physical difficulties confronting a reporter told off to cover so vast and widely dispersed a thing as a national convention are extremely trying. What goes on in the actual hall is only part of it, and seldom the most important part. There are also four or five committees to think of, not to mention forty-eight

State delegations, any one of which may throw a monkey-wrench into the machinery at any moment. Each of the candidates also has his headquarters, and sometimes those headquarters are extensive labyrinths, with chambers that are secret as well as chambers where every comer is welcomed. Moreover, various other politicians of high potency are also on the scene, and every one of them, at very short notice or no notice at all, may begin to sweat important news." HLM *Making a President*—Preface.

Baltimore *Evening Sun* Monday Articles, specifically dealing with conventions and campaign tours, are listed as *See also* references at the end of each section.

1920

[Dispatches] Republican National Convention, Chicago. [Baltimore] Sun and Evening Sun June 7-13, 1920.

Presidential Candidate, Warren G. Harding; Vice-Presidential Candidate, Calvin Coolidge.

Mencken Looks Over Field and Decides That Johnson [Hiram Walker Johnson, U. S. Senator, R. Calif.] is Keenest of Candidates. June 7, p. 1, Home edition.
Really Strong Men Lacking at Chicago, Mencken Finds. June 8, p. 1, Home edition.
Mencken Yet Thinks Johnson Will Win. June 9, p. 1, Home edition.
Mencken Finds Show Dullest in History. June 10, p. 1, Home edition.
Henry Mencken Sees Death of Liberalism. June 11, p. 1, Home edition.
Mencken Declares Delegates Wabbled. June 12, p. 2, Night final.
GOP Ticket Triumph for Old Bosses. Sunday June 13, p. 1, [no edition indicated].

[Dispatches] Democratic National Convention, San Francisco. [Baltimore] Sun and Evening Sun June 26—July 7, 1920.

Presidential Candidate, James M. Cox; Vice-Presidential Candidate, Franklin D. Roosevelt.

Mencken Counts on [William Jennings] Bryan to Make San Francisco Hum if They Try to Coffin Him. June 26, p. 1, Financial edition.
Chaos in Frisco, Mencken Declares. June 28, p. 1, Home edition.
It's All in Wilson's Hands, Mencken Concludes After Looking Around at Frisco. June 29, p. 1, Home edition.
Mencken Finds Convention is Genuinely Democratic. June 30, p. 1, Home edition.
Mencken Says All's Set to Put 'Young William' [William G. McAdoo] Over if Wilson Gives the Word. July 1, p. 1, Financial edition.
Dull Day at San Francisco is Brightened for Mencken by Eloquent Widow Lady. July 2, p. 2, Financial edition.
Mencken Describes Session in Which Wm. J. Bryan Was "Murdered in Cold Blood." July 3, p. 3, Financial edition.
Eyes Turning to [John W.] Davis With Dark Horse Talk. Sunday July 4, p. 2, [no edition indicated].

End, As Viewed by Mencken, Was Strangely Undramatic. July 6, p. 2, **Financial edition.**

Battle at San Francisco Absolutely Free and Open, Henry Mencken Affirms. July 7, p. 1, Financial edition.

See also Monday Articles. [Baltimore] Evening Sun 1920: San Francisco: A Memory, July 21; Bayard vs. Lionheart, July 26.

1924

[Dispatches] Republican National Convention, Cleveland. [Baltimore] Evening Sun June 9–13, 1924.

Presidential Candidate, Calvin Coolidge; Vice-Presidential Candidate, Charles G. Dawes.

Mencken Finds Cleveland a Silent Sahara on Eve of Republican Convention. June 9, p. 1, 5:30 Financial edition.

Shackled Delegates Stalk Disconsolate at Butler's [Nicholas Murray Butler, Pres. Columbia Univ.] Convention, Mencken Says. June 10, p. 1, 5:30 Financial edition.

Mencken Forced to Flee Before Burton's [Theodore Elijah Burton, Congressman, R. Ohio] Oratory; "Babbittry" Appalls Him. June 11, p. 1, 5:30 Financial edition.

Mencken Diagnoses Butler, Finding Him Superior to Professional Politicians. June 12, p. 1, 5:30 Financial edition.

Vice-Presidential Battle Thrills Mencken After Dull Business of Naming 'Cal.' June 13, p. 1, 5:30 Financial edition.

[Dispatches] Democratic National Convention, New York. [Baltimore] Sun and Evening Sun June 23—July 9, 1924.

Presidential Candidate, John W. Davis; Vice-Presidential Candidate, Charles W. Bryan.

Mencken Finds Candidates Ready to do Anything but Take a Clean-Cut Stand. June 23, p. 1, 5:30 Financial edition.

Mencken Turns to Prophecy and Forecasts Nominee's Stand on Leading Issues. June 24, p. 1, 5:30 Financial edition.

Convention's Only Reality is the Struggle for Jobs, H. L. Mencken Concludes. June 25, p. 1, 5:30 Financial edition.

Mencken Decides Klan's Enemies Have Hurt Their Cause by Drawing Issue. June 26, p. 1, 5:30 Financial edition.

Mencken Senses Success for Ritchie [Albert C. Ritchie, Gov. of Md.] or Some Other Aspirant Now in Oblivion. June 27, p. 1, 5:30 Financial edition.

Conventions Have Become Ill Managed and Inefficient Carnivals, Thinks Mencken. June 28, p. 1, 5:30 Financial edition.

New York Firmly Convinced Its "Demigod" [Alfred E. Smith] Will Succeed. Sunday June 29, p. 4, C edition.

Seeing Party's Hopes Ruined by Klan, Mencken Suggests the Nomination of Coolidge. June 30, p. 1, 5:30 Financial edition.

Nominate Today, Advises Mencken, or Give Reins to Delegates Themselves. July 1, p. 1, 5:30 Financial edition.

McAdoo a Corpse, But, to Mencken's Surprise, Won't Go in the Grave. July 2, p. 1, 5:30 **Financial edition.**

Klan, With Religious Issue Underlying, Has Dominated From Start, Says Mencken. July 3, p. 1, 5:30 Financial edition.
Too Late to Compromise, With Defeat in November Certain, Declares Mencken. July 5, p. 5, 5:30 Financiall edition.
Even Ku Kluxers Past Caring, Says Mencken of Convention Collapse. July 7, p. 2, 5:30 Financial edition.
Mencken Finds That Politicians' Sagacity is Mostly a Legend. July 8, p. 3, 5:30 Financial edition.
Finds Convention Devoid of Common Sense as Well as Real Leadership. July 9, p. 2, 5:30 Financial edition.

See also Monday Articles. [Baltimore] Evening Sun 1924: The Clowns March In, June 2; Machiavelli Groans, July 10; Post-Mortem, July 14; Breathing Space, August 4; Labor in Politics, August 11; The New Woodrow, August 18.

1928

[Dispatches] Republican National Convention, Kansas City. [Baltimore] Evening Sun June 11-16, 1928.

Presidential Candidate, Herbert Hoover; Vice-Presidential Candidate, Charles W. Curtis.

Mencken Finds GOP Convention is Colorless and Likely to be Worse. June 11, p. 1, Financial edition.
Air of Deceit and Fraud Pervades Whole GOP Meeting, Says Mencken. June 12, p. 1, Financial edition.
Mencken Says Grateful Hoover Ought to Make Vare [William Scott Vare, Congressman, R. Pa.] Secretary of State. June 13, p. 1, Financial edition.
Committee Works Hard Trying to Hew Wet-Dry Plank, Mencken Reports. June 14, p. 1, Financial edition.
Hoover Leaves Crowd Cool and Spiritless, in Eyes of H. L. Mencken. June 15, p. 1, Financial edition.
This, Says Mencken, Was the "Most Low-Down" Convention Ever Held. June 16, p. 1, Financial edition.

[Dispatches] Democratic National Convention, Houston. [Baltimore] Evening Sun June 23–30, 1928.

Presidential Candidate, Albert E. Smith; Vice-Presidential Candidate, Joseph T. Robinson.

Scene Set, Foes Arriving, For Democracy's Usual Warfare, Says Mencken. June 23, p. 1, Financial edition.
Strife Rends Democrats, Says Mencken, Making Smith Men Less Secure. June 25, p. 1, Financial edition.
Mencken Thinks Ritchie the Man Who Will Profit from Houston Turmoil. June 26, p. 1, Financial edition.
Bowers [Claude Gernade Bowers, Chairman and Keynote speaker] is Too Mild, Thinks Mencken Who Sighs for Bryan's Fire. June 27, p. 1, Financial edition.
Al Smith a Bitter Pill for Democrats, Despite Display, Says Mencken. June 28, p. 1, Financial edition.
Drys Emerge in Defeat, Says Mencken; Plank a 'Hollow Compromise.' June 29, p. 1, Financial edition.
Honest Candidate Comes Out of Convention That Met Truth, Says Mencken. June 30, p. 1, Financial edition.

See also Monday Articles. [Baltimore] Evening Sun 1928: The Show Begins, June 4.

[Dispatches] Al Smith Campaign Tour. [Baltimore] Evening Sun October 12–30, 1928.

Comfort, But Not Always Conviction, Report of Mencken on Smith Tour. October 12, p. 1, 5 Star edition, Greensboro, N.C.

Mencken Says Smith's Nashville Speech was Better Than it Appears. October 13, p. 1, 5 Star edition, Nashville, Tenn.

Mencken Says Audience and Radio Too Much for Man to Handle at Once. October 15, p. 1, 5 Star edition, Belleville, Ill.

Reports from Territory Smith Covered Permit Optimism, Says Mencken. October 16, p. 1, 5 Star edition, Sedalis, Mo.

Analysis Fails Mencken, Pondering Smith's Sway of Crowds; Just Has 'It.' October 17, p. 1, 5 Star edition, Sedalis, Mo.

Border States Will Give Smith 390,955 Majority, Mencken's Dope Says. October 18, p. 1, 5 Star edition, Chicago.

Refinement is Keynote of Smith's Reception in Chicago, Says Mencken. October 19, p. 1, 5 Star edition, Chicago.

Mencken Says Chicago Audience Disappointed With Smith's Address. October 20, p. 1, 5 Star edition, Chicago.

Mencken Calls Smith's Speech Great Success, Just What Was Wanted. October 30, p. 1, 5 Star edition [Baltimore].

See also Monday Articles. [Baltimore] Evening Sun 1928: Episode, October 15; Al in the Free State, October 29.

1932

[Dispatches] Republican National Convention, Chicago. [Baltimore] Evening Sun June 13-18, 1932.

Presidential Candidate, Herbert Hoover; Vice-Presidential Candidate, Charles W. Curtis.

Mencken Sees More Whoops Than Votes for Repeal Plank. June 13, p. 1, 6 Star edition.

Mencken Pictures GOP Nonentities' Moment of Glory. June 14, p. 1, 6 Star edition.

Drys Are Done For, Mencken Says, and Is Sad at the Thought. June 15, p. 1, 6 Star edition.

Drys Out in Cold in Platform Fight, Mencken Declares. June 16, p. 1, 6 Star edition.

Maryland Man Hustled From GOP Meeting. June 16, p. 1, 6 Star edition.

GOP Wet Revolt Amazing in Extent, Mencken Declares. June 17, p. 1, 6 Star edition.

Mencken Sees Fight Left in Doomed Drys. June 18, p. 1, 6 Star edition.

[Dispatches] Democratic National Convention, Chicago. [Baltimore] Sun and Evening Sun June 26—July 2, 1932.

Presidential Candidate, Franklin D. Roosevelt; Vice-Presidential Candidate, John N. Garner.

Bishop Cannon [Chairman of Anti-Saloon League of America] Tells Mencken Prohibition is "In The Rough." Sunday June 26, p. 1, C edition.

Mencken Sees Smith Collapsed, Raskob [John J. Raskob, Chairman Dem. Nat. Committee, 1928] Done as Statesman. June 27, p. 1, 6 Star edition.

Farley [James A. Farley, Chairman Dem. Nat. Committee, 1932-1940] Surrender on Rules Leaves 4 Bitter Battles. June 28, p. 1, 6 Star edition.

Ritchie Lauded by Happy Wets. June 28, p. 1, 6 Star edition.

Irish Catholic Drys Due Some Democratic Sop, Mencken's Told by One. June 28, p. 2, 6 Star edition.

Mencken Finds Dry Mourners Dry-Eyed as Prohibition Dies. June 29, p. 1, 6 Star edition.

Dry Law a Fugitive in Bible Belt Bogs Now, Says Mencken. June 30, p. 1, 6 Star edition.

Marylanders Storm Ritchie Headquarters. June 30, p. 1, 6 Star edition.

Mencken Calls Night Session "Horrible"; Stampede Blocked. July 1, p. 1, 6 Star edition.

Mencken Finds Both Sides Sour, Thinking Only of Their Losses. July 2, p. 1, 6 Star edition.

The dispatches for July 1 and July 2 are reprinted in: *The Vintage Mencken,* gathered by Alistair Cooke. (N.Y. Vintage Books, 1955) p. 204–215, "The Nomination of F.D.R."

See also Monday Articles. [Baltimore] Evening Sun 1932: The Impending Carnage, May 2; The Battle Joins, May 9; Aftermath, June 20; Where Are We At?, July 5; The End of Prohibition, July 11.

The dispatches for both 1932 conventions were reprinted in: *Making A President, a Footnote to the Saga of Democracy,* by H. L. Mencken. (N.Y. Knopf, 1932).

MENCKEN TELLS HOW MAGIC WORD "BEER" BROUGHT THE CHEERS, Watches Roosevelt Draw Yells from Armory Audience, Attentive But Unmoved at Discussion of Tariffs and Such. [Baltimore] Evening Sun, Wednesday October 26, 1932, p. 1, 6 Star edition.

Franklin D. Roosevelt's campaign speech in Baltimore.

1936

[Dispatches] Republican National Convention, Cleveland. [Baltimore] Sun and Evening Sun June 8–13, 1936.

Presidential Candidate, Alfred M. Landon; Vice-Presidential Candidate, Frank Knox.

Mencken Finds Confidence in Convention City Almost Cornered by Landon Bloc. June 8, p. 1, D edition.

Borah [William Edgar Borah, Senator, R. Idaho] Puts on Grand Show, Mencken Says, But Leaves GOP Outlook Unchanged. June 9, p. 1, D edition.

Steiwer [William Hoover Steiwer, State Senator, R. Oregon] in Fine Voice, Brings Roard from Crowd with Shots at New Deal. June 10, p. 1, D edition.

Publisher [William F. Knox] Backs Return to Gold Basis. June 10, p. 3, D edition.

Noah Advises Mencken He's Planning a Flood, Asks Him Aboard Ark. Evening, June 10, 1936, p. 3, 6 Star edition.

"Three Long Years" Usurps Honor Given "Oh, Susanna" as GOP Campaign Song. June 11, p. 1, D edition.

Hoover Draws First Big House at Convention. June 11, p. 1, D edition.

Landon's Backers Parade with Pitchforks (Corked) as They Await Nomination. June 12, p. 1, D edition.

Farmer Sure of Victory, Taxpayer Sure of Defeat in Fall, Mencken Writes. June 13, p. 1, D edition.

[Dispatches] Democratic National Convention, Philadelphia. [Baltimore] Sun June 22–28, 1936.

Presidential Candidate, Franklin D. Roosevelt; Vice-Presidential Candidate, John N. Garner.

Farley Staging His Show to Keep Convention from Becoming Mammoth Bore. June 22, p. 1, D edition.

Exhibits Showing Benefits of New Deal Found Lacking in Reference to Taxpayer. June 23, p. 1, D edition.

Speech of Keynoter Cut to Keep Him from Going on into Today's Session. June 24, p. 1, D edition.

Mencken Finds Robinson [Joseph Taylor Robinson, Senator, D. Ark.] Oration Like Keynoter's, Only Not So Much of It. June 25, p. 1, D edition.

Presentation of Platform Marked by Convention's Poky Pace, Says Mencken. June 26, p. 1, D edition.

Ballots Won by Roosevelt, But Show Was Stolen by Lehman [Herbert H. Lehman, Gov. of N.Y.], Mencken Writes. June 27, p. 1, D edition.

Roosevelt and Garner Told of Nomination in Open-Air Ceremony at Philadelphia. June 28, p. 1, C edition.

Convention is Filled with Ringers as John N. Garner Gets Nomination. June 28, p. 2, C edition.

See also Monday Articles. [Baltimore] Evening Sun 1936: Rough Stuff Ahead, February 3; The Show Begins, March 9; Turning on the Heat, May 4; The Combat Joins, July 6.

[Dispatches] Landon Campaign Tour. [Baltimore] Sun July 23— October 30, 1936.

Topeka Fears Rain May Spoil Its Great Day. July 23, p. 1, D edition, Topeka, Kansas.

Landon Hears He's Chosen While Thousands Look On As Clouds Lift for GOP. July 24, p. 1, D edition, Topeka, Kansas.

Landon Is Neither Vacuum Nor Kansas Gang's Stooge, Mencken Notes at Topeka. July 26, p. 1, C edition, Topeka, Kansas.

Many GOP Notables Hear Landon Open Campaign in East at Birthplace. August 23, p. 1, C edition, Middlesex, Pa.

Landon Goes to Old Church in Birthplace. August 24, p. 1, D edition, New Castle, Pa.

Gov. Landon is Received with Chautauqua Salute Waved by 7,000 Hearers. August 25, p. 1, D edition, Chautauqua, N.Y.

Chilly Wind Sweeps Field as Governor Landon Makes Major Eastern Address. August 27, p. 1, D edition, Buffalo, N.Y.

Landon Taking Back Porch to People, He Tells Them from Train on Way East. September 12, p. 1, D edition, Fort Wayne, Ind.

Nominee Gives Eleven Talks in Day's Ride. September 13, p. 1, C edition, Portland, Maine.

Maine Election Today Called Risk to Landon. September 14, p. 1, Final edition, Portland, Maine.

Landon Offers Dual Plan to Promote World Peace. October 25, p. 1, C edition, Indianapolis, Ind.

Landon Opens Final Bid for East with Speech in Baltimore This Morning. October 26, p. 1, D edition, Aboard Governor Landon's special train.

Landon Appeals to Voters of Eastern Pennsylvania; Kansan Speaks to Big Crowd in Philadelphia. October 27, p. 1, D edition, Philadelphia.

Landon Makes Attack upon Spoils System. October 28, p. 1, D edition, Pittsburgh.

Roosevelt and Landon Cross Trails as They Bid for Empire State. October 29, p. 1, D edition, New York.

Landon Gives His Creed Ending Eastern Campaign; Gives Pledge to End Waste and Spending. October 30, p. 1, D edition, New York.

See also Monday Articles. [Baltimore] Evening Sun 1936: The Challenger, August 31; Stumping Tour, September 21.

[Dispatches] Townsend Convention, Cleveland. [Baltimore] Sun July 14–20, 1936.

Lemke [William Lemke, Candidate for Pres. on Union Party Ticket] Far From His Hero, Dr. Townsend [Francis Everett Townsend, author of old-age pension plan] Discloses, After Hop to Cleveland. July 14, p. 1, D edition.

Dr. Townsend, Threatened by Revolt, Plans to Grant More Democratic Control. July 15, p. 1, D edition.

Rev. Gerald Smith Stars at Townsend Convention in Rabble-Rousing Talk. July 16, p. 1, D edition.

Enemies of Roosevelt Triumph as Townsend Orders Defenders Ousted. July 17, p. 1, D edition.

Ban Upon Indorsements by Townsend Convention Makes Combat a Squall. July 18, p. 1, D edition.

Townsendites Toss in Cash to Defend Leader in Suit; Lemke Takes His Bow Today. July 19, p. 1, C edition.

Lemke Pledges His Support to Townsend Plan. July 20, p. 1, D edition.

See also Monday Articles. [Baltimore] Evening Sun 1936: The Townsend Circus, July 27. *See also* Miscellaneous Articles. Sunpapers, 1939.

[Dispatches] Coughlin Convention, Cleveland. [Baltimore] Sun August 13–18, 1936.

Endorsed William Lemke, Presidential Candidate of the Union Party.

Coughlinites in Cleveland at Odds Over Townsend and Gerald Smith as Speakers. August 13, p. 1, D edition.

Father Coughlin [Charles Edward Coughlin, Head of National Union for Social Justice] Settles Row in NUSJ Ranks Over Speeches by Outsiders. August 14, p. 1, D edition.

Roosevelt Competition Takes Edge off Opening of Coughlin Convention. August 15, p. 1, D edition.

Single Dissenter Escapes Steam-Roller of Coughlin to Cry out Against Lemke. August 16, p. 1, C edition.

Blistering Heat is Braved by 25,000 to Hear Coughlin and Other Speakers at Rally. August 17, p. 1, D edition.
Townsend Ill; Finds Hearing is Postponed. August 18, p. 1, D edition.

See also Monday Articles. [Baltimore] Evening Sun 1936: The Radio Priest, August 24.

1940

[Dispatches] Republican National Convention, Philadelphia. [Baltimore] Sun June 22–29, 1940.

Presidential Candidate, Wendell L. Willkie; Vice-Presidential Candidate, Charles L. McNary.

GOP Defense Plank Waits on Roosevelt and Hitler. June 22, p. 1, 6AM edition.
All Republican Candidates to be Present at Convention. June 23, p. 1, D edition.
Willkie Cuts Luncheon to See Delegates. June 24, p. 1, 6AM edition.
Youthful Keynoter [Harold E.] Stassen Gets Free Rein for Oratory. June 25, p. 1, 6AM edition.
Hon. Herbert Hoover Brings Down House at Convention. June 26, p. 1, 6AM edition.
Wild Cheers and Boos Greet Willkie's Name. June 27, p. 1, D edition.
Willkie Win Held Victory of Amateur. June 28, p. 1, 6AM edition.
Willkie Visits Convention to Give Thanks. June 29, p. 1, 6AM edition.

[Dispatches] Democratic National Convention, Chicago. [Baltimore] Sun July 13–19, 1940.

Presidential Candidate, Franklin D. Roosevelt; Vice-Presidential Candidate, Henry Wallace.

Shadow of Roosevelt Heavy Over Chicago. July 13, p. 1, 6AM edition.
Chicago Delegates Devoting Themselves to Futile Acts. July 14, p. 1, 6AM edition.
Farley Talk Described as Only Half a Farewell. July 16, p. 1, 6AM edition.
Roosevelt Statement Flabbergasts Delegates. July 17, p. 1, 6AM edition.
Delegates Toe the Mark, Throwing Tradition Out. July 18, p. 1, 6AM edition.
Roosevelt Closes "Show"—By Remote Control. July 19, p. 1, 6AM edition.
Apathy Rules Day Session of Convention. July 19, p. 4, 6AM edition.

See also Monday Articles. [Baltimore] Evening Sun 1940: Wonder Man, June 30; Triumph of Democracy, July 21.

[Dispatches] Willkie Campaign Tour. [Baltimore] Sun and Evening Sun August 16—November 3, 1940.

Mencken Goes to Elwood. Morning, August 16, p. 1, 6AM edition, Elwood, Ind.
Two Idealists Underwrite Bill for GOP Notification Orgies. August 17, 6AM edition, Elwood, Ind.
Vast Crowd, Possibly 200,000 Strong, Hears Willkie's Acceptance. Sunday August 18, p. 1, D edition, Elwood, Ind.
Rushville Idyll: Mr. Willkie's Share-Croppers. Evening, August 20, editorial page.
Willkie Urges Utmost Assistance to England in New York Tour. October 9, p. 1, 6AM edition, New York.

Willkie Says New Deal is Wrecking Land. October 10, p. 1, 6AM edition, New Haven.

Willkie Makes 6-Hour Tour of Rhode Island. October 11, p. 1, 6AM edition, Providence.

Willkie Says Rivals Mulct New England. October 12, p. 1, 6AM edition, Boston.

Willkie Assails "Scurrilous" Pamphlet—Says New Deal Tries to Raise Racial Issue. Sunday, October 13, p. 1, D edition, Albany.

Willkie Heads East. Evening, October 29, p. 3, 6 Star edition, Jackson, Ohio.

W. Va. Hails Willkie. Evening, October 30, p. 1, 6 Star edition, Grafton, W. Va.

Turnout for Willkie Huge in Wilmington. Evening, October 31, p. 1. 6 Star edition, Aboard the special train.

Willkie Heartened by Camden Cheers. Evening, November 1, p. 1, 6 Star edition, Aboard the Willkie train in New Jersey.

Music and Spellbinders Entertain Willkie Crowd. Sunday, November 3, p. 1, D edition, New York.

See also [Sunday Articles]. [Baltimore] Sun 1940: There He Is! September 15; Heil Roosevelt! September 22; Touring With Willkie, October 13; Notes On The Campaign, October 20; Ninth Inning: Willkie At Bat, November 3.

1948

[Dispatches] Republican National Convention, Philadelphia. [Baltimore] Sun June 19–22, 1948.

Presidential Candidate, Thomas E. Dewey; Vice-Presidential Candidate, Earl Warren.

Mencken Tunes In: Expects Blitz of Sound from Heirs of Lincoln. June 19, p. 1, Final edition.

Mencken Listens: But About All He Hears from GOP is Vague Talk. June 20, p. 1, 5AM edition.

Mencken's Bottlescope: Television Lamps Stir Up 2-Way Use for Beer. June 21, p. 1, Final edition.

Mencken Counts 'Em: Decibels Hit Ceiling in Keynote-Night Din. June 22, p. 1, Final edition.

[Dispatches] Democratic National Convention, Philadelphia. [Baltimore] Sun July 10–15, 1948.

Presidential Candidate, Harry S. Truman; Vice-Presidential Candidate, Alben W. Barkley.

Mencken At Gettysburg: Yank Democrats Tense as Rebel Army Nears. July 10, p. 1, Final edition.

Mencken Hears the Drums: Anti-Rights Rebs Due, All Armed to the Jaws. July 11, p. 1, D edition.

Mencken is Let Down: Trumanocide Rebel's Verbal Guns Go Phut. July 12, p. 1, Final edition.

Mencken Wipes Brow: 'Dear Alben,' All Het Up Over GOP, Mops His Too. July 13, p. 1, Final edition.

Mencken Lifts an Eyebrow: The Pretty Lady-Democrats Brighten Up a Dull Scene. July 13, p. 4, Final edition.

Mencken Gets His Battle: Rebs Breach Doghouse, Defiant Guns A-Barkin.' July 14, p. 1, Final edition.

Doves For the Victors: Truman and Barkley Emerge Amid Uproar. July 15, p. 1, Final edition.

[Dispatches] Progressive Party National Convention, Philadelphia. [Baltimore] Sun July 23–26, 1948.

Presidential Candidate, Henry A. Wallace; Vice-Presidential Candidate, Glen H. Taylor.

Mencken and the Swami: Marx, Lenin, Uncle Joe Missing at Convention. July 23, p. 1, Final edition.

Mencken and the Votaries: Sudden Flap of Wings Would be no Surprise. July 24, p. 1, Final edition.

Mencken at Hall and Park: Sees Comrades Emerge and Wallace Nominated. July 25, p. 1, D edition.

Mencken Tastes the Cake: Finds Several Raisins in Paranoiac Confection. July 26, p. 1, Final edition.

Reprinted in: *The Vintage Mencken,* gathered by Alistair Cooke. (N.Y., Vintage Books, 1955) p. 223–226, "The Wallace Paranoia."

See also [Articles]. [Baltimore] Sun August 1—November 9, 1948.

WORKS BY H. L. M.

Miscellaneous Articles

1921

LIST OF 100 RECENT AMERICAN BOOKS WORTH READING. [Baltimore] Evening Sun January 22, 1921, page opposite book page, in "More Book Talk."

REED VIEWS WILSONIAN DEBACLE WITH SARDONIC CHUCKLE, SAYS MENCKEN. [Baltimore] Evening Sun February 14, 1921, p. 1.

[Harding Inauguration]. [Baltimore] Evening Sun March 2–4, 1921, p. 1, Financial edition.

Old-Time Inauguration Joy is Lacking, Mencken Finds; Blames It on Prohibition. March 2.
Mencken Finds Wilson "A Ghost of Sad Music in an Unlistening Street." March 3.
Harding Faces Task With Air of Confidence. March 4.
See also Monday Articles. [Baltimore] Evening Sun 1921: Gamalielese, March 7.

[Dempsey-Carpentier Fight]. [Baltimore] Evening Sun July 1–3, 1921.

Big Fight to be Square Because Honesty Insures Most Cash, Says Mencken. July 1, p. 1, Financial edition.
Horde of Ring "Experts" Squander Infinite Care on Circle, Mencken Finds. July 2, p. 2, Financial edition.
Sob Sisters' Paens in Praise of Carpentier Bear Odds, Says Mencken. July 2. This article apparently appeared in an early edition, which is no longer available. Unverified.
Brief Battle Was Hopeless for Carpentier from First. July 3, p. 1, Financial edition.
See also Monday Articles. [Baltimore] Evening Sun 1921: How Legends Are Made, July 5.

MENCKEN EXPLAINS STORM OVER CASE OF COMMUNISTS. [Baltimore] Evening Sun October 20, 1921, p .1.

Concerning Sacco-Vanzetti case retrial.

1922

MENCKEN THINKS TALES OF FILM ORGIES FALSE. [Baltimore] Sun July 9, 1922, Part 6, p. 8.

EXILE AT WIERINGEN [FRIEDRICH WILHELM VIKTOR ALBERT] SAYS HE LONGS FOR DAY WHEN HE CAN ASSIST GERMANY. [Baltimore] Sun October 11, 1922, p. 1.

See also Monday Articles. [Baltimore] Evening Sun 1922: Notes from a Lonely Shore, October 23.

WHO'S LOONEY NOW? [Baltimore] Sun November 5, 1922, Part 10, p. 1.

Brief answer to the question, Do women have souls?

1923

MAX WAYS AS H. L. MENCKEN KNEW HIM. [Baltimore] Evening Sun June 5, 1923, editorial page.

"Max Ways [March 7, 1869—June 5, 1923] died this morning. He was City Editor of the old Baltimore *Herald* when Henry L. Mencken got his first newspaper job there. Mr. Mencken wrote this article this morning when he was told of the death of his old boss."

10 DULLEST AUTHORS PICKED BY EXPERTS, INCLUDING MENCKEN. [Baltimore] Evening Sun July 28, 1923, book page.

1925

PARADE UNLIKE ANYTHING SINCE DAYS OF ROOSEVELT. [Baltimore] Sun August 9, 1925, p. 1.

Ku Klux Klan parade in Washington, D.C.

1926

ENGLISH COMPLACENCY WRECKED BY SHAW, IS MENCKEN'S VIEW. [Baltimore] Sun July 27, 1926, p. 1.

Written on the occasion of George Bernard Shaw's 70th birthday.

WHY THEY HAVE NOT MARRIED YET. IMPOSSIBLE HUSBAND, SAYS MENCKEN. [Baltimore] Sun November 7, 1926, Part 2, Section 2, p. 8.

Mencken and others give their views as to why they have not married.

BACHELOR MENCKEN ASSAILS POLYGAMY. [Baltimore] Sun November 20, 1926, p. 2.

HLM answers the challenge issued by Mrs. Anna Garlin Spencer, special lecturer at Columbia University Teacher's College.

1927

ADAMS AS AN EDITOR. [Baltimore] Sun October 14, 1927, p. 13.

John Haslup Adams, January 31, 1871—October 13, 1927, was made Editor of the *Evening Sun* when that paper was started; Mencken was his chief of staff. Mencken also wrote the unsigned editorial about Adams that appears in this same issue.

1932

MAN WHO REALLY BUSTED PROHIBITION GIVES ALL CREDIT TO OPPOSITE SEX. [Baltimore] Sun October 30, 1932, p. 1, C edition.

"Captain [Thomas Moses] Stayton, founder of Wet Group, details fight towards repeal of Volstead Act—believes "'Archbishop' Cannon did Dry cause most damage."

1935

MENCKEN CALLS MISS REESE ONE OF GREATEST OF TIME. [Baltimore] Evening Sun December 17, 1935, back page.

"Paying tribute to 'Tears' as a masterful sonnet." HLM praises the work of Lizette Woodworth Reese, 1856-1935.

1937

THE MORE ABUNDANT LIFE FOR JUDGES. [Baltimore] Sun February 7, 1937, p. 1.

A PROPOSED NEW CONSTITUTION FOR MARYLAND. [Baltimore] Sun April 12, 1937, p. 11–12.

"The Constitution of 1867, Article XIV, Section 2, provides that the Legislature, every twenty years, shall 'take the sense of the people in regard to calling a convention for altering this Constitution.' The Legislature did so in 1887, 1907 and 1930, but politics got into the matter each time and there was no action. Of late the need for a general overhauling of the Constitution has become painfully manifest. It is, as it stands, quite inadequate to its purpose, and its inadequacy is proved anew every time the Legislature meets. We labor under a wasteful, incompetent and archaic system of government, and its defects offer a standing invitation to fanatical reformers to tinker with it. In the hope that a beginning, however insufficient, may induce better men to undertake a well-considered and thorough revision, I offer herewith a proposed draft of an entirely new Constitution." Introduction. Reprinted as a pamphlet.

"Novum Organum" by Thomas F. Cadwalader. [Baltimore] Evening Sun April 16, 1937, editorial page. A discussion of H. L. Mencken's proposed new Constitution for Maryland.

"A New Atlantis" by Garrard Glenn, Professor of Law, Univ. of Va. [Baltimore] Evening Sun April 30, 1937, editorial page. A discussion of H. L. Mencken's proposed new Constitution for Maryland.

"Unfit For What?" by Clarence Stone. [Baltimore] Evening Sun May 21, 1937, editorial page. A discussion of H. L. Mencken's proposed new Constitution for Maryland: Article I, Section 2, dealing with the vote; Article III, Section 7, dealing with the "unfit."

TWO TRAITS GAINED RENOWN FOR HOWE. [Baltimore] Sun October 4, 1937, p. 7.

Unsigned, obituary, Edgar Watson Howe, May 3, 1853—October 3, 1937.

1939

CREATOR OF PHILO VANCE. [Baltimore] Sun April 14, 1939, editorial page.

Unsigned obituary, Williard Huntington Wright, 1888–1939.

[National Right to Work Congress, Washington]. [Baltimore] Sun June 4–8, 1939, p. 1, D edition.

Money, By Lobby and Printing Press, Called for at Right-To-Work Rally. June 4.
Workers' Alliance Congress, Only Barely Started, Seems to be Petering Out Already. June 6.
Right-To-Work Congress Perks Up to Give Ear to Speech by Mrs. Roosevelt. June 8.

See also [Sunday Articles]. [Baltimore] Sun 1939: The Worker's Alliance, June 11.

[Townsend Rally, Indianapolis]. [Baltimore] Sun June 22–25, 1939, p. 1, D edition.

Townsend Rallies His Men to Smite the Congressmen Who Voted Against His Bill. June 22.
Dr. Townsend is Cheered by 10,000 Backers. June 23.
Old Folks Get Run-Around at Pension Rally. June 24.
Townsendites End Business of Convention. June 25.

See also Conventions 1936, Townsend Convention.

See also [Sunday Articles]. [Baltimore] Sun 1939: Dr. Townsend and His Plan, July 2.

[Fifth American Youth Congress, New York]. [Baltimore] Sun July 2–4, 1939, p. 1, D edition.

Youth Congress Opens Parley Under Tunney Group's Attack. July 2.
Youth Group Balks at Fight on Communism. July 3.
Anti-Marxists in Youth Group Snowed Under. July 4.

A FAR FROM ADEQUATE FAREWELL TO THE RENNERT. [Baltimore] Sun December 15, 1939, editorial page.

Unsigned editorial. Rennert Hotel in Baltimore.

1940

RAYMOND PEARL, HOPKINS BIOLOGIST, DIES SUDDENLY AT HERSHEY, PA. [Baltimore] Sun November 18, 1940, back page.

Mencken also wrote the unsigned editorial about Pearl, 1879–1940, that appears in this same issue.
See also [Sunday Articles] [Baltimore] Sun November 24, 1940.

1941

MAX BROEDEL. [Baltimore] Sun October 28, 1941, editorial page.
Unsigned editorial, obituary. Anatomical artist of Johns Hopkins, 1870-1941.

1954

MENCKEN ON HERGESHEIMER. [Baltimore] Sun May 2, 1954, Section A, p. 12.

WORKS BY H. L. M.

"Some years ago, when his intimate friend and literary colleague, Joseph Hergesheimer, was seriously ill, H. L. Mencken wrote the following appreciation of the novelist, with the understanding that it would be printed after Mr. Hergesheimer's death." Joseph Hergesheimer, 1880–1954.

As H.L.M. Sees It

As H.L.M. SEES IT. [Baltimore] Evening Sun November 8, 1924 —January 28, 1928, page opposite editorials.

Weekly articles written for the *Chicago Sunday Tribune*. *The Evening Sun,* by special arrangement, received the articles free. The articles were published in the *Evening Sun* every Saturday as long as the series ran. The first article, November 8, 1924, appeared on the editorial page in "Books to be Read or Read About;" the next three articles: November 22, November 29, and December 6, 1924, appeared under individual headings on the page opposite editorials; from December 13, 1924 until the end of the series the articles appeared under the boxed head "As H.L.M. Sees It" on the page opposite editorials.

The Evening Sun published the articles on Saturday, the *Chicago Sunday Tribune* on Sunday, therefore the articles actually appeared first in Baltimore. *The Evening Sun* published two articles which the *Chicago Sunday Tribune* did not use, omitted several which were rewritings of articles previously published, and HLM used three as part of his "Monday Articles" series.

See—Chicago Sunday Tribune.

Scopes Trial

[Scopes Trial]. [Baltimore] Evening Sun July 9–18, 1925, p. 1, 5:30 Financial edition.

Trial of public-school teacher, John T. Scopes, for teaching Darwinian theory contrary to state statute. Clarence Seward Darrow was chief defense attorney, William Jennings Bryan was chief prosecutor.

Mencken Finds Daytonians Full of Sickening Doubts About Value of Publicity. July 9.
Impossibility of Obtaining Fair Trial Insures Scopes' Conviction, Says Mencken. July 10.
Mencken Likens Trial to Religious Orgy, With Defense a Beelzebub. July 11.
Yearning Mountaineers' Souls Need Reconversion Nightly, Mencken Finds. July 13.
This article, partially rewritten and expanded, was reprinted as "The Hills of Zion" in: *Prejudices: Fifth Series.* p. 75–86; *The Borzoi Reader,* edited with an introduction and notes by Carl Van Doren. (N. Y. Knopf, 1936), p. 656–662; *The Vintage Mencken,* gathered by Alistair Cooke. (N.Y. Vintage Books, 1955) p. 153–161.
Darrow's Eloquent Appeal Wasted on Ears That Heed Only Bryan, Says Mencken. July 14.
Law and Freedom, Mencken Discovers, Yield Place to Holy Writ in Rhea County. July 15.
Mencken Declares Strictly Fair Trial is Beyond Ken of Tennessee Fundamentalists. July 16.

[Dudley F.] Malone [Defense attorney] the Victor, Even Though Court Sides with Opponents, Says Mencken. July 17.
Battle Now Over, Mencken Sees; Genesis Triumphant and Ready for New Jousts. July 18.
See also Monday Articles. [Baltimore] Evening Sun 1925: The Tennessee Circus, June 15; Homo Neandertalensis, June 29; Tennessee in The Frying-Pan, July 20; Bryan, July 27; Round Two, August 10; Aftermath, September 14.
Reprinted in: *Chattanooga News* [Tennessee], July 9–18, 1925; *Star Reporters and 34 of Their Stories,* collected, with notes and an introduction by Ward Greene. (N.Y.: Random House, 1948) "The Baltimore Nonpareil," p. 226–255.
Mencken's dispatches from the trial were syndicated and stirred up a storm of protest all over the South.
"Mr. Goldsborough Writes a Letter" by A. S. Goldsborough, Executive Secretary of the Baltimore Association of Commerce. [Baltimore] Evening Sun August 13, 1925, editorial page. Accusing HLM of hurting Baltimore's trade with the South through his Scopes Trial dispatches.
"South Carolina Speaks to Mr. Goldsborough" by Charlton Wright. [Baltimore] Evening Sun August 21, 1925, editorial page.
"Mencken, Mr. Goldsborough and The South" by Julian Harris. [Baltimore] Evening Sun August 25, 1925, editorial page.
"Mencken and The South—Finale." [Baltimore] Evening Sun August 27, 1925, editorial page. Excerpts from Southern newspapers on the Goldsborough affair.

Pan American Conference

[Pan American Conference, 6th, Havana]. [Baltimore] Evening Sun January 18–25, 1928, p. 1, Financial edition.
Diplomats Fagged Out Doffing Hats to Flags. January 18.
Static Carefully Tuned Out of Havana Program. January 18.
Article appeared in an edition no longer available on microfilm. Unverified.
Though Blood's Shed, Wise Ones Quiet at Havana. January 19.
Mr. [Charles Evans] Hughes [American delegate, Secretary of State 1921–1925] Runs Things, Though Not a Spaniard. January 24.
Gin Guzzling American Tourists Crowd Havana. January 24.
Mencken Misses Pupils at University of Havana. January 25.

See also Monday Articles. [Baltimore] Evening Sun 1928: The Goosegreasers at Work, January 23; The Spanish Main, January 30; The Clowns Go Home, February 21.

London Naval Conference

[London Naval Conference]. [Baltimore] Evening Sun January 27—February 10, 1930, p. 1, 5 Star edition.
Mencken Sees Navy Pact Keeping Peace for While as Best to be Hoped for. January 27.
Shelving Real Issues is Main Naval Parley Work, Mencken Finds. January 29.
Etiquette Makes Rapid Progress Impossible at London, Mencken Says. January 31.
Sees Few Signs Parley Result Will Be Worth Name of Disarmament. February 4.
Mencken Believes U.S. Proposals Clear Way for Some Real Action. February 7.

Anglo-American Accord is Noticeable Drift at Parley, Mencken Finds. February 10.

See also Monday Articles. [Baltimore] Evening Sun 1930: The Naval Conference, February 21; The Naval Conference, March 31.

The University of Maryland

THE UNIVERSITY OF MARYLAND. [Baltimore] Sun May 17—June 5, 1937.

I. A Brief Outline of Its History. May 17, p. 11.
II. The College of Agriculture. May 18, p. 15.
III. The Greater University. May 19, p. 13.
IV. The Princess Anne Academy. May 20, p. 13.
V. Its Auxiliary Services. May 21, p. 15.
VI. The Growth of the Student Body. May 22, p. 11.
VII. The School of Law. May 24, p. 11.
VIII. The Baltimore College of Dental Surgery. May 25, p. 13.
IX. The School of Pharmacy. May 26, p. 13.
X. The Lost-Colleges. May 27, p. 13.
XI. The School of Medicine. May 28, p. 15.
XII. More About the School of Medicine. May 29, p. 11.
XIII. The University Hospital. May 31, p. 9.
XIV. The Extension Service. June 1, p. 11.
XV. The Summer School. June 2, p. 13.
XVI. The School of Nursing. June 3, p. 15.
XVII. The Commander-In-Chief. June 4, p. 15.
XVIII. Summary and Conclusion. June 5, p. 11.

The Johns Hopkins Hospital

THE JOHNS HOPKINS HOSPITAL. [Baltimore] Sun July 6–28, 1937.

I. The Dispensary. July 6, p. 11.
II. The Clinics. July 7, p. 13.
III. The Osler Clinic. July 8, p. 13.
IV. The Halsted Clinic. July 9, p. 13.
V. The Woman's Clinic. July 10, p. 7.
VI. Housekeeping. July 12, p. 9.
VII. The Harriet Lane Home for Invalid Children. July 13, p. 13.
VIII. The Wilmer Ophthalmological Institute. July 14, p. 13.
IX. The James Buchanan Brady Urological Institute. July 15, p. 11.
X. The Henry Phipps Psychiatric Clinic. July 16, p. 13.
XI. The Marburg Memorial Building. July 17, p. 9.
XII. The Thayer and the Diagnostic Clinic. July 19, p. 7.
XIII. The School of Nursing. July 20, p. 11.
XIV. The Day's Mail. July 21, p. 11.
XV. The Social Service. July 22, p. 11.
XVI. The Special Clinics. July 23, p. 13.
XVII. Its Finances. July 24, p. 9.
XVIII. The Medical School. July 26, p. 7.
XIX. Its Needs. July 27, p. 11.
XX. Conclusion. July 28, p. 9.
Reprinted as mimeographed pamphlet.

NEWSPAPER WORK

Editorship

"Effective today, Hamilton Owens, who for many years has been editor of *The Evening Sun,* becomes editor of *The Sun.* H. L. Mencken becomes editor temporarily of *The Evening Sun* and will serve for a period of three months, after which he will again give his attention to his own writing." [Baltimore] Evening Sun January 24, 1938, editorial page.

The first entry in HLM's clipping book for this period is "Jail for Dr. Townsend," appearing on February 8.

"Philip M. Wagner, who joined the editorial staff of *The Evening Sun* in February, 1930, becomes editor of *The Evening Sun* with this issue, succeeding H. L. Mencken, who became acting editor in February, and now retires in accordance with an arrangement then made." [Baltimore] Evening Sun May 9, 1938, editorial page.

"My best newspaper writing was done over my own name, and it dealt mainly with topics that editorial writers seldom tackle." HLM (EPFL—A30)

The editorials HLM wrote during this period are listed to illustrate how HLM handled editorial topics.

[Acting Editor]. [Baltimore] Evening Sun February 8—May 7, 1938.

Jail for Dr. Towsend. February 8. (Francis Everett Townsend, head of the Townsend Recovery Plan.)
A Respectable Tradition. February 9. (Civil liberties.)
Object Lesson. February 10. (An entire page of dots, each representing a Federal jobholder.)
'Raus Mit 'Em! February 17. (Directorates of the city's art museums.)
Off Again, On Again. February 17. (The President and the rise in prices.)
A-B-C Class for Wizards. February 21. (Incompetents in government.)
Getting Rid of the Unfit. February 21. (Reproduction control.)
Man of an Extinct Species. February 22. (George Washington, a gentleman.)
How Nebraska Does It. February 22. (Taxes.)
The Love of Money. February 28. (Franklin D. Roosevelt.)
A Mate for Hugo. March 1 (National Bar Association demands a Negro lawyer be given the vacant seat on Supreme Bench.)
An Alarming Proposal. March 1. (Bill to restore Washington, D.C. to Maryland.)
Second Thoughts. March 1. (On "An alarming proposal," *see* above.)
The Cost of Being Saved. March 2. (New Deal and the railroads.)
Socialized Medicine. March 2.
The Beauties of Charity. March 2. (Roosevelt's memoirs syndicated in newspapers, free.)
The Taxpayer as Maecenas. March 3.

Five Years of the New Deal. March 4.
　Entire page, probably the longest editorial ever written, by Mencken and Wagner. Gerald Johnson, who favored Roosevelt, replied to it on March 8.
The Way to Fascism. March 7. (Bill to "take the profits out of war.")
Mr. Barton's Crusade. March 8. (Repealing laws.)
The End of a Yardstick. March 9. (TVA.)
The Bridges Case. March 9. (Harry Bridges, boss of Longshoremen's Union.)
Sermon or Announcement? March 10. (President's choice of the 15th Psalm.)
The Bogus Yardstick. March 11. (TVA.)
A Statesman Takes a Ride. March 11. (John Main Coffee Bill for Bureau of Fine Arts.)
Senator Norris on Himself. March 11.
The Next Justice. March 12. (Robert L. Vann, a possibility.)
Indiscretion of a Wizard. March 14. (TVA.)
A Gladiator of the Law. March 14. (Clarence Darrow.)
Helping Business. March 15. (Borden Co. and the New Deal.)
Wien Bleibt Wien. March 17. (Austria and Hitler.)
A Few Figures. March 21 . (National debt.)
The Leftist Seers. March 21. (Pink prophets.)
Idealist into Jobholder. March 21. (Nebraska's one chamber legislature.)
Dr. Morgan on the TVA. March 23.
The Care of the Sick. March 24. (Socialized medicine.)
A Foolish Law. March 30. (McNaboe-Devaney Bill.)
Public Spirit by Force. March 31. (Baltimore Dahlia Society.)
Decency in the Courtroom. April 2.
Do the Japs Agree? April 2. (Night flying manoeuvers around Hawaii cancelled.)
The Reorganization Bill. April 4. (Reorganization of the Federal government.)
Chance for Publicists. April 4. (Robert L. Vann for the Supreme Court.)
The Moscow Camp Meeting. April 5. (New state trials.)
An Apparently Sound Idea. April 6. (Judges' financial troubles.)
The Byrd Boom Busts. April 8. (Federal funds for the University of Maryland.)
A Non-Dictator Blows Up. April 9. (Sam Rayburn.)
The Big Smash. April 11. (Roosevelt and the New Deal.)
The Reds and Fair Play. April 11.
Confession and Avoidance. April 15. (On a previous editorial.)
Why Not Lead the Way? April 15. (Roosevelt.)
The Halt and The Maimed. April 15. (4th report of the National Health Survey.)
Off Again, On Again. April 16. (Roosevelt.)
Where the Money Goes. April 18. (Consolidated Edison Co. of N.Y.)
A Good Beginning. April 18. (Roosevelt's plans to cure the depression.)
Fellow-Travelers. April 19. (Communists.)
The End of a Sure Cure. April 19. (Townsend Movement.)
The Outlook Brightens. April 19. (GOP to join battle against spending.)
Aesthetes Hot for Jobs. April 20. (Claude Denson Pepper—John Main Coffee Bill.)
Happy Days in Mexico. April 20. (President Cardenas' announcement that he will pay for confiscated oil wells.)
The Joys of Competition. April 23. (Borden Co. and National Dairy Products Corp.)
Note on Human Progress. April 25.
The State Health Report. April 27.
A New Witch-Hunt. April 28. (Dickstein Bill on naturalization.)

Greeks Bearing Gifts. April 28. (Pacifists.)
More and Worse. April 29. (May Bill.)
Who Will Be General? April 30. (For a division of Negro soldiers.)
The Mexican New Deal. April 30. (Mexican Claims Commission.)
Fairy Tale. May 2. (Albania.)
A Law Against Lynching. May 7.

Sunday Articles

[Sunday Articles]. [Baltimore] Sun May 16, 1958—February 2, 1941, editorial page.

A few of these articles appeared neither on Sunday nor on the editorial page and are so indicated. As a whole, however, the articles form a continuous series.

1938

Heretics on Trial. May 16. (State trials in Moscow.)
Democracy as a Check on Governmental Powers. June 6.
Life in the Tropics is Far From Easy. June 13, page opposite editorials. (West Indies.)
The New Deal and The Doctors. August 5, page opposite editorials.
"The New Deal Regime and The Doctors," Letter to the Editor, by Walton H. Hamilton. Appeared in the [Baltimore] Sun August 13, 1938, editorial page. An answer to HLM's article.
Pacifism in Extremis. August 10, page opposite editorials. (Few people are actually against war.)
A Third Term? Well, Why Not? August 17, page opposite editorials.
Medicine Under the New Deal. August 21.
Twilight of an Idealist. August 28. (David John Lewis, 1869–1952, Maryland congressman.)
After the Ball is Over. September 4. (Government and democracy.)
Thirty Dollars Every Thursday. September 11. (Old-age pensions.)
Triumph of the Wicked. September 18. (The election and Roosevelt.)
Chenaniah and His Sons. September 25. (Maryland judiciary.)
The Cards Are Reshuffled. October 9. (Neville Chamberlain, British Prime Minister 1937–1940, and the profits of his betrayal.)
Forerunners of Utopia. October 16. (New Deal vs. democracy.)
Degrees, But No Jobs. October 23.
Free Speech for Its Enemies. October 30. (Frank Hague, Mayor of Jersey City 1917–1947, and the Communists.)
Of the People, By the People. November 6. (New Deal democracy.)
The Wreckage of the Storm. November 13. (The Liberals.)
Job for the Wrecking Crew. November 20. (When the New Deal goes up in smoke.)
Help for the Jews. November 27. (English and American proposals for dealing with the refugees.)
The New Deal Band of Justice. December 4. (Wagner Labor Relations Act, passed in 1935.)
Uproars in the Mediterranean. December 11. (Italy, France, Tunisia.)
Warming Up the Bugles. December 18. (Roosevelt, war and the Pan-American Conference.)
Mercy for the Merciless. December 25. (The new penology.)

WORKS BY H. L. M.

1939

The Problem of the Refugee. January 1. (English and American proposals.)
New Deal Cant. January 8. (Government and religion.)
The Crusade to Save Democracy. January 15. (U.S. aid to Russia.)
The Truth About Spain. January 22. (Spanish Civil War.)
Memoirs of a Bookkeeper. January 29. (Income tax returns.)
Loud Sounds the Offertory. February 5. (Taxes.)
The Marxian Blight. February 12. (Spain and Communism.)
The Two-Party System. February 19.
The Way to War. February 26. (New Deal.)
The Right to Free Speech. March 5.
Hopkins Place [Baltimore] Redivivus. March 12. (Local politics.)
Equality Before the Law. March 19.
The Nine Old Men. March 26. (William O. Douglas' appointment to the Supreme Court.)
The Same Old Gang. April 2. (Maryland legislature.)
The Great Game of War. April 9.
Another Barcelona Falls. April 16. (The local election.)
Call for a Khaki Election. April 22. (Roosevelt and Europe.)
The Marxians in Spain. April 30.
Starving the Pratt Library. May 7.
The Art of Selling War. May 9, page opposite editorials.
Approach to the Goose Step. May 14. (Conscript army.)
On Bogus Neutrality. May 16, page opposite editorials.
Biopsy on Baltimore. May 21. (Dr. E. L. Thorndike's *Your City*.)
The Balance Sheet. May 23, page opposite editorials. (New Deal spending.)
Disaster in Moronia. May 28. (Steinbeck's *Grapes of Wrath*.)
The Downhill Road. May 30, page opposite editorials. (Government spending.)
Reflections on Homicide. June 4.
The Great Scramble. June 6, page opposite editorialls. (Immigration.)
The Worker's Alliance. June 11. (Right-to-work Congress.)
Where the Money Goes. June 13, page opposite editorials.
The Third-Term Campaign. June 18.
Maryland Loses Again. June 22, page opposite editorials. (National Youth Administration.)
The New Democracy. June 25. (New Deal.)
The Dust Bowl Revives. June 27, page opposite editorials.
Dr. Townsend and His Plan. July 2. (Old-age pensions.)
Third-Term Prospects. July 4, page opposite editorials.
The New Deal Kindergarden. July 9. (Youth and Communism.)
The Jobholders' Share. July 11, page opposite editorials. (Taxes.)
The Standard of Living. July 14, page opposite editorials. (Minimum living standard.)
Polemic for a Third Term. July 16.
Up, Guards and At 'Em! July 23. (Neutrality and the allies.)
The Dead Horse. August 6. (New Deal chances in next election.)
A Word for the Japs. August 13.
The Fruits of Fraud. August 20. (New Deal.)
Triumph of Idealism. August 25, page opposite editorials. (Russo-German pact.)
The Valley of Megiddo. August 27. (Looming war, the allies and neutrality.)

The War Upon Medicine. September 3. (New Deal vs. medicine.)
Why Not Be Honest? September 10. (Fake neutrality.)
    Reprinted in: *An American Editor Speaks.* Mount Vernon, Washington
    (State): The Concord Press, n.d., pamphlet.
On False News. September 17. (Newspapers and newspapermen.)
Heavyweight Bout. September 24. (England and fake neutrality.)
    Reprinted in: *An American Editor Speaks. See* above.
Sham Battle. October 1. (U. S. neutrality.)
Notes on a Moral War. October 8. (World War II.)
    Reprinted in: *An American Editor Speaks. See* above; also reprinted as a
    pamphlet, Sargent Bulletin #10.
Idealism Marches On. October 15. (War and the New Deal.)
    Reprinted in: *An American Editor Speaks. See* above.
Poker Game. October 22. (Europe.)
More Headaches for Pinks. October 29. (The Women's International League
    for Peace and Democracy.)
We Shall See. November 5. (New Deal and neutrality.)
The House of Its Friends. November 12. (Roosevelt, war and neutrality.)
Leaves from a Notebook. November 19.
The Third-Term Campaign. November 26.
The Reign of Waste. December 3. (New Deal.)
More Leaves from a Notebook. December 10.
Progress of a Moral War. December 17. (Finland.)
Justice for Labor. December 24. (New Deal administration of the Wagner Labor
    Relations Act.)
Happy New Year. December 31. (Russia, Finland, and the New Deal.)

1940

Salvage from a Wastebasket. January 7.
A Martyr to Service. January 14. (England and the war.)
The State of the World. January 21.
Jobholder Help Jobholder. January 28. (National Labor Relations Board.)
The 1940 Sweepstakes. February 4.
The Moral Front. February 11. (Finland, England and Japan.)
Counter-Reformation. February 18. (New Deal.)
Pages from a Notebook. February 25.
The Campaign Opens. March 3.
Political Notes. March 10. (George L. Radcliffe and William Cabell Bruce,
    Democratic senatorial candidates for Maryland.)
Descent to Avernus. March 17. (Investigation of the *New Masses* by the govern-
    ment.)
Seven Months of War. March 24. (Outlook for France and England.)
The British Empire. March 31.
The Wicked Earl. April 7. (Bertrand Russell and the nature of the public
    school.)
The Channels of Trade. April 14. (Hull Trade Agreements Act.)
The Call of Service. April 21. (Franklin D. Roosevelt, John L. Lewis, the
    campaign and the war.)
On Academic Freedom. April 28. (Bertrand Russell and the nature of the public
    school.)
The Right to Picket. May 5. (Rights of the individual and of groups.)
The Suicide of Democracy. May 12. (New Deal.)

Onward, Christian Soliders! May 19. (New Deal.)
The Campaign Opens. May 26. (Arming and the New Deal.)
From the Journal of a Plague Year. June 22. (Preparing for national defense.)
Heating up the Heroes. June 9. (National defense and the threat of invasion.)
Walk-Over. June 16. (Roosevelt and the election.)
Preparations for War. June 23.
Wonder Man. June 30. (Wendell L. Willkie.)
Campaign Prospects. July 7. (Effects of the war on the campaign.)
Advances in Moral Science. July 14. (Government of the world and the policies
of the New Deal.)
Triumph of Democracy. July 21. (Democratic convention.)
    Reprinted as a pamphlet, Sargent Bulletin #70.
The Gong Sounds. July 28. (Campaign prospects.)
Quickstep War. August 4. (Neutral aid to England.)
    Reprinted as a pamphlet, Sargent Bulletin #74.
Notes on Conscription. August 11. (Draft Bill.)
The French Have an Idea. August 18. (Judiciary systems and the French
"who's to blame trials?")
The Days Ahead. August 25. (Campaign, constitution and war.)
Mid-Channel. September 8. (Campaign.)
There He Is! September 15. (Willkie's campaign.)
Heil Roosevelt! September 22. (Willkie's campaign.)
The Primrose Path. September 29. (Roosevelt and Willkie.)
War and No War. October 6. (Roosevelt and England.)
Touring with Willkie. October 13. (Willkie's campaign.)
Notes on the Campaign. October 20. (Willkie's campaign.)
The Old Order Changeth. October 27. (Roosevelt and his effect on democracy.)
Ninth Inning: Willkie at Bat. November 3. (Willkie's campaign.)
Coroner's Inquest. November 10. (The election.)
The Call to Lovey-Dovey. November 17 . (Effect of Roosevelt on U.S.)
Raymond Pearl [Hopkins biologist]. November 24. (Memorial tribute after
his death.)
The Pattern of Revolution. **December 1.**
Nuisance Value. December 8. (Academic freedom and the University of
Michigan.)
Christmas Cheer. December 15. (Roosevelt, keeping us out of war.)
Taxes. **December 22.**

1941

Happy New Year. January 5. (U.S., England and the war.)
The Gospel of Hatred. January 12. (War.)
Below the Rio Grande. January 19. (South American Republics.)
Walter Abell and The Sun. January 26. (Obituary. Abell had actively controlled
the Sun from 1904–1910.)
Progress of the Great Crusade. February 2. (World War II.)

Articles

Mencken rejoined the staff of the Sunpapers, at the urging
of Paul Patterson, President of the A. S. Abell Co., after a period
of seven years, to cover the National Conventions of 1948;

and remained to contribute occasional articles to the pages of
The Sun.

[Articles] [Baltimore] Sun August 1—November 9, 1948.

Home to Roost: Mencken Calls Dixie Chickens 'Spavined.' August 1, editorial
page. (The South's civil-rights rebellion.)

Mencken Probes Mystery: Is [Henry A.] Wallace a Goon or Sucker? He Asks.
August 4, editorial page.

[Harry S.] Truman and Herring: Mencken Meditates on Great Red Hunt.
August 8, p. 1, D edition.

Mencken on the Red Blight: Finds Truman's Remedy Too Little and Too
Late. August 22, p. 1, D edition.

Mencken Hears Wallace: Finds No Eggs, No Tomatoes, No Excuse for Enthusiasm. September 13, p. 28, Final edition. (Speech at the Armory in
Baltimore.)

Wallace's Motives: Mencken Thinks Aim is to Defeat Truman. September 15,
editorial page.

Mencken In Gloomy Mood: View of Candidates Leaves Him Uninspired. September 22, editorial page.

Mencken on [J. Strom] Thurmond, Suh: Looks on Bull Run Ticket's Rally
as Elegant But Futile. October 2, p. 24, Final edition. (Confederate pow-wow
at the Lyric Theatre in Baltimore.)

Mencken and GOP Decorum: [Earl] Warren's Doctrine Found Impeccable—
But No Zowie. October 3, p. 30, D edition. (Speech at the Lyric Theatre in
Baltimore.)

War Scare in Campaign?: Mencken Suggests it May be Used by Truman.
October 6, editorial page.

Mencken Thanks [Norman] Thomas: Rare Political Hullabaloo by Really Intelligent Man. October 18, editorial page. (Speech at the Lyric Theatre in
Baltimore.)

Mencken's For Hanging: Tired of Freudian 'Hooey.' He'd 'Squeeze the Weazand.'
October 21, p. 36, Final edition.

Mencken on [Alben W.] Barkley: A Competent Rabble-Rouser, But Plenty
of Empty Seats. October 23, p. 24, Final edition. (Speech at the Lyric Theatre
in Baltimore.)

Two Truman Mistakes: Mencken Lists His Views on New Deal and Wallace.
October 26, editorial page.

Truman's Election: Mencken Says Country Jolly Well Deserves It. November
7, editorial page.

Equal Rights in Parks: Mencken Calls Tennis Order Silly, Nefarious. November
9, editorial page.

This is the last newspaper article written by H.L.M. His last article is typical
of his career. If there is one theme that runs throughout HLM's newspaper
writing it is a belief in, and defense of, the rights of the individual. Reprinted in: *The Vintage Mencken,* gathered by Alistair Cooke. (N.Y. Vintage
Books, 1955), p. 227–230, "Mencken's Last Stand."

"These articles were suggested by Joseph Medill Patterson, . . . one of the proprietors of the *Chicago Tribune*. . . . He had read some of my Monday articles in the Baltimore *Evening Sun,* and proposed that I rework the material for a wider audience. His plan was to print the new articles in the *Sunday Tribune* weekly, and try to sell them to other papers through the Tribune Syndicate. . . . the papers that bought the articles from time to time always got into difficulties. I started out by discussing relatively safe literary matters, but soon got into politics and religion, and some of the articles caused violent local uproars, and forced harassed editors to suspend the series. On one occasion the Tribune itself set up and distributed an article ["Lame Ducks," for April 11, 1926] but notified its clients that it would not print it. The Baltimore *Evening Sun,* which got the articles for nothing by my arrangement with J. M. Patterson, printed this article. [Baltimore *Evening Sun,* Saturday, April 10, 1926, "As H.L.M. Sees It," "A Noose or Poison for Beaten Presidential Candidates"] The New York *World* stuck pretty faithfully: it ran the articles on its 'page opposite to editorials' under the standing heading of 'Hiring a Hall.' Once, while I was in Chicago, I called on Arthur M. Crawford, manager of the Tribune Syndicate, and found that he had just received a cancellation from a San Francisco paper. Five minutes later the editor of another San Francisco paper was announced, and in my presence Crawford sold him the series. He began it at once and advertised it heavily, hoping to win readers from his rival. He figured that the storm would soon blow over. But in a while the clergy of San Francisco raised such a pother that he had to suspend too." HLM (EPFL—A25)

[Syndicated Articles]. Chicago Sunday Tribune November 9, 1924 —January 29, 1928; Magazine Section November 9, 1924—February 8, 1925; Drama Section February 15, 1925—January 29, 1928.

1924

The Young Writer. November 9. (Advice to writers.)
Cabell and His Ideas. November 16.
Call For a Plebiscite. November 23. (To elect an author to represent letters.)
Poetry in America. November 30.

The South Rebels Again. December 7. (*Journal of Social Forces,* University of North Carolina.)

Robert Louis Stevenson. December 14.*

Comstockery. December 21. (Crusade against sex books.)

The Trade of Letters. December 28.

1925

Sherwood Anderson. January 4.

A Chance for Novelists. January 11. (Non-political novel on Washington, D.C.)

Literature and the Schoolmarm. January 18. (Style not learned from text-books.)

Women as Novelists. January 25. (Hampered by convention.)

On Book Collecting. February 1.

Mark Twain. February 8.*

The Author and His Market. February 15. (Hack writers and the fiction magazines.)

Short Story Courses. February 22. (Do more harm than good.)

Ambrose Bierce. March 1.

Sinclair Lewis' "Arrowsmith." March 8.

The Case of Dreiser. March 15.*

The Last New Englander. March 22. (Barrett Wendell of Harvard.)

The National Letters Today. March 29.

Greenwich Village. April 5. (Kreymborg's autobiography.)

The American Language. April 12.

Reflections on Journalism. April 19. (Schools of and professional dignity.)

Two Wasted Lives. April 26. (Alexander Berkman and Emma Goldman.)

Scott Fitzgerald and His Work. May 3.

Literature and Geography. May 10.

The Trade of Beautiful Letters. May 17.

The Heirs of Conrad. May 24. (William McFee and Francis Brett Young.)

Ring W. Lardner. May 31.

A Forgotten Great American. June 7. (Daniel C. Gilman, 1st Pres. of Johns Hopkins University.)

Intelligence Tests. June 14.

Painting and Its Critics. June 21.

The Case of Edward W. Bok. June 28.

The Critic and His Job. July 5.

Biography. July 12. (More good ones needed.)

The English Begin to Slip. July 19. (Contemporary American novels better.)

The Pedagogues Come under Fire. July 26. (From intelligent students.)

Huxley. August 2.

On Free Speech. August 9. (American people against it.)

A Chance for a Bright Young Man. August 16. (Sound history of American letters.)

Nietzsche. August 23.

Outside, Looking In. August 30. (Americanization of Europe.)

On the Enlightenment of Our Modern Youth. September 6. (Sex-hygiene books.)

Treason at the Domestic Hearth. September 13. (Biography of Arnold Bennett by wife.)

Fundamentalism: Divine and Secular. September 20.*

The Decay of Idealism. September 27. (Gay cavortings supplant Chautauqua.)

The Gospel of Service. October 4. (Kiwanis.)

Edgar Saltus. October 11.

A Long Felt Want. October 18. (Textbook on art and science of politics in democracy.)*
O. Henry. October 25. (William Sydney Porter.)
Poe's Start in Life. November 1. (Letters to John Allan.)*
Cousin Jocko. November 8. (Evolution.)*
The Music of the American Negro. November 15.*
A Short View of Literary Gents. November 22. (Hack writers.)*
The New Inquisition. November 29. (Religious animosities based on fear.)
American Books in England. December 6. (English novel down with diabetes.)
Johann Strauss. December 13. (The younger.)
The Comstockian Imbecility. December 20. (Censorship.)*
Hints for Novelists. December 27.*

1926

Jacquerie. January 3. (Darwinism beyond fundamentalist comprehension.)*
Notes on Government. January 10.*
The Bill of Rights. January 17.*
A Chance for a Millionaire. January 24.
Padlocks. January 31. (Use of injunction process.)*
The United States Senate. February 7.*
Optimistic Reflections. February 21. (Liberalism.)
Equality Before the Law. February 28. (Volstead Act.)*
The Emperor of Dictionaries. March 7. (Oxford English Dictionary.)*
The Sad Case of Tennessee. March 14.*
On Liberty. March 21.
Essay on Constructive Criticism. March 28. (Businessmen, turn to the arts.)*
The Birth Control Hullabaloo. April 4.*
Babbitt Starts a Counter Offensive. April 18. (Necessity has made him articulate.)
Women as Politicians. April 25.
More Tips for Novelists. May 2. (Novel on the American journalist.)
Another Attempt at Constructive Criticism. May 9. (Businessmen, try science.)
On Encyclopedias. May 16.
Melancholy Reflections. May 23. (About bathtub hoax.)*
On War Books. May 30.
The Delusion of Law. June 6. (Only capital punishment can stamp out heresy.)
Victualry as a Fine Art. June 13.*
On Literary Gents. June 20.
Yet More Hints for Novelists. June 27.*
Proposals for a Valuable Work. July 4. (English-American Dictionary.)
Havelock Ellis. July 11.*
Holy Writ. July 18. (Translators have botched it.)*
Hymn to the Truth. July 25. (Battle between truth and fiction.)*
The Battle of Ideas. August 1. (Man must be free to express them.)*
The Believing Mind. August 8. (Socialists will believe anything.)*
On Realism. August 15.*
On Metaphysicians. August 22. (Philosophy moonshine and wind music.)
Man as a Mammal. August 29. (Recommended reading on evolution.)*
Dreams of Peace. September 5. (Eloquence not enough to insure it.)*
Another Long-Awaited Book. September 12. (Of advice to young men.)*
Notes on Journalism. September 19. (Current state of tabloid.)
Reflections on War. September 26.
Remarks on Reds. October 3. (Red peril killed by Bolshevism.)

The Rewards of Virtue. October 10. (Bricklayers better paid than professors, deserve it.)

The Postoffice. October 17.

On Controversy. October 24. (Hollow and futile.)*

The Prohibition Buffoonery. October 31.

The Psychic Follies. November 7. (Patriotism, Sunday schools corrupt youth.)

Life Under Bureaucracy. November 14.

New States. December 19. (Unrealistic representation between rural & urban areas.)

The Human Mind. December 26. (Greatest minds occasionally slip into imbecilities.)

1927

On Railroad Travel. January 2.

The Yearning to Save. January 9. (Not from piety but enjoyment of the sport.)

Human Monogamy. January 16. (Natural instinct.)*

The Black Country. January 23. (Unnecessary ugliness of mill towns, Pa.)

Why Liberty? January 30. (Enthusiasm for it in America cooling.)

The Battle Below the Potomac. February 6. (South begins to look well barbered.)

Chiropractic. February 13.
Reprinted as a pamphlet.

The Executive Secretary. February 20. (Swarm in every city.)

The Anatomy of Wowserism. February 27. (Envy behind moral endeavor.)*

Blackmail Made Easy. March 6. (Charging authors with plagiarism.)*

Justice and the Press. March 13.

On Connubial Bliss. March 20. (In spite of laws and propaganda.)*

Beethoven, Obit. March 26, 1827. March 27.*

Another Inquisition Fails. April 3. (Against Darwinian heresy.)

The Telephone Nuisance. April 10.*

On Human Progress. April 17 . (Proceeds at leisurely pace.)*

The Rev. Clergy. April 24.*

The Pedagogue's Utopia. May 1. (U.S. emphasis on schools.)*

The National Conventions. May 8.*

On Eugenics. May 15.*

The Silver Lining. May 22. (Prohibition has waked America.)

Babel. May 29. (Only man among mammals cannot speak to all his species.)*

Chanson Americaine. June 5. (Eminence, aspiration, patriotism, faith—American style.)

Advice to Young Authors. June 12.

Vive le Roi! June 19. (Coolidge.)*

Journalism in the Republic. June 26.

The Movies. July 3. (Fodder for half-wits.)*

The Ancestry of Man. July 10.

The Colored Brother. July 17.

The War Against War. July 24. (Pacifists.)

Prohibition Today. July 31.

Aesthetic Note. August 7.

The Revival of Philosophy. August 14.

The Training of the Writer. August 21. (Fallacy that journalism is royal road.)

The American Scene. August 28.*

The Language We Speak. September 4.*

Millionaires and Their Money. September 11.

Reflections on Government. September 18.
The Dark American. September 25.
The Radicals and Their Ideas. October 2.
On Going to College. October 9.*
An American Saint. October 16. (Henry Ward Beecher.)
Manifest Destiny. October 23. (Secretary of State, hardest post.)
A Glance Ahead. October 30. (Professor Thomas Griffith Taylor's prophecy.)
The Sport of Emperors. November 6. (War.)
The Literary Life. November 13. (Get a good job and hold on to it.)
San Francisco. November 20.
Debates. November 27.
On Home Life. December 4.
On Law Enforcement. December 11.
On the Movies. December 18.
The Avalanche of Books. December 25.*

1928

The Future Looks Damper. January 1. (Prohibition.)
The Holy Estate. January 8. (Companionate marriage.)
On Crime. January 15. (Criminology on level with chiropractic.)
Souls Marching On. January 22. (Sacco-Vanzetti, etc.)
The Choice of a Career. January 29. (Make your boys businessmen.)
  "With the present lines this series of articles is suspended. I hope to resume it at some time in the future, but of such things no man can be certain in a world of change. I am going on furlough to write a book. [*Treatise On The Gods.*] How long it will take I don't know. But I shall be grateful to any persons who may be moved to assist the business with their prayers."

These articles, with a few noted exceptions, were published in the [Baltimore] *Evening Sun* on the "page opposite editorials" every Saturday as long as the series ran under the standing heading "As H.L.M. Sees It." Since the articles were printed on Saturday in *The Evening Sun* and on Sunday in the *Chicago Sunday Tribune* they actually appeared first in Baltimore. The following articles, which were rewritings of articles previously published, were not used by *The Evening Sun:* "Cabell and His Ideas," November 16, 1924; "A Forgotten Great American," June 7, 1925; "Biography," July 12, 1925; "Huxley," August 2, 1925; "Treason at the Domestic Hearth," September 13, 1925; "The Sad Case of Tennessee," March 14, 1926; "Justice and the Press," March 13, 1927. Three of the articles appeared in *The Evening Sun* as part of the Monday Articles series: "The Human Mind," December 26, 1926 appeared on Thursday December 30, 1926; "On Railroad Travel," January 2, 1927 appeared on Wednesday January 5, 1927; "The Avalanche of Books," December 25, 1927 appeared on December 26, 1927. Two articles written for this series but not used by the *Chicago Tribune* were published in *The Evening Sun:* "The Old-fashioned Saloon Finds A Defender," February 13, 1926; "A Noose or Poison for Beaten Presidential Candidates" [Lame Ducks], April 10, 1926.

  The following papers subscribed to all or parts of the series: *Allahabad* [India] *Pioneer, Boston* [Mass.] *Herald, Charlotte* [N.C.] *Observer, Christchurch* [N.Z.] *Star, Columbia* [S.C.] *Record,* [Columbia, S.C.] *State, Darlington* [Eng.] *Northern Echo, Dayton* [Ohio] *Daily News, Detroit* [Mich.] *News, Greensboro* [N.C.] *Daily News, Hartford* [Conn.] *Courant, Johnstown* [Pa.] *Democrat, Kansas City* [Mo.] *Star, Kobe* [Japan] *Herald, Los Angeles* [Calif.] *Record, Louisville* [Ky.] *Courier-Journal, Macon* [Ga.] *Telegraph,*

[Manchester, Eng.] *Sunday Chronicle, Memphis* [Tenn.] *Commercial Appeal, New Orleans* [La.] *Item,* [New York] *World, Norfolk* [Va.] *Journal and Guide, Norfolk* [Va.] *Virginian-Pilot and Norfolk Landmark, Nottingham* [Eng.] *Journal and Express, Paris Chicago Tribune, Pekin* [China] *Leader, North China Star, Raleigh* [N.C.] *News and Observer, St. Louis* [Mo.] *Post-Dispatch, St. Paul* [Minn.] *Pioneer Press,* [San Francisco] *Bulletin, San Francisco Chronicle, Shanghai* [China] *Times, Springfield* [Mass.] *Union, Syracuse* [N.Y.] *Herald, Youngstown* [Ohio] *Vindicator.*

"Much of the material in the articles was later re-worked for my various 'Prejudices' books." HLM (EPFL—A25)

* Reprinted in *The Bathtub Hoax and Other Blasts and Bravos from the Chicago Tribune by H. L. Mencken,* edited, with an introduction and notes by Robert McHugh. (N.Y. Knopf, 1958)

"I was asked at different times to contribute to [the New York *American*], but did not do so until 1934, when B. A. Bergman, then the editor of it, proposed that I do a small weekly article on some aspect of American English. Inasmuch as I was engaged upon the fourth edition of 'The American Language' at the time, this proposal fitted into my plans very well, and I consented. Later Bergman suggested that I widen the scope of the articles somewhat. But inasmuch as there was a rule in the *American* office forbidding the printing of political articles on the page [page opposite editorials], and it was very strictly interpreted, I found the going impossible. Once, when I sent in an article on beer, it was transferred to the editorial page on the ground that any discussion of beer was political. I didn't want to contribute to the Hearst editorial page. . . . [The articles] were printed not only by the [New York] *American,* but also by the [Chicago] *Herald and Examiner,* the [San Francisco] *Examiner,* the [Los Angeles] *Examiner,* the [Milwaukee] *Wisconsin News,* the [Pittsburgh] *Sun-Telegraph,* the [Seattle] *Post-Intelligencer,* the [Atlanta] *Georgian,* and the [Detroit] *Times.* The [Baltimore] *News-Post* should have been included, but Coblenz left it out at my request in order that there should be no conflict with my work for the Baltimore *Sunpapers.*" HLM (EPFL—A115)

[Philological Articles]. [New York] American July 9, 1934—May 20, 1935, page opposite editorials.

1934

Dialects: Examination of American Language Underway. July 9.
You-All: Confederate Trademark's Mysterious Origin. July 16.
Delicacy's Decay: Old Prudery Preserved Only in Remote Backwaters. July 23.
Hopeful Purists: War Against Bad English Appalling Task. July 30.
English Sneers: Mother Tongue May Become American Dialect. August 6.
Pacifism: Modest Reflections on a Romantic Delusion. August 13.
Philosophy: Organized Nonsense as a Form of Learning. August 20.
On Liberty: It Begins to Go Out of Fashion in the World. August 23, editorial page.
New Verbs: Their Manufacture Mostly an American Industry. August 27.*
Dying Words: They Have Their Life-Spans Like Living Creatures. September 3.*
Needed Words: Gaps in the Language That Should be Filled. September 10.

NEWSPAPER WORK

Counter-Words: Common Coins of Speech Worn Smooth and Thin. September 17.
Euphemisms: Linguistic Disguises for the Harsh Facts of Life. September 24.
Madeira: A Noble Wine Returns to the American Table. October 1.
Spelling Reform: A Great Cultural Movement Makes Haste Slowly. October 8.
Orter Be A Law!: Efforts to Make American an Official Language. October 15.
Who's Who: The Biennial Roster of a Great Nation's Glories. October 22.
Surnames: How They Are Modified in the United States. October 29.
Place-Names: Efforts to Make Them the Same Everywhere. November 5.
English Grows: How It Has Outdistanced All Other Languages. November 12.*
The League of Nations: A Transparent False Face for Dog-Eat-Dog Diplomacy. November 14, editorial page.
Outlawry: A New Need Revives an American Punishment. November 19.
Human Progress: Some of Its Pearls Are Commonly Overlooked. November 26.
Foreign Words: They Are Quickly Naturalized in American. December 3.
American Dialects: A Comprehensive Study of Regional Speech. December 10.
Paying the Piper: It Will be a Blue Day When the New Deal Bills Come In. December 17, editorial page.
In Defense of the Fat: Consolation from England for the Over-Weight. December 17.
Table Words: American Has Borrowed Many, Mostly From Dutch. December 24.*
Language Cops: Their Traffic Regulations Always Fail. December 31.

1935

Why Are We Yankees?: A Philological Mystery That Remains Unsolved. January 7.
Mr. Kipling: A Belated Memorial to an Obscure But Honest Man. January 14. (Baltimore expressman from Mencken's youth.)*
An American Nuisance: Some Unkind Words About Our Mistering Custom. January 21.
Italo-American: It Is Spoken by Nearly 2,000,000 People. January 28.
Exit the Banquet: Human Progress Overtakes an American Institution. February 7.
"The Banquet: Mr. Mencken's Gloomy Views Contradicted," by James M. Cain. Appeared [New York] American February 26, 1935, page opposite editorials.
Indian Words: Not Many of Them Are in the American Vocabulary. February 14.*
A Dangerous Age: Brainstorms Are the Rule in the Late Teens. February 21.
O.K.—A Mystery: An Everyday Term Whose Origin Remains Unknown. February 28.
Making New Words: Their Birth, Death and Ofttimes Amazing Popularity. March 7.
Malt Liquor: Kind Words for a Great Boon to Mankind. March 11, editorial page.
Press-Engineers: The Yearning to be Something Greater Than One Is. March 14.
Blatta Orientalis: An Ancient, Indestructible Companion of Homo Sapiens. March 21. (Cockroaches.)
Saurkraut, Bum, Poker: Many German Words Are Now Good American. March 28.*
Man of Means: An Obscure Chapter in the History of Capitalism. April 4. (Baltimore local of Mencken's youth.)

115

Diet and Exercise: Two Fetishes That Have Seen Their Best Day. April 11.
The Cafeteria: Its Origin is Still Clouded in Mystery. April 18.
Property in Words: Some That Everybody Uses Have Private Owners. April 25.*
Lasso, Cinch, Hoosegow: Spanish Words That Have Become Good American. May 15.
Matzoth, Mazuma: Yiddish Words That Have Enriched American. May 20.

* Reprinted: *See* Magazine Articles by HLM.

[Miscellaneous Articles]. [New York] American December 20, 1935—April 22, 1936, page opposite editorials.

H. L. Mencken: On Realism and Romance. December 20. (Cabell.)
Barabbas the Romantic. December 27. (Books and publishers.)
Hooch for the Artists. January 3. (Brief jail term do them good.)
Common Politeness. January 6.
The Man of Science. January 13.
The Higher Learning. January 20.
A Dangerous Fallacy. April 22, editorial page. (That extensive government is good government.)

ARTICLES AND INTERVIEWS FOR THE
ASSOCIATED PRESS AND MISCELLANEOUS NEWSPAPERS

During his early newspaper days on the Baltimore *Herald* HLM acted as correspondent for a variety of out-of-town newspapers.

"Something would happen in Baltimore, for example, that was of interest to Philadelphia and I would wire to the Philadelphia papers giving them a brief outline of the facts and asking them how much they wanted. . . . The first customer I ever had was the Philadelphia *Inquirer,* . . . It bought a small news item from me in 1899 and paid me sixty-six cents for it. During 1900 I had relations of the same sort with many other newspapers but I soon found that selling actual news was troublesome and unprofitable and I therefore turned to more leisurely articles for the Sunday supplements . . . Sometimes I made as much as seven or eight dollars a week. At another time I became American correspondent for a number of Far Eastern newspapers, among them the Colombo *Observer,* the Kobe *Chronicle* and the Hong Kong *Free Press.* I got nothing in cash for this service, but received the subscribing newspapers by every mail and sold the news in them to American papers. The net profit, of course, was small. What interested me was the romance." HLM (EPFL—A29)

In *Autobiographies and Sketch of the Vagabonds,* published in 1905, the article on HLM includes the following statement. "He has done newspaper work for the New York Evening Post, the Chicago Tribune, the New York Telegraph, the Hong Kong Daily Press, the Pittsburgh Dispatch, the New Orleans Picayune, the Kobe (Japan) Chronicle, the Ceylon Observer, and the Nagasaki (Japan) Press, not to speak of fifty or sixty other daily papers."

During HLM's long association with the *Sunpapers,* excepting the three series of articles he wrote for the New York *Evening Mail* in 1917–1918, the *Chicago Sunday Tribune* in 1924–1928, and the *New York American* in 1934–1935, he rarely wrote for other newspapers; and with rare exceptions, the Scopes Trial material being one, the *Sunpapers* did not syndicate HLM's articles.

The bulk of the early material was unsigned and is now no longer available, either because it is impossible to trace or because the papers are no longer in existence and back files are no longer available.

The Associated Press

1930

Mencken Spanks Lewis For Nobel Prize Speech, Declares Times Were Never Better for Young American Writers—Hopes "Red" Will Stop Talking and Return to His Pen. [Baltimore] Evening Sun December 31, 1930, p. 1.

1931

What's Going On—Today—In This World of Ours, The Chances of an American Literary Prodigy Appearing Tomorrow Are Much Better Than They Were Last Year, In the Opinion of H. L. Mencken, Editor and Critic, Who Believes That the Depression Has Made It Harder for the Beginner to Market His Wares, Thus Discouraging Half-Baked Work and Encouraging Young Writers to Learn Their Business. [Baltimore] Evening Sun June 10, 1931, p. 2.

1932

Nation Favors Slapstick Films; Mencken Concurs. [Baltimore] Evening Sun March 28, 1932, p. 1.

1933

Mencken Comments on Novelist's [Galsworthy] Death. [Baltimore] Evening Sun January 31, 1933, p. 6.

Politicos Decent for Once, is H. L. Mencken's Response, Protagonist of Liquor Takes Time From Rejoicing at Repeal to Toss Barb at "Political Parsons" and Bouquet to Captain Stanton. [Baltimore] Sun December 6, 1933, p. 26.

1935

Mencken Assails Lynching in State, Advocates Costigan-Wagner Bill, He Says Citizens Need Federal Aid. [Baltimore] Sun February 15, 1935, p. 3.

Mencken Offers College Sanctuary in Maryland, Assures Arkansas Institution, Facing Probe, That It Can Expound "Isms" Here—Willing Himself to Occupy Its Chair of Theology. [Baltimore] Evening Sun February 22, 1935, p. 42.

Anybody Can Beat Roosevelt But Hoover, Mencken Thinks. [Baltimore] Sun December 17, 1935, p. 1.

1936

Mencken Says Edward [VIII] Has Failed His People, Declares Everyone Loves a Lover, But Respect of the World Is Reserved for Him Who Plays the Game According to the Rules. [Baltimore] Evening Sun December 7, 1936, p. 1.

1937

Book Publishing Isn't a Business, It's a Sport, Says H. L. Mencken, Now Cynical. Columbus [Ohio] Sunday Dispatch December 26, 1937, Section A, p. 10.

1946

How To Be a Book Collector, From Ibsen on Up the Mencken Family Tree. Washington Post May 5, 1946, Section 2, p. 6B.

Miscellaneous Newspapers

1900

Daring Dashes for Freedom, Exploits by Convicts to Break Their Fetters. Baltimore American March 4, 1900, p. 27, 5 columns, unsigned.

"Written for a syndicate started by L. J. de Bekker and G. W. Hobbs, members of the staff of the *American*. It seems to have got no further than this first article for which I got nothing." HLM (EPFL—A54)

1902

The Shame of "Shorty" Ferguson. [Syracuse] Evening Herald February 27, 1902, p. 14.

Short story.

1906

Nectar of the Eastern Sho'. [New York] Sun November 11, 1906, Third Section, p. 12, unsigned.

Hustled His Way to Congress. [New York] Sun December 2, 1906, Third Section, p. 5, unsigned.

Harry B. Wolf, of the Third Maryland District.

1917

Americans Not Badly Treated, Newspaperman Arriving in Havana from Berlin Tells of Conditions There. Havana Post March 6, 1917, p. 8.

1921

Liquor and Literature, To the Editor of The Literary Review. [New York] Evening Post January 22, 1921, Section 3, p. 14.

The charms of liquor are preserved in the names of prominent literary people, such as Gertrude Stein.

Criticism, By Our Own H. L. Mencken. [New York] Sun April 23, 1921, editorial page, "The Sun Dial."

A prose skit, appearing in Don Marquis' column and purporting to be by HLM.

To the Editor of the Evening Post. [New York] Evening Post November 12, 1921, p. 8.

A testimonial written for the 120th anniversary of the founding of the paper.

1922

My Country, 'Tis of Thee. [London] Sunday Express August 27, 1922.

1923

The United States a British Colony. Is Mencken's Prediction. [New York] World January 7, 1923, editorial section p. 1.

The American Tradition. [New York] Evening Post November 24, 1923, Literary Review, p. 1.

"Doughty vs. Mencken," Letter to the Editor, by Leonard Doughty. Appeared in [New York] Evening Post January 19, 1924, The Literary Review, p. 466.

1924

I Have Been Faithful to Thee, Cynara, In My Fashion, Mr. Mencken Restates It In His Own American Mercurial Fashion. New York Tribune March 9, 1924, Magazines and Books Section, p. 22, "The Dome" by Samuel Hoffenstein.

1926

A Nomination by Mr. Mencken, To the Editor of The World. [New York] World September 27, 1926, editorial page.

Good Life, Good Death, Says Mencken. San Francisco Chronicle November 18, 1926, p. 3.
    About George Sterling, written at the time of his suicide.

1928

Mencken, Romantic Love the Bunk. Washington [D.C.] Daily News March 13, 1928, p. 16.

Aid Sought for an Author, To the Editor of the New York Times. New York Times March 17, 1928, editorial page.
    HLM asks financial aid for a struggling author, received only facetious replies.

1930

What We Are Doing to Your Language. [London] Daily Express January 15, 1930.

What Is To Be Done About Divorce? Article IV. [New York] World January 26, 1930. The World's Magazine Section, p. 2.

To The Dogs. Manchester Guardian February 1, 1930, p. 11.
    "There are prevailing ideas, as there are prevailing winds."

H. L. Mencken Recalls, Bob Davis's Remarkable Gastronomical Attainments. [New York] Sun July 15, 1930, editorial page.
    "While Bob Davis is recovering from injuries received on a Southern trip a number of his writer friends are pinch hitting for him."

1931

Your Governors. [London] Daily Express April 10, 1931.
    On English government.

1933

Thus Spake Mr. Mencken. [New York] Daily Mirror April 6, 1933, p. 2.
    A short, exclusive beer message.

What America Thinks of Things. Manchester Evening News April 24, 1933, p. 6.
    On America's two problems, as HLM sees them, foreign trade, debt.

1935

To Whom It May Concern, Mr. Mencken Replies. New York American January 11, 1935, page opposite editorials.

A reply to the article, " 'Sensible Men,' A Dissenting Note on H. L. Mencken's Democracy," by G. K. Chesterton, which appeared on the same day and page.

1936

Mencken Calls Hapgood Action Typical of New Deal Policy. Baltimore News-Post February 27, 1936, p. 4.

1937

Personal View. Manchester Evening News May 28, 1937.

"One can only admire the hopeful pertinacity of the persons who labor sincerely for peace in the world."

1941

Henry L. Mencken Calls Times His Professional 'Alma Mater.' The Ellicott City Times, Century Edition March 17, 1941, Section A, p. 3.

Interviews

1921

Jones, Stacy V. Intrepid Herald Staff Man Beards Mencken in His Den, Emerges Intact From Interview With Baltimore Iconoclast, Finding Him Human After All. Washington Herald August 28, 1921, Section 4, p. 3.

1922

Mencken May Think It's True, But Do You. [New York] World August 19, 1922, p. 3.

From an interview in London; HLM's thesis, that America is rotten with money.

Mencken in England. [Baltimore] Evening Sun September 6, 1922, editorial page.

"This is the manner in which a correspondent of a London Newspaper [Sunday Express] greeted H. L. Mencken on his arrival in England." Editor's note.

1923

What Is the Soul? It's a Difficult Question. [Atlanta] Sunday Constitution Magazine February 4, 1923, p. 12.

"There is no such thing as a soul says Mencken; 'The only evidence supporting this notion lies in the hope that it is true.' But Amiel, the Swiss philosopher,
says Mencken is a 'pensée' writer who doesn't perceive that our real life is
composed of ideas and ideals."

1924

Wilson, B. F. I Like Women But Not Too Young, Says Henry
L. Mencken. [Denver] Rocky Mountain News April 20, 1924,
Magazine Section, p. 3.

American Taste Best, Says Mencken. [Baltimore] Sun November 30, 1924, Part 2, Section 5, p. 3.

1925

Kaufman, S. Jay. Round the Town. New York Telegram September
24, 1925, editorial page.

"The Round the Town Questionnaire. Some twenty-three questions. Which
we round the towned some days ago. And which are thus answered by
H. L. Mencken."

1928

Stein, Hannah. Companionate Marriage, H. L. Mencken In-
tends to Take a Wife for Better or Worse If He Ever Decides to
Marry. Buffalo Evening News May 7, 1928, Magazine Features,
p. 19.

Hughes, Alice. Interview With H. L. Mencken On Why He's For
Smith. Washington [D.C.] Daily News August 21, 1928, p. 11.

1929

Baker, Gladys. Henry L. Mencken Interviewed. Birmingham News
January 20, 1929, Magazine Section, p. 12.

Butterly, George P. Jr. Says Too Many People Marry, H. L.
Mencken, Baltimore's Bad Boy, Calls Marriage an Art and Like
All Arts is Cluttered Up With Quacks. Brooklyn Daily Eagle
September 8, 1929, Brooklyn Eagle Magazine, p. 10.

De la Llana, Pedro. Two Apostles of Gloom, Pedro de la Llana
Who Sees Little Good in Philippine Government, Interviews H.
L. Mencken, Chief Prophet of America's Political Doom. [Manila]
Philippines Free Press September 28, 1929, p. 2.

1930

Mencken Sees U. S. As Diurnal Comic Feature, Hoover and Prohibition Provide Iconoclastic Editor With Daily Laugh. Here on Honeymoon. Worried Over Inability to Get His Favorite Drink—Gibes at War Profiteers. [Montreal] Gazette August 29, 1930, p. 4.

Pomeroy, Hally. A Lucky Mrs. Mencken the Editor Admits That As a Husband He's Perfect. Kansas City Star September 16, 1930, p. 1.

Lewis, Lloyd. The Married Mr. Mencken. Chicago Daily News October 8, 1930, Midweek Section, p. 3.

1931

MacDonald, A. B. After Again Blasting "Yokels" of the Southwest, H. L. Mencken Defends His Views to Visitor. Kansas City Star March 1, 1931, Section D, p. 1.

1932

Smith, Harry Allen. Depression Exaggerated Greatly, Mencken Says, Capitalistic System Working Badly, But so Would Any Other, He Says—Sees Rascality, Stupidity and Quackery Finally Exposed. [Baltimore] Evening Sun May 25, 1932, p. 1.

"Have the political dissenters in America any pertinent suggestions for a solution to our current economic dilemma? What do they think is wrong? And what remedy can they offer? The United Press has interviewed several of their number and presents their ideas in a series of articles."

I Believe America Will Reject Hoover Says H. L. Mencken. [London] Daily Mail October 31, 1932, p. 12.

1933

Sills, Kenneth C. M. What Do Americans Think of the French? Milwaukee Journal February 10, 1933, editorial page.

A Paris newspaper which sent questionaires to several prominent U.S. literary men received quite frank answers and advised its readers to take the criticism as a tonic probably containing grains of truth. The article was reprinted in various U.S. newspapers.

Wolff, Miles H. Mencken Says Heavy Tax on Beer Means Whisky Era. [Baltimore] Evening Sun September 6, 1933, p. 2.

America Still in Literary Doldrums, Critic, In Associated Press Interview, Notes Signs of Improvement, However, In Waning

Vogue for "Gushing" Books About Russia. [Baltimore] Sun September 8, 1933, p. 24.

Mencken Urges 3.6 Beer With 5-Qt Schooner. [Wilmington] Evening Journal September 28, 1933, p. 4.

1934

Mencken Prefers J. P. Morgan to Professors Who Guide U. S., Says on Return From Abroad, "There's Enough Messianic Complex in Jack" for Him to Take Job. Predicts Worse Mess Due to Present Planning. [Baltimore] Sun April 6, 1934, p. 28.

1935

What U. S. Needs Is a King, Says Mencken On His Return [from Europe]. [Baltimore] Sun July 13, 1935, p. 18.

Anderson, Paul Y. Anybody Can Beat Roosevelt But Hoover, Mencken Thinks. [Baltimore] Sun December 17, 1935, p. 1.

1936

Mencken Tongue-Lashing Everybody. Pittsburgh Sun-Telegraph June 7, 1936, Part I, p. 2.

1939

Mencken Going to Wake for Expiring Rennert. [Baltimore] Evening Sun December 14, 1939, p. 54.

> Rennert Hotel in Baltimore. Mencken also wrote the editorial, "A Far From Adequate Farewell to the Rennert," which appeared in *The Sun* on December 15, 1939.

1940

Van Gelder, Robert. Mr. Mencken on Literature and Politics, An Interview In Which He Makes Some Caustic Remarks About Writing in the Thirties, New York Times February 11, 1940, Book Review, p. 12.

> Reprinted in: Van Gelder, Robert. *Writers and Writing.* (N.Y., Scribner, 1946), p. 20–22.

Baker, Gladys. Mencken, At 60, Rated Best Paid of Writers, Don't Believe a Word of What He Says About His Failing Fitness Gladys Baker Suggests. Birmingham News October 6, 1940, Section 4, p. 1.

1941

Tinney, Cal. Thus Spake Mr. Mencken. Philadelphia Record February 20, 1941, Section 2, p. 17.

Reid, Louis. Ripe Slang Enriches American Language, Says H. L. Mencken. New York Journal American August 3, 1941, Pictorial review, p. 5.

1942

Smith, Harry Allen. The Totem Pole. Louisville Times April 22, 1942, Section 3, p. 3.

1946

Sherman, John K. Mencken of Baltimore, Author, Sage, Dog Hater. Minneapolis Sunday Tribune February 17, 1946, p. 19.

Morehouse, Ward. Report on America, H. L. Mencken Speaks a Piece. [New York] Sun June 5, 1946, p. 31.

Reprinted in: *The Sun Digest*, A Literary Harvest from the Pages of The New York Sun. July, 1946, p. 13–14, "Quiet Chat."

1948

Cloud, Joseph. Mencken Talks, But What You Believe Is Something Else Again. Baltimore American March 7, 1948, Section A, p. 2.

1954

Manchester, William. Mencken, 73, Mellows; Does Not 'Dislike Ike.' [Baltimore] Sun January 11, 1954, p. 26.

MAGAZINE ARTICLES

Here are listed chronologically HLM's contributions to magazines: articles, comments, answers to symposiums, letters to the editor, and the like. Book reviews, due to their prodigious quantity, have been listed separately. Only a few of the translated articles have been located. "I have got hold of only a few [of the Spanish translations published in Latin America]. I have heard of others published in Russia but have managed to see but one or two. The German translations predominate because, in the years following the war, Herman George Scheffauer, who was living in Berlin, interested himself in promoting them." HLM (EPFL—A174)

Pseudonyms abound in his early years, many of them shared by the entire writing staff of the *Smart Set*. Only those items known to have been written by HLM are included. For a detailed listing of pseudonyms he used *see* section so entitled.

Complete entry has been cited whenever possible. *New Yorker* pagination is cited for the out-of-town edition.

"My attempts at fictioneering had begun on March 28, 1896, with a brief and dreadful piece entitled 'Idyl,' done in one evening. After 1898, as the poetical sap began to ooze out of me, I did more and more prose, and on April 28, 1900, my first published short story. . . . I must have sold, altogether, nearly twenty-five short stories. In fact, my market was very good . . . but after 1904 I turned to other things." HLM, 1937 (EPFL—A52)

1899

TO RUDYARD KIPLING [poem], by W. G. L. [pseud.] Bookman 10: 337, Dec., 1899.

"I was so diffident that I signed the poem 'W.G.L.' and did not send my address. When it came out in the December number I was enormously pleased and soon mustered up courage to confess the authorship. The *Bookman* promptly sent me a check and invited me to send in more poems." HLM— (EPFL—A29, p. 121). Reprinted in *Ventures into Verse.*

1900

AURORAL [poem] New England Magazine, n.s. 22: 275, May, 1900.
Reprinted in *Ventures into Verse.*

THE COOK'S VICTORY. Short Stories 39: 238-247, Aug., 1900.
Reprinted in *Deep Waters, an Anthology of Stories of the Sea,* edited by Charles W. Grayson (New York, Holt, 1926. p. 257–270); *The Man Mencken,* by Isaac Goldberg (New York, Simon, 1925. p. 313–324); *Ship Ahoy, Nautical Tales and Verse* (New York, Avon, 1954. p. 23–34); and *Stories for Men, an Anthology,* edited by Charles Grayson (Boston, Little, 1936. p. 367–377).

THE FOUR-FOOT FILIPINO, a Ballad of the Trenches. Leslie's Weekly 90: 18, Jan. 6, 1900.

THE TIN CLADS [poem] National Magazine 11: 649, March, 1900.
Reprinted in *Ventures into Verse.*

1901

THE FLIGHT OF THE VICTOR, illustrated by Charles Grunwald. Frank Leslie's Popular Magazine 52: 482-487, Sept., 1901. illus.

LIKE A THIEF IN THE NIGHT. Short Stories 43: 212-218, Aug., 1901.

THE TRANSPORT GEN'RAL FERGUSON [poem] Life 37: 532, June 20, 1901.
Reprinted in *Ventures into Verse.*

THE WOMAN AND THE GIRL, illustrated by Florence England Nosworthy. Short Stories 41: 229-243, Feb., 1901. illus.

1902

A BALLADE OF PROTEST [poem] Bookman 15: 140, April, 1902.
Reprinted in *Ventures into Verse.*

THE CRIME OF McSWANE, illustrated by R. Emmett Owen. Frank Leslie's Popular Monthly 54: 253-257, July, 1902. illus.
Reprinted in *Esquire 32: 74, 132, Oct., 1949.*

A DOUBLE REBELLION! Short Stories 45: 78-85, Jan., 1902.

FIRING AND A WATERING, an Episode of a South American Revolution. Short Stories 47: 206–214, Aug., 1902.

HURRA LAL, PEACEMAKER. Short Stories 46: 148-156, May, 1902.

1903

CHARLES J. BONAPARTE, a Useful Citizen, by John F. Brownell [pseud.] Frank Leslie's Popular Magazine 57: 166–169, Dec., 1903.

THE PASSING OF A PROFIT, the Story of a Losing Venture. Short Stories 49: 117-128, Jan., 1903.

1904

ARTHUR PUE GORMAN, Past-Master in Politics and Presidential Possibility, by John F. Brownell [pseud.] Leslie's Monthly Magazine 57:527-534, March, 1904. port. as front.

THE FEAR OF THE SAVAGE. Criterion 5: 16–19, Nov., 1904.

THE HEATHEN RAGE. Criterion 5: 36–40, Sept., 1904.

JAMES, CARDINAL GIBBONS, by John F. Brownell [pseud.] Leslie's Monthly Magazine 58: 99-102, May, 1904. port. as front.

1905

THE BEND IN THE TUBE. Red Book Magazine 4: 495-501, Feb., 1905.

> Reprinted in *The Man Mencken,* by Isaac Goldberg (New York, Simon, 1925. p. 325–339).

MARKETING WILD ANIMALS, by Charles F. Brownell [pseud.] Leslie's Monthly Magazine 60: 287–295, July, 1905. illus.

ON PASSING THE ISLAND OF SAN SALVADOR [poem] New England Magazine, n.s. 33: 133, Oct., 1905.

THE STAR SPANGLED BANNER, by Henry Lewis [sic] Mencken. The Monthly Story Magazine 1: 858-865, Sept., 1905.

1906

THE KING AND TOMMY CRIPPS, illustrated by Gustavus C. Widney. Red Book Magazine 7: 307–316, July, 1906. illus.

THE LAST CAVALRY CHARGE. Red Book Magazine 7:487-497, Aug., 1906. illus.

1908

In Nov., 1908, HLM began his monthly book review column as literary critic of the *Smart Set,* continuing until Dec., 1923.

WHAT YOU OUGHT TO KNOW ABOUT YOUR BABY, by Leonard K. Hirshberg. Delineator 72: 592–3; 812–813; 1014–1015; 73: 106; 262, 264–265; 438–440; 574, Oct., 1908—April, 1909. 74: 327, Oct., 1909.

> Each of the eight parts has its own subtitle, from "The New Born Baby" to "The Child Ready for School." HLM wrote the articles from information supplied by Hirshberg. *See* Contributions to Books and Pamphlets, 1910.

1909

THE ARTIST. Bohemian Magazine 17: 805-808, Dec., 1909. *See* Books and Pamphlets, 1912.

THE BALDHEADED MAN. Bohemian Magazine 17: 431–432, Oct., 1909.

CARDINAL GIBBONS. American Magazine 69: 168, Dec., 1909.

E PLURIBUS UNUM. Bohemian Magazine 17: 428-429, Oct., 1909.

THE FINE ART OF CONJUGAL BLISS. Bohemian Magazine 17: 419-420, Oct., 1909.

THE GASTRONOMIC VALUE OF THE KNIFE. Bohemian Magazine 17: 709, Dec., 1909.

IN DEFENSE OF PROFANITY. Bohemian Magazine 17: 567-568, Nov., 1909.

INTERESTING PEOPLE: DR. WILLIAM OSLER. American 68: 555, Oct., 1909.

> HLM suggested and started this column, which became one of the magazine's most enduring ones.

THE PSYCHOLOGY OF KISSING. Bohemian Magazine 17: 714, Dec., 1909.

THE SLAP-STICK BURLESQUE. Bohemian Magazine 17: 425–426, Oct., 1909.

MAGAZINE ARTICLES

1912

HORSETALES. Smart Set 36: iii-iv, Jan., 1912.

PERTINENT AND IMPERTINENT, by Owen Hatteras [pseud.] Smart Set 36: 157 — 43: 74 April, 1912 — July, 1914.

These comments appeared in April and May 1912, were resumed in April 1913, and continued monthly thereafter until July 1914.

1913

THE AMERICAN. Smart Set June — Oct., 1913; Feb., 1914.

"The American" 40: 87–94, June; "The American: His Morals" 40: 83–91, July; "The American: His Language" 40: 89–96, Aug. (incorporated into *The American Language*); "The American: His Ideas of Beauty" 41: 91–98, Sept.; "The American: His Freedom" 41: 81–88, Oct.; "The American: His New Puritanism" 42: 87–94, Feb., 1914.

AT LARGE IN LONDON, by George Weems Peregoy [pseud.] Smart Set 40: 99–107, June, 1913.

Reprinted in *Europe After 8:15*.

THE BEERIAD. Smart Set 39: 103–111, April, 1913.

Reprinted in *Europe After 8:15*.

GOOD OLD BALTIMORE. Smart Set 40: 107–114, May, 1913.

Reprinted in *The Souvenir Program of the Baltimore Canned Goods Exchange*, 1914. p. 3–7.

POST-IMPRESSIONS OF CITIES, by Amelia Hatteras [pseud?] Smart Set 41: 84, Nov., 1913.

1914

SMART SET. v. 44, no. 3—v. 72, no. 4. Nov., 1914—Dec., 1923.

HLM and George Jean Nathan began their joint editorship of *Smart Set; a Magazine of Cleverness* in Nov., 1914 (v. 44, no. 3) and continued until Dec., 1923 (v. 72, no. 4).

AFTER ALL, WHAT'S THE USE? by J. D. Gilray [pseud.] Smart Set 44: 276–278, Dec., 1914.

AH, CHE LA MORTE! by Raoul della Torre [pseud.] Smart Set 44: 1–2, Nov., 1914.

Burlesque of opera libretto.

THE BALLADE OF COCKAIGNE [poem], by Herbert Winslow Archer [pseud.] Smart Set 44: 29, Nov., 1914.

WORKS BY H. L. M.

THE BARBAROUS BRADLEY (story). Smart Set 44: 31–46, Nov., 1914.

THE BLIND GODDESS, by George Weems Peregoy [pseud.] Smart Set 44: 61, Nov., 1914.

THE BRIDGE GAME, and How I Beat It to a Finish, by Owen Hatteras [pseud.] Smart Set 43: 75–81, June, 1914.

THE CITY OF SEVEN SUNDAYS, by Owen Hatteras [pseud.] Smart Set 44: 71–78, Nov., 1914.

DEATH: A Discussion, by Robert W. Woodruff [pseud.] Smart Set 44: 213–216, Dec., 1914.

EPITHALAMIUM, by Francis Clegg Thompson [pseud.] Smart Set 44: 68–70, Nov., 1914.

THE INNUMERABLE CARAVAN, by Owen Hatteras [pseud.] Smart Set 44:184, Dec., 1914.

LITANY FOR MAGAZINE EDITORS, by Owen Hatteras [pseud.] Smart Set 45: 122, Feb., 1914.

THE MAILED FIST AND ITS PROPHET. Atlantic Monthly 114: 598–607, Nov., 1914.

MR. JOHN SMITH, by Irving S. Watson [pseud.] Smart Set 44: 203–206, Dec., 1914.

NEWSPAPER MORALS. Atlantic Monthly 113: 289–297, March, 1914.

> Reprinted in *The Profession of Journalism; a Collection of Articles on Newspaper Editing and Publishing Taken from the Atlantic Monthly,* edited with an introduction and notes by Willard Grosvenor Bleyer (Boston, Atlantic Monthly Press, 1918. p. 68–69). Ralph Pultizer wrote a refutation, *Atlantic Monthly* 113: 773–778, June, 1914.

AN ODE TO MUNICH [poem], by Pierre D'Aubigny. Smart Set 44: 201–202, Dec., 1914.

THE OLD TRAILS [poem], by Harriet Morgan [pseud.] Smart Set 44: 25, Nov., 1914.

THE REWARDS OF SCIENCE, by R. B. McLoughlin [pseud.] Smart Set 44: 3, Nov., 1914.

SONG [poem], by Janet Jefferson [pseud.] Smart Set 44: 46, Nov., 1914.

THOUGHTS ON MORALITY, by William Fink [pseud.] Smart Set 44: 19-21, Nov., 1914.

VENERATION [poem] by Marie de Verdi [pseud.] Smart Set 44: 61, Nov., 1914.

WATER-WAGON ENCHANTMENTS, by Owen Hatteras [pseud.] Smart Set 44: 178, Dec., 1914.

1915

PARISIENNE, v. 1, no. 1—July, 1915—

"In 1915, being short of money, Warner [Eltinge F., publisher of *Smart Set* and *Field and Stream*], Crowe [Eugene F., paper magnet, part owner of *Smart Set*], Nathan and I decided to start a 15 cent fiction magazine. In those days the United States was full of French propagandists. We decided to take a satirical advantage of the fact, and so started a monthly called the *Parisienne*. We would buy stories and novelettes from hacks, and have them change the scene to France. The magazine ran to elegant and gaudy stuff . . . made an immense success, and was soon earning $4,000 a month. . . . Once the Comstocks tackled it, but it was really quite harmless, and the case was thrown out on a demurrer. I tired of this nonsense very soon, despite its profitableness, and in 1916 Nathan and I sold our interest to Warner and Crowe." HLM (EPFL—A29, p. 113–114)

AN AMERICAN STATESMAN (burlesque), by William Fink [pseud.] Smart Set 45: 119–121, Feb., 1915.

THE BALLAD OF SHIPS IN HARBOR. [unsigned] Smart Set 45: 226, March, 1915.

Reprinted from *Ventures into Verse*. Later set to music by Franz Bornschein.

BEETHOVEN [unsigned] Smart Set 45: 240, March, 1915.

CHILDREN OF APOLLO, by William Drayham [pseud.] Smart Set 47: 48, Dec., 1915.

CONTRIBUTIONS TO A THESAURUS OF AMERICAN SYNONYMS FOR "WHISKERS," by James P. Ratcliffe, Ph.D. [pseud.] Smart Set 45: 29–30, Feb., 1915.

THE EXILE RETURNS, by Owen Hatteras [pseud.] Smart Set 47: 120, Oct., 1915.

WORKS BY H. L. M.

A FEW PAGES OF NOTES, by William Drayham [pseud.] Smart Set 45: 435–438, Jan., 1915.

Eighteen paragraphs in the style of *The American Credo*.

THE FLAPPER, [unsigned] Smart Set 45: 1–2, Feb., 1915.

A FOOTNOTE FOR CRITICS, by William Drayham [pseud.] Smart Set 47: 128, Oct., 1915.

FOUR NOTES, by William Drayham [pseud.] Smart Set 46: 64, Aug., 1915.

FROM THE MEMOIRS OF THE DEVIL. [unsigned] Smart Set 45: 363–366, Jan., 1915.

THE GREATEST GIFT, by Owen Hatteras [pseud.] Smart Set 47: 156, Nov., 1915.

THE INCOMPARABLE PHYSICIAN, by William Fink [pseud.] Smart Set 47: 241–242, Nov., 1915. *See* Books and Pamphlets, 1935.

THE INTERIOR HIERARCHY, by Owen Hatteras [pseud.] Smart Set 45: 413–415, Jan., 1915.

INVOCATION [poem], by James Wharton [pseud.] Smart Set 45: 211, March, 1915.

IS CIVILIZATION, THEN, A FAILURE? [Unsigned] Smart Set 45: 402, Jan., 1915.

A LITANY FOR MUSIC LOVERS, by Owen Hatteras [pseud.] Smart Set 45: 389, Jan., 1915.

THE MEMORY OF EDNA, by Owen Hatteras [pseud.] Smart Set 47: 59–61, Dec., 1915.

NEAPOLITAN NIGHTS, by Owen Hatteras [pseud.] Smart Set 46: 61–67, May, 1915.

A PANORAMA OF WOMEN, by W. L. D. Bell [pseud.] Smart Set 46: 278, June, 1915.

POST-IMPRESSIONS OF POETS, by Owen Hatteras [pseud.] Smart Set 46: 402, June, 1915.

MAGAZINE ARTICLES

A PRAYER FOR PURITANS. [unsigned] Smart Set 45: 228, March, 1915.

THE PRAYER OF A LITTLE FROG, by William Drayham [pseud.] Smart Set 47: 294, Sept., 1915.

THE SCHOLAR, by Owen Hatteras [pseud.] Smart Set 46: 1-2, July, 1915.

A SNAPSHOT OF AN IDEAL HUSBAND, by Owen Hatteras [pseud.] Smart Set 47: 225, Sept., 1915.

THE VOICES [poem], by W. H. Trimball [pseud.] Smart Set 45: 248, March, 1915.

THE WEDDING, a Stage Direction, by Robert W. Woodruff [pseud.] Smart Set 45: 255–262, March, 1915.

1916

SAUCY STORIES. v. 1, no. 1— Aug., 1916—

"There existed a 15-cent thriller called *Snappy Stories,* beloved of shop girls. Col. W. D. Mann had started it shortly after he had sold the *Smart Set,* and had appropriated for it the long S's of the latter's cover. The fact irked us. We found that we could do nothing about it legally. So we decided to start a long S imitation of our own. The result was *Saucy Stories,* which . . . made a great success, but Nathan and I tired of it, and sold it to Warner and Crowe." HLM (EPFL—A29, p. 114)

THE BLEEDING HEART, by Owen Hatteras [pseud.] Smart Set 48: 262, May, 1916.

CHANSON D'AMOUR À LA CARTE, by Owen Hatteras [pseud.] Smart Set 50: 128, Dec., 1916.

A CONTRIBUTION TOWARD A LIST OF EUPHEMISMS FOR "DRUNK," by James P. Ratcliffe, A.M.,Ph.D. (Harvard), LL.D. (Oxon.) [pseud.] Smart Set 49: 99-100, June, 1916.

THE DEATHBED, by William Drayham [pseud.] Smart Set 48: 276, May, 1916.

DEGENERATE DAYS, by William Drayham [pseud.] Smart Set 49: 112, Aug., 1916.

A FOOTNOTE ON THE DUEL OF SEX, by Owen Hatteras [pseud.] Smart Set 49: 1-2, Aug., 1916.

135

HALLS, by Owen Hatteras [pseud.] Smart Set 48: 65, April, 1916.

A LITANY FOR HANGMEN, by Owen Hatteras [pseud.] Smart Set 49: 112, Aug., 1916.

NOTES FROM A DAYBOOK, by Owen Hatteras [pseud.] Smart Set 48: 66, April, 1916.

A PANORAMA OF BABIES, by W. L. D. Bell [pseud.] Smart Set 49: 54, Aug., 1916.

THE PURITAN, by Owen Hatteras [pseud.] Smart Set 49: 219-222, July, 1916.

THE RESCUERS, a Study in the Art of Protecting Ladies, by Owen Hatteras [pseud.] Smart Set 48: 205–206, Jan., 1916.

SAVED! by William Drayham [pseud.] Smart Set 48: 48, Feb., 1916.
   The play is saved because G. J. Nathan says it is "absolutely rotten."

1917

ADDENDA TO WILSTACH, by W. L. D. Bell [pseud.] Smart Set 53: 108, Dec., 1917.

BLUEBEARD'S GOAT, by William Drayham [pseud.] Smart Set 52: 94-96, July, 1917.

THE CHARMED CIRCLE (Complete Novelette), by William Drayham [pseud.] Smart Set 52: 3-28, Aug., 1917.

THE CONCLUSIONS OF A MAN AT SIXTY, by Owen Hatteras [pseud.] Smart Set 52: 117-118; 43-44, July, Aug., 1917.

THE CONQUEROR, by Owen Hatteras [pseud.] Smart Set 52: 114-116, Aug., 1917.

THE CYNIC, by W. L. D. Bell [pseud.] Smart Set 52: 72, Aug., 1917.

THE DREISER BUGABOO. The Seven Arts 2: 507-517, Aug., 1917.

THE GENIUS, by Owen Hatteras [pseud.] Smart Set 52: 76, June, 1917.

IBSEN: JOURNEYMAN DRAMATIST. Dial 63: 323-326, Oct. 11, 1917.

MAGAZINE ARTICLES

LUDENDORFF. Atlantic Monthly 119: 823-832, June, 1917.

THE OMISSION, by Owen Hatteras [pseud.] Smart Set 50: 212, Nov., 1917.

ROSEMARY, Being Selections from a Romantic Correspondence, by Owen Hatteras [pseud.] Smart Set 52: 60-62; 53: 59-60, July, Oct., 1917.

WALL PAPER (story), by Owen Hatteras [pseud.] Smart Set 53: 121-126, Nov., 1917.

THE WINDOW OF HORRORS [story] by William Drayham [pseud.] Smart Set 53: 109-118, Sept., 1917.

1918

THE CAROUSEL, by W. L. D. Bell [pseud.] Smart Set 55: 92, Aug., 1918.

THE HOMERIC SEX, by Owen Hatteras [pseud.] Smart Set 56: 33-39, Sept., 1918.

THE HYPOCRITE [story] by William Drayham [pseud.] Smart Set 57: 125-127, Nov., 1918.

THE MAN OF GOD [story] by William Drayham [pseud.] Smart Set 57: 95-103, Oct., 1918.

SHE DID NOT BELIEVE ME, by W. L. D. Bell [pseud.] Smart Set 54: 102, Feb., 1918.

UNMENTIONABLES, an Inquiry into the Advertising Pages (essay), by Owen Hatteras [pseud.] Smart Set 54: 53-57, April, 1918.

THE VICTIM (story), by Owen Hatteras [pseud.] Smart Set 55: 33-38, Aug., 1918.

1919

ALONG THE POTOMAC, by C. Farley Anderson [pseud.] Smart Set 60: 73-75, Sept., 1919.

HERE'S TO THE DEAD! [story] by William Drayham [pseud.] Smart Set 58: 121-128, Feb., 1919.

MEDITATION (essay), by Major Owen Hatteras, D.S.O. [pseud.] Smart Set 58: 97-99, April, 1919.

RÉPÉTITION GÉNÉRALE, by H. L. Mencken and George Jean Nathan. Smart Set 58: 49-53—72: 51-56, April, 1919—Dec., 1923.

> This new department was announced in the April 1919 issue, and continued monthly during their tenure of the editorship of the magazine.

WIVES [story], by William Drayham [pseud.] Smart Set 58: 29-34, Jan., 1919.

1920

BLACK MASK. v. 1, no. 1—April, 1920—

> "A year or two later we started *Black Mask,* devoted to stories of mystery. It, also, was a success. Its readers included many judges, statesmen, and other Eminentisimos. Nathan and I sold our interest in it to Warner and Crowe after running it for six months. Such enterprises begin as good sport, but soon become bores. Crowe was then near death. He was a very rich man, and liked us. He therefore gave us an excellent price. This price, with what we had already got out of the organization, sufficed to relieve Nathan and me from want permanently. Since then we have done nothing primarily for money—that is, in the magazine field." HLM (EPFL—A29, p. 114)

CONVERSATIONS, set down by Major Owen Hatteras [pseud.] Smart Set Dec., 1920—March, 1923.

> II. "On Anatomy and Physiology," 63: 93-98, Dec., 1920. III. "On Women," 64: 71-76, Jan., 1921. IV. "On Politics," 64: 93-98, Feb., 1921. V. "On Literature," 64: 89-94, April, 1921. VI. "On Dress," 65: 97-102, May, 1921. VII. "On Editing a Magazine," 65: 99-106, June, 1921. VIII. "On Marriage," 65: 91-96, July, 1921. IX. "On the Darker Races," 70: 93-98, March, 1923.

A LITANY FOR BIBULI, by Major Owen Hatteras [pseud.] Smart Set 63: 1-2, Nov., 1920.

LITERARY CAPITAL OF THE UNITED STATES. Nation [London] 27: 90-92, April 17, 1920.

> Reprinted in *On American Books, a Symposium of Five American Critics as Printed in the London Nation,* edited by Francis Hackett (New York, Huebsch, 1920. p. 31-38. The Freeman Pamphlets).

MEDITATIONS IN E MINOR. New Republic 24: 38-40, Sept. 8, 1920; reprinted 131: 81, Nov. 22, 1954.

> Reprinted in *The New Republic Anthology 1915:1935,* edited by Groff Conklin (New York, Dodge 1936. p. 125-129).

A MYSTERIOUS MATTER. The Freeman 1: 200-202, May 12, 1920.

Reprinted as "Der Rätselhafte Fall Wilson, Übersetzung von Tony Noah, in *Die Glocke* p. 499-505, June 21, 1920.

THE NATIONAL LITERATURE. Yale Review, n.s. 9: 804-817, July, 1920.

Reprinted as "Amerikanisches," Übersetzung von Tony Noah, in *Die Neue Rundschau* p. 1017-1029, Oct., 1921. Also in *Essays Toward Truth, Studies in Orientation,* selected by Kenneth Allan Robinson, William B. Pressey, and James D. McCallum (New York, Holt, 1924. p. 353–367).

A PANORAMA OF PATRIOTS, by Owen Hatteras [pseud.] Smart Set 63: 70, Nov., 1920.

THE SO-CALLED FAIR, by Owen Hatteras [pseud.] Smart Set 61: 1-2, April, 1920.

STAR-SPANGLED MEN. New Republic 24: 118-120, Sept. 29, 1920.

ZWEIFEL AM STIMMZETTEL. Das Tagebuch p. 826-830, July 3, 1920.

Translated from the Baltimore *Evening Sun.*

1921

NATION. v. 112, no. 2914—v. 135, no. 3521 May 11, 1921—Dec. 28, 1932.

HLM was Contributing Editor during this period.

AD IMAGINEM DEI CREAVIT ILLUM, by Owen Hatteras [pseud.] Smart Set 64: 2, March, 1921.

THE AMERICAN NOVEL. Voices [London] 5: 46-47, Feb., 1921.

THE BOOK OF REUBEN. The Freeman 2: 397-398, Jan. 5, 1921.

THE CAT AND HIS SHADOW, by W. L. D. Bell [pseud.] Smart Set 64: 84, March, 1921.

DIANTHUS CARYOPHYLLUS, by Major Owen Hatteras [pseud.] Smart Set 65: 18, May, 1921.

THE DIVINE AFFLATUS. Voices [London] 5: 115-121, Nov., 1921.

THE FOLLIES OF WASHINGTON. The Outlook [London] 48: 483-484, Dec. 10, 1921.

AN ICONOCLAST AT WASHINGTON. The Outlook. [London] 48: 436-437, Nov. 26, 1921.

La Infamia de los Labios, Tésis Práctica Sobre el Arte del Beso. Trad. de Addie B. Deering y Eugenio Vera. La Revista Mexicana. 1921.

Translated from *In Defense of Women*. Miss Deering was HLM's secretary.

Iron Infallibility, by Major Owen Hatteras [pseud.] Smart Set 66: 118, Nov., 1921.

James Huneker. Century Magazine 102: 191-197, June, 1921.

Melomania, by Major Owen Hatteras [pseud.] Smart Set 64: 56, April, 1921.

Morning Song in C Major. The Reviewer 2: 1-5, Oct., 1921.

The Motive of the Critic. New Republic 28: 249-251, Oct. 26, 1921.

Reprinted, slightly revised, as "Footnote on Criticism" in *Prejudices: Third Series*, p. 84-104; and *Criticism in America* (New York, Harcourt, 1924. p. 261-286).

Der Nächste Krieg. Die Grenzboten 80: 241-243, Aug. 31, 1921.

The Novels of W. L. George. Vanity Fair 15: 33,80, Feb., 1921.

A Panorama of Holy Clerks, by Major Owen Hatteras [pseud.] Smart Set 65: 2, June, 1921.

A Panorama of Idiots, by Major Owen Hatteras [pseud.] Smart Set 64: 2, Jan., 1921.

Release from Puritans, Pedagogues and Anglo-Saxons. Independent 107: 249, Dec. 10, 1921.

A Short View of Gamalielese. Nation 112: 621-622, Aug. 27, 1921.

Reprinted in *The Shock of Recognition*, edited by Edmund Wilson (Garden City, N.Y., Doubleday, 1943. p. 1233-1237).

Things I Remember, by Major Owen Hatteras [pseud.] Smart Set 64: 2, Feb., 1921.

1922

American Puritanism at Bay. The Outlook [London] 49: 110-112, Feb. 11, 1922.

Reprinted as "Decadenza del Puritanismo," in *Il Mundo* [Roma] May 12, 1922.

EHE UND SCHEIDUNG, Übersetzung von Theamaria Lenz. Das Tagebuch p. 1204-1207, Aug. 26, 1922 (Sondernummer über Amerika).

From *In Defense of Women.*

FOOTNOTE ON JOURNALISM. Nation 114: 493-494, April 26, 1922.

THE HARVARD AFFAIR. Jewish Tribune 39: 2, June 9, 1922.

HLM's answer to inquiry about restriction of number of Jewish students admitted to Harvard University.

MARYLAND: APEX OF NORMALCY. Nation 114: 517-519, May 3, 1922.

"2nd of a series on the commonwealths that compose this Republic." Reprinted in *These United States, a Symposium,* edited by Ernest Gruening (New York, Boni, 1923. p. 13-24). Also in the Baltimore *Evening Sun,* p. 7, May 6, 1922.

MR. MENCKEN REPLIES. Bookman 55: 364, June, 1922.

Answer to "An Open Letter to H. L. Mencken," by Hugh Walpole in 55: 225-228, May, 1922. Reprinted in *The Bookman Anthology of Essays,* edited by John Farrar (New York, Doran, 1923. p. 54-68).

THE NEW FREEDOM. Issues of Today March 11, 1922.

PÍO BAROJA. Now and Then [London] p. 9-10, March, 1922.

THE PROHIBITION SWINDLE. The Outlook [London] 50: 87-88, July 29, 1922.

THREE YEARS OF PROHIBITION IN AMERICA. The Outlook [London] 49: 502-503, June 24, 1922.

Reprinted as "Tre Anni di Proibizione Alcoolica negli Stati Uniti" in *Enotria* [Milano] Sept., 1922.

WHAT I AM GOING TO READ THIS SUMMER. Answers from persons of various occupations and interests. The Independent 108: 554, June 24, 1922.

1923

À LA MARYLAND. Nation 117: 731, Dec. 26, 1923.

AMERICAN TRADITION. Literary Review 4: 277-278, Nov. 24, 1923.

AMERICANA, by Major Owen Hatteras, D.S.O. [pseud.] Smart Set 71: 59-60—72: 65-69, March—Dec., 1923.

A regular monthly feature from May until the end of HLM and GJN's editorship.

WORKS BY H. L. M.

Aus dem Wörterbuch "Jazz Webster," Übersetzung von Theamaria Lenz. Das Tagebuch p. 222-228, 451-452, Feb. 17, March 31, 1923.

Translation of a chapter from *A Book of Burlesques.*

Calvinism: New Style. The Outlook [London] 52: 237-238, Sept. 29, 1923.

The Dead Letter of Prohibition. The Outlook [London] 52: 148-149, Aug. 25, 1923.

Dr. Saleeby on Prohibition. The Outlook [London] 51: 243, March 24, 1923.

The Field of Biography and History; Opinions of Prominent Editors As to Works That Are Needed. The Independent 110: 130, Feb. 17, 1923.

HLM's opinion entitled "Paltry Professors and History."

Fifteen Years. Smart Set 72: 138-144, Dec., 1923.

HLM's farewell to the *Smart* Set, consisting of a review of his own work and a critical appraisal of the national literary scene.

From an Editor and a Gentleman. Nation 116: 151, Feb. 7, 1923.

HLM's forwarding letter in answer to Frank F. Miles' reply to his criticism. *See* below, Hoch Iowisch.

H. L. Mencken, by Himself. Nation 117: 647-648, Dec. 5, 1923.

Help for German Authors. New Republic 33: 254, Jan. 31, 1923.

Letter urging contributions.

Hoch Iowisch. Nation 116: 72, Jan. 17, 1923.

Letter to the editor, dated Dec. 25, spoofing *Iowa Legionnaire* for advertising German and radical books. Reply from Legion Commander Frank F. Miles, and HLM's further answer, published in "From an Editor and a Gentleman," *see* above.

Is the South a Desert. Southern Literary Magazine 1: 4,34, Oct. 23, 1923.

John Strom, Thrice Doctor, by James Dryham [pseud.] Smart Set 71: 122, May, 1923.

Mr. Harding's Second Term. The Outlook [London] 51: 344-345, April 23, 1923.

MAGAZINE ARTICLES

1924

HLM and George Jean Nathan began their joint editorship of *The American Mercury* in January, 1924.

ARTS AND DECORATION. v. 22, no. 1—v. 39, no. 3 Nov., 1924—July, 1933.

> HLM served on the Board of Consulting Editors, which was later called the Board of Advisory Editors.

CLINICAL NOTES, by George Jean Nathan and H. L. Mencken. American Mercury v. 1, no. 1—v. 5, no. 19 Jan., 1924—July, 1925.

> This column appeared as a monthly feature and continued to be written by Nathan after HLM assumed sole editorship.

THE CLOWN SHOW. Nation 119: 8-9, July 2, 1924.

EDITORIAL. American Mercury v. 1, no. 1—v. 24, no. 9 Jan., 1924—Dec., 1931.

> These political and literary comments were a regular monthly feature, except for Aug., 1924; Jan., April—Sept., 1925; Feb. 1926; Jan. and Dec., 1927; Jan. and May 1929; April 1930. For the Aug. 1931 issue it bore the title "Leaves from a Waste-Basket". With the Feb., 1930 issue they began to have separate titles. The editorials continued from Jan., 1932—Nov., 1933 under the title of "What is Going On In the World," except for Nov., 1932 when it was called "Commentary."

HOW THE QUACKS SUCCEED. Illinois Medical Journal 46: 240-242, Oct., 1924.

JOSEPH CONRAD. Nation 119: 179, Aug. 20, 1924.

RUTH SUCKOW. The Borzoi Broadsides 3: 3, May, 1924. 1 *l.*

> Reprinted in the *American Mercury* 2: ix, June, 1924.

SEX UPROAR. Nation 119: 191-193, July 23, 1924.

> HLM's letter in answer to attack by Bernard Sobel, "Mr. Mencken on the Sex Comedy" 119: 444-445, Oct. 22, 1924.

1925

"With the August 1925 issue [v. 5, no. 20] Mr. Mencken will assume the sole editorship of *The American Mercury*. Mr. Nathan becomes a Contributing Editor . . . " 5: x, July, 1925.

ADVICE TO YOUNG AUTHORS, The Triad [Melbourne] p. 247-248, April, 1925.

THE AMATEUR THEATRE. The Vagabond [Baltimore] 1: 3,20, Dec., 1925.

EFFECT NOTHING. The Writer 37: 204, Nov. 25, 1925.

H. L. MENCKEN on *The Nation*. American Mercury 6: xiv, Sept., 1925 (as advertisement)

Reprinted from the Baltimore *Evening Sun,* July 6, 1925. Also issued as a separate.

IN TENNESSEE. Nation 121: 21-22, July 1, 1925. port. by Hugo Gellert.

MY DEAR WALPOLE. An Open Letter from H. L. Mencken. Bookman 62: 438-439, Dec., 1925.

In answer to Hugh Walpole's "My Dear Mencken" 62: 246-248, Nov., 1925. Issued as a separate.

NOBLESSE OBLIGE. The Sniper 1925.

1926

AN AMERICAN LITERARY PHENOMENON, THEODORE DREISER. Vanity Fair 26: 50, May, 1926.

A CINCINNATI COINAGE. American Speech 1: 246, Jan., 1926.

THE DEFEAT OF ALFONSO. Youth's Companion 100: 23-24 Jan. 14, 1926. illus.

"This story was accepted Dec. 5, 1900, but languished in its office safe for 25 years. In 1925 the editor asked me if I objected to its publication. After looking it over I said no." HLM (EPFL—A112, p. 61). Story retold in *Time* 7: 24, Jan. 25, 1926.

ENGLISH IN FIRST PLACE. World Review 3: 144, Nov. 15, 1926.

MAN OF SCIENCE, ARTIST AND GENTLEMAN. Birth Control Review 10: 46, Feb., 1926.

Reprinted in *Havelock Ellis, in Appreciation,* compiled, edited and printed by Joseph Ishill (Berkeley Hts., N.J. Priv. print. by the Oriole Press, 1929. p. 59–60).

MYSTERY OF POE. Nation 122: 289-290, March 17, 1926.

ON LIVING IN THE UNITED STATES. Nation 113: 655-656, Dec. 7, 1926. (Holiday Book Suppl.)

MAGAZINE ARTICLES

PER YEAR. American Speech 1: 456, May, 1926; discussion 1: 509-510, June, 1926.

SHOOTING-THE-CHUTES WITH ENGLISH. World Review 3: 175, Dec. 6, 1926.

SONGS OF THE AMERICAN NEGRO. World Review 1: 279, Feb. 8, 1926.

VICTUALRY AS A FINE ART. American Restaurant 9: 59-60, Sept., 1926.

> Reprinted from the *Chicago Sunday Tribune,* June 13, 1926. Also contains comments by editors of institutional publications. Editorial reply to article, p. 52, Dec., 1926.

1927

AMERIKANISCHE FREIHEIT, übersetzt von Herman George Scheffauer. Weltbühne [Berlin] 23: 896-899, June 7, 1927; Prager Tageblatt, June 11, 1927.

> Reprinted from Baltimore *Evening Sun.*

AS MENCKEN SEES IT. *See* "Testament" below.

ENGLISH TERMS FOR AMERICAN READERS; A List from the Appendix of *"Let's Go to the Movies,"* by Iris Barry. American Speech 3: 68-69, Oct., 1927.

THE GREAT DEFENDER [Darrow] Vanity Fair 28: 44, March, 1927.

JITNEY. American Speech 2: 214, Jan., 1927.

LEBEN UNTER BÜROKRATEN, Übersetzung aus dem Amerikanischen von Trude Norden. Die Neue Bücherschau [Berlin] 7: 160-163, Oct., 1927.

> Reprinted from Baltimore *Evening Sun.*

THE LOW-DOWN ON HOLLYWOOD. Photoplay 32: 36-37, 118-120 April, 1927. port.

ON THE NEED OF THE UNITED STATES. Riverdale Review April 14, 1927.

DIE PHILOSOPHIE ALS LEERES GEREDE. Das Tagebuch p. 544-547, April, 1927; Prager Tageblatt April 31, 1927.

> Translated from the Baltimore *Evening Sun.*

TESTAMENT. Review of Reviews 76: 413-416, Oct., 1927.

Editor's introduction "Mencken and his Isms", p. 412. "We have asked Mr. Mencken to tell our readers what he finds to be his underlying convictions . . . " HLM's Testament, "What I do believe, at bottom and immovably," is continued with an article entitled "As Mencken Sees It," p. 417–418.

THWACKS FROM THE MOTHERLAND. Nation 124: 434, April 20, 1927. *See also* Book Reviews. Joad.

TWO NOTES. American Speech 2: 408, June, 1927.

1928

CLOWN SHOW. Nation 126: 713, June 27, 1928.

DIE DEUTSCHAMERIKANER. Die Neue Rundschau [Berlin] p. 486-493, Nov., 1928.

UN ENCUENTRO CON RODOLFO VALENTINO. Trad. por J. M. Valdés-Rodriguez. Carteles [Habana] ports. Sept. 2, 1928. "Der Unglückliche Valentino," übersetzt von E. Haag. Weltbühne [Berlin] p. 821-823, Nov. 3, 1928. "Valentino." Der Tag [Berlin] Nov. 12, 1928.

Various translations of the "Monday Article" from the Baltimore *Evening Sun*, Oct. 27, 1927.

ESTADOS UNIDOS Y CENTRO AMÉRICA. Trad. por J. M. Valdés-Rodriguez. Carteles [Habana] port. May 6, 1928.

Reprinted from the *American Mercury* editorial, 13: 409-411, April, 1928.

PANAMERICANISMO? Versión español de Alvaro A. Araújo. La Pluma [Montevideo] 9: 133-136, Dec., 1928.

Reprinted from the Baltimore *Evening Sun*.

THE RIGHTS OF A COLUMNIST; a Symposium on the Case of Heywood Broun Versus the New York *World*. Nation 126: 608-609, May 30, 1928.

STATEMENTS OF BELIEF II. Further "Credos" of America's Leading Authors. Bookman 68: 206-207, Oct., 1928.

Same three fundamental concepts as stated fuller in "Testament," *see* above, 1927.

VIAJANDO POR EL MUNDO. Trad. por M. Primello de Fernández de Castro. Social [Habana] 13: 12, 58-59, 85 April, 1928.

Translation of "Seeing the World" from *A Book of Burlesques*.

HLM checking galley proofs in his study. (*Photograph by A. Aubrey Bodine.*)

First issue edited by HLM and Nathan.

August 1916
15 Cents

America's most Entrancing Magazine

First issue edited by HLM and Nathan.

Post-Mencken cover. (*Reproduced from the Collections of the Library of Congress.*)

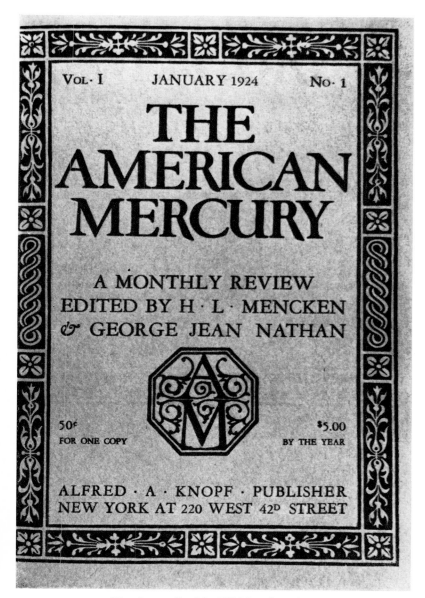

First issue edited by HLM and Nathan.

December 1933

The Fallacies of the N. R. A. See page 415

The Mystery of Retail Price. See page 388

The American Mercury

Edited by
H. L. MENCKEN

Alfred A. Knopf, *Publisher*

$1.00 *for one copy—By the year* $10.00

Last issue under editorship of HLM.

The Mencken home—1524 Hollins Street, Baltimore, Maryland.
(*Photograph by Bob Brown.*)

The H. L. Mencken Room, Enoch Pratt Free Library. *(Photograph by Sussman-Ochs.)*

MAGAZINE ARTICLES

WHAT IS THIS TALK ABOUT UTOPIA? Nation 126: 662-663, June 13, 1928.

Third of a series in which "various persons describe the world they would like to live in."

WHAT'S WRONG WITH *The Nation?* Nation 127: 542-543, Nov. 21, 1928.

1929

APPRECIATION OF SCHUBERT, an Editorial. Etude 47: 25-26, Jan., 1929. port.

Reprint of an *American Mercury* editorial, 15: 284-286, Nov., 1928.

THOSE TWO MEN! Comments on the Sacco-Vanzetti Case. The Lantern [Boston] 2: 5-6, Aug., 1929.

1930

FOOD FOR THOUGHT, by Clarence W. Lieb, cartoon by Ralph Barton. Woman's Home Companion 57: 30, June, 1930. port.

HLM answers questions about his diet and the influence of food on creativity.

LITTLE CONCERT-HALLS, by Atwood C. Bellamy [pseud.] American Mercury 20: 244-246, June, 1930.

MASTER PEDAGOGUE. Nation 131: 617, Dec. 3, 1930.

ON BREAKING INTO TYPE. The Colophon v. 1, pt. 1, 8p. Feb., 1930.

" . . . was written especially for *The Colophon* in the month of August, 1929, and is set in a type face now used in America for the first time, designed by Emil Rudolf Weiss and cast in the Bauerische Giesserei of Frankfurt, Germany." Reprinted in: *Breaking into Print*, compiled by Elmer Adler (New York, Simon, 1937. p. 139–146) and in *Carrousel for Bibliophiles*, edited by William Targ (New York, Duschnes, 1947. p. 344–349) with title "On Getting into Print."

WHAT I BELIEVE. Living Philosophies XII. Forum 84: 133-139, Sept. 1930; discussion 84 suppl.: 40-41, Nov., 1930.

Reprinted in *Living Philosophies* (New York, Simon, 1931. p. 179-193).

1931

THE BURDEN OF CREDULITY. Opportunity, Journal of Negro Life 9: 40-41, Feb., 1931.

IS THE COLLEGE STUDENT RADICAL? The Liberal April, 1931.

LEAVES FROM A WASTE-BASKET. American Mercury 23: 408-410, Aug., 1931.

The only "Editorial" bearing this title.

LITERARY MARKET NOTE. Junior League Magazine 18: 11-22, Dec., 1931. port.

Letter to Miss Richardson praising the magazine, in "Open Forum" column, p. 3, 106.

PRESIDENT HOOVER. Vanity Fair 36: 40, April, 1931. port. (of Hoover by Garretto).

THE REVEREND BRETHREN. The World Tomorrow 14: 225, July, 1931.

SINCLAIR LEWIS. Vanity Fair 35: 48 Jan., 1931. port. (col. caricature of Lewis by William Cotton).

STAGE CENSORSHIP IS CERTAIN UNLESS . . . Theatre Guild Magazine 8: 12,17, Feb., 1931.

THE ULTIMATE MUSICAL CHOICE, pt. I. Representative Men and Women in All Callings State Their Choice. Etude 19: 10, Jan., 1931. port.

THE WORST AMERICAN STATE, by Charles Angoff and H. L. Mencken. American Mercury Pt. I, 24: 1-16; pt. II, 24: 175-188; pt. III, 24: 355-371; Sept.—Nov., 1931.

1932

CARIBBEAN CARAVEL, Newssheet Aboard S. S. Columbus, North German Lloyd.

"Historical Notes," no. 9, p. 1, Jan. 18, 1932. "Confidential Information," no. 12, p. 1, Jan. 25, 1932. "New York Ahoy!!" no. 13, p. 1, Jan. 26, 1932.

COMMENTARY. American Mercury 27: 377-383, Nov., 1932.

Continuation of "Editorial," and only issue so titled. After this issue editorials appeared as "What Is Going on in the World." *See* below.

A FAITHFUL PUBLIC OFFICIAL. Baltimore Health News 9: 36-37, April, 1932.

Obituary for Dr. C. Hampson Jones.

GOETHE, as Viewed by American Writers and Scholars, a Symposium. Monatshefte für Deutschen Unterricht 24: 88-89, March—April, 1932.

JAMES BRANCH CABELL. Wings 6: 5-7, Feb., 1932. port.

METANTHROPOLOGICAL CRISIS, an Enquête. Transition 2: 128, March, 1932.

> Answer to questions on collectivism and metaphysicians, written June, 1931.

PRODDING THE NOBEL PRIZE COMMITTEE [a Symposium] Books Abroad 6: 373, July, 1932.

WHAT IS GOING ON IN THE WORLD. American Mercury 25: 1-6—30: 257-262, Jan., 1932—Nov., 1933.

> Monthly editorial and lead article. Not issued July 1932, nor June—Aug., 1933.

1933

BOOKS I HAVE NEVER READ, a Symposium. Nation 137: 537, Nov. 8, 1933.

JEWS ARE EASY MARKS: Exclusive Interview by Maxwell Weinberg. Chicago Sentinel Sept. 28, 1933; Jewish Times [Baltimore] 29: 2, Sept. 29, 1933.

NOTES AND QUERIES. American Speech 8: 72-73, Feb., 1933.

NOTES ON EDUCATION. The Black and Blue Jay [Johns Hopkins University] 14: 11, 24 Nov., 1933. port.

OVERNIGHT SAINTS. Delineator 123: 4, 50, Oct., 1933. port. (HLM and wife by A. A. Bodine)

SHALL WE ABOLISH SCHOOL 'FRILLS?' YES. The Rotarian 42: 16-17, 48, May, 1933. illus.

> The negative was upheld by John Dewey. Digest in *School Management* 2: 5, 16, June, 1933. The controversy caused by this article continued to be printed in *School Management*: "A Letter to H. L. Mencken" by J. Morris Jones, editor of this magazine, 52: 336-337, June, 1933. "H. L. Mencken Answers Our Letter" and "We Reply" p. 362–363, July. "The Mencken Correspondence" two letters from HLM and one from Jones, p. 400, Aug., 1933.

TEN YEARS. American Mercury. 30: 385-387, Dec., 1933.

> A summation upon "my retirement from the editorship of the *American Mercury* to take effect at the end of the present year . . . yielding to Mr. Henry Hazlitt."

1934

THE ADRIATIC: EAST SIDE. The Seven Seas 13: 9-10, June, 1934. illus.

AMERICA'S HOSTILITY TO ART. Vanity Fair 42: 21-22, April, 1934.

THE BRAIN TRUST. Liberty 11: 16-18 March 3, 1934. illus., port. (photo by Ray Lee Jackson)

DYING WORDS. American Commentator p. 3, Oct., 1934; Words 1: 7, Jan., 1935.

> Reprinted by permission from the New York *American* and the Los Angeles *Examiner.*

FOREIGN PARTS. New Yorker May—July, 1934.

> "Athens" 10: 39-40, May 12. "Istanbul" 10: 72-73, May 19. "Granada" 10: 68-69, June 2. "Gibraltar" 10: 71-72, June 16. "Jerusalem" 10: 52, June 23. "Venice" 10: 37-38, June 30. "Madeira" 10: 50, July 14. "Rabat" 10: 51-52, July 21. "Cairo" 10: 34, July 28. Venice and Cairo do not appear in the out-of-town editions.

FOUR GLAD YEARS. College Humor 1: 8-9, 66, Nov., 1934.

HENRY L. MENCKEN ON RADIO. Broadcasting 7: 16, Nov. 1, 1934.

> Testimony submitted to Federal Communications Commission, Broadcasting Division, on their proposal to turn over a quarter of all stations to so-called educational and religious agencies.

HITLER HAS BUT HIS OWN THROAT TO CUT. American Hebrew and Jewish Tribune 135: 293, Sept. 7, 1934. port.

HOW FREE DO YOU WANT TO BE? Liberty 11: 26-27, Aug. 25, 1934. illus., port.

ILLUMINATORS OF THE ABYSS. Saturday Review of Literature 11: 155-156, Oct. 6, 1934. port.

INDIVIDUALISM CHEATS THE CORONER. Vanity Fair 42: 35,65, June, 1934.

MEMOIRS OF AN EDITOR. Vanity Fair 41: 16,54, Feb., 1934.

> Letter telling of plans for future writing on p. 9.

THE NETHER FRINGE. Panorama, a Monthly Survey of People and Ideas, edited by Isaac Goldberg. no. 9, p. 1 June, 1934.

> On unemployment.

NEW VERBS. Words 1: 5, Nov., 1934.

Reprinted by permission from the New York *American* and the Los Angeles *Examiner.*

NOT AN IDEA MISSING. Readers Digest, back cover, v. 25, Sept., 1934; issued also as advertising brochure by contributors, p. 5.

NOTES ON NEGRO STRATEGY. Crisis 41: 298,304, Oct., 1934.

NOTES ON THE NEW DEAL. Current History 40: 521-527, Aug., 1934.

Reprinted in *Survey of Current Economics,* edited by Norman Buck (New York, Nelson, 1934. p. 819–826).

SCHOOLHOUSES IN THE RED. Liberty 11: 26-28, June 16, 1934. illus., port. (by Davart).

WAS EUROPE A SUCCESS? Nation 139: 374-375, Oct. 3, 1934.

Answer in a symposium to a series by Joseph Wood Krutch, Aug. 15—Sept. 4, 1934.

WELLS NEARING THREE SCORE. Nation 139: 567, Nov. 14, 1934.

WHAT TO DO WITH CRIMINALS. Liberty 11: 7-10, July 28, 1934. illus.

Condensed in *Readers Digest* 25: 10-12, Sept., 1934 (biog. sketch, p. 111–112)

WHY NOBODY LOVES A POLITICIAN. Liberty 11: 16-17, Oct. 27, 1934. illus.

WHY NOT AN AMERICAN MONARCHY? Vanity Fair 43: 21-22 Nov., 1934.

A YEAR OF LEGAL LIQUOR. Nation 139: 666-667, Dec. 12, 1934.

"Issues and Men, a Reply to H. L. Mencken" 140: 35, Jan. 9, 1935. To which HLM answers "Mr. Mencken Has the Last (to Date) Word" 140: 72-73 Jan. 16. 1935.

1935

ANNIVERSARY POSTBAG. Yale Review, n.s. 25: 18-19, Sept., 1935.

HLM's contribution to the twenty-fifth anniversary issue, written July 25, 1935, dealt with politics.

ANSWERS TO THE GREAT VANITY FAIR QUESTIONNAIRE. Vanity Fair 45: 54, Oct., 1935, questions #9 and 10.

THE ARTS, in a Symposium "Five Years and What They Have Done to Us." Cosmopolitan. 98: 24, Jan., 1935. port.

WORKS BY H. L. M.

CAPITALISM WON'T DIE. Liberty 12: 7-9, June 1, 1935. illus.
Condensed in *Readers Digest* 27: 11-14, July, 1935.

ENGLISH GROWS. American Commentator p. 3-4, Jan., 1935; Words 1: 6,13, Sept., 1935.

FUTURE OF ENGLISH. Harper 170: 541-548, April, 1935.
Condensed in *Readers Digest* 26: 27-30, May, 1935.

HOW TO DRINK LIKE A GENTLEMAN. Liberty 12: 42-45, Jan. 12, 1935. illus.

MR. KIPLING. American Commentator p. 14, April, 1935.

ONWARD AND UPWARD WITH THE ARTS. New Yorker May 11, 1935—March 7, 1936.

"The Advance of Nomenclatural Eugenics in the Republic," 11: 44-52, May 11, 1935. "The Advance of Onomatology, the Art and Science of Naming Babies," 11: 32-40, May 25, 1935. "The Advance of Honorifics," 11: 30-37, Aug. 17, 1935. "Report on the Progress of Euphenism," 11: 39-42, Aug. 31, 1935. "The Advance of Municipal Onomastics," 11: 54-57, Feb. 8, 1936. "The Dizzy Rise (and Ensuing Bust) of Simplified Spelling," 12: 37-44, March 7, 1936.

PROPERTY IN WORDS. Words 1: 6, May, 1935.

Reprinted by permission from the New York *American* and the Los Angeles *Examiner*.

THE RED BUGABOO. Liberty 12: 13-17, Jan. 26, 1935. illus.

SAUERKRAUT, BUM, POKER. Words 1: 10,23, Nov., 1935.

SHOULD THE COSTIGAN-WAGNER ANTI-LYNCHING BILL BE PASSED BY CONGRESS? Congressional Digest 14: 186, June, 1935.

THE SOUTH ASTIR. Virginia Quarterly Review 11: 47-60, Jan., 1935.

TABLE WORDS. Words 1: 6, March, 1935.

Reprinted by permission from the New York *American* and Los Angeles *Examiner*.

WISHES JEWS WOULD STOP ALARMING GOYIM. American Hebrew and Jewish Times 137: 295 Sept. 20, 1935. port.

1936

THE AMERICAN LANGUAGE. Yale Review, n.s. 25: 538-552, March, 1936.

MAGAZINE ARTICLES

Abridged in *Readers Digest* 28: 67-70, May, 1936. Reprinted in: *The American Reader*, edited by Claude M. Simpson and Allan Nevins, with a foreword and editorial advice by Henry Seidel Canby (Boston, Heath, 1941. p. 251–259); *Essay Annual* p. 1–15, 1937, p. 15–25, 1941; *Readings for Liberal Education*, edited by Louis G. Locke, William M. Gibson, George Arms (New York, Rinehart, 1948. p. 111–118); *This America*, edited by John D. Kern and Irwin Griggs (New York, Macmillan, 1942. p. 340–352); *The Yale Review Anthology*, edited with an introduction by Wilbur Cross and Helen MacAfee (New Haven, Yale University Press; London, Oxford University Press, 1942. p. 27–39).

AMERICANA. American Speech 11: 82, Feb., 1936.

BUILDING PROBLEMS, a Symposium of Nine Questions Posed by Architectural Forum. Architectural Forum 65: 61,64,114,120, Oct., 1936.

THE CASE OF DR. LANDON. American Mercury 39: 129–134 Oct., 1936.

CHOOSING THE CANDIDATE. American Mercury Digest 12: 19, Spring, 1936.

Reprinted from "What is Going On in the World," 26: 129-138 June, 1932.

CONVENTION DAYS ARE HERE AGAIN. Cosmopolitan 100: 32, May, 1936.

THE DOLE FOR BOGUS FARMERS. American Mercury 39: 400-408, Dec., 1936.

INDIAN WORDS. Words 2: 5,9, May, 1936.

Reprinted by permission from the New York *American* and Los Angeles *Examiner*.

MAKING YOUR MUSIC LIVE. Etude 54: 277-278, May, 1936.

THE NEW DEAL MENTALITY. American Mercury 38: 1-11, May, 1936.

ORDEAL OF A PHILOSOPHER. New Yorker 12: 21-24, April 11, 1936.

Used as a chapter in *Happy Days*.

PEACE ON EARTH—WHY WE HAVE WARS. Liberty 13: 24-25, Dec. 26, 1936. port.

Condensed in *Readers Digest* as "Peace—When Human Nature Changes" 30: 55-56, June, 1937.

WORKS BY H. L. M.

THE REDS AND CIVIL RIGHTS. American Mercury 38: 284-289, July, 1936.

SUCH LANGUAGE! American 122: 65,72, Oct., 1936.

THIS SHOW MUST END. The Trumpeter v. 1, no. 12, Oct. 10, 1936. on verso of cover. port.
One page endorsement of Alfred M. Landon.

THREE YEARS OF DR. ROOSEVELT. American Mercury 37: 257-265, March, 1936.

WHAT IS SLANG? Readers Digest 29: 67-70, Oct., 1936.
Condensed from *The American Language,* fourth edition.

WILL A WOMAN BE PRESIDENT? Eve 2: 10-11, Nov., 1936.
Answer to a symposium started by Mae C. Hurwitch in the July 1 issue.

1937

THE AMERICAN FUTURE. American Mercury 40: 129-136, Feb., 1937.

CONSTITUTION FOR THE NEW DEAL. American Mercury 41: 129-136, June, 1937.
Abridged in *Readers Digest* 31: 27-29, July, 1937.

GOVERNOR MURPHY'S LABOR POLICY—FOR AND AGAINST. Survey Graphic 26: 465-466, Sept., 1937.
HLM's opinion entitled " . . . extinct vermin . . . "

HYMN TO THE TRUTH. Readers Digest 31: 53-54, Oct., 1937.
Condensed from *Prejudices: Sixth Series,* about the Bathtub Hoax.

INNOCENCE IN A WICKED WORLD. New Yorker 13: 16-18, Feb. 20, 1937.
Used as a chapter in *Happy Days.*

SEMPER FIDELIS. American Mercury 42: 436-439, Dec., 1937.

UTOPIA BY STERILIZATION. American Mercury 41: 399-408, Aug., 1937.
Excerpts in *Literary Digest* 124 (Digest 1): 22, Aug. 7, 1937.

1938

AMERICAN CIVIL LIBERTIES UNION. American Mercury 45: 182-189, Oct., 1938.

MAGAZINE ARTICLES

FORBIDDEN WORDS. Better English 2: 1-9, Nov., 1938.

HAVANA REVISITED. Seven Seas Feb. 22, 1938.

TRIUMPH OF THE HAVE-NOT. American Mercury 43: 16-22, Jan., 1938.

1939

BRIEF GUST OF GLORY. New Yorker 15: 25-32, Aug. 5, 1939.

Used as a chapter in *Happy Days.*

BRINGING ROOSEVELT UP TO DATE. American Mercury 46: 257-264, March, 1939.

FARMERS, REAL AND BOGUS. Country Home Magazine Oct. 9, 1939.

IN THE FOOTSTEPS OF GUTENBERG. New Yorker 15: 30-34, Oct. 14, 1939.

Used as a chapter in *Happy Days.* Reprinted in *Scholastic* 36: 21-22, 28, April, 1940. port. Same in *Readers Digest,* as "Portrait in Ink" 38: 97-98, April, 1941.

ITALIAN LIBRARY OF INFORMATION. The Beydom of Tunisia . . . Outline Studies. p. 13-15, Jan., 1939. (HLM quoted from the *Sun,* Dec. 21, 1938.)

LARVAL STAGE OF A BOOKWORM. New Yorker 15: 28-32, Sept. 23, 1939.

Used as a chapter in *Happy Days.*

MEMOIRS OF DECEASED PEDAGOGUES. New Yorker 15: 26-31, June 3, 1939.

Used as a chapter in *Happy Days.*

MEMORIALS OF GOURMANDIZING. New Yorker 15: 26-33, Aug. 26, 1939.

Used as a chapter in *Happy Days.*

RECOLLECTIONS OF ACADEMIC ORGIES. New Yorker 15: 29-34, June 17, 1939.

Used as a chapter in *Happy Days.*

RECREATIONS OF A REACTIONARY. New Yorker 15: 56-60, Nov. 4, 1939.

Used as a chapter in *Happy Days.*

WORKS BY H. L. M.

THE RUIN OF AN ARTIST. New Yorker. 15: 23-26, May 27, 1939.

Used as a chapter in *Happy Days.*

THE SCHOOLING OF A THEOLOGIAN. New Yorker 15: 31-39, July 8, 1939.

Used as a chapter in *Happy Days.*

THOUGHTS ON CURRENT DISCONTENTS. American Mercury 46: 447-448; 47: 215, April, June, 1939.

TWO CLEAR DUTIES. Editor & Publisher 72: 72, April 22, 1939.

1940

AMERICAN AND ENGLISH. Scholastic 37: 21-22, 27, Nov. 18, 1940

Excerpts from *The American Language,* fourth edition.

AMERICANS VERSUS FIFTH COLUMNISTS; a Symposium. Survey Graphic 29: 550, Nov., 1940.

HLM's answer to Werner Guttmann's article "Don't Penalize the German-Americans" in the Oct., 1940 issue.

BRITISH SPEECH INVADED. Saturday Review of Literature 22: 10, June 1, 1940. port. (by Gene Markey); Comment by Burton Rascoe, 22: 9, June 15, 1940.

Editors Note: "This is first of a series of monthly articles . . . on . . . the state of the American language." There followed: "Our Borrowed Vocabulary," 22: 13, June 29, 1940. port. (by Schreiber); reprinted in *Scholastic* 45: 17, Oct. 23, 1944. "Vocabulary Glorification," 22: 11, Aug. 3, 1940; reprinted in *Essay Annual* p. 26-27, 1941. "Some Southern Given Names," 22: 11, Sept. 14, 1940. "All these were written for the *Reader's Digest,* which farmed them out to the *Saturday Review.*" HLM (EPFL—A22.2)

DOWNFALL OF A REVOLUTIONARY. Esquire 14: 27, 122, Sept., 1940.

Used as a chapter in *Heathen Days.* Reprinted in *The Esquire Treasury,* edited by Arnold Gingrich (New York, Simon, 1953. p. 423–428); *A Treasury of Laughter,* edited by Louis Untermeyer (New York, Simon, 1946. p. 478–484).

NOTES ON THE AMERICAN LANGUAGE. Readers Digest April—June, 1940.

I. "Bizarre Nomenclature, Mostly Feminine," 36: 71-72, April, 1940. II "War Slang," 36: 39, May, 1940 (Notes on the Mother Tongue). III. "Scrambled Parts of Speech," 36: 99-100, June, 1940.

1941

DAYS OF INNOCENCE. New Yorker Feb. 15, 1941—Sept. 25, 1943.

Only the first seven of this long series were numbered. The first nine articles, from "The Girl from Red Lion, Pa." to "The Synthesis of the News" were used in *Newspaper Days*; the following seven, from "Notes on Paleozoic Publicists" to "Memoirs of a Stable Boy" in *Heathen Days*.

1941: I. "The Girl from Red Lion, Pa." 17: 15-18, Feb. 15. II. "Slaves of Beauty" 17: 18-20, March 1. III. "The Judicial Arm" 17: 20-21, March 29. IV. "The Gospel of Service" 17: 17-20, April 26. V. "Giants at the Bar" 17: 20-22, May 24. VI. "Souvenirs de la Noblesse Française" 17: 72-76, June 14. VII. "Fire Alarm" 17: 21-26, July 5. "Recollections of Notable Cops" 17: 27-29, Sept. 20. "The Synthesis of the News" 17: 22-25, Oct. 18; condensed in *Readers Digest* as "Reporter and the Arc Lights" 39: 39-40, Nov., 1941. "Notes on Paleozoic Publicists" 17: 92-97, Dec. 20.

1942: "A Dip into Statecraft" 17: 18-20, Feb. 14. "Old Home Day" 18: 17-19, March 7. "Master of Gladiators" 18: 18-20, April 25. "Romantic Intermezzo" 18: 17-20, Nov. 7. "Gore in the Caribbees" 18: 20-23, Dec. 19.

1943: "Memoirs of a Stable Boy" 18: 18-21, Jan. 16; condensed in *Readers Digest* as "Adventures with a Pony" 42: 88-90. April. "Surdi Audiunt" 19: 17-20. June 12. "The Life of Tone" 19: 21-25, Sept. 25.

HAPPY DAYS. American Mercury. 52: 769-794, June, 1941.

Excerpts in Book Supplement. Excerpts also in *Readers Digest* 38: 97-98, April, 1941.

1942

AMBROSE BIERCE. Encore 1: 211-214, March, 1942.

Reprinted from *Prejudices: Sixth Series.*

THE CULT OF HOPE. Encore 2: 52-56, July, 1942.

Reprinted from *Prejudices: Second Series.*

EXEUNT OMNES. Encore 1: 592-599, June, 1942.

Reprinted from *Prejudices: Second Series.*

FORBIDDEN WORDS. Encore 2: 548-556, Nov., 1942.

Reprinted from *The American Language,* fourth edition.

A GLIMPSE OF H. L MENCKEN'S LATEST WORK: A New Dictionary of Quotations. Encore 1: 461-471, May, 1942.

THE HILLS OF ZION. Encore 1: 125-131, Feb., 1942.

Reprinted from *Prejudices: Fifth Series.*

'O.K.' 1840. American Speech 17: 126-127, April, 1942.

SCIENTIFIC EXAMINATION OF A POPULAR VIRTUE. Encore 1: 315-319, April, 1942.

Reprinted from *Prejudices: Second Series.*

THE WORST TRADE OF THEM ALL. Liberty 19: 19-20, April 4, 1942.

WORKS BY H. L. M.

1943

ADVENTURES OF A Y.M.C.A. LAD. Encore 3: 529-534, May, 1943.

Reprinted from *Heathen Days.*

AN EVENING ON THE HOUSE. Esquire 20: 63, 233-234, 236, 238-239, Dec., 1943.

Reprinted in the *Armchair Esquire,* edited by Arnold Gingrich and L. Rust Hills (New York, Putnam, 1958. p. 172–180); and also in its Popular Library edition (Popular Library Special W-1100, 1960. p. 140–154).

THE FRINGES OF LOVELY LETTERS. Encore 4: 257-268, 436-447, Sept. —Oct., 1943.

Reprinted from *Prejudices: Fifth Series.*

PORTRAIT OF AN IMMORTAL SOUL. Encore 3: 129-135, Feb., 1943.

Reprinted from *Prejudices: First Series.*

1944

AMERICAN AND ENGLISH. Encore 5: 265-271, 415-418, March—April, 1944.

Reprinted from *The American Language.*

AMERICAN PROFANITY. American Speech 19: 241-249, Dec., 1944.

DESIGNATIONS FOR COLORED FOLK. American Speech 19: 161-174, Oct., 1944.

Reprinted in *The Twentieth Century English,* edited by William S. Knicker-bocker (New York, Philosophical Library, 1946. p. 139–157).

EPIGRAMS IN C MAJOR. Encore 6: 160-162, Aug., 1944.

Reprinted from *A Little Book in C Major.*

GEORGE ADE—MEMORIAL ISSUE. Magazine of Sigma Chi 63: 38-39, Oct.—Nov., 1944.

OBSEQUIES IN THE GRAND MANNER. Esquire 21: 43, 133-135, Jan., 1944.

STARE DECISIS. New Yorker 20: 17-21, Dec. 30, 1944.

Reprinted as *Christmas Story, see* Books and Pamphlets, 1946. Also as "Christmas With The Bums," illustrated by James Gorth in *True, the Men's Magazine* 36: 36-37, 82-84, Dec., 1956.

WAR WORDS IN ENGLAND. American Speech 19: 3-15, Feb., 1944; Comments by Bob Trout of CBS 19: 292-295, Dec., 1944.

MAGAZINE ARTICLES

1945

AMERICAN SPEECH: 1925—1945. The Founders Look Back. American Speech 20: 241-242, Dec., 1945.

"The record informs me that I was pa of *American Speech*—a fact that somewhat surprises me, for I have a poor memory and I am not normally given to good works." p. 241. Reminiscences by Louise Pound, Kemp Malone and A. G. Kennedy, p. 242-246, further attest HLM's role and support. The birth of this magazine was saluted in the *American Mercury* 6: xlviii, Dec., 1925.

EARLY DAYS, drawings by Warren Chappell. Borzoi Battledore 1: 1-2, 4, 1945. illus.

TALE OF A TRAVELLER. New Yorker 21: 48-53, Oct. 20, 1945.

1946

BULLETIN ON 'HON.' American Speech 21: 81-85, April, 1946.

THE CURRENT SUFFIXES. American Speech 21: 67-69, Feb., 1946.

MISCELLANY. [Againster used in an editorial in the Chicago Times.] American Speech 21: 68-69, Feb., 1946.

NOTES ON AMERICAN. Word Study 21: 2-3, May, 1946.

VERBS NEW AND OLD. American Speech 21: 303-305, Dec., 1946; 23: 69-70, Feb., 1948.

1947

THE BOOBOISIE AGAIN. Fortune 35: 29, April, 1947.

Letter to the editor in answer to an article on the radio in the March, 1947 issue.

ETYMOLOGICAL NOTES. American Speech 22: 232-234, Oct., 1947.

NAMES FOR AMERICANS. American Speech 22: 241-256, Dec., 1947. bibliog. footnotes.

WHY MENCKEN ESCHEWS THE THEATRE. Scents, Sweatshop Size, Buncombe Keep Baltimore Sage from Theatre. Variety 165: 3, 73, Jan. 8, 1947.

1948

AN AMERICAN REACTION TO BERNARD SHAW'S FORTY LETTER ALPHABET. Quarterly Journal of Speech 34: 503, Dec., 1948.

AMERICAN STREET NAMES. American Speech 23: 81-88, April, 1948. bibliog. footnotes

THE IDIOM OF THE HAM. Theatre Arts Monthly 32: 20-21, June— July, 1948, illus.

"Examples of theatrical argot are reprinted from *Supplement Two: The American Language.*"

THE LANGUAGE OF THE FLOUR MILL. Horizon [General Mills] p. 9, March, 1948. port. p. 8.

LOVE STORY. New Yorker 23: 23-26, Jan. 17, 1948.

MARYLAND SPEECH. Gardens, Houses and People [Baltimore] 23: 11-12, Feb., 1948. port.

Reprinted from *The American Language. Supplement II.*

MY CURRENT READING. Saturday Review of Literature 31: 14, May 22, 1948. port.

OUR MOST POPULAR NAMES. Science Digest 24: 52-55, July, 1948.

POSTSCRIPTS TO THE AMERICAN LANGUAGE. New Yorker Sept. 25, 1948 —Oct. 1, 1949.

"The Podunk Mystery" 24: 71-77, Sept. 25, 1948. "Hell and its Outskirts" 24: 52-57, Oct. 23, 1948. "The Vocabulary of the Drinking Chamber" 24: 62-67, Nov. 6, 1948; "Dept. of Amplification" Dec. 4, 1948, not carried in out-of-town edition. "Video Verbiage" 24: 102-105, Dec. 11, 1948. "Scented Words" 25: 70-74, April 2, 1949. "The Life and Times of O.K." 25: 56-61, Oct. 1, 1949; reprinted as "Woher Stammt der Ausdruck 'Okeh'" *Neue Auslese* 5: 115, 118, March, 1950. port.

THE STATE OF AMERICAN WRITING, 1948; a Symposium. Partisan Review. 15: 893-894, Aug., 1948.

Excerpts from a letter sent in reply to questionnaire.

THAT WAS NEW YORK. The Life of an Artist [Theodore Dreiser] New Yorker 24: 53-57, April 17, 1948.

WHAT THE PEOPLE OF AMERICAN TOWNS CALL THEMSELVES. American Speech 23: 161-184, Oct.—Dec., 1948. bibliog. p. 172–184.

1949

SOME OPPROBRIOUS NICKNAMES. American Speech 24: 25-30, Feb., 1949.

MAGAZINE ARTICLES

1951

WILLIAM JENNINGS BRYAN. American Mercury 73: 70-74, Oct., 1951.

Reprinted "to give our readers, especially those under forty, a taste of Mencken's therapeutically acid pen." From an editorial 4: 158-159, Oct., 1925. Also included in *The American Mercury Reader*; a selection of distinguished articles, stories and poems published in *The American Mercury* during the past twenty years, edited by Lawrence E. Spivak and Charles Angoff (Philadelphia, Blakiston, 1944. p. 34–37).

1952

IN THE MERCURY'S OPINION. American Mercury 75: 3-8, Aug., 1952.

Reprint from political editorials July, 1924; June and December, 1932.

MENCKEN ON THE MILITARY. American Mercury 74: 21-25, Jan., 1952.

Reprint from editorial, 18: 22-24, Sept., 1929.

PAST AND PRESENT. American Mercury 75: 121-126, Dec., 1952.

A few reprints from "Clinical Notes"; also "Truth and Temptation," p. 126, from *Prejudices*.

1957

THE INCOMPARABLE BUZZ-SAW; excerpts from A Mencken Chrestomathy. Readers Digest 70: 127, May, 1957.

Reprinted from p. 40 of the *Chrestomathy*, part of "Appendix on a Tender Theme."

BOOK REVIEWS

This section consists of an alphabetical listing by author of the books reviewed by HLM in magazines and newspapers. Exceedingly brief reviews consisting at times of a sentence or a pertinent word, as well as the many notices he wrote in the "Check List of New Books" in the *American Mercury* have been omitted. From time to time HLM reviewed one of his own books; these reviews are listed. General comments concerning an author's work are entered after the reviews of specific writings.

When an entire month or section is devoted to a plethora of books of a single category, e.g. poetry, there has been no attempt to list individually the authors briefly mentioned. Instead, the review has been entered by its title under its specific classification: Poetry, or Plays and Theater, at the end of the author alphabet. There is no further attempt at subject classification. This section is not included in the general Index, as the alphabetical arrangement was deemed sufficient.

To facilitate locating a specific work, the title of the review is always listed after the reference. At times this may give an odd impression, because HLM chose the *Smart Set* monthly titles to fit the first, or main, book featured that month.

All reviews were signed, with the exception of those which appeared serially in *Town Topics,* the latter continuing to appear under the name of "The Ringmaster." "Those contributed . . . during 1914 were done at the nomination of Percival Pollard. . . . He was going abroad and suggested to the editor that I be asked to supply his place. As I recall it I was paid $15 apiece for the reviews." HLM (EPFL—A109)

[My book reviews] "began in the *Smart Set* in 1908, and thus have been running twenty-five years. How many books I have reviewed in that time, God alone knows, for I used to plow through whole shelves of them in an issue." (from "Ten Years," in the *American Mercury* 30: 387, Dec., 1933)

ABBOTT, ELEANOR HALLOWELL. The White Linen Nurse. Smart Set 42: 157-158, March, 1914. The Raw Material of Fiction.

ABBOTT, LAWRENCE FRASER. Impressions of Theodore Roosevelt. Smart Set 61: 140-141, Feb., 1920. From the Diary of a Reviewer—Dec. 8; 61: 138-144, March, 1920. Roosevelt and others.

ABBOTT, WILBUR CORTEZ. The New Barbarians. American Mercury 5: 122-124, May, 1925. Woes of a 100% American.

ABDULLAH, ACHMED. Night Drums. Smart Set 67: 142-143, April 1922. The Niagara of Novels—III.

ADAM, KARL. The Spirit of Catholicism. American Mercury 18: 253-254, Oct. 1929. Ghostly Matters.

ADAMS, CHARLES FRANCIS. Studies Military and Diplomatic. Smart Set 36: 151-154, April, 1912. An Antidote to "Yankee Doodle."

ADAMS, FRANKLIN PIERCE. In Other Words. Smart Set 39: 146-147, April, 1913. The Burbling of the Bards.

ADAMS, GEORGE B. Outward Bound. Smart Set 49: 304-305, May, 1916. Tra-la! Tra-la-la! Tra-la-la-la!

ADAMS, JAMES TRUSLOW.
The Adams Family. Nation 131: 70, July 16, 1930. An American Dynasty.
The Founding of New England. Smart Set 66: 144, Sept., 1921. From the Diary of a Reviewer—VII; 66: 138-141, Dec., 1921. Variations on a Familiar Theme.

ADAMS, SAMUEL HOPKINS.
The Clarion. Town Topics 72: 21-22, Oct. 22, 1914. An Uplifter Put to Torture; Smart Set 44: 306-307, Dec., 1914. Mush for the Multitudes.
The Health Master. Smart Set 44: 157-158, June, 1914. The Anatomy of the Novel.

ADE, GEORGE.
Ade's Fables. Smart Set 39: 154-155, Feb., 1913. The Burden of Humor; Town Topics 71: 19, June 4, 1914. More Fables by Ade.
Single Blessedness and Other Observations. Smart Set 70: 144, Feb., 1923. Specimens of Current Fiction—VI.

ADLER, ALFRED.
The Neurotic Constitution. Smart Set 56: 138-140, Sept., 1918. Rattling the Subconscious.
The Practice and Theory of Individual Psychology, translated by P. Radin. American Mercury 2: 255, June, 1924. Brief Notices.

AGAR, HERBERT. The People's Choice from Washington to Harding: A Study in Democracy. American Mercury 30: 249-252, Oct., 1933. The Nordic Utopia.

AHAD HA—'AM. *See* Ginzberg, Asher.

WORKS BY H. L. M.

AIKMAN, DUNCAN. Calamity Jane and the Lady Wildcats. American Mercury 13: 251-252, Feb., 1928. Three Americans.

AIKMAN, HENRY G., *pseud. See* Armstrong, Harold Hunter.

AINSLEE, PETER. The Scandal of Christianity, a Symposium Review. Christian Union Quarterly 19: 125-127, Oct., 1929.

AKINS, ZOË. Papa. Smart Set 45: 154, Feb., 1915. Lachrymose Love.

ALBEE, JOHN. Confessions of Boyhood. Smart Set 31: 157, Aug., 1910. A Hot Weather Novelist.

ALBRIGHT, VICTOR EMANUEL. The Shakespearean Stage. Smart Set 30: 158-159, Jan., 1910. George Bernard Shaw As A Hero.

ALLEN, HERBERT WARNER. The Wines of France. American Mercury 3: 381-382, Nov., 1924. Paradise Lost.

ALLEN, JAMES LANE.
The Doctor's Christmas Eve. Smart Set 33: 162-163, March, 1911. A Stack of Novels.
The Heroine in Bronze. Smart Set 39: 157, Feb., 1913. The Burden of Humor.

AMERICAN ACADEMY OF ARTS AND LETTERS. Academy Papers: Addresses on Language Problems. American Mercury 7: 122-123, Jan., 1926. Speech-Day in the Greisenheim.

THE AMERICAN CARAVAN: A Yearbook of American Literature. American Mercury 12: 382-383, Nov., 1927. Literary Shock Troops.

THE AMERICAN COLLEGE DICTIONARY, edited by Clarence L. Barnhart. Partisan Review 15: 371-374, March, 1948. Thousands of Words—All Good Ones.

AMERICAN LABOR YEAR BOOK 1923–24. The Rand School of Social Science. American Mercury 2: 383, July, 1924. The Slave and His Ways.

ANDERSON, MARGARET C. My Thirty Years' War: An Autobiography. American Mercury 20: 379-381, July, 1930. Schwärmerei.

ANDERSON, SHERWOOD.
Dark Laughter. American Mercury 6: 379-380, Nov., 1925. Fiction Good and Bad.
Hello Towns! American Mercury 17: 253-254, June, 1929. Experiments by Old Hands.
Horses and Men. [Baltimore] Evening Sun, Dec. 8, 1923. Meed of Praise to Anderson's Stories; American Mercury 1: 252, Feb., 1924. Three Volumes of Fiction.
Many Marriages. Smart Set 71: 138-139, July, 1923. Some New Books.
Marching Men. Smart Set 53: 143, Dec., 1917. Critics Wild and Tame—IV.
Poor White. Smart Set 63: 138-139, Dec., 1920. Chiefly Americans.
Tar: A Midwest Childhood. American Mercury 10: 382-383, March, 1927. Literary Confidences.
The Triumph of the Egg. Smart Set 67: 143, Feb., 1922. Frank Harris and Others—IV.
Windy McPherson. Smart Set 50: 144, Oct., 1916. The Creed of a Novelist.
Winesburg, Ohio. Smart Set 59: 140,142, Aug., 1919. Novels, Chiefly Bad—II.

BOOK REVIEWS

ANDREEV, LEONID NIKOLAEVICH.
Anathema. Smart Set 33: 165-166, Feb., 1911. The Revival of the Printed Play.

The Dilemma. Smart Set 31: 158, July, 1910. A Fictioneer of the Laboratory.

The Life of Man. Smart Set 44: 154-155, Sept., 1914. Thirty-Five Printed Plays.

Love of One's Neighbor, translated by Thomas Seltzer. Town Topics 72: 16, Aug. 29, 1914. The Printed Drama.

The Seven Who Were Hanged. Smart Set 28: 153-155, July, 1909. The Best Novels of the Year.

Silence. Smart Set 27: 158, Jan., 1909. A Road Map of the New Books.

ANTHONY, JOSEPH, ed. The Best News Stories of 1923. American Mercury 2: 508-510, Aug., 1924. The Reporter at Work.

ANTHONY, KATHARINE SUSAN. Margaret Fuller. Smart Set 63: 142-144, Dec., 1920. Chiefly Americans—III.

ANTHONY, NORMAN. Noble Experiment, by Judge, Jr. [pseud.] American Mercury 21: 253-254, Oct., 1930. Books About Boozing.

APOLLINAIRE, GUILLAUME. The Poet Assassinated, translated from the French, with a biographical notice and notes, by Matthew Josephson. American Mercury 1: 377-379, March, 1924. A Modern Masterpiece.

ARCHER, WILLIAM.
Play-Making, a Manual of Craftsmanship. Smart Set 38: 151-152, Oct., 1912. Synge and Others.

Through Afro-America. [Baltimore] Evening Sun, p. 6, May 7, 1910. A Negro State?

ARKWRIGHT, FRANK. The ABC of Technocracy. American Mercury 28: 505-507, April, 1933. Old Dr. Scott's Bile Beans.

ARMSTRONG, HAMILTON FISH. Hitler's Reich: The First Phase. American Mercury 30: 506-510, Dec., 1933. Hitlerismus.

ARMSTRONG, HAROLD HUNTER.
The Groper, by Henry G. Aikman [pseud.] Smart Set 60: 143, Oct., 1919. Mark Twain—IV.

Zell, by Henry G. Aikman [pseud.] [Baltimore] Evening Sun, Feb. 12, 1921. A New Novel That Is Original and Meritorious; Smart Set 64: 142, March, 1921. A Soul's Adventures—II.

ARMSTRONG, PAUL. The Escape. Smart Set 44: 154, Nov., 1914. Critics of More or Less Badness.

ARTSYBASHEV, MIKHAIL PETROVICH.
The Millionaire. Smart Set 47: 309-310, Nov., 1915. After All, Why Not?
Sanine. Smart Set 45: 293-294, March, 1915. The Bugaboo of the Sunday Schools.

ASBURY, HERBERT.
Carry Nation. American Mercury 18: 509-510, Dec., 1929. Portrait of a Christian Woman.

The Gangs of New York. American Mercury 14: 383, July, 1928. Chronicles of Sin.

Up from Methodism. [Baltimore] Evening Sun, Sept. 20, 1926. The Escape from Zion; American Mercury 9: 380-381, Nov., 1926. Three Lively Lives.

ASCH, SHALOM.
The God of Vengeance, translated by Isaac Goldberg. Smart Set 55: 143-144, Aug., 1918. A Sub-Potomac Phenomenon—IV.

Mottke the Vagabond. Smart Set 54: 140-141, March, 1918. Literae Humanistes.

ASKEW, ALICE. J. DE C. (LEAKE). Testimony, by Alice and Claude Askew. Smart Set 31: 158, May, 1910. In Praise of a Poet.

ASQUITH, MARGOT. See Oxford and Asquith, Margot Asquith, countess of.

ATHERTON, GERTRUDE FRANKLIN (HORN).
Black Oxen. Smart Set 71: 138-141, May, 1923. Nordic Blond Art.

The Crystal Cup. American Mercury 6: 249-251, Oct., 1925. The Gland School.

Julia France and Her Times. Smart Set 38: 152-154, Sept., 1912. Prose Fiction Ad Infinitum.

Mrs. Belfame. Smart Set 49: 151, July, 1916. A Soul's Adventures.

Tower of Ivory. Smart Set 31: 156, June, 1910. The Greatest of American Writers.

The Alpine School of Fiction. Smart Set 71: 138-141, May, 1923. Nordic Blond Art. Answer to article in the Bookman 55: 26-33, March, 1922.

[ATKINSON, W. W.] Mind Power. Smart Set 28: 158-159, July, 1909. The Best Novels of the Year.

ATWATER, RICHARD TUPPER. Rickety Rimes of Riq. American Mercury 6: 251-254, Oct., 1925. Poetry.

AUBRY, GEORGES JEAN. Joseph Conrad: Life and Letters. Nation 125: 384, 386, Oct. 12, 1927. The Life of Joseph Conrad.

AUER, LEOPOLD. My Long Life in Music. [Baltimore] Evening Sun, Oct. 20, 1923.

AUGIER, GUILLAUME VICTOR ÉMILE. Four Plays from the French of Émile Augier, translated by Barrett H. Clark. Smart Set 68: 153-155, Feb., 1916. A Massacre in a Mausoleum.

AUSTIN, MARY (HUNTER).
The Arrow Maker, a Drama in Three Acts. [Baltimore] Evening Sun, p. 6, May 4, 1911. The Arrow Maker.

A Woman of Genius. Smart Set 38: 157, Dec., 1912. A Visit to a Short Story Factory.

THE AUTOBIOGRAPHY OF AN EX-COLORED MAN. Smart Set 53: 138-142, Sept., 1917. Si Mutare Potest Aethiops Pellum Suam.

AYRES, CLARENCE EDWIN.
Huxley. Nation 134: 374, March, 30, 1932. Darwin's Bulldog.

Science: The False Messiah. American Mercury 12: 126-127, Sept., 1927. Caveat Against Science.

AYRES, HARRY MORGAN, comp. The Modern Student's Book of English Literature, edited by Harry Morgan Ayres, Will David Howe and Frederick Morgan Padelford. American Mercury 3: 509, Dec., 1924. Anthologies.

BOOK REVIEWS

BABBITT, IRVING. Democracy and Leadership. American Mercury 3: 123-125, Sept., 1924. The State of the Country.

BACON, PEGGY. Funeralities. American Mercury 6: 251-254, Oct., 1925. Poetry.

BAKER, ELIZABETH. Chains, a Play in Four Acts. Smart Set 42: 155, Sept., 1913. Getting Rid of the Actor.

BAKER, GEORGE PIERCE. Dramatic Technique. Smart Set 59: 138, 141, July, 1919. The Coroner's Inquest.

BAKER, RAY STANNARD.
Adventures in Friendship, by David Grayson [pseud.] Smart Set 33: 162, March, 1911. A Stack of Novels.
Woodrow Wilson; Life and Letters, v. 1-2. American Mercury 13: 251-252, Feb., 1928. Three Americans.
Woodrow Wilson; Life and Letters. v. 3-4. American Mercury 25: 250-253, Feb., 1932. Nine American Statesmen.

BALLANTINE, WILLIAM GAY. The Logic of Science. American Mercury 30: 379-380, Nov., 1933. Science vs. Religion.

BALMER, EDWIN. Waylaid by Wireless. Smart Set 29: 159, Sept., 1909. The Books of the Dog Days.

BALZ, ALBERT GEORGE ADAM. The Basis of Social Theory. American Mercury 2: 507, Aug., 1924. Mankind in the Mass.

BANGS, JOHN KENDRICK.
A Little Book of Christmas. Smart Set 38: 158, Nov., 1912. Novels Bad, Half Bad and Very Bad.
Songs of Cheer. Smart Set 31: 160, Aug., 1910. A Hot Weather Novelist.

BARING, MAURICE. Diminutive Dramas. Smart Set 34: 153, Aug., 1911. The New Dramatic Literature.

BARKER, ELSA. Frozen Grail, and Other Poems. Smart Set 31: 160, Aug., 1910. A Hot Weather Novelist.

BARNABEE, HENRY CLAY. Reminiscences: My Wanderings [cover title]. Smart Set 41: 157-158, Dec., 1913. The Russians.

BARNES, EARL. Woman in Modern Society. Smart Set 38: 154, Dec., 1912. A Visit to a Short Story Factory.

BARNES, ERNEST WILLIAM, *Bp. of Birmingham*. Scientific Theory and Religion. American Mercury 30: 379-380, Nov., 1933. Science vs. Religion.

BARNES, HARRY ELMER.
The New History and the Social Studies. American Mercury 6: 124-126, Sept., 1925. The Historian and His Job.

The Story of Punishment. American Mercury 21: 380-383, Nov., 1930. The Criminal.

The Twilight of Christianity. Nation 129: 722, Dec. 11, 1929. Religion in America.

BARNETT, AVROM. Foundations of Feminism, a Critique. Smart Set 64: 143-144, March, 1921. A Soul's Adventures—III.

BAROJA Y NESSI, PÍO. Caesar or Nothing, translated by Louis How. Smart Set 59: 143, June, 1919. The Infernal Mystery—III.

BARRETT, EDWARD JOHN.
The Jesuit Enigma. American Mercury 13: 123-125, Jan., 1928. Shock Troops.
While Peter Sleeps. American Mercury 17: 123-125, May, 1929. The Gods and Their Agents.

BARRY, DAVID S. Forty Years in Washington. American Mercury 2: 510, Aug., 1924. Brief Notices.

BARRY, JOHN DANIEL. Outlines. Smart Set 44: 155, Nov., 1914. Critics of More or Less Badness.

BARTHOLDT, RICHARD. From Steerage to Congress. American Mercury 22: 508-509, April, 1931. Sidelights on an Heroic Epoch.

BARTLETT, FREDERICK ORIN.
New Lives for Old, by William Carleton [pseud.] Smart Set 40: 156, Aug., 1913. A Counterblast to Buncombe.
On Way Out, by William Carleton [pseud.] Smart Set 33: 163-164, April, 1911. The Meredith of Tomorrow.
The Prodigal Pro Tem. Smart Set 33: 161, March, 1911. A Stack of Novels.
The Seventh Noon. Smart Set 30: 158, April, 1910. A Glance at the Spring Fiction.

BARTON, WILLIAM ELEAZAR. The Soul of Abraham Lincoln. Smart Set 62: 140-142, May, 1920. More Notes From A Diary—II.

BARWELL, NOEL. Someone Pays. Smart Set 28: 155, July, 1909. The Best Novels of the Year.

BASS, ARCHER BRYAN. Protestantism in the United States. American Mercury 17: 123, 125, May, 1929. The Gods and Their Agents.

BAVINK, BERNHARD. The Natural Sciences. American Mercury 30: 379-380, Nov., 1933. Science vs. Religion.

BAZALGETTE, LÉON. Walt Whitman: The Man and His Work, translated from the French by Ellen FitzGerald. Smart Set 62: 140,142, May, 1920. More Notes From A Diary—II.

BEARD, CHARLES A. and MARY R. The Rise of American Civilization. American Mercury 12: 250-252, Oct., 1927. Kultur in the Republic.

BEASLEY, GERTRUDE. My First Thirty Years. American Mercury 7: 123-125, Jan., 1926. A Texas Schoolmarm.

BECHHOFER, C. E. *See* Roberts, Carl Eric Bechhofer.

BECK, L. ADAMS. The Story of Oriental Philosophy. American Mercury 15: 254-255, Oct., 1928. Blather from the East.

BECKLEY, ZOË. A Chance To Live. Smart Set 58: 141, March, 1919. Mainly Fiction.

BEDFORD, JESSIE. The Cradle of a Poet, by Elizabeth Godfrey [pseud.] Smart Set 32: 165, Dec., 1910. Mainly About Novels.

BOOK REVIEWS

BEER, THOMAS.

The Fair Rewards. Smart Set 67: 141-142, April, 1922. The Niagara of Novels —II.

Hanna. American Mercury 19: 122-125, Jan., 1930. American Worthies.

The Mauve Decade: American Life at the End of the Nineteenth Century. American Mercury 8: 382-383, July, 1926. The End of the Century.

Stephen Crane; a Study in American Letters. [Baltimore] Evening Sun, Jan. 19, 1924; Dial 76: 73-74, Jan. 24, 1924.

BEERBOHM, MAX.

Yet Again. Smart Set 31: 159, June, 1910. The Greatest of American Writers.

Zuleika Dobson. Smart Set 37: 153-156, July, 1912. A Dip into the Novels; 46: 294, June, 1915. Here are novels!

BEHIND THE SCENES IN POLITICS; a Confession. American Mercury 3: 252-253, Oct., 1924. Hornswoggling the Rabble.

BEITH, JOHN HAY. The Right Stuff, by Ian Hay [pseud.] Smart Set 31: 155, Aug., 1910. A Hot Weather Novelist.

BEKKER, PAUL. Beethoven. American Mercury 7: 509-510, April, 1926. Old Ludwig.

BELL, CLIVE. Civilization. American Mercury 16: 122-124, Jan., 1929. What Is Civilization?

BELL, LILIAN. The Concentrations of Bee. Smart Set 30: 156, Feb., 1910. Books To Read and Books To Avoid.

BENEDICT, A. L. Why We Are Men and Women. American Mercury 18: 126-127, Sept., 1929. The Fruits of Emancipation.

BENEFIELD, BARRY. Short Turns. American Mercury 9: 382, Nov., 1926. Certain Works of Fiction.

BENN, ERNEST J. P. The Confessions of a Capitalist. American Mercury 9: 126-127, Sept., 1926. Babbitt as Philosopher.

BENNETT, ARNOLD.

Books and Persons. Smart Set 54: 143-144, April, 1918. Business—IV.

Denry the Audacious. Smart Set 34: 166, May, 1911. Novels—The Spring Crop.

The Gates of Wrath. Smart Set 48: 155, April, 1916. The Publishers Begin Their Spring Drive.

Hilda Lessways. Smart Set 36: 157-158, Jan., 1912. Conrad, Bennett, James, Et Al.

Lilian. Smart Set 71: 140, July, 1923. Some New Books—II.

The Lion's Share. Smart Set 57: 140-142, Dec., 1918. The Late Mr. Wells—II.

Paris Nights. Smart Set 42: 153, 154-155, Feb., 1914. Anything But Novels!

The Pretty Lady. Smart Set 55: 140-141, Aug., 1918. A Sub-Potomac Phenomenon—II.

The Roll-Call. Smart Set 59: 141-142, June, 1919. The Infernal Mystery—III.

These Twain. Smart Set 48: 156, Feb., 1916. A Massacre in a Mausoleum.

WORKS BY H. L. M.

Things That Have Interested Me. Smart Set 65: 143-144, July, 1921. Literary Notes—III.

What the Public Wants. Smart Set 35: 153-154, Oct., 1911. Brieux and Others. [Appraisal.] Smart Set 60: 138-144, Sept., 1919.

BENSON, ALLEN L. The New Henry Ford. [Baltimore] Evening Sun, Sept. 15, 1923.

BENSON, E. F.
The Climber. Smart Set 27: 158, April, 1909. The Novels That Bloom in the Spring, Tra-La!

The Fascinating Mrs. Halton. Smart Set 31: 158, July, 1910. A Fictioneer of the Laboratory.

The Freaks of Mayfair. Smart Set 54: 141-142, Feb., 1918. The National Letters—III.

Mrs. Ames. Smart Set 38: 155-156, Dec., 1912. A Visit to a Short Story Factory.

Thorley Weir. Smart Set 42: 153-154, Jan., 1914. A Pestilence of Novels.

BENT, SILAS. Justice Oliver Wendell Holmes. American Mercury 26: 123-126, May, 1932. The Great Holmes Mystery.

BERCOVICI, KONRAD. Ghitza. Smart Set 67: 142-143, April, 1922. The Niagara of Novels—III.

BERESFORD, J. D.
The Candidate for Truth. Smart Set 38: 156-157, Sept., 1912. Prose Fiction Ad Infinitum.

The Early History of Jacob Stahl. Smart Set 34: 157-158, Aug., 1911. The New Dramatic Literature.

God's Counterpoint. Smart Set 58: 141-142, Jan., 1919. Nothing Much Is Here, Alas!—III.

These Lynnekers. Smart Set 50: 283, Nov., 1916. Professors at the Bat—III.

BERGSON, HENRI. Dreams. Smart Set 44: 157, Oct., 1914. A Review of Reviewers.

BERKMAN, ALEXANDER. The Bolshevik Myth. Chicago Sunday Tribune, April, 26, 1925. Two Wasted Lives.

BERL, EMMANUEL. The Nature of Love. American Mercury 3: 510, Dec., 1924. Brief Notices.

BERNAYS, EDWARD L. Crystallizing Public Opinion. American Mercury 7: 123-124, May, 1924. Training for Press Agents.

BETTS, GEORGE HERBERT. The Beliefs of 700 Ministers. American Mercury 17: 509-510, Aug., 1929. The Pastors and Their Dogmas.

BEVERIDGE, ALBERT J. Abraham Lincoln, 1809-1858. American Mercury 16: 381-382, March, 1929. The Early Lincoln.

BHARTRIHARI. The Satakas, or Wise Sayings of Bhartrihari, translated by J. M. Kennedy. Town Topics 71: 18-19, June 4, 1914. Buncombe from the Orient.

BIBESCO, MARTHE LUCIE (LAHOVARY) "Princess G. V. Bibesco." I Have Only

Myself To Blame. Smart Set 67: 143, April, 1922. The Niagara of Novels—III.

BIBLE. N. T. English. The Riverside New Testament, a translation from the original Greek into the English of today by William G. Ballentine. Smart Set 72: 138-142, Oct., 1923. Holy Writ.

BIBLE. O. T. Translated by J. M. Powis Smith. N. T. translated by Edgar J. Goodspeed. [Baltimore] Evening Sun., Dec. 5, 1931. New Translation of the Bible.

BIERCE, AMBROSE. In the Midst of Life. Smart Set 57: 144, Oct., 1918. Suite Élégiaque—III.

BIGGERS, EARL DERR.
Love Insurance. Town Topics 72: 16, Oct. 29, 1914. Novels of No Importance.
The Seven Keys to Baldpate. Smart Set 40: 157, May, 1913. Weep for the White Slave!

BINDLOSS, HAROLD. Sidney Carteret, Rancher. Smart Set 33 :164, April, 1911.
The Meredith of Tomorrow.

BIRD, WILLIAM. A Practical Guide to French Wines. American Mercury 3: 381-382, Nov., 1924. Paradise Lost.

BIRMINGHAM, G. A., pseud. See Hannay, James Owen.

BISHOP, JOHN PEALE. The Undertaker's Garland, by John Peale Bishop and Edmund Wilson, Jr. Smart Set 70: 143-144, March, 1923. Adventures Among Books—III.

BJÖRKMAN, EDWIN AUGUST.
The Modern Drama Series. Smart Set 44: 157-159, Sept., 1914. Thirty-five Printed Plays.
Voices of Tomorrow. Smart Set 41: 157-158, Nov., 1913. Marie Corelli's Sparring Partner.

BJØRNSON, BJØRNSTJERNE. Plays, Second Series. Smart Set 43: 156, July, 1914. Galsworthy and Others.

BLACK, GEORGE FRASER. The Surnames of Scotland. New York Herald Tribune Books p. 7, Dec. 29, 1946. 7,000 Scottish Family Names.

BLACKWELL, ALICE STONE. Lucy Stone; Pioneer of Woman's Rights. American Mercury 21: 506-508, Dec., 1930. A Primeval Uplifter.

BLACKWOOD, ALGERNON.
Incredible Adventures. Smart Set 45: 153, Feb., 1915. Lachrymose Love.
Jimbo, a Fantasy. Smart Set 28: 158, May, 1909. Some Novels—and a Good One.
John Silence, Physician Extraordinary. Smart Set 28: 156, June, 1909. Books for the Hammock and Deck Chair.

BLAKE, MARGARET, pseud. See Schem, Lida Clara.

BLAMFIELD, CHARLES. Basic Aims. American Mercury 6: 251-254, Oct., 1925.
Poetry.

BLAND, EDITH (NESBIT). The House with No Address, by E. Nesbit. Smart Set 28: 156, June, 1909. Books for the Hammock and Deck Chair.

BLANKENSHIP, RUSSELL. American Literature As an Expression of the National Mind. American Mercury 24: 507-508, Dec., 1931. The American As Literatus.

BLATCHFORD, ROBERT. Not Guilty. Smart Set 57: 143, Oct., 1918. Suite Élégiaque —III.

BLEACKLEY, HORACE WILLIAM. Ladies Fair and Frail. Smart Set 28: 158, June, 1909. Books for the Hammock and Deck Chair.

BLEYER, WILLARD GROSVENOR, ed. The Profession of Journalism. Smart Set 55: 140, July, 1918. The Public Prints—II.

BLUNT, WILFRID SCAWEN. My Diaries. Smart Set 69: 143, Sept., 1922. The Coroner's Inquest; 69: 140-143, Nov., 1922. Chiefly Pathological—II.

BLYTHE, SAMUEL GEORGE. The Old Game. Smart Set 44: 158, Oct., 1914. A Review of Reviewers; Town Topics 72: 14, Aug. 13, 1914. Good-Bye, Booze!

BOAS, FRANZ. Anthropology and Modern Life. American Mercury 16: 122-124, Jan., 1929. What Is Civilization?

BODENHEIM, MAXWELL.
Blackguard. Smart Set 71: 140-141, June, 1923. Notices of Books—IV— Nietzsche in Greenwich Village.
Replenishing Jessica. American Mercury 5: 507, 509-510, Aug., 1925. Novels Good and Bad.

BOGARDUS, EMORY STEPHEN. Fundamentals of Social Psychology. [Baltimore] Evening Sun, June 7, 1924. Mencken Lambasts a "Diligent and Dreadful Effort"; American Mercury 2: 506, Aug., 1924. Mankind in the Mass.

BOJER, JOHAN.
The Great Hunger. Smart Set 58: 141-142, March, 1919. Mainly Fiction.
The Power of a Lie, translated from the Norwegian by Jessie Muir. Smart Set 28: 154-156, May, 1909. Some Novels—and a Good One; 28: 153-154, July, 1909.

BOK, EDWARD WILLIAM.
The Americanization of Edward Bok. Smart Set 64: 140-142, Jan., 1921. Consolation—II—The Incomparable Bok.
A Man from Maine. [Baltimore] Evening Sun, May 26, 1923; Smart Set 71: 139-141, Aug., 1923. Biography and Other Fiction—II.

BOOTH, EDWARD CHARLES. The Doctor's Lass. Smart Set 32: 165, Dec., 1910. Mainly About Novels.

BOOTH, MEYRICK. Women and Society. American Mercury 18: 126-127, Sept., 1929. The Fruits of Emancipation.

BORDEAUX, HENRY. The Fear of Living, [translated] by Ruth Helen Davis. Smart Set 40: 155-157, July, 1913. Various Bad Novels.

BORUP, GEORGE. A Tenderfoot with Peary. Smart Set 34: 152, June, 1911. The Horse Power of Realism.

BOOK REVIEWS

THE BORZOI CLASSICS [ser.] American Mercury 3: 508-509, Dec., 1928. Reprints.

THE BORZOI PLAYS. Smart Set 52: 398-399, May, 1917. Shocking Stuff—3.

BOULE, MARCELLIN. Fossil Man. Chicago Sunday Tribune, Aug. 29, 1926. Man as a Mammal.

BOULTON, WILLIAM B. In the Days of the Georges. Smart Set 31: 159, July, 1910. A Fictioneer of the Laboratory.

BOURNE, RANDOLPH SILLIMAN. The History of a Literary Radical, edited by Van Wyck Brooks. Smart Set 64: 142-143, March, 1921. A Soul's Adventures—III.

BOWDEN, ROBERT DOUGLAS. In Defense of Tomorrow. American Mercury 25: 379-383, March, 1932. The Case for Democracy.

BOWER, B. M., pseud. See Sinclair, Bertha (Muzzy).

BOWER, LAHMAN FORREST. The Economic Waste of Sin. American Mercury 4: 253-255, Feb., 1925. Babbitt als Philosoph.

BOWERS, CLAUDE GERNADE.
Jefferson and Hamilton: The Struggle for Democracy in America. American Mercury 7: 381-383, March, 1926. The Heroic Age.
The Tragic Era: The Revolution After Lincoln. American Mercury 18: 381-382, Nov., 1929. Memorials of Dishonor.

BOYD, ERNEST AUGUSTUS.
Appreciations and Depreciations. Smart Set 54: 140, Feb., 1918. The National Letters—II.
The Contemporary Drama of Ireland. Smart Set 53: 144, Sept., 1917. Si Mutare Protest Aethiops Pellum Suam—IV.
Ireland's Literary Renaissance. Smart Set 51: 138-141, March, 1917. The Books of the Irish.
Ireland's Literary Renaissance. (new edition) Smart Set 70: 140-141, March, 1923. Adventures Among Books—II. Reprinted as pamphlet.
Literary Blasphemies. American Mercury 13: 254-255, Feb., 1928. The Third Degree.
Studies From Ten Literatures. American Mercury 5: 252-254, June, 1925. Four Critics of Letters.

BOYD, WOODWARD, pseud. See Shane, Peggy (Smith).

BOYESEN, ALGERNON. Napoleon. Smart Set 30: 158, March, 1910. The Literary Heavyweight Champion.

BRABY, MAUD CHURTON. Modern Marriage and How To Bear It. Smart Set 27: 153-154, March, 1909. The Literary Clinic.

BRADFORD, GAMALIEL.
American Portraits: 1875-1900. New York Evening Post Literary Review, p. 562, April 8, 1922. Spiritual Autopsies.
Bare Souls. American Mercury 5: 510, Aug., 1925. Other Biographies.
D. L. Moody: Worker in Souls. American Mercury 13: 251-252, Feb., 1928. Three Americans.

Damaged Souls. New York Evening Post Literary Review, p. 746, June 9, 1923. Gentlemen With Complexes.

The Soul of Samuel Pepys. American Mercury 2: 377-380, July, 1924. The Bradford Formula.

BRAINERD, ELEANOR HOYT. The Personal Conduct of Belinda. Smart Set 31: 157, June, 1910. The Greatest of American Writers.

BRANDES, GEORG. Friedrich Nietzsche. Town Topics 72: 16, July 30, 1914. The Prophet of the Superman.

BRANN, WILLIAM COWPER. The Complete Works of Brann, the Iconoclast. Smart Set 71: 144, Aug., 1923. Biography and Other Fiction—VI.

BRASOL, BORIS LEE. The Elements of Crime. [Baltimore] Evening Sun, Jan. 14, 1928. Criminology is on a Level with Chiropractic and Fortune Telling; American Mercury 13: 379-381, March, 1928. The Ways of the Wicked.

BRATTER, CARL ADOLF. Amerika von Washington bis Wilson. American Mercury 1: 507-508, April, 1924. God's Country: Exterior View.

BRAY, MARY MATTHEWS. My Grandmother's Garden. Smart Set 33: 168, March, 1911. A Stack of Novels.

BREGENZER, DON, ed. A Round-Table in Poictesme: A Symposium. American Mercury 2: 254-255, June, 1924. Cabelliana.

BRENNECKE, ERNEST. The Life of Thomas Hardy. American Mercury 5: 510, Aug., 1925. Other Biographies.

BRIEUX, EUGÈNE.
Blanchette. Smart Set 42: 156-157, Feb., 1914. Anything But Novels!

The Escape. Smart Set 42: 156-157, Feb., 1914. Anything But Novels!

Three Plays by Brieux, with Preface by Bernard Shaw; English versions by Mrs. Bernard Shaw [and others]. Smart Set 35: 151-153, Oct., 1911. Brieux and Others.

BRIFFAULT, ROBERT. Sin and Sex. American Mercury 23: 253-255, June, 1931. A Gloss upon Christian Morality.

THE BROADWAY TRANSLATIONS [ser.] American Mercury 3: 508, Dec., 1924. Reprints.

BROCK, HENRY IRVING. Meddlers, Uplifting Moral Uplifters. American Mercury 20: 254, June, 1930. The Smut-Snufflers.

BROGAN, DENNIS WILLIAM. Government of the People: A Study in the American Political System. Nation 137: 487, Oct. 25, 1933. American Politics.

BRONNER, MILTON. Maurice Hewlett, Being a Critical Review of His Prose and Poetry. Smart Set 32: 168, Oct., 1910. Meredith's Swan Song.

BROOKE, RUPERT. Collected Poems. Smart Set 49:306, May, 1916. Tra-la! Tra-la la! Tra-la la la!

BROOKS, JOHN GRAHAM. As Others See Us. Smart Set 27: 158-159, Feb., 1909. The Literary Olio.

BOOK REVIEWS

BROOKS, VAN WYCK.

Letters and Leadership. Smart Set 58: 138-142, Feb., 1919. Sunrise on the Prairie.

The Ordeal of Mark Twain. Smart Set 68: 138-144, Oct., 1920. Groping in Literary Darkness.

BROUN, HEYWOOD.

Anthony Comstock, by Heywood Broun and Margaret Leech. New York Herald Tribune Books, p. 1, March 6, 1927. The Emperor of Wowsers.

Christians Only, by Heywood Broun and George Britt. American Mercury 23: 123-126, May, 1931. The Curse of Prejudice.

BROUSSON, JEAN JACQUES. Anatole France Himself. American Mercury 5: 510, Aug., 1925. Other Biographies.

BROWN, DEMETRA (VAKA).

The Duke's Price. Smart Set 30: 159, April, 1910. A Glance at the Spring Fiction.

Haremlik. Smart Set 28: 154-155, Aug., 1909. Novels and Other Books—Chiefly Bad.

In the Shadow of Islam. Smart Set 36: 155, Feb., 1912. Rounding up the Novels.

BROWN, IVOR JOHN CARNEGIE. First Player: The Origin of Drama. American Mercury 16: 122-124, Jan., 1929. What Is Civilization?

BROWN, JOSEPH M. Astyanax. Smart Set 31: 159, June, 1910. The Greatest of American Writers.

BROWNE, LEWIS. Since Calvary. American Mercury 25: 506-510, April, 1932. Quod Est Veritas?

BROWNE, WALDO RALPH. Altgeld of Illinois. American Mercury 3: 250-251, Oct., 1924. Heretics.

BROWNELL, WILLIAM CRARY. The Genius of Style. American Mercury 4: 381-382, March, 1925. What Is Style?

BRULLER, JEAN. 21 Recettes Pratiques de Mort Violente. American Mercury 13: 125-126, Jan., 1928. A Useful Textbook.

BRUNO, GUIDO. The Sacred Band: A Litany of Ingratitude. Smart Set 67: 140-141, Feb., 1922. Frank Harris and Others—II.

BRYCE, JAMES, viscount.

Modern Democracies. Smart Set 66: 138-141, Sept., 1921. From the Diary of a Reviewer.

The Story of a Plough Boy. Smart Set 38: 156, Sept., 1912. Prose Fiction Ad Infinitum.

BUCHHOLZ, HEINRICH EWALD.

Of What Use Are the Common People? [Baltimore] Evening Sun, July 21, 1923. Common People Dissected.

U.S. A Second Study in Democracy. Nation 123: 374, Oct. 13, 1926. A Cure for Democracy.

BUCK, ALBERT HENRY. The Dawn of Modern Medicine. Nation 112: 87-88, Jan. 19, 1921. Chapters of Medical History.

BUCKNER, JAMES DYSART MONROE. How I Lost My Job As a Preacher. Smart Set 70: 143-144, Jan., 1923. Confidences—IV.

BULWER-LYTTON, EDWARD ROBERT. *See* Lytton, Edward Robert Bulwer-Lytton, *1st earl* of.

BURGESS, GELETT. Lady Méchante. Smart Set 30: 155, Feb., 1910. Books To Read and Books To Avoid.

BURGESS, JOHN WILLIAM. Recent Changes in American Constitutional Theory. American Mercury 1: 121-122, Jan., 1924. The New Freedom.

BURHANS, VIOLA. The Cave Woman, a Novel of Today. Smart Set 32: 168, Nov., 1910. A Guide to Intelligent Eating.

BURKE, KENNETH. The White Oxen, and Other Stories. American Mercury 6: 381, Nov., 1925. Fiction Good and Bad.

BURLINGAME, ANNE ELIZABETH. The Battle of the Books. Smart Set 65: 141, June, 1921. Books About Books—II.

BURNS, WALTER NOBLE. The Saga of Billy the Kid. American Mercury 8: 125-127, May, 1926. A Hero of the Open Spaces.

BURR, JANE, *pseud*. The Glorious Hope. Smart Set 58: 142, Jan., 1919. Nothing Much Is Here, Alas!—III.

BURTT, EDWIN ARTHUR. Religion in an Age of Science. American Mercury 18: 253-254, Oct., 1929. Ghostly Matters.

BUTLER, FRANK HEDGES. Wine and the Wine Lands of the World. American Mercury 11: 381-382, July, 1927. A Book for Bibbers.

BUTLER, SAMUEL. The Collected Works of Samuel Butler. Shrewsbury edition American Mercury 14: 251-253, June, 1928. Two Gay Rebels.

BYNNER, WITTER. Tiger. Smart Set 41: 159, Nov., 1913. Marie Corelli's Sparring Partner.

BYWATER, HECTOR CHARLES. The Great Pacific War: A History of The American-Japanese Campaign of 1931-33. American Mercury 6: 507-508, Dec., 1925. The Next War.

CABELL, JAMES BRANCH.
Beyond Life. Smart Set 58: 142-143, March, 1919. Mainly Fiction—II.

Cords of Vanity. Smart Set 28: 155-156, June, 1909. Books for the Hammock and Deck Chair.

The Cream of the Jest. Smart Set 53: 143, Dec., 1917. Critics Wild and Tame —IV.

Figures of Earth. Smart Set 65: 142-143, May, 1921. The Land of the Free —III; [Baltimore] Evening Sun, March 12, 1921. New Cabell Book on Snouters.

Gallantry. Smart Set 69: 144, Nov., 1922. Chiefly Pathological.

The High Place. American Mercury 1: 380-381, March, 1924. Three Gay Stories.

BOOK REVIEWS

Jurgen. Smart Set 61: 138-140, Jan., 1920. The Flood of Fiction.

The Silver Stallion: A Comedy of Redemption. American Mercury 8: 509-510, Aug., 1926. Fiction.

Something About Eve. American Mercury 12: 510, Dec., 1927. A Comedy of Fig-Leaves.

The Storisende Edition of the Works of James Branch Cabell. American Mercury 14: 251-253, June, 1928. Two Gay Rebels.

Straws and Prayer-Books: Dizain des Diversions. American Mercury 3: 509-510, Dec., 1924. Cabell.

The Way of Ecben: A Comedietta Involving a Gentleman. American Mercury 19: 126-127, Jan., 1930. Fiction by Adept Hands.

The White Robe. American Mercury 16: 508-509, April, 1929. The story of a Saint.

[Appraisal—Chicago Applauds.] Smart Set 55: 138-140, Aug., 1918. A Sub-Potomac Phenomenon.

CABOT, RICHARD CLARKE. What Men Live By: Work, Play, Love, Worship. Smart Set 44: 156, Oct., 1914. A Review of Reviewers.

CAHAN, ABRAHAM. The Rise of David Levinsky. Smart Set 55: 138-140, May, 1918. The Stream of Fiction. [Comments] 58: 141, Jan., 1919.

CAIN, JAMES MALLAHAN. Our Government. American Mercury 21: 126-127, Sept., 1930. Risum Teneatis?

CAINE, HALL.
My Story. Smart Set 29: 154-155, Sept., 1909. The Books of the Dog Days.

The White Prophet. Smart Set 29: 154-155, Dec., 1909. "A Doll's House"— with a Fourth Act.

The Woman Thou Gavest Me. Smart Set 41: 154-155, Nov., 1913. Marie Corelli's Sparring Partner.

CALTHROP, DION CLAYTON. Perpetua, or The Way To Treat a Woman. Smart Set 35: 157, Oct., 1911. Brieux and Others.

CALVERTON, VICTOR FRANCIS. The Newer Spirit. American Mercury 5: 252-253, June, 1925. Four Critics of Letters.

THE CAMBRIDGE ANCIENT HISTORY, v. 5: Athens. American Mercury 12: 254-255, Oct., 1927. The Greeks.

THE CAMBRIDGE HISTORY OF AMERICAN LITERATURE. Smart Set 54: 138-140, Feb., 1918 (v.3) The National Letters; 59: 138,142, July, 1919 (v.2) The Coroner's Inquest; 65: 138-141, June, 1921 (last 2 v.) Books About Books.

CANBY, HENRY SEIDEL. American Estimates. Saturday Review of Literature 5: 849-850, April 6, 1929. Light and Reading.

CANNAN, GILBERT.
The Anatomy of Society. Smart Set 61: 142-143, Feb., 1920. From the Diary of a Reviewer (Dec., 1913).

Round the Corner. Smart Set 43: 159, June, 1914. The Anatomy of the Novel.

WORKS BY H. L. M.

CANNON, WALTER BRADFORD. The Wisdom of the Body. American Mercury 26: 282-283, July, 1932. The Machine That Is Man.

CANTOR, NATHANIEL FREEMAN. Crime, Criminals and Criminal Justice. American Mercury 26: 379-382, July, 1932. Notes on an Insoluble Problem.

CARDOZO, BENJAMIN NATHAN. The Paradoxes of Legal Science. American Mercury 15: 123-125, Sept., 1928. The Curse of Government.

CARLETON, WILLIAM, *pseud. See* Bartlett, Frederick Orin.

CARLISLE, DONALD THOMPSON. Wining and Dining with Rhyme and Reason, by D. T. Carlisle and Elizabeth Dunn. Nation 138: 193, Feb. 14, 1934. For Thy Stomach's Sake.

CARMAN, BLISS. The Making of Personality. Smart Set 26: 155, Dec., 1908. Oyez! Oyez! All Ye Who Read Books.

CARMICHAEL, WAVERLY TURNER. From the Heart of a Folk. Smart Set 58: 142-143, April, 1919. Notes of a Poetry-Hater—V.

CAROTTI, GIULIO. A History of Art. American Mercury 1: 380, March, 1924. Art Criticism.

CARPENTER, EDWARD. The Dream of Love and Death. Smart Set 38: 153, Dec., 1912. A Visit to a Short Story Factory.

CARPENTER, NILES. The Sociology of City Life. American Mercury 25: 123-125, Jan., 1932. How Americans Live.

CARRINGTON, HEREWARD. Eusapia Palladino and Her Phenomena. Smart Set 30: 159-160, April, 1910. A Glance at the Spring Fiction.

CARSON, ROSE M. Through the Valley of the Shadow and Beyond. Smart Set 27: 154, Feb., 1909. The Literary Olio.

CARSON, WILLIAM ENGLISH. Northcliffe; Britain's Man of Power. Smart Set 55: 140-141, July, 1918. The Public Prints—II.

CARTER, WILLIAM GILES HARDING. The American Army. Smart Set 46: 296, June, 1915. Here Are Novels!

CASE, SHIRLEY JACKSON. Jesus through the Centuries. American Mercury 25: 506-510, April, 1932. Quod Est Veritas?

CASTAIGNE, ANDRÉ. The Bill-Toppers. Smart Set 29: 155, Oct., 1909. The Last of the Victorians.

CASTLE, AGNES (SWEETMAN). Panther's Cub, by Agnes and Egerton Castle. Smart Set 34: 154, July, 1911. Novels for Hot Afternoons.

CATHER, WILLA SIBERT.
Alexander's Bridge. Smart Set 38: 156-157, Dec., 1912. A Visit to a Short Story Factory.
Death Comes for the Archbishop. American Mercury 12: 508-510, Dec., 1927. The Desert Epic.
A Lost Lady. American Mercury 1: 253, Feb., 1924. Three Volumes of Fiction.

My Antonia. Smart Set 58: 143-144, Feb., 1919. Sunrise on the Prairie; 58: 138-141, March, 1919. Mainly Fiction.

One of Ours. Smart Set 69: 140-142, Oct., 1922. Portrait of an American Citizen—II.

The Professor's House. American Mercury 6: 380, Nov., 1925. Fiction Good and Bad.

The Song of the Lark. Smart Set 68: 306-307, Jan., 1916. Partly About Books —4—Cinderella the Nth.

Youth and the Bright Medusa. Smart Set 63: 139-140, Dec., 1920. Chiefly Americans.

CATLIN, GEORGE BYRON. The Story of Detroit. American Mercury 1: 505,507, April, 1924. Provincial Literature.

CAVAN, RUTH SHONLE. Suicide. American Mercury 13: 508-510, April, 1928. Swing Low, Sweet Chariot!

CAWEIN, MADISON JULIUS. New Poems. Smart Set 31: 160, Aug., 1910. A Hot Weather Novelist.

CHAFEE, ZECHARIAH.
Freedom of Speech in War Times. Smart Set 65: 138-140, May, 1921. The Land of the Free.

The Inquiring Mind. American Mercury 15: 123-125, Sept., 1928. The Curse of Government.

CHAFER, LEWIS SPERRY. Satan. Smart Set 29: 158, Oct., 1909. The Last of the Victorians.

CHAMBERLAIN, LUCIA. Son of the Wind. Smart Set 33: 163, March, 1911. A Stack of Novels.

CHAMBERS, ROBERT WILLIAM.
The Adventures of a Modest Man. Smart Set 34: 166, May, 1911. Novels— The Spring Crop.

Ailsa Page. Smart Set 33: 164, Jan., 1911. The Leading American Novelist.

The Business of Life. Smart Set 41: 159, Dec., 1913. The Russians.

The Gay Rebellion. Smart Set 40: 155-156, July, 1913. Various Bad Novels.

CHASE, STUART. Technocracy: An Interpretation. American Mercury 28: 505-507, April, 1933. Old Dr. Scott's Bile Beans.

CHATTERTON-HILL, GEORGES. The Philosophy of Nietzsche. Smart Set 40: 156-157, Aug., 1913. A Counterblast to Buncombe.

CHEEVER, EZEKIEL, pseud. See Buchholz, Heinrich Ewald.

CHEKHOV, ANTON PAVLOVICH. Nine Humorous Tales, translated by Isaac Goldberg and Henry T. Schmittkind. Smart Set 55: 141-142, July, 1918. The Public Prints—III.

CHENEY, SHELDON. A Primer of Modern Art. American Mercury 2: 510, Aug., 1924. Brief Notices.

CHERRY-GARRAND, APSLEY GEORGE BENET. The Worst Journey in the World. American Mercury 21: 123-124, Sept., 1930. Penguin's Eggs.

CHESTER, GEORGE RANDOLPH.
The Cash Intrigue. Smart Set 30: 154, Feb., 1910. Books To Read and Books To Avoid.

The Making of Bobby Burnit. Smart Set 29: 155-156, Oct., 1909. The Last of the Victorians.

CHESTERTON, GILBERT KEITH.
Alarms and Discursions. Smart Set 34: 168, May, 1911. Novels—The Spring Crop.

The Ball and the Cross. Smart Set 30: 153-154, March, 1910. The Literary Heavyweight Champion.

The Flying Inn. Smart Set 42: 151-152, April, 1914. Roosevelt, Bulwer-Lytton and Anthony Comstock.

George Bernard Shaw. Smart Set 30: 153-154, Jan., 1910. George Bernard Shaw As A Hero.

Gilbert K. Chesterton: A Criticism. Smart Set 28: 159, May, 1909. Some Novels—and a Good One.

Orthodoxy. Smart Set 27: 154-155, Feb., 1909. The Literary Olio.

What's Wrong with the World. Smart Set 33: 165, Jan., 1911. The Leading American Novelist.

CHILDS, JESSIE DOW (HOPKINS). The Sea of Matrimony. Smart Set 30: 157, April, 1910. A Glance at the Spring Fiction.

CHINARD, GILBERT. Thomas Jefferson: The Apostle of Americanism. American Mercury 19: 122-125, Jan., 1930. American Worthies.

CHURCHILL, JENNIE (JEROME) "Lady Randolph Churchill." The Reminiscences of Lady Randolph Churchill, by Mrs. George Cornwallis-West. Smart Set 27: 157-158, Jan., 1909. A Road Map of the New Books.

CHURCHILL, WINSTON.
A Far Country. Smart Set 46: 150-154, Aug., 1915. The Sawdust Trail.

The Inside of the Cup. Smart Set 41: 158-160, Sept., 1913. Getting Rid of the Actor.

A Modern Chronicle. Smart Set 31: 156, July, 1910. A Fictioneer of the Laboratory.

CLARK, BARRETT HARPER.
Contemporary French Dramatists. Smart Set 47: 308, Nov., 1915. After All, Why Not?

European Theories of the Drama, edited by Barrett H. Clark. Smart Set 58: 142, Feb., 1919. Sunrise on the Prairie—IV.

CLARK, ELLERY HARDING. Loaded Dice. Smart Set 28: 157, June, 1909. Books for the Hammock and Deck Chair.

CLARK, EMILY. Stuffed Peacocks. American Mercury 14: 127, May, 1928. Fiction.

CLARK, EVANS, ed. The Internal Debts of the United States. American Mercury 30: 122-126, Sept., 1933. Laugh, Suckers, Laugh!

CLEMENS, SAMUEL LANGHORNE. See Twain, Mark, pseud.

BOOK REVIEWS

[CLEMENTS, MRS. M. E.] The Den of the Sixteenth Section. Smart Set 36: 155, Feb., 1912. Rounding up Novels.

CLENDENING, LOGAN. The Human Body. Nation 125: 427, Oct. 19, 1927. Man as a Mechanism.

CLIFFORD, SIR HUGH CHARLES.
The Further Side of Silence. Smart Set 51: 268, Jan., 1917. Suffering Among Books.

Malayan Monochromes. Smart Set 44: 152, Nov., 1914. Critics of More or Less Badness; Town Topics 72: 16, Aug. 29, 1914. Conrad and His Discoverer.

CLIFFORD, LUCY (LANE) "Mrs. W. K. Clifford." Plays: Hamlet's Second Marriage; Thomas and the Princess; The Modern Way, by Mrs. W. K. Clifford. Smart Set 31: 159, Aug., 1910. A Hot Weather Novelist.

COBB, FRANK IRVING. Cobb of the *World*; A Leader in Liberalism, compiled from his editorial articles and public addresses by John L. Heaton. American Mercury 3: 127, Sept., 1924. Frank I. Cobb.

COBB, IRVIN SHREWSBURY.
Anatomy. Smart Set 39: 155, Feb., 1913. The Burden of Humor.

Speaking of Operations. Smart Set 48: 157, Feb., 1916. A Massacre in a Mausoleum; 48: 307-310, March, 1916. The Great American Art.

Those Times and These. Smart Set 53: 143, Sept., 1917. Si Mutare Potest Aethiops Pellum Suam—III.

COHEN, LESTER. Sweepings. American Mercury 9: 382, Nov., 1926. Certain Works of Fiction.

COHEN, MORRIS RAPHAEL. Reason and Nature. American Mercury 24: 123-124, Sept., 1931. In the Grove of Athene.

COLEMAN, LOYD RING. Psychology; a Simplification. American Mercury 11: 382-383, July, 1927. Psychology.

COLEMAN, MCALLISTER. Eugene V. Debs; a Man Unafraid. American Mercury 20: 507-508, Aug., 1930. An American Dreamer.

COLERIDGE, STEPHEN. Memories. Smart Set 40: 155, Aug., 1913. A Counterblast to Buncombe.

COLLIER, PRICE. Germany and the Germans, from an American Point of View. Smart Set 41: 156-158, Sept., 1913. Getting Rid of the Actor.

COLLINS, JOSEPH. The Doctor Looks at Literature. Smart Set 72: 138-140, Nov., 1923. Notices of Books.

COLMORE, G., *pseud. See* Weaver, Gertrude (Renton).

COLYER, W. T. Americanism; a World Menace. Smart Set 70: 138-141, April, 1923. Americanism: Exterior View. Issued as pamphlet.

COMFORT, WILL LEVINGTON.
Down Among Men. Smart Set 42: 160, Jan., 1914. A Pestilence of Novels.

Fate Knocks at the Door. Smart Set 38: 153-155, Nov., 1912. Novels Bad, Half Bad and Very Bad.

Midstream. Town Topics 71: 19, June 25, 1914. Comfort As His Own Hero; Smart Set 43: 158-159, Aug., 1914. Adventures Among the New Novels.

Routledge Rides Alone. Smart Set 31: 157, July, 1910. A Fictioneer of the Laboratory.

She Buildeth Her House. Smart Set 35: 157-158, Oct., 1911. Brieux and Others.

CONGER, SARAH (PIKE), "Mrs. E. H. Conger." Letters From China. Smart Set 39: 157, Dec., 1909. "A Doll's House"—With a Fourth Act.

CONNOLLY, MARGARET. The Life Story of Orison Swett Marden, a Man Who Benefited Men. American Mercury 7: 252-254, Feb., 1926. A Master of Platitude.

CONRAD, JESSIE (GEORGE). Joseph Conrad and His Circle. Nation 141: 444, Oct. 16, 1935. Contribution to Martyrology.

CONRAD, JOSEPH.
The Arrow of Gold. Smart Set 59: 141-142, Aug., 1919. Novels, Chiefly Bad—III.

Chance. Smart Set 42: 153-157, March, 1914. The Raw Material of Fiction.

The Nigger of the Narcissus. Town Topics 72: 14, Aug. 13, 1914. A Glance at the Novels; 72: 16, Aug. 29, 1914. Conrad and His Discoverer.

Notes on Life and Letters. [Baltimore] Evening Sun, May 21, 1921. Conrad's "Notes" Lack Coherence; Smart Set 65: 142, July, 1921. Literary Notes—III.

A Personal Record. Smart Set 38: 147, 149-150, Oct., 1912. Synge and Others.

The Point of Honor. Smart Set 26: 153-155, Dec., 1908. Oyez! Oyez! All Ye Who Read Books.

The Rescue. Smart Set 62: 138-140, Aug., 1920. Books More or Less Amusing.

The Rover. American Mercury 1: 252-253, Feb., 1924. Three Volumes of Fiction.

Set of Six. Smart Set 45: 432-433, April, 1915. The Grandstand Flirts with the Bleachers.

The Shadow Line. Smart Set 52: 144, Aug., 1917. Criticism of Criticism of Criticism.

The Shorter Tales of Joseph Conrad, with a preface by the author. American Mercury 4: 505-507, April, 1924. The Conrad Wake.

Suspense. American Mercury 6: 379, Nov., 1925. Fiction Good and Bad.

Tales of Hearsay. American Mercury 4: 505-507, April, 1924. The Conrad Wake.

Under Western Eyes. Smart Set 36: 153-157, Jan., 1912. Conrad, Bennett, James Et Al.

Victory. Smart Set 45: 430-432, April, 1915. The Grandstand Flirts with the Bleachers.

Within the Tides. Smart Set 48: 156, April, 1916. The Publishers Begin Their Spring Drive.

Youth. Smart Set 40: 159-160, July, 1913. Various Bad Novels: 63: 142-143, Nov., 1920. Notes in the Margin—IV; 69: 141-144, Dec., 1922. The Monthly Feuilleton—IV.

COOKE, GRACE MACGOWAN. The Power and the Glory. Smart Set 32: 167, Nov., 1910. A Guide to Intelligent Eating.

BOOK REVIEWS

COOKE, MARJORIE BENTON. Bambi. Town Topics 72: 16, Oct. 29, 1914. A Dearth of Masterpieces; Smart Set 44: 305-306, Dec., 1914. Mush for the Multitudes.

COOLIDGE, CALVIN.
The Autobiography of Calvin Coolidge. American Mercury 19: 122-125, Jan., 1930. American Worthies.

The Price of Freedom. [Baltimore] Evening Sun, April 19, 1924. Coolidge, as Author, Drives Mencken into Superlatives; American Mercury 2: 252-254, June, 1924. The Heir of Lincoln.

COOPER, COURTNEY RYLEY. Lions 'N Tigers 'N Everything. American Mercury 3: 510, Dec., 1924. Brief Notices.

CORBIN, JOHN. Husband, and The Forbidden Guests. Smart Set 33: 167, Feb., 1911. The Revival of the Printed Play.

[CORDAY, MICHEL and COUVREUR, ANDRÉ.] The Inner Man, adapted from the French by Florence Crewe-Jones. Smart Set 42: 156-157, Jan., 1914. A Pestilence of Novels.

CORELLI, MARIE.
Holy Orders. Smart Set 26: 158, Nov., 1908. The Good, the Bad and the Best Sellers.

Innocent, Her Fancy and His Fact. Smart Set 45: 150-152, Feb., 1915. Lachrymose Love.

COREY, HERBERT. The Truth About Hoover. American Mercury 26: 506-508, Aug., 1932. Hoover as Archangel.

CORNERS, GEORGE F. Rejuvenation; How Steinach Makes People Young. American Mercury 1: 251, Feb., 1924. Pseudo-Science.

CORNWALLIS-WEST, MRS. GEORGE. See Churchill, Jennie (Jerome) "Lady Randolph Churchill."

COSTELLO, PIERRE. A Sinner of Israel. Smart Set 34: 166, May, 1911. Novels— The Spring Crop.

COTES, SARA JEANNETTE (DUNCAN) "Mrs. Everard Cotes." The Burnt Offering. Smart Set 31: 156, Aug., 1910. A Hot Weather Novelist.

COTTON, EDWARD HOWE, ed. Has Science Discovered God? American Mercury 25: 506-510, April, 1932. Quod Est Veritas?

COUCH, STATA B. In the Shadow of the Peaks. Smart Set 29: 157, Oct., 1909. The Last of the Victorians.

COVEY, ELIZABETH (ROCKFORD). The One and I, by Elizabeth Freemantle [pseud.] Smart Set 27: 155-156, Feb., 1909. The Literary Olio.

COX, MARIAN (METCALF).
The Crowds and the Veiled Woman. Smart Set 31: 157, June, 1910. The Greatest of American Writers.

Spiritual Curiosities. Smart Set 37: 156-157, July, 1912. A Dip into the Novels.

CRADDOCK, CHARLES EGBERT, pseud. See Murfree, Mary Noailles.

CRAIG, EDWARD GORDON. On the Art of the Theatre. Smart Set 36: 154-155, April, 1912. An Antidote to "Yankee Doodle."

WORKS BY H. L. M.

CRAM, RALPH ADAMS.
The Nemesis of Mediocrity. Smart Set 54: 141-142, April, 1918. Business—II.
The Substance of Gothic. Smart Set 55: 144, May, 1918. The Stream of Fiction—IV.
Walled Towns. Smart Set 61: 144, Feb., 1920. From the Diary of a Reviewer—(Dec., 1916)

CRAMB, JOHN ADAM. Germany and England. Smart Set 45: 463-464, Jan., 1915.
A Gamey Old Gaul.

CRANE, LEO. Indians of the Enchanted Desert. Atlantic Monthly 136: [12] Nov.
25, 1925. (No title). Reprinted in *Current Reviews*, compiled by Lewis
Worthington Smith. (New York, Holt, 1926.) p. 358-359.

CRANSTON, RUTH.
Compensation, by Anne Warwick [pseud.] Smart Set 34: 167, May, 1911.
Novels—The Spring Crop.
The Meccas of the World, by Anne Warwick [pseud.] Smart Set 42: 160,
Feb., 1914. Anything But Novels!

CRAPSEY, ALGERNON SIDNEY. The Last of the Heretics. American Mercury 3:
251-252, Oct., 1924. Heretics.

CRAVEN, PRISCILLA, *pseud. See* Shore, Mrs. Teignmouth.

CRAVEN, THOMAS. Men of Art. American Mercury 23: 379-380, July, 1931.
Painters and Their Craft.

CRAWFORD, FRANCIS MARION.
The Diva's Ruby. Smart Set 26: 159, Dec., 1908. Oyez! Oyez! All Ye Who Read
Books.
Stradella. Smart Set 29: 155, Dec., 1909. "A Doll's House"—With a Fourth Act.
The Undesirable Governess. Smart Set 31: 156, July, 1910. A Fictioneer of the
Laboratory.
Wandering Ghosts. Smart Set 34: 154, June, 1911. The Horse Power of
Realism.

CRAWFORD, MARY CAROLINE. Goethe and His Woman Friends. Smart Set 36: 156,
March, 1912. The Prophet of the Superman.

CRAWFORD, NELSON ANTRIM.
The Ethics of Journalism. American Mercury 2: 248-250, June, 1924. The
Newspaper Man.
A Man of Learning. American Mercury 14: 127, May, 1928. Fiction.

CRILE, GEORGE WASHINGTON. Man—An Adaptive Mechanism. Smart Set 60: 138-
143, Dec., 1919. Exeunt Omnes.

CROCKETT, ALBERT STEVENS. When James Gordon Bennett Was Caliph of Bagdad.
American Mercury 9: 254-255, Oct., 1926. Bennett and the Herald.

CROWNINSHIELD, FRANCIS WELCH. Manners for the Metropolis. Smart Set 27: 156,
Feb., 1909. The Literary Olio.

CROY, HOMER.
R. F. D. No. 3. American Mercury 5: 124-126, May, 1925. Fiction.

BOOK REVIEWS

West of the Water Tower. [Baltimore] Evening Sun, May 5, 1923. Mid-western Novel in Manner of the Bike and Bustle Era; Smart Set 71: 140-141, Sept., 1923. Some New Books—III.

CUNEO, SHERMAN A. From Printer to President: The Story of Warren G. Harding. Smart Set 70: 142-143, Jan., 1923. Confidences—III.

CURIE, MARIE. Pierre Curie. [Baltimore] Evening Sun, Nov. 17, 1923.

CURLE, RICHARD. Joseph Conrad; a Study. Smart Set 44: 151-152, Nov., 1914. Critics of More or Less Badness.

CURRIER, ANDREW FAY. How To Keep Well. American Mercury 3: 510, Dec., 1924. Brief Notices.

CURWOOD, JAMES OLIVER. The Danger Trail. Smart Set 30: 159, April, 1910. A Glance at the Spring Fiction.

CUSHING, HARVEY WILLIAMS. The Life of Sir William Osler. American Mercury 5: 505-507, Aug., 1925. Osler.

DABNEY, VIRGINIUS. Liberalism in the South. American Mercury 28: 251-253, Feb., 1933. The Agonies of Dixie.

DAKIN, EDWIN FRANDEN. Mrs. Eddy: The Biography of a Virginal Mind. American Mercury 18: 379-381, Nov., 1929. The Career of a Divinity.

DALEY, MYRA, *i.e.* PEARL SIMIRA. Jerd Cless. Smart Set 30: 156, Feb., 1910. Books To Read and Books To Avoid.

DANLEY, FRANK, *pseud. See* Frankau, Julia (Davis).

DARROW, CLARENCE SEWARD. Crime; Its Cause and Treatment. American Mercury 4: 122-123, Jan., 1925. Crime and Punishment.

DASGUPTA, SURENDRA NATH. Hindu Mysticism. American Mercury 12: 253, Oct., 1927. Nonsense out of the East.

D'AUVERGNE, EDMUND BASIL FRANCIS. Lola Montez. Smart Set 29: 156, Sept., 1909. The Books of the Dog Days.

DAVENPORT, WALTER. Power and Glory; the Life of Boise Penrose. American Mercury 25: 250-253, Feb., 1932. Nine American Statesmen.

DAVIDSON, JOHN.
Fleet Street and Other Poems. Smart Set 29: 159, Sept., 1909. The Books of the Dog Days.
The Man Forbid, and Other Essays. Smart Set 33: 166-167, March, 1911. A Stack of Novels.

DAVIS, CHARLES BELMONT. The Lodger Overhead. Smart Set 28: 154, Aug., 1909. Novels and Other Books—Chiefly Bad.

DAVIS, HAROLD L. Honey in the Horn. New York Herald Tribune Books, p. 1, Aug. 25, 1935. History and Fable and Very Good Stuff.

DAVIS, JEROME, *ed.* Labor Speaks for Itself on Religion. American Mercury 18: 253-254, Oct., 1929. Ghostly Matters.

DAVIS, RICHARD HARDING. The Man Who Could Not Lose. Smart Set 35: 158, Dec., 1911. An Overdose of Novels.

DAVIS, SUSAN LAWRENCE. Authentic History of the Ku Klux Klan, 1965–1877. American Mercury 2: 120, May, 1924. Bravos in Bed-Sheets.

DAVISON, HENRY POMEROY. The American Red Cross in the Great War. Smart Set 68: 144, Nov., 1920. Notes in the Margin—V.

DAWSON, FRANCIS WARRINGTON.
The Scar. Smart Set 31: 155, June, 1910. The Greatest of American Writers.
The Scourge. Smart Set 33: 165, March, 1911. A Stack of Novels.

DEACON, RENÉE M. Bernard Shaw As Artist—Philosopher. Smart Set 33: 167-168, Feb., 1911. The Revival of the Printed Play.

DEAN, SARA. A Disciple of Chance. Smart Set 31: 155, June, 1910. The Greatest of American Writers.

DE BEKKER, LEANDER JAN.
The Serio-Comic Profession. Smart Set 48: 150-151, April, 1916. The Publishers Begin Their Spring Drive.
Stoke's Encyclopedia of Music and Musicians. Smart Set 27: 157, March, 1909. The Literary Clinic.

DE COULEVAIN, PIERRE. See Favre de Coulevain, Hélène.

DE KRUIF, PAUL.
Hunger Fighters. Nation 127: 523, Nov. 14, 1928. The Battle for Food.
Men Against Death. American Mercury 28: 123-124, Jan., 1933. The Siege of Nature.
Microbe Hunters. Nation 122: 235-236, March 3, 1926. The War upon the Unseen.
Seven Iron Men. Nation 129: 495, Oct. 30, 1929. A Saga of the North.

DELL, FLOYD.
The Briary-Bush. Smart Set 67: 141, Jan., 1922. Book Article No. 158—II.
Moon-Calf. Smart Set 64: 142, Feb., 1921. The Anatomy of Ochlocracy—III; 64: 141-142, March, 1921. A Soul's Adventures—II—American Novels.
Were You Ever A Child? Smart Set 61: 143-144, Feb., 1920. From the Diary of a Reviewer (Dec., 1913).
Women As World Builders. Smart Set 41: 157, Oct., 1913. "With Your Kind Permission—."

DEMAREST, VIRGINIA. The Fruit of Desire. Smart Set 33: 161, March, 1911. A Stack of Novels.

DE MORGAN, JACQUES. See Morgan, Jacques Jean Marie de.

DENNETT, MARY (WARE). Who's Obscene? American Mercury 20: 253-254, June, 1930. The Smut-Snufflers.

DENNIS, CHARLES HENRY. Eugene Field's Creative Years. American Mercury 3: 507, Dec., 1924. Two Journalists.

DENNIS, CLARENCE JAMES. Doreen and the Sentimental Bloke. Smart Set 51: 271-272, Jan., 1917. Suffering Among Books.

BOOK REVIEWS

DENNIS, GEOFFREY POMEROY. Harvest in Poland. American Mercury 5: 507-509, Aug., 1925. Novels Good and Bad.

DENNY, LUDWELL. America Conquers Britain. American Mercury 20: 251-253, June, 1930. Twilight in England.

DE PRATZ, CLAIRE. See Pratz, Claire de.

DE SÉLINCOURT, HUGH. A Fair House. Smart Set 34: 154, July, 1911. Novels for Hot Afternoons.

DESSAUER, FRIEDRICH. Auslandsraetsel; Nord Amerikanische und Spanische Reisebriefe. American Mercury 1: 507-508, April, 1924. God's Country: Exterior View.

DEWING, ELIZABETH BARTOL. See Kaup, Elizabeth Bartol (Dewing).

DIBBLE, ROY FLOYD.
John L. Sullivan. American Mercury 5: 510, Aug., 1925. Other Biographies.
Strenuous Americans. American Mercury 2: 377-380, July, 1924. The Bradford Formula.

DIBELIUS, WILHELM. England. American Mercury 20: 251-253, June, 1930. Twilight in England.

DICKINSON, EMILY. The Complete Poems of Emily Dickinson, edited by Martha Dickinson Bianchi. American Mercury 6: 251-254, Oct., 1925. Poetry.

DICKSON, HARRIS. An Old-Fashioned Senator: A Story-Biography of John Sharp Williams. Nation 121: sup. 426, Oct. 14, 1925. Yazoo's Favorite. Reprinted in *Book Reviewing*, by Wayne Gard. (New York, Knopf, 1927) p. 117–121.

DICTIONARY OF AMERICAN ENGLISH ON HISTORICAL PRINCIPLES, edited by Sir William Craigie . . . [and others.] Part I. Chicago Sunday Tribune, April 12, 1925. The American Language; New York Herald Tribune Books, p. 2, Oct. 4, 1936. Printing the American Lingo.

DIDIER, EUGÈNE LEMOINE. The Poe Cult. Smart Set 29: 157-158, Nov., 1909. What About Nietzsche?

DILNOT, GEORGE. Scotland Yard: Its History and Associations. American Mercury 10: 380-382, March, 1927. Die Polizei.

DIXON, ROLAND BURRAGE. The Building of Cultures. American Mercury 16: 122-124, Jan., 1929. What Is Civilization?

DIXON, THOMAS.
Comrades. Smart Set 27: 156, April, 1909. The Novels That Bloom in the Spring, Tra-La!
The Love Complex. American Mercury 6: 122-124, Sept., 1925. A Reverend Novelist.
The Root of Evil. Smart Set 33: 163, April, 1911. The Meredith of Tomorrow.

DIXON, WILLIAM MACNEILE. The Englishman. American Mercury 24: 509-510, Dec., 1931. Two Views of the English.

DOBELL, CLIFFORD. Antony van Leeuwenhoek & His "Little Animals." American Mercury 28: 124-125, Jan., 1933. The Siege of Nature.

DONNELLY, FRANCIS PATRICK. Art Principles in Literature. American Mercury 5: 252, June, 1925. Four Critics of Letters.

DORAN, GEORGE HENRY. Chronicles of Barabbas, 1884–1934. Nation 40: 662, June 5, 1935. A Friend of Letters. Reprinted in the 1952 edition of the book, p. 442–444.

DOS PASSOS, JOHN.
Manhattan Transfer. American Mercury 7: 507, April, 1926. Fiction Good and Bad.
Streets of Night. American Mercury 2: 380-381, July, 1924. Rambles in Fiction.
Three Soldiers. Smart Set 66: 143–144, Dec., 1921. Variations of a Familiar Theme—5; 69: 141, Oct., 1922.

DOSTOEVSKY, FEDOR MIKHAILOVICH. Letters and Reminiscences. Smart Set 72: 141-142, Nov., 1923. Notices of Books—II.

DOUGHERTY, GEORGE S. The Criminal as a Human Being. American Mercury 4: 122-123, Jan., 1925. Crime and Punishment.

DOUGHTY, CHARLES MONTAGU. Travels in Arabia Deserta. American Mercury 1: 510, April, 1924. Brief Notices.

DOUGLAS, LORD ALFRED BRUCE. Oscar Wilde and Myself. Smart Set 44: 150–151, Nov., 1914. Critics of More or Less Badness.

DOUGLAS, JAMES. Adventures in London. Smart Set 30: 159, Jan., 1910. George Bernard Shaw As A Hero.

DOUGLAS, NORMAN. Good-Bye to Western Culture. American Mercury 21: 383, Nov., 1930. Katzenjammer.

DOYLE, SIR ARTHUR CONAN.
The Last Galley. Smart Set 36: 158, Feb., 1912. Rounding Up the Novels.
The Lost World. Smart Set 39: 158, Jan., 1913. Again the Busy Fictioneers.
The New Revelation. Smart Set 55: 141-142, Aug., 1918. A Sub-Potomac Phenomenon—III.
The Valley of Fear. Smart Set 46: 294, June, 1915. Here Are Novels!

DRAMATIC INDEX, 1909. Smart Set 31: 159, Aug., 1910. A Hot Weather Novelist.

DRAWBRIDGE, CYPRIAN LEYCESTER, ed. The Religion of Scientists. American Mercury 27: 123-126, Sept., 1932. Science and Theology.

DREISER, THEODORE.
An American Tragedy. American Mercury 7: 379-381, March, 1926. Dreiser in 840 Pages.
A Book About Myself. Smart Set 70: 143-144, March, 1923. Adventures Among Books—III.
The Color of a Great City. [Baltimore] Evening Sun, Jan. 12, 1924.
Dawn. American Mercury 23: 383, July, 1931. Footprints on the Sands of Time.
The Financier. New York Times Book Review, Nov. 10, 1912. The Story of a Financier Who Loved Beauty; Smart Set 39: 153, 155-157, Jan., 1913. Again the Busy Fictioneers.

Free and Other Stories. Smart Set 57: 143-144, Nov., 1918. Dithyrambs Against Learning—II.

A Gallery of Women. American Mercury 19: 254-255, Feb., 1930. Ladies, Mainly Sad.

The 'Genius.' Smart Set 67: 150-154, Dec., 1915. A Literary Behemoth.

Hey-Rub-a-Dub-Dub. Smart Set 62: 138-140, May, 1920. More Notes from a Diary.

A Hoosier Holiday. Smart Set 50: 138-143, Oct., 1916. The Creed of a Novelist.

Jennie Gerhardt. Smart Set 35: 153-155, Nov., 1911. A Novel of the First Rank; American Mercury 19: 255, Feb., 1930.

Plays of the Natural and the Supernatural. Smart Set 69: 154, June, 1916. A Soul's Adventures.

Sister Carrie. Chicago Sunday Tribune, March 15, 1925. The Case of Dreiser; New York Evening Mail, Aug. 4, 1917. Sister Carrie's History.

The Titan. Town Topics 71:17-18, June 18, 1914. Dreiser and His Titan; Smart Set 43: 153-157, Aug., 1914. Adventures Among the New Novels; American Mercury 19: 255, Feb., 1930.

A Traveler at Forty. Smart Set 42: 153-154, Feb., 1914. Anything But Novels!

Twelve Men. New York Sun, April 13, 1919; Smart Set 59: 140-141, Aug.. 1919. Novels, Chiefly Bad—II.

DRUMMOND, HAMILTON. The Justice of the King. Smart Set 54: 166-167, May, 1911. Novels—The Spring Crop.

DRYSDALE, CHARLES VICKERY. Small Family System, Is It Injurious or Immoral? Smart Set 45: 462-463, Jan., 1915. A Gamey Old Gaul.

DUDENEY, ALICE, "Mrs. Henry Dudeney." Trespass. Smart Set 30: 157-158, Jan., 1910. George Bernard Shaw As A Hero.

DU MAURIER, GUY LOUIS BUSSON. An Englishman's Home; a Play in Three Acts. Smart Set 28: 158, July, 1909. The Best Novels of the Year.

DUNCAN, ISADORA. My Life. American Mercury 13: 506-508, April, 1928. Two Enterprising Ladies.

DUNSANY, EDWARD JOHN MORETON DRAX PLUNKETT, *18th baron.*
The Book of Wonder. Town Topics 72: 16-17, Sept. 24, 1914. Two Books by a Noble Lord.

Time and the Gods. *See* above.

[Comment.] Smart Set 44: 157-159, Sept., 1914. Thirty-Five Printed Plays; 52: 138-139, July, 1917. The Cult of Dunsany.

DURANT, WILLIAM JAMES.
Philosophy and the Social Problem. Smart Set 54: 140-141, April, 1918. Business—II.

The Tragedy of Russia. American Mercury 30: 252-255, Sept., 1933. The Slav Utopia.

DURNING-LAWRENCE, *Sir* EDWARD. Bacon Is Shakespeare. Smart Set 33: 167-168, Feb., 1911. The Revival of the Printed Play.

DWIGHT, HARRISON GRISWOLD. Stamboul Nights. Smart Set 49: 153, June, 1916. A Soul's Adventures—III.

DYER, WALTER ALDEN. The Lure of the Antique. Smart Set 33: 167, Jan., 1911. The Leading American Novelist.

DYLLINGTON, ANTHONY. The Unseen Thing. Smart Set 31: 154-155, Aug., 1910. A Hot Weather Novelist.

EATON, GEOFFREY DELL. Backfurrow. American Mercury 5: 124-126, May, 1925. Fiction.

EATON, WALTER PRICHARD.
The American Stage of To-Day. Smart Set 27: 158-159, Feb., 1909. The Literary Olio.
At the New Theatre and Others. Smart Set 33: 167-168, Feb., 1911. The Revival of the Printed Play.

ECHEGARAY Y EIZAGUIRRE, JOSÉ. The Great Galeoto. Smart Set 44: 159, Sept., 1914. Thirty-Five Printed Plays.

ECKSTEIN, GUSTAV. Noguchi. American Mercury 23: 383, July, 1931. Footprints on the Sands of Time.

EDDINGTON, Sir ARTHUR STANLEY. The Nature of the Physical World. American Mercury 16: 509-510, April, 1929. The Riddle of the Universe.

EDGAR, WILLIAM GROWELL. The Medal of Gold. American Mercury 7: 127, Jan., 1926. Brief Notices.

EDGELL, GEORGE HAROLD. The American Architecture of Today. American Mercury 14: 123-124, May, 1928. American Architecture.

EDWARDS, LYFORD PATERSON. The Natural History of Revolution. American Mercury 12: 379-382, Nov., 1927. Revolutions.

EISLER, ROBERT. The Messiah Jesus and John The Baptist, according to Flavius Josephus . . . American Mercury 25: 125-127, Jan., 1932. Light on Christian Origins.

ELIOT, THOMAS STEARNS. For Lancelot Andrewes. American Mercury 18: 123-124, Sept., 1929. The New Humanism.

ELLIOTT, MABEL AGNES. Conflicting Penal Theories in Statutory Criminal Law. American Mercury 24: 124-127, Sept., 1931. What Is To Be Done About It?

ELLIS, HAVELOCK.
Impressions and Comments. Chicago Sunday Tribune, July 11, 1926. Havelock Ellis; Second Series 1914–1920. New York Evening Post Literary Review, p. 37, Sept. 24, 1921.
Impressions and Opinions. Smart Set 50: 285, Nov., 1916. Professors at the Bat.
Studies in the Psychology of Sex. Smart Set 38: 153-154, Dec., 1912. A Visit to a Short Story Factory.
The Task of Social Hygiene. Smart Set 40: 152, June, 1913. A Nietzschean, a Swedenborgian and Other Queer Fowl.
The World of Dreams. Smart Set 35: 153-154, Sept., 1911. A 1911 Model Dream Book.

BOOK REVIEWS

ELLIS, WILLIAM THOMAS. Billy Sunday; the Man and His Message. Smart Set 49: 292-296, July, 1916. Savonarolas A-Sweat.

ELSER, FRANK B. The Keen Desire. American Mercury 9: 382, Nov., 1926. Certain Works of Fiction.

THE ENCYCLOPAEDIA BRITANNICA, 14th edition. American Mercury 19: 125-126, Jan., 1930. The New Britannica; 26: 254-255, June, 1932. Comments.

THE ENCYCLOPEDIA AMERICANA. American Mercury 26: 254-255, June., 1932. Wisdom up to Date.

ERNST, BERNARD MORRIS LEE and HEREWARD CARRINGTON. Houdini and Conan Doyle, the Story of a Strange Friendship. American Mercury 26: 250-254, June, 1932. The Believing Mind. Reprinted in *Modern English Composition*, by John C. McCloskey. (New York, Farrar, 1934) p. 140–141, entitled "Mediums and Nonsense."

ERSKINE, JOHN. Sonata and Other Poems. American Mercury 6: 251-254, Oct., 1925. Poetry.

ERVINE, ST. JOHN GREER.
The Foolish Lovers. Smart Set 63: 141-142, Oct., 1920. Gropings in Literary Darkness.

Mrs. Martin's Man. Smart Set 45: 433, April, 1915. The Grandstand Flirts with the Bleachers.

ETIQUETTE FOR AMERICANS, by a Woman of Fashion. Smart Set 29: 158, Nov., 1909. What About Nietzsche?

EVANS, CARADOC.
Capel Sion. Smart Set 57: 142-143, Dec., 1918. The Late Mr. Wells—III.

My Neighbours. Smart Set 62: 140-141, Aug., 1920. Books More or Less Amusing—II.

My People. Smart Set 55: 141, Aug., 1918. A Sub-Potomac Phenomenon—II.

THE EVERYMAN ENCYCLOPEDIA. Smart Set 49: 156, June, 1916. A Soul's Adventures.

EWERS, HANNS HEINZ. Edgar Allan Poe; translated from the German by Adele Lewisohn. Smart Set 54: 143-144, April, 1918. Business—IV.

FABER, KNUD HELGE. Nosography in Modern Internal Medicine. American Mercury 1: 255, Oct.. 1924. Brief Notices.

FARMER, FANNIE MERRITT. The Boston Cooking-School Cook-Book. American Mercury 21: 508-509, Dec., 1930. The American Cuisine. Reprinted in *Our Land and Its Literature*, edited by Orton Lowe. (New York, Harper, 1936) p. 559–561.

FARNOL, JEFFERY.
The Broad Highway. Smart Set 34: 165-166, May, 1911. Novels—The Spring Crop.

The Money Moon. Smart Set 37: 158, July, 1912. A Dip into the Novels.

My Lady Caprice. Smart Set 37: 158, July, 1912. A Dip into the Novels.

FARRAR, GERALDINE. The Story of an American Singer. Smart Set 49: 154, June, 1916. A Soul's Adventures—5.

WORKS BY H. L. M.

FAVRE DE COULEVAIN, HÉLÈNE. On the Branch, by Pierre de Coulevain [pseud.] Smart Set 30: 153, 155, April, 1910. A Glance at the Spring Fiction.

FEILER, ARTHUR. The Russian Experiment, translated by H. J. Stenning. American Mercury 22: 506-508, April, 1931. Life in the Marxian Utopia.

FERBER, EDNA.
The Girls. [Baltimore] Evening Sun, Oct. 15, 1921. Gleams of Hope; Smart Set 67: 140, Jan., 1922. Book Article No. 158—II.

Show Boat. American Mercury 9:127, Sept., 1926. Three Novels.

FERGUSSON, HARVEY.
The Blood of the Conquerors. Chicago Sunday Tribune, May 10, 1925. Literature and Geography; Smart Set 67: 140, Jan., 1922. Book Article No. 158—II.

Capitol Hill. Smart Set 71: 141-142, July, 1923. Some New Books—IV; Chicago Tribune, Jan. 11, 1925. A Chance for Novelists; [Baltimore] Evening Sun, April 7, 1923.

Wolf Song. American Mercury 12: 508-510, Dec., 1927. The Desert Epic.

Women and Wives. American Mercury 2: 381, July, 1924. Rambles in Fiction.

FINCK, HENRY THEOPHILUS.
Food and Flavor. Smart Set 41: 155-156, Oct., 1913. "With Your Kind Permission—."

Richard Strauss, the Man and His Works. Smart Set 53: 142, Dec., 1917. Critics Wild and Tame—III.

FISHBEIN, MORRIS S. Fads and Quackery in Healing. American Mercury 27: 510, Dec., 1932. The Charlatans' Paradise.

FISHER, HARRIET WHITE. A Woman's World Tour in a Motor. Smart Set 36: 158, March, 1912. The Prophet of the Superman.

FISHMAN, JOSEPH FULLING. Crucibles of Crime; the Shocking Story of the American Jail. Smart Set 72: 143-144, Nov., 1923. Notices of Books—III.

FITCH, CLYDE.
Clyde Fitch and His Letters, by Montrose J. Moses and Virginia Gerson. American Mercury 4: 124-125, Jan., 1925. A Butterfly of Yesterday.

A Wave of Life. Smart Set 30: 156, Feb., 1910. Books To Read and Books To Avoid.

FITCH, GEORGE HELGESON. Homeburg Memories. Smart Set 45: 434, April, 1915. The Grandstand Flirts with the Bleachers. Includes "Sentimental Interlude" by HLM.

FITHIAN, ISAAC NEWTON. A Pilgrim's Thoughts. Smart Set 43: 153-154, May, 1914. The Harp, The Sackbut and the Psaltery.

FITZGERALD, FRANCIS SCOTT KEY.
The Beautiful and the Damned. Smart Set 67: 140-141, April, 1922. The Niagara of Novels—II.

Flappers and Philosophers. Smart Set 68: 140, Dec., 1920. Chiefly Americans.

The Great Gatsby. American Mercury 5: 382, July, 1925. New Fiction; Chicago Sunday Tribune, May 3, 1925. Scott Fitzgerald and His Work.

Tales of the Jazz Age. Smart Set 7: 141, July, 1923. Some New Books—IV.

This Side of Paradise. Smart Set 62: 140, Aug., 1920. Books More or Less Amusing—II.

FLAMMARION, CAMILLE. At the Moment of Death. Smart Set 68: 139-140, Aug., 1922. The Intellectual Squirrel-Cage—II. Camille at the Bat Again.

FLEMING, SANDFORD. Children and Puritanism. American Mercury 29: 508-510, Aug., 1933. Infants in Hell.

FLETCHER, ELLA ADELIA. The Law of the Rhythmic Breath. Smart Set 27: 154, Feb., 1909. The Literary Olio.

FLETCHER, JOHN GOULD. Japanese Prints. Smart Set 58: 143-144, April, 1919. Notes of a Poetry-Hater—VI.

FLEXNER, ABRAHAM. Universities, American, English, German. American Mercury 22: 250-252, Feb., 1931. The Higher Learning in America.

FLEXNER, BERNARD and ROGER N. BALDWIN. Juvenile Courts and Probation. Smart Set 44: 156-157, Oct., 1914. A Review of Reviewers.

FLINT, LEON NELSON. The Conscience of the Newspaper. American Mercury 5: 379-382, July, 1925. Learning How To Blush.

FLOWER, JOHN CYRIL. An Approach to the Psychology of Religion. American Mercury 13: 124-126, May, 1928. The Powers of the Air.

FLYNN, JOHN THOMAS. God's Gold: The Story of Rockefeller and His Times. American Mercury 27: 507-510, Dec., 1932. John the Baptist (Secular).

FOERSTER, NORMAN, ed. Humanism and America: Essays on the Outlook of Modern Civilization. American Mercury 20: 125-127, May, 1930. Pedagogues A-Flutter.

FOLLETT, WILSON.
Joseph Conrad. Smart Set 48: 305-306, Jan., 1916. Partly About Books—3—Conrad Again.
The Modern Novel. Smart Set 58: 142, Feb., 1919. Sunrise on the Prairie—VI.

FOLLETT, WILSON and HELEN THOMAS. Some Modern Novelists. Smart Set 56: 140-143, Sept., 1918. Rattling the Subconscious—II.

FOOTNER, HULBERT. New Rivers of the North. Smart Set 60: 144, Dec., 1919. Exeunt Ones—III.

FORAKER, JOSEPH BENSON. Notes of a Busy Life. Smart Set 49: 155-156, June, 1916. A Soul's Adventures.

FORBES, ROSITA (TORR). The Sultan of the Mountains. American Mercury 2: 510, Aug., 1924. Brief Notices.

FORD, FORD MADOX.
The Half Moon, by Ford Madox Hueffer. Smart Set 29: 159, Sept., 1909. The Books of the Dog Days.
Joseph Conrad: A Personal Remembrance. American Mercury 4: 505-507, April, 1924. The Conrad Wake.

WORKS BY H. L. M.

FORD, HENRY.
My Life and Work. Smart Set 70: 138-140, Jan., 1923. Confidences.

Today and Tomorrow. American Mercury 9: 125-127, Sept., 1926. Babbitt as Philosopher.

FORD, JAMES LAUREN, Forty-Odd Years in the Literary Shop. Smart Set 67: 142, Feb., 1922. Frank Harris and Others—II.

FORD, SEWELL.
Cherub Devine. Smart Set 28: 153-155, July, 1909. The Best Novels of the Year.

Just Horses. Smart Set 31: 159, July, 1910. A Fictioneer of the Laboratory.

FORMAN, JUSTUS MILES. Jason: A Romance. Smart Set 29: 160, Nov., 1909. What About Nietzsche?

FORT, CHARLES. Wild Talents. American Mercury 26: 508-510, Aug., 1932. Nonsense as Science.

FOSTER, ROBERT FREDERICK. Car No. 44. Smart Set 30: 158, April, 1910. A Glance at the Spring Fiction.

FOSTER, WILLIAM ZEBULON. The Great Steel Strike, and Its Lessons. [Baltimore] Evening Sun, p. 6, Aug. 14, 1920. Foster's Own Story of the Steel Strike that Failed; Smart Set 68: 144, Oct., 1920. Gropings in Literary Darkness—VI.

FRANCE, ANATOLE.
On Life and Letters, edited by Frederic Chapman. Smart Set 30: 160, Jan., 1910. George Bernard Shaw As A Hero.

The Opinions of Anatole France, recorded by Paul Gsell, translated from the French by Ernest A. Boyd. Smart Set 68: 140, Aug., 1922. The Intellectual Squirrel Cage—II—Camille at the Bat Again.

The Revolt of the Angels. Smart Set 45: 458-459, Jan., 1915. A Gamey Old Gaul.

FRANCESCO, GRETE DE. The Power of the Charlatan, translated from the German by Miriam Beard. Yale Review, n.s. 29: 181, Autumn, 1939. Quacks, Faddists, and Others.

FRANCK, HARRY ALVERSON.
A Vagabond Journey Around the World. Smart Set 31: 160, June, 1910. The Greatest of American Writers.

Zone Policeman 88. Smart Set 41: 158, Sept., 1913. Getting Rid of the Actor.

FRANK, WALDO DAVID.
City Block. Smart Set 69: 144, Nov., 1922. Chiefly Pathological—III.

Holiday. Smart Set 72: 143-144, Oct., 1923. Holy Writ—III.

Our America. Smart Set 61: 141, Feb., 1920. From the Diary of a Reviewer (Dec., 1910).

FRANKAU, GILBERT. Jack—One of Us, a Novel in Verse. Smart Set 39: 156, Feb., 1913. The Burden of Humor.

FRANKAU, JULIA (DAVIS). Joseph in Jeopardy, by Frank Danby [pseud.]. Smart Set 37: 157, July, 1912. A Dip into the Novels.

BOOK REVIEWS

FREDERICK, JOHN TOWNER. Druida. Smart Set 71: 141, July, 1923. Some New Books—IV.

FREEMAN, DOUGLAS SOUTHALL. R. E. Lee [Baltimore] Evening Sun, May 13, 1935. Twilight of a God.

FREEMANTLE, ELIZABETH, *pseud. See* Covey, Elizabeth (Rockford).

FREIENFELS, RICHARD MILLER. *See* Müller—Freienfels, Richard.

FRENCH, ALICE. By Inheritance, by Octave Thanet [pseud.] Smart Set 31: 155, June, 1910. The Greatest of American Writers.

FRENCH, ANNE (WARNER).
How Leslie Loved. Smart Set 34: 157-158, June, 1911. The Horse Power of Realism.
An Original Gentleman. Smart Set 26: 158, Dec., 1908. Oyez! Oyez! All Ye Who Read Books.
The Panther. Smart Set. *See* above, An Original Gentleman.
Sunshine Jane. Smart Set 43: 156, June, 1914. The Anatomy of the Novel.

FRENCH, JOSEPH LEWIS, *ed.* Sixty Years of American Humor. American Mercury 3: 509, Dec., 1924. Anthologies.

FRENCH, LILLIE HAMILTON. The House Dignified. Smart Set 28: 159, May, 1909. Some Novels—and a Good One.

FRENSSEN, GUSTAV. Klaus Hinrich Baas, the Story of a Self-Made Man. Smart Set 34: 154, June, 1911. The Horse Power of Realism.

FREUD, SIGMUND.
Beyond the Pleasure Principle. American Mercury 3: 380, Nov., 1924. Marvels From Vienna.
Group Psychology and the Analysis of the Ego, translated by James Strachey. *See* entry above.
Totem and Taboo. Smart Set 56: 138-140, Sept., 1918. Rattling the Subconscious.

FRIEDMAN, ELISHA MICHAEL. Russia in Transition: A Business Man's Appraisal. American Mercury 28: 253-255, Feb., 1933. The Russian Imposture.

FROHMAN, DANIEL. Memoirs of a Manager. Smart Set 34: 154, Aug., 1911. The New Dramatic Literature; [Baltimore] Evening Sun, p. 6, April 17, 1911.

FULLER, HENRY BLAKE.
On the Stairs. Smart Set 55: 142-143, July, 1918. The Public Prints—III.
Waldo Trench and Others. Smart Set 26: 159, Nov., 1908. The Good, The Bad and the Best Sellers.

FURNISS, HARRY. Some Victorian Men. American Mercury 4: 383, March, 1925. Brief Notices.

FUTRELLE, JACQUES.
Elusive Isabel. Smart Set 28: 157, July, 1909. The Best Novels of the Year.
My Lady's Garter. Smart Set 38: 158, Dec., 1912. A Visit to a Short Story Factory.

195

FYVIE, JOHN. Wits, Beaux and Beauties of the Georgian Era. Smart Set 29: 158, Dec., 1909. "A Doll's House"—With a Fourth Act.

GAFFNEY, THOMAS ST. JOHN. Breaking the Silence. American Mercury 22:508-509, April, 1931. Sidelights on an Heroic Epoch.

GALE, ZONA.
Miss Lulu Bett. Smart Set 63: 141-142, Oct., 1920. Gropings in Literary Darkness.
When I Was a Little Girl. Smart Set 42: 158, Jan., 1914. A Pestilence of Novels.

GALLICHAN, WALTER M. Modern Woman and How To Manage Her. Smart Set 31: 156-157, Aug., 1910. A Hot Weather Novelist.

GALSWORTHY, JOHN.
The Dark Flower. Smart Set 43: 153-156, July, 1914. Galsworthy and Others.
Fraternity. Smart Set 28: 154, June, 1909. Books for the Hammock and Deck Chair; 28: 153-154, July, 1909.
The Fugitive. Smart Set 43: 153-155, July, 1914. Galsworthy and Others.
In Chancery. Smart Set 64: 143, Feb., 1921. The Anatomy of Ochlocracy—III.
Justice. Smart Set 33: 164-165, Feb., 1911. The Revival of the Printed Play.
A Motley. Smart Set 32: 168, Oct., 1910. Meredith's Swan Song.
The Patrician. Smart Set 34: 155, June, 1911. The Horse Power of Realism.
Plays. Smart Set 29: 153-154, Sept., 1909. The Books of the Dog Days.

GAMBLE, ELIZA BURT. The Sexes in Science and History. Smart Set 53: 138-144, Oct., 1917. Woman, Lovely Woman.

GANCEL, JOSEPH. Gancel's Ready Reference of Menu Terms. Smart Set 32: 165-166, Nov., 1910. A Guide to Intelligent Eating.

GANNETT, HENRY. American Names: A Guide to the Origin of Place Names in the United States. Mississippi Valley Historical Review 35: 148-149, June, 1948.

GARÇON, MAURICE and JEAN VINCHON. The Devil, an Historical, Critical and Medical Study, translated by Stephen Haden Guest from the sixth French edition American Mercury 20: 254-255, June, 1930. The Ghostly Realm.

GARLAND, HAMLIN.
The Shadow World. Smart Set 27: 153-154, Feb., 1909. The Literary Olio.
A Son of the Middle Border. New York Evening Mail, Sept. 29, 1917.

GARRISON, THEODOSIA (PICKERING).
The Earth Cry, and Other Poems. Smart Set 33: 168, Feb., 1911. The Revival of the Printed Play.
The Joy of Life, and Other Poems. Smart Set 28: 158-159, Aug., 1909. Novels and Other Books—Chiefly Bad.

GASKELL, AUGUSTA. What Is Life? American Mercury 16: 253-254, Feb., 1929. The Origin Of Life.

GASTON, CHARLES ROBERT, ed. Forum Papers: Second Series. American Mercury 5: 378-379, July, 1925. The Pedagogue at Work.

BOOK REVIEWS

GEE, WILSON. Research Barriers in the South. American Mercury 28: 251-253, Feb., 1933. The Agonies of Dixie.

GEISERT, HENRY A. The Criminal. American Mercury 21: 380-383, Nov., 1930. The Criminal.

GENETIC STUDIES OF GENIUS. v.3 The Promise of Youth. American Mercury 23: 126-127 May, 1931. Superiority in the Young.

GENTHE, ARNOLD. The Book of the Dance. Smart Set 50: 284-285, Nov., 1916. Professors at the Bat.

GEORGE, WALTER LIONEL.

A Bed of Roses. Smart Set 36: 157-158, Feb., 1912. Rounding Up the Novels.

Blind Alley. Smart Set 59: 138-139, Aug., 1919. Novels, Chiefly Bad.

Caliban. Smart Set 63: 144, Nov., 1920. Notes in the Margin—V.

Hail, Columbia! [Baltimore] Evening Sun, July 16, 1921. Shows Very Sharp Eyes; Smart Set 66: 142-144, Sept., 1921. From the Diary of a Reviewer—IV.

The Intelligence of Woman. Smart Set 51: 266-272, April, 1917. The Infernal Feminine.

The Making of an Englishman. Smart Set 43: 153-156, June, 1914. The Anatomy of the Novel; 45: 294, March, 1915. The Bugaboo of the Sunday Schools.

The Second Blooming. *See* entry above. p. 294-296.

The Strangers' Wedding. Smart Set 48: 154, April, 1916. The Publishers Begin Their Spring Drive.

Ursula Trent. Smart Set 67: 139-140, Jan., 1922. Book Article No. 158—II.

GEROULD, KATHARINE FULLERTON. Modes and Morals. Smart Set 62: 143-144, May, 1920. More Notes from a Diary—IV.

GERTSEN, ALEXANDER IVANOVICH. The Memoirs of Alexander Herzen, My Past and Thoughts, translated by Constance Garnett. American Mercury 3: 382-383, Nov., 1924. Barbary in Europe.

GIBBS, GEORGE FORT.

The Bolted Door. Smart Set 34: 166, May, 1911. Novels—The Spring Crop.

Madcap. Smart Set 42: 157, March, 1914. The Raw Material of Fiction.

[GILBERT, CLINTON WALLACE.] The Mirrors of Washington. Smart Set 66: 143-144, Nov., 1921. More Notes on Books—4.

GILBERT, GEORGE HOLLEY. The Christian Content of the Bible. American Mercury 20: 255, June, 1930. The Ghostly Realm.

GILBERT, *Sir* WILLIAM SCHWENK. The Mikado. Smart Set 48: 308, Jan., 1916. Partly About Books—8.

GILBRETH, LILLIAN EVELYN (MOLLER). Living with Our Children. American Mercury 14: 510, Aug., 1928. The Family as a Corporation.

GILMAN, LAWRENCE. Aspects of Modern Opera. Smart Set 27: 156-157, March, 1909. The Literary Clinic.

GINZBERG, ASHER. Selected Essays, by Ahad ha-'Am [pseud.] Smart Set 54: 141-142, Jan., 1918. Seven Pages About Books—III.

WORKS BY H. L. M.

GLASGOW, ELLEN ANDERSON GHOLSON.

Barren Ground. American Mercury 5: 383, July, 1925. New Fiction.

Life and Gabriella. Smart Set 48: 155, April, 1916. The Publishers Begin Their Spring Drive.

The Miller of Old Church. Smart Set 35: 155, Dec., 1911. An Overdose of Novels.

The Romance of a Plain Man. Smart Set 28: 153, Aug., 1909. Novels and Other Books—Chiefly Bad.

They Stooped to Folly, a Comedy of Morals. American Mercury 18: 251-253, Oct., 1929. Two Southern Novels.

Virginia. Smart Set 40: 158, July, 1913. Various Bad Novels.

Works . . . The Old Dominion ed. American Mercury 29: 504-506, Aug., 1933. A Southern Skeptic.

GLASS, MONTAGUE.

Abe and Mawruss, Being Further Adventures of Potash and Perlmutter. Smart Set 35: 151-153, Dec., 1911. An Overdose of Novels.

The Competitive Nephew. Smart Set 46: 450, July, 1915. The Prometheus of the Western World.

Elkan Lubliner: American. Smart Set 39: 155-156, Feb., 1913. The Burden of Humor.

Object: Matrimony. Smart Set 39: 158, Jan., 1913. Again the Busy Fictioneers.

GLOVER, TERROT REAVELEY. The World of the New Testament. American Mercury 23: 506-510, April, 1932. Quod Est Veritas?

GLUECK, SHELDON, ed. Probation and Criminal Justice. American Mercury 29: 381-383, July, 1933. The Job of the Judge.

GOBINEAU, JOSEPH ARTHUR, comte de. The Renaissance, translated by Paul V. Cohn. Smart Set 42: 156, Feb., 1914. Anything But Novels!

GODDARD, MABEL, LOUISE SCHAFER CAMP and EVA HANDS LYCAN. American English. [Baltimore] Sun, Sec. 1, p. 11, Aug. 6, 1939. For Teaching English.

GODFREY, ELIZABETH, pseud. See Bedford, Jessie.

GODFREY, HOLLIS. The Man Who Ended War. Smart Set 26: 157, Dec., 1908. Oyez! Oyez! All Ye Who Read Books.

GOEPP, PHILIP HENRY. Symphonies and Their Meaning. Smart Set 43: 159-160, July, 1914. Galsworthy and Others.

GOING, CHARLES BUXTON. David Wilmot, Free-Soiler. American Mercury 3: 510, Dec., 1924. Brief Notices.

GOLD, MICHAEL. Jews without Money. American Mercury 19: 381-382, Mar., 1930. The Life of the Poor.

GOLDBERG, BEN ZION. The Sacred Fire. American Mercury 20: 254-255, June, 1930. The Ghostly Realm.

GOLDBERG, ISAAC.

Brazilian Literature. Smart Set 70: 141, March, 1923. Adventures Among Books—II.

BOOK REVIEWS

Six Plays of the Yiddish Theatre. Smart Set 52: 399, May, 1917. Shocking Stuff —4.

GOLDMAN, EMMA.

My Disillusionment in Russia. American Mercury 2: 122-123, May, 1924. Two Views of Russia.

The Social Significance of the Modern Drama. Smart Set 44: 152-154, Nov., 1914. Critics of More or Less Badness.

GOLDMAN, SOLOMON. A Rabbi Takes Stock. American Mercury 23: 306-310, April, 1932. Quod Est Veritas?

GOMPERS, SAMUEL. Seventy Years of Life and Labor; an Autobiography. American Mercury 5: 510, Aug., 1925. Other Biographies.

GONZALES, AMBROSE ELLIOTT.

The Black Border: Gullah Stories of the Carolina Coast. Smart Set 70: 143-144, Feb., 1923. Specimens of Current Fiction—V.

With Aesop Along the Black Border. American Mercury 3: 383, Nov., 1924. Brief Notices.

GOODMAN, DANIEL CARSON.

Hagar Revelly. Smart Set 41: 158-159, Oct., 1913. "With Your Kind Permission —."

The Taker. Smart Set 60: 143-144, Oct., 1919. Mark Twain—IV.

GOODNOW, ELIZABETH. The Market for Souls. Smart Set 31: 158, May, 1910. In Praise of a Poet.

GORE, JOHN. The Barmecide's Feast. Smart Set 38: 155, Nov., 1912. Novels Bad, Half Bad and Very Bad.

GORKY, MAXIM.

Fragments from My Diary. American Mercury 4: 127, Jan., 1925. The Land of Lunacy.

My Childhood. Smart Set 67: 154-155, Dec., 1915. Literary Behemoth.

The Spy. Smart Set 27: 158, March, 1909. The Literary Clinic.

Tales of Two Countries. Smart Set 45: 153, Feb., 1915. Lachrymose Love.

GOSSIP, GEORGE HATFIELD DINGLEY. Forsaken, by Ivan Trepoff [pseud.] Smart Set 32: 165-166, Sept., 1910. The MacKaye Mystery.

GRAÇA ARANHA, JOSÉ PEREIRA DA. Canaan, translated from the Portuguese by Mariano Joaquin Lorente. American Mercury 62: 141, Aug., 1920. Books More or Less Amusing.

GRAF, ARTURO. The Story of the Devil. American Mercury 25: 506-510, April, 1932. Quod Est Veritas?

GRANT, ROBERT. The Chippendales. Smart Set 28: 155-156, July, 1909. The Best Novels of the Year.

GRANT, WATSON ELLIOTT LOVEGOOD.

Mainland. Smart Set 54: 142, March, 1918. Literae Humaniores; 55: 141, May, 1918. The Stream of Fiction.

WORKS BY H. L. M.

Where Bonds Are Loosed. Smart Set 55: 138, 140-141, May, 1918. The Stream of Fiction—II.

GRANVILLE—BARKER, HELEN MANCHESTER (GATES). The Sovereign Good, by Helen Huntington. Smart Set 27: 158-159, March, 1909. The Literary Clinic.

GRATTAN, CLINTON HARTLEY, ed. The Critique of Humanism, a Symposium. American Mercury 20: 508-509, Aug., 1930. Sassing Teacher.

GRAY, DAVID. Mr. Carteret and Others. Smart Set 31: 154, June, 1910. The Greatest of American Writers.

GRAY, JUDD. Doomed Ship, the Autobiography of Judd Gray, prepared for publication by his sister, Margaret Gray. American Mercury 16: 254-255, Feb., 1929. A Good Man Gone Wrong.

GRAYSON, DAVID, pseud. See Baker, Ray Stannard.

GREEN, ANNA KATHARINE. See Rohlfs, Anna Katharine (Green.)

GREEN, HELEN. The Maison de Shine. Smart Set 27: 156-157, Feb., 1909. The Literary Olio.

GREENE, WARD. Cora Potts, a Pilgrim's Progress. American Mercury 18: 251-253, Oct., 1929. Two Southern Novels.

GRUENING, ERNEST HENRY. Mexico and Its Heritage. American Mercury 15: 508-509, Dec., 1928. Across the Border.

GUÉRARD, ALBERT LÉON. Reflections on the Napoleonic Legend. American Mercury 1: 510, April, 1924. Brief Notices.

GUIGNEBERT, CHARLES ALFRED HONORÉ. Christianity, Past and Present. American Mercury 14: 124-126, May, 1928. The Powers of the Air.

HACKETT, FRANCIS.
Henry The Eighth. American Mercury 17: 508-509, Aug., 1929. The Slave of Love.
Horizons. Smart Set 56: 142-143, Sept., 1918. Rattling the Subconscious—II.
The Invisible Censor. Smart Set 65: 141-142, June, 1921. Books About Books —II.
That Nice Young Couple. American Mercury 5: 507-509, Aug., 1925. Novels Good and Bad.

HAGEDORN, HERMANN. Roosevelt, Prophet of Unity. American Mercury 3: 255, Oct., 1924. Brief Notices.

HAGGARD, Sir HENRY RIDER. Queen Sheba's Ring. Smart Set 32: 166, Dec., 1910. Mainly About Novels.

HALDEMAN-JULIUS, EMANUEL AND ANNA MARCET HALDEMAN-JULIUS. Dust. Smart Set 65: 140-141, July, 1921. Literary Notes—II—The Husbandman.

HALDEMAN-JULIUS COMPANY. Ten Cent Pocket Series. Smart Set 68: 140-142, Aug., 1922. The Intellectual Squirrel-Cage—III.

HALE, LOUISE CLOSSER. The Married Miss Worth. Smart Set 34: 155, July, 1911. Novels for Hot Afternoons.

BOOK REVIEWS

HALE, WILLIAM BAYARD. The Story of a Style. Smart Set 64: 142-143, Jan., 1921. Consolation—III—The Late Master-Mind.

HALÉVY, ÉLIE. A History of the English People in 1815, translated from the French by E. I. Watkins and D. A. Barker. American Mercury 4: 383, March, 1925. Brief Notices.

HALIBURTON, THOMAS CHANDLER. Sam Slick; edited with a critical estimate by Ray Palmer Baker. American Mercury 1: 510, April, 1924. Brief Notices.

HALL, BOLTON. What Tolstoy Taught. Smart Set 37: 158, Aug., 1912. Zola.

HALSEY, FORREST. Fate and the Butterfly. Smart Set 28: 153-154, Aug., 1909. Novels and Other Books—Chiefly Bad.

HAMILL, JOHN. The Strange Career of Mr. Hoover under Two Flags. American Mercury 25: 250-253, Feb., 1932. Nine American Statesmen.

HAMILTON, CICELY MARY. Marriage as a Trade. Smart Set 30: 158-159, Feb., 1910. Books To Read and Books To Avoid.

HAMILTON, GILBERT VAN TASSEL and KENNETH MACGOWAN. What Is Wrong With Marriage? American Mercury 17: 125-127, May, 1929. The Holy Estate.

HAMILTON, MARY AGNES (ADAMSON). England's Labor Rulers, by Iconoclast [pseud.] with a foreword by S. K. Ratcliffe. American Mercury 2: 382-383, July, 1924. The Slave and His Ways.

HAMMERTON, JOHN ALEXANDER. George Meredith in Anecdote and Criticism. Smart Set 29: 159, Oct., 1909. The Last of the Victorians.

HAMSUN, KNUT.
The Growth of the Soil. Smart Set 65: 143, May, 1921. The Land of the Free—IV.
Hunger. Smart Set 64: 141-142, Feb., 1921. The Anatomy of Ochlocracy—III.

HANNAY, JAMES OWEN. The Red Hand of Ulster, by G. A. Birmingham [pseud.] Smart Set 40: 156-157, May, 1913. Weep for the White Slave!

HANSCOM, ELIZABETH DEERING, ed. The Heart of the Puritan. Smart Set 54: 138-139, March, 1918. Literae Humaniores.

HANSEN, HARRY. Midwest Portraits. American Mercury 1: 253-254, Feb., 1924. The Chicago Outfit.

HAPGOOD, HUTCHINS.
An Anarchist Woman. Smart Set 29: 156-157, Sept., 1909. The Books of the Dog Days.
The Story of a Lover. Smart Set 60: 143-144, Dec., 1919. Exeunt Omnes—III.

HAPGOOD, NORMAN, ed. Professional Patriots. American Mercury 12: 123-126, Sept., 1927. Autopsy.

HARBERTON, ERNEST ARTHUR GEORGE POMEROY, 7th viscount. How To Lengthen Our Ears. Smart Set 57: 138-141, Nov., 1918. Dithyrambs Against Learning.

HARLAND, HENRY. The Royal End. Smart Set 28: 157-158, June, 1909. Books for the Hammock and Deck Chair.

WORKS BY H. L. M.

HARLOW, REX.

A Biography of Everett Wentworth Hill. American Mercury 21: 509-510, Dec., 1930. Portrait of an Idealist.

Oklahoma City's Younger Leaders. American Mercury 24: 382-383, Nov., 1931. Men of Vision.

HARRÉ, T. EVERETT. The Eternal Maiden. Smart Set 40: 150, June, 1913. A. Nietzschean, a Swedenborgian and Other Queer Fowl.

HARRIS, FRANK.

Bernard Shaw. American Mercury 25: 253-255, Feb., 1932. Harris on Shaw.

Contemporary Portraits. Pearson's 27: 298, Dec., 1921.

Love in Youth. Smart Set 50: 143, Oct., 1916. The Creed of a Novelist—5.

The Man Shakespeare and His Tragic Life Story. Smart Set 30: 158-159, Jan., 1910. George Bernard Shaw As A Hero.

Montes the Matador. Smart Set 31: 159, July, 1910. A Fictioneer of the Laboratory.

My Life: v. 2. American Mercury 6: 254-255, Oct., 1925. Frank Harris Again.

My Life and Loves. Smart Set 71: 139-140, June, 1923. Notices of Books—III —In the Altogether.

Oscar Wilde. Smart Set 50: 280-284, Sept., 1916. Portrait of a Tragic Comedian.

The Women of Shakespeare. Smart Set 39: 157-158, March, 1913. Gerhart Hauptmann.

[Comment] Smart Set 67: 138-140, Feb., 1922. Frank Harris and Others.

HARRIS, JULIA COLLIER. The Life and Letters of Joel Chandler Harris. Smart Set 58: 142-143, Feb., 1919. Sunrise on the Prairie—VI.

HARRISON, HENRY SYDNOR.

Andrew Bride of Paris. American Mercury 7: 508-509, April, 1926. Fiction Good and Bad.

Pots and Pans: The Study of Ceramics. American Mercury 16: 122-124, Jan., 1929. What Is Civilization?

Queed. Smart Set 34: 155, July, 1911. Novels for Hot Afternoons.

V.V.'s Eyes. Smart Set 40: 160, Aug., 1913. A Counterblast to Buncombe.

HARRISON, MARY ST. LEGER (KINGSLEY). The Score, by Lucas Malet [pseud.]. Smart Set 29: 157, Oct., 1909. The Last of the Victorians.

HARRISON, PAUL W. The Arab At Home. American Mercury 4: 127, Jan., 1925. Brief Notices.

HART, ETHEL GERTRUDE. The Dream Girl. Smart Set 40: 155-156, July, 1913. Various Bad Novels.

HARTT, ROLLIN LYNDE. The People At Play. Smart Set 29: 157, Sept., 1909. The Books of the Dog Days.

HARVEY, ALEXANDER. William Dean Howells; a Study of the Achievement of a Literary Artist. Smart Set 53: 141, Dec., 1917. Critics Wild and Tame—II.

HASKIN, FREDERIC J.

The American Government. Smart Set 37: 156-157, Aug., 1912. Zola.

The Immigrant. Smart Set 41: 157, Oct., 1913. "With Your Kind Permission—."

HASTINGS, WELLS SOUTHWORTH. The Man in the Brown Derby. Smart Set 36: 152, Feb., 1912. Rounding Up the Novels.

HATTON, HENRY and ADRIAN PLATE. Magicians' Tricks and How They Are Done. Smart Set 33: 167, Jan., 1911. The Leading American Novelist.

HAUPTMANN, GERHART JOHANN ROBERT.

Atlantis. Smart Set 39: 155, March, 1913. Gerhart Hauptmann.

The Dramatic Works of Gerhart Hauptmann, translated and edited by Ludwig Lewisohn. Smart Set 39: 154-155, March, 1913. Gerhart Hauptmann; 41: 156-157, Dec., 1913. The Russians; 44: 159-160, Sept., 1914. Gerhart Hauptmann; 45: 436, April, 1915. The Grandstand Flirts with the Bleachers.

The Fool in Christ, Emanuel Quint. Smart Set 36: 155-156, Feb., 1912. Rounding Up the Novels.

The Sunken Bell [Drama League]. Smart Set 44: 159-160, Sept., 1914. Thirty-Five Printed Plays.

The Weavers. Smart Set 34: 152, Aug., 1911. The New Dramatic Literature.

HAY, IAN, *pseud. See* Beith, John Hay.

HAYWARD, CHARLES WILLIAMS. Re-Creating Human Nature. American Mercury 3: 255, Oct., 1924. Brief Notices.

HAZELTON, GEORGE COCHRANE. The Raven, the Love Story of Edgar Allan Poe. Smart Set 28: 155, June, 1909. Books for the Hammock and Deck Chair.

HAZEN, CHARLES DOWNER. Europe Since 1815. [Baltimore] Evening Sun, p. 6, July 15, 1910. Europe Since 1815.

HEARD, GERALD. Social Substance of Religion. American Mercury 25: 506-510, April, 1932. Quod Est Veritas?

HEARN, LAFCADIO.

Creole Sketches. American Mercury 2: 255, June, 1924. Brief Notices.

Fantastics and Other Fancies. Smart Set 61: 144, Jan., 1920. The Flood of Fiction—V.

HECHT, BEN.

Count Bruga. American Mercury 8: 509-510, Aug., 1926. Fiction.

Erik Dorn. Smart Set 66: 140-142, Oct., 1921. Notes on Books—III.

Fantazius Mallare. Smart Set 70: 139-140, Feb., 1923. Specimens of Current Fiction—II.

Gargoyles. *See* above, Fantazius Mallare.

1001 Afternoons in Chicago. Smart Set 70: 138-139, March, 1923. Adventures Among books.

HEINE, HEINRICH. Atta Troll, translated by Hermann Scheffauer. Smart Set 42: 156, Feb., 1914. Anything But Novels!

HELLER, OTTO.

Henrik Ibsen; Plays and Problems. Smart Set 38: 151, Oct., 1912. Synge and Others.

Prophets of Dissent. Smart Set 56: 143-144, Sept., 1918. Rattling the Subconscious—III.

HELSTON, JOHN. "Thracian Sea," a Novel. Town Topics 72: 16, Nov. 12, 1914.
Novels of Small Importance.

HEMINGWAY, ERNEST.

Death in the Afternoon. American Mercury 27: 506-507, Dec., 1932. The
Spanish Idea of a Good Time.

A Farewell to Arms. American Mercury 19: 126-127, Jan., 1930. Fiction by Adept
Hands.

Men without Women. American Mercury 14: 127, May, 1928. Fiction.

HENDERSON, ARCHIBALD.

Bernard Shaw, Playboy and Prophet. American Mercury 28: 507-510, April,
1933. Shaw and His Frankenstein.

The Changing Drama. Smart Set 45: 154-155, Feb., 1915. Lachrymose Love.

George Bernard Shaw, His Life and Works. Smart Set 36: 156, March, 1912.
The Prophet of the Superman.

Interpreters of Life. Smart Set 34: 156, June, 1911. The Horse Power of
Realism.

HENDERSON, ERNEST FLAGG. A Lady of the Old Régime. Smart Set 30: 159, Jan.,
1910. George Bernard Shaw As A Hero.

HENNESSY, MICHAEL EDMUND. Calvin Coolidge, from a Green Mountain Farm
to the White House. American Mercury 2: 252-254, June, 1924. The Heir of
Lincoln.

HERGESHEIMER, JOSEPH.

Berlin. American Mercury 27: 251-254, Oct., 1932. A Novelist on Furlough.

Biography & Bibliographies. American Mercury 27: 251-254, Oct., 1932. A
Novelist on Furlough.

The Bright Shawl. Smart Set 69: 138-139, Dec., 1922. The Monthly Feuilleton
—I—Cuba in Stained Glass. Reprinted in Current Reviews, edited by Lewis
Worthington Smith (New York, Holt, 1926) p. 189–191.

Cytherea. Smart Set 67: 138-140, April, 1922. The Niagara of Novels.

Gold and Iron. Smart Set 55: 143-144, July, 1918. The Public Prints—III.

The Happy End. Smart Set 61: 142-143, Jan., 1920. The Flood of Fiction—IV.

Java Head. Smart Set 58: 138-141, March, 1919. Mainly Fiction.

The Lay Anthony. Town Topics 72: 20-21, Oct. 22, 1914. The Sufferings of a
Virgin Hero; Smart Set 44: 307-308, Dec., 1914. Mush for the Multitude.

Mountain Blood. Smart Set 46: 154-155, Aug., 1915. The Sawdust Trail.

San Cristóbal de la Habana. Smart Set 64: 144, Feb., 1921. The Anatomy of
Ochlocracy—IV.

Sheridan: A Military Narrative. American Mercury 27: 251-254, Oct., 1932.
A Novelist on Furlough.

Swords and Roses. American Mercury 17: 253-254, June, 1929. Experiments by
Old Hands.

Tampico. American Mercury 9: 383, Nov., 1926. Certain Works of Fiction.

The Three Black Pennys. Smart Set 53: 142-143, Dec., 1917. Critics Wild and
Tame—IV.

BOOK REVIEWS

[Appraisal Obit.] [Baltimore Sunday] Sun, May 2, 1954. Mencken on Hergesheimer.

HERRICK, ROBERT.

His Great Adventure. Smart Set 42: 154, Jan., 1914. A Pestilence of Novels.

One Woman's Life. Smart Set 40: 149, June, 1913. A Nietzschean, a Swedenborgian and Other Queer Fowl.

HERTER NORTON, MARY DOWE. String Quartette Playing. American Mercury 6: 507, Dec., 1925. Books About Music.

HERTS, BENJAMIN RUSSELL. Depreciations. Smart Set 48: 152-153, Feb., 1916. A Massacre in a Mausoleum.

HERTZ, EMANUEL. Abraham Lincoln. American Mercury 25: 250-253, Feb., 1932. Nine American Statesmen.

HERVEY, HARRY. Caravans by Night. Smart Set 67: 142-143, April, 1922. The Niagara of Novels—II.

HERVIEU, PAUL ERNEST. The Labyrinth (Le Dédale). Smart Set 42: 157, Feb., 1914. Anything But Novels!

HERZEN, ALEXANDER. *See* Gertsen, Alexander Ivanovich.

HEWLETT, MAURICE HENRY.

Brazenhead the Great. Smart Set 34: 155, June, 1911. The Horse Power of Realism.

Mrs. Lancelot, a Comedy of Assumptions. Smart Set 39: 157, Jan., 1913. Again the Busy Fictioneers.

Rest Harrow, a Comedy of Resolution. Smart Set 32: 166-167, Nov., 1910. A Guide to Intelligent Eating.

The Song of Renny. Smart Set 36: 156-157, Feb., 1912. Rounding up the Novels.

HIBBEN, PAXTON.

Henry Ward Beecher, an American Portrait. [Baltimore] Evening Sun, March, 21 and Oct. 15, 1927.

The Peerless Leader; William Jennings Bryan. American Mercury 19: 122-125, Jan., 1930. American Worthies.

HICHENS, ROBERT SMYTHE.

Bella Donna. Smart Set 30: 157, Jan., 1910. George Bernard Shaw As A Hero.

The Dweller on the Threshold. Smart Set 34: 154-155, June, 1911. The Horse Power of Realism.

A Spirit in Prison. Smart Set 27: 157, Jan., 1909. A Road Map to the New Books.

HICKEY, WILLIAM. The Memoirs of William Hickey. Smart Set 17: 143-144, Jan., 1922. Book Article No. 158—I.

HICKS, SEYMOUR. Seymour Hicks, Twenty-Four Years of an Actor's Life. Smart Set 34: 154, Aug., 1911. The New Dramatic Literature.

WORKS BY H. L. M.

HILL, JAMES J. Civilization. Smart Set 32: 163-164, Sept., 1910. The Mackaye Mystery.

HILLQUIT, MORRIS and JOHN A. RYAN. Socialism: Promise or Menace? Smart Set 44: 154-155, Nov., 1914. Critics More or Less Bad.

HINKLE, BEATRICE M. The Re-creating of the Individual. American Mercury 1: 251, Feb., 1924. Pseudo-Science.

HINTON, JAMES. The Mystery of Pain. Smart Set 44: 157-158, Oct., 1914. A Review of Reviewers.

THE HISTORY OF CHRISTIANITY IN THE LIGHT OF MODERN KNOWLEDGE, a Collective Work. American Mercury 18: 253-254, Oct., 1929. Ghostly Matters.

HITLER, ADOLF. My Battle. American Mercury 30: 506-510, Dec., 1933. Hitlerismus.

HOBBS, SAMUEL HUNTINGTON. North Carolina: Economic and Social. American Mercury 20: 509-510, Aug., 1930. The Tarheel Empire.

HOLDEN, RAYMOND PECKHAM. Abraham Lincoln, the Politician and the Man. American Mercury 19: 122-125, Jan., 1930. American Worthies.

HOLLAND, RUPERT SARGENT. The Man in the Tower. Smart Set 29: 156, Dec., 1909. "A Doll's House"—With a Fourth Act.

HOLLOPETER, WILLIAM CLARENCE. Hay-Fever, Its Prevention and Cure. Smart Set 69: 138-140, Nov., 1922. Chiefly Pathological.

HOLMES, OLIVER WENDELL. The Dissenting Opinions of Mr. Justice Holmes, arranged by Alfred Lief, with a foreword by George W. Kirchwey. American Mercury 23: 122-124, May, 1930. Mr. Justice Holmes.

HOLMES, SAMUEL JACKSON.

An Introduction to General Biology. American Mercury 10: 251-252, Feb., 1927. The Science of Life.

The Trend of the Race. Smart Set 66: 142-144, Oct., 1921. Notes on Books —IV.

HOLT, GUY. A Bibliography of the Writings of James Branch Cabell. American Mercury 2: 254-255, June, 1924. Cabelliana.

HOOKER, BRIAN. The Right Man. Smart Set 26: 157, Dec., 1908. Oyez! Oyez! All Ye Who Read Books.

HOOVER, CALVIN BRYCE.

The Economic Life of Soviet Russia. American Mercury 22: 506-508, April, 1931. Life in the Marxian Utopia.

Germany Enters the Third Reich. American Mercury 30: 506-510, Dec., 1933. Hitlerismus.

HOOVER, DONALD D. "Copy!" A Handbook for Reporters and Students of Journalism. American Mercury 24: 254-255, Oct., 1931. American Journalism.

HOPKINS, WILLIAM JOHN. Old Harbor. Smart Set 30: 157, Feb., 1910. Books To Read and Books To Avoid.

HOPPER, JAMES and FRED R. BECHDOLT. "9009." Smart Set 27: 155, Feb., 1909. The Literary Olio; 28: 153-154, July, 1909.

BOOK REVIEWS

HORNBLOW, ARTHUR.

By Right of Conquest. Smart Set 29: 160, Nov., 1909. What About Nietzsche?

Training for the Stage. Smart Set 57: 269-271, Jan., 1917. Suffering Among Books.

HORWILL, HERBERT WILLIAM. A Dictionary of Modern American Usage. New York Herald Tribune Books, p. 6, Aug. 18, 1935. How Americans Speak American.

HOUGH, EMERSON.

54-40 or Fight. Smart Set 27: 158, April, 1909. The Novels That Bloom in the Spring, Tra-La!

Getting a Wrong Start, a Truthful Autobiography [Anon.] Smart Set 46: 293, June, 1915. Here Are Novels!

HOUGHTON, STANLEY. Hindle Wakes, a Play in Three Acts. Smart Set 42: 154, 155-156, Sept., 1913. Getting Rid of the Actor.

HOWARD, GEORGE FITZALAN BRONSON.

Birds of Prey. Smart Set 59: 144, June, 1919. The Infernal Mystery.

The Red Light of Mars. Smart Set 43: 157-158, July, 1914. Galsworthy and Others.

HOWARD, KATHLEEN. Confessions of an Opera Singer. Smart Set 58: 138-139, Jan., 1919. Nothing Much Is Here, Alas!

HOWARD, WILLIAM LEE. Lila Seri. Smart Set 27: 155-156, Jan., 1909. A Road Map of the New Books.

HOWARD, WILLIAM TRAVIS. Public Health Administration and the Natural History of Disease in Baltimore, Md., 1797-1920. American Mercury 4: 378-380, March, 1925. Man vs. the Microbe.

HOWE, EDGAR WATSON.

The Anthology of Another Town. Smart Set 64: 140, Jan., 1921. Consolation.

The Blessing of Business. Smart Set 54: 138-140, April, 1918. Business.

Plain People. American Mercury 17: 255, June, 1929. American Worthies.

Success Easier Than Failure. Smart Set 54: 139-141, Jan., 1918. Seven Pages About Books—II; 54: 138-140, April, 1918. Business.

HOWE, FREDERIC CLEMSON. The Confessions of a Reformer. American Mercury 7: 125-126, Jan., 1926. Katzenjammer.

HOWE, MARK ANTHONY DEWOLFE. Barrett Wendell and His Letters. American Mercury 4: 509-510, April, 1925. A New England Worthy.

HOWE, PERCIVAL PRESLAND. J. M. Synge, a Critical Study. Smart Set 38: 147-149, 150, Oct., 1912. Synge and Others.

HOWELLS, WILLIAM DEAN.

The Leatherwood God. Smart Set 51: 266-268, Jan., 1917. Suffering Among Books.

My Mark Twain. Smart Set 33: 166-167, Jan., 1911. The Leading American Novelist.

New Leaf Mills. Smart Set 40: 145-147, June, 1913. A Nietzschean, a Swedenborgian and Other Queer Fowl.

[Remarks.] Smart Set 34: 151-152, June, 1911. The Horse Power of Realism.

HOYT, NANCY. Roundabout. American Mercury 8: 509-510, Aug., 1926. Fiction.

HUDSON, WILLIAM HENRY. Letters from W. H. Hudson, 1901-1922, edited with an introduction by Edward Garnett. American Mercury 1: 510, April, 1924. Brief Notices.

HUEFFER, FORD MADOX. *See* Ford, Ford Madox.

HUEFFER, OLIVER MADOX. A Vagabond in New York. Smart Set 42: 158-159, Feb., 1914. Anything But Novels!

HUGHES, CHARLES EVANS. The Supreme Court of the United States. American Mercury 15: 123-125, Sept., 1928. The Curse of Government.

HUGHES, RUPERT. The Old Nest. Smart Set 37: 160, July, 1912. A Dip into the Novels.

HULL, EDITH MAUDE. The Sheik. Smart Set 66: 138-140, Oct., 1921. Notes on Books.

HUNEKER, JAMES GIBBONS.

Bedouins. Smart Set 62: 140, May, 1920. More Notes From A Diary.

Egoists: a Book of Supermen. [Baltimore Sunday] Sun, p. 21, April 11, 1909. A Book of Criticism; Smart Set 28: 153-154, June, 1909. Books for the Hammock and Deck Chair.

Ivory, Apes and Peacocks. Smart Set 47: 155-156, Dec., 1915. A Literary Behemoth.

New Cosmopolis. Smart Set 46: 444-447, July, 1915. The Prometheus of the Western World.

Old Fogy. Smart Set 43: 158-159, July, 1914. Galsworthy and Others; Town Topics 72: 21, Oct. 22, 1914. Huneker At His Best.

The Pathos of Distance. Smart Set 41: 153-155, Oct., 1913. "With Your Kind Permission—."

Steeplejack. New York Evening Post Literary Review, p. 2, Sept. 25, 1920. Huneker II, on Huneker I; Smart Set 63: 140-142, Dec., 1920. Chiefly Americans —II Huneker's Confessions.

Unicorn. Smart Set 53: 138-140, Dec., 1917. Critics Wild and Tame.

Variations. Smart Set 67: 141, Feb., 1922. Frank Harris and Others—II.

HUNTINGTON, ELLSWORTH. The Character of Races, as Influenced by Physical Environment, Natural Selection and Historical Development. American Mercury 4: 252-253, Feb., 1925. Homo Sapiens.

HUNTINGTON, HELEN MANCHESTER (GATES). *See* Granville-Barker, Helen Manchester (Gates).

HUTCHINSON, ARTHUR STUART-MENTETH. Once Abroad the Lugger—. Smart Set 32: 166-167, Sept., 1910. The Mackaye Mystery.

HUXLEY, ALDOUS LEONARD.

Antic Hay. American Mercury 1: 381, March, 1924. Three Gay Stories.

BOOK REVIEWS

Chrome Yellow. Smart Set 68: 142-143, May, 1922. Reflections on Prose Fiction—II—Scherzo for Bassoon; The Reviewer [Richmond, Va.] 3: 406-407, April, 1922.

Limbo. Smart Set 67: 140, Aug., 1920. Books More or Less Amusing—II.

Mortal Coils. Smart Set 69: 144, Nov., 1922. Chiefly Pathological.

Two or Three Graces. American Mercury 9: 127, Sept., 1926. Three Novels.

HUXLEY, THOMAS HENRY.

Essays. Chicago Sunday Tribune, Aug. 2, 1925. Huxley.

Science and Christian Tradition. *See* above.

HYAMSON, ALBERT MONTEFIORE. Palestine, the Rebirth of an Ancient People. Smart Set 54: 142-143, Jan., 1918. Seven Pages About Books—III.

IBSEN, HENRIK.

A Doll's House. Town Topics 72: 16, Aug. 27, 1914. The Printed Drama; Smart Set 66: 141-142, Nov., 1921. More Notes on Books.

[Compared to Strindberg.] Smart Set 37: 153-154, June, 1912. The Terrible Swede.

IBSEN, SIGURD.

Human Quintessence. Smart Set 40: 152, June, 1913. A Nietzschean, a Swedenborgian and Other Queer Fowl.

Robert Frank. Smart Set 45: 156, Feb., 1915. Lachrymose Love.

ICONOCLAST, *pseud. See* Hamilton, Mary Agnes (Adamson).

I'LL TAKE MY STAND; the South and the Agrarian Tradition, by Twelve Southerners. American Mercury 22: 379-381, March, 1931. Uprising in the Confederacy.

INGRAM, ELEANOR MARIE.

A Man's Hearth. Smart Set 48: 309, Jan., 1916. Partly About Books—10.

Stanton Wins. Smart Set 34: 156, July, 1911. Novels for Hot Afternoons.

The Unafraid. Smart Set 42: 157, Jan., 1914. A Pestilence of Novels.

IRONSIDE, JOHN. The Red Symbol. Smart Set 31: 156, July, 1910. A Fictioneer of the Laboratory.

IRVINE, ALEXANDER FITZGERALD. From the Bottom Up. Smart Set 31: 157, Aug., 1910. A Hot Weather Novelist.

IRWIN, WILLIAM HENRY. The House of Mystery, an Episode in the Career of Rosalie La Grange, Clairvoyant. Smart Set 31: 157, June, 1910. The Greatest of American Writers.

ISAACSON, CHARLES DAVID. Face to Face with Great Musicians. Smart Set 58: 138-139, Jan., 1919. Nothing Much Is Here, Alas!

ISHMAN, FREDERIC STEWART.

Half a Chance. Smart Set 29: 156, Oct., 1909. The Last of the Victorians.

Nothing but the Truth. Town Topics 72: 16, Nov. 12, 1914. Other Novels; Smart Set 44: 309, Dec., 1914. Mush for the Multitudes.

ISMAN, FELIX. Weber & Fields. American Mercury 4: 383, March, 1925. Brief Notices.

JACKS, LAWRENCE PEARSALL. My American Friends. Nation 137: 79-80, July 19, 1933. These Here States.

JACKSON, CHARLES TENNEY. The Day of Souls. Smart Set 30: 153, 155-156, April, 1910. A Glance at the Spring Fiction.

JACKSON, WILFRED SCARBOROUGH. Trial by Marriage. Smart Set 31: 158, May, 1910. In Praise of a Poet.

JAMES, HENRY.
Charles W. Eliot, President of Harvard University. Nation 131: 617, Dec. 3, 1930. A Master-Pedagogue.
The Finer Grain. Smart Set 33: 161-162, March, 1911. A Stack of Novels.
The Henry James Year Book, edited by Evelyn Garnaut Smalbey. See below, The Outcry.
Julia Bride. Smart Set 30: 156, Jan., 1910. George Bernard Shaw As A Hero.
The Outcry. Smart Set 36: 158, Jan., 1912. Conrad, Bennett, James et al.

JAMES, MARQUIS. The Raven: A Biography of Sam Houston. American Mercury 19: 122-125, Jan., 1930. American Worthies.

[JAMES, WINIFRED LEWELLIN.] Letters to My Son. Smart Set 31: 156, Aug., 1910. A Hot Weather Novelist.

JANVIER, MEREDITH. Baltimore in the Eighties and Nineties. [Baltimore] Evening Sun, April 15, 1933. Vignettes of Old Baltimore.

JEAN-AUBRY, G. See Aubry, Georges Jean.

JEANS, Sir JAMES HOPWOOD.
The Mysterious Universe. American Mercury 22: 252-254, Feb., 1931. The Eternal Conundrum.
The New Background of Science. American Mercury 30: 379-380, Nov., 1933. Science vs. Religion.

JEFFERS, JOHN ROBINSON. Flagons and Wine. Smart Set 43: 155-156, May, 1914. The Harp, the Sackbut and the Psaltery.

JEFFERSON, ALFRED. Thirty-Five Years of Public Life. Smart Set 48: 304-307, March, 1916. The Great American Art.

JENKS, GEORGE C. The Climax. Smart Set 31: 154-155, June, 1910. The Greatest of American Writers.

JENNINGS, HERBERT SPENCER. The Universe and Life. American Mercury 30: 379-381, Nov., 1933. Science vs. Religion.

JEPSON, EDGAR. Whitaker's Dukedom. Town Topics 72: 16, Nov. 12, 1914. Other Novels.

JESPERSEN, OTTO.
An International Language. American Mercury 15: 382-383, Nov., 1928. The Siege of Babel.

BOOK REVIEWS

Language: Its Nature, Development and Origin. Smart Set 68: 143-144, May, 1922. Reflections on Prose Fiction—III—Philological.

JESSE, FRYNTWYEL TENNYSON. Murder & Its Motives. American Mercury 4: 122-123, Jan., 1925. Crime and Punishment.

JOAD, C. E. M. The Babbitt Warren. Nation 124: 434, April 20, 1927. Thwacks from the Motherland.

JOHNSON, GERALD WHITE.

Andrew Jackson: An Epic in Homespun. American Mercury 13: 382-383, March, 1928. Andrew Jackson.

Randolph of Roanoke: A Political Fantasy. American Mercury 17: 255, June, 1929. American Worthies.

JOHNSON, JAMES WELDON. The Book of Negro Spirituals. American Mercury 6: 507, Dec., 1925. Books About Music.

JOHNSON, OWEN McMAHON.

The Eternal Boy, Being the Story of the Prodigious Hickey. Smart Set 27: 154-156, April, 1909. The Novels That Bloom in the Spring, Tra-La!; 28: 153-154, July, 1909.

The Salamander. Town Topics 71: 18, June 18, 1914. Lesser Novels; Smart Set 43: 159, Aug., 1914. Adventures Among the Novels.

Virtuous Wives. Smart Set 57: 142-143, Nov., 1918. Dithyrambs Against Learning—II.

The Woman Gives. Smart Set 50: 284, Nov., 1916. Professors at the Bat.

JOHNSON, ROBERT UNDERWOOD. Remembered Yesterdays. American Mercury 1: 249-250, Feb., 1924. Little One of the Immortals.

JOHNSON, WILLIS FLETCHER. George Harvey: 'A Passionate Patriot.' American Mercury 19: 122-125, Jan., 1930. American Worthies.

JOHNSTON, MARY.

Lewis Rand. Smart Set 27: 153-155, Jan., 1909. A Road Map of the New Books; 28: 153-154, July, 1909. The Best Novels of the Year.

The Long Roll. Smart Set 34: 155-156, Aug., 1911. The New Dramatic Literature.

JOLINE, ADRIAN HOFFMAN.

At the Library Table. Smart Set 31: 159-160, June, 1910. The Greatest of American Writers.

Edgehill Essays. Smart Set 34: 168, May, 1911. Novels—The Spring Crop.

JONES, HENRY ARTHUR.

The Foundations of a National Drama. Smart Set 41: 158, Nov., 1913. Marie Corelli's Sparring Partner.

Mary Goes First. Smart Set 44: 159, Sept., 1914. Thirty-Five Printed Plays.

JORDAN, DAVID STARR. The Days of a Man. Smart Set 71: 137-139, June, 1923. Notices of Books—II—An American Pedagogue.

JORDAN, KATE. The Creeping Tides. Smart Set 40: 154-155, July, 1913. Various Bad Novels.

WORKS BY H. L. M.

Josephson, Matthew. Zola and His Time. American Mercury 15: 506-508, Dec., 1928. The Father of Them All.

Josey, Charles Conant. Race and National Solidarity. American Mercury 1: 122-123, Jan., 1924. The Uplift: Export Department.

Joyce, James. A Portrait of the Artist as a Young Man. Smart Set 52: 142-143, Aug., 1917. Criticism of Criticism of Criticism.

Judge, Jr. *pseud. See* Anthony, Norman.

Jung, Carl Gustav. Analytical Psychology. Smart Set 56: 138-140, Sept., 1918. Rattling the Subconscious.

Kallen, Horace Meyer. Indecency and the Seven Arts. American Mercury 20: 253-254, June, 1930. The Smut-Snufflers.

Kammerer, Paul.
The Inheritance of Acquired Characteristics, translated by A. Paul Maerker-Branden. American Mercury 3: 380, Nov., 1924. Marvels from Vienna.

Rejuvenation and the Prolongation of Human Efficiency. American Mercury 1: 251, Feb., 1924. Pseudo-Science.

Kauffman, Reginald Wright.
The House of Bondage. Smart Set 32: 165, Dec., 1910. Mainly About Novels; 40: 153-154, May 1913. Weep for the White Slave!

My Heart and Stephanie. Smart Set 31: 155, June, 1910. The Greatest of American Writers.

Kaun, Alexander Samuel. Leonid Andreyev: A Critical Study. American Mercury 1: 127, Jan., 1925. The Land of Lunacy.

Kaup, Elizabeth Bartol (Dewing).
A Big Horse To Ride, by Elizabeth Bartol Dewing. Smart Set 35: 155-156, Sept., 1911. A 1911 Model Dream Book.

Other People's Houses. Smart Set 30: 155, March, 1910. The Literary Heavyweight Champion.

Kavanagh, Marcus A. You Be The Judge. American Mercury 21: 380-383, Nov., 1930. The Criminal.

Kaye-Smith, Sheila. The Three Furlongers. Town Topics 72: 16, Oct. 29, 1914. Rita and Laurence; Smart Set 44: 308-309, Dec., 1914. Mush for the Multitude.

Keays, Hersilia A. Mitchell (Copp). I and My True Love. Smart Set 26: 158-159, Dec., 1908. Oyez! Oyez! All Ye Who Read Books.

Keller, Albert Galloway. Man's Rough Road. American Mercury 27: 254-255, Oct., 1932. The Travail of Man.

Kelley, Francis Clement. The Bishop Jots It Down. [Baltimore] Evening Sun, p. 10, May 28, 1939. Reminiscences of a Bishop.

Kellner, Leon. American Literature, translated from the German by Julia Franklin. Smart Set 42: 150-153, Oct., 1915. The Literature of a Moral Republic.

BOOK REVIEWS

KELLOCK, HAROLD. "Mr. Hobby," a Cheerful Romance. Smart Set 40: 155-156, July, 1913. Various Bad Novels.

KELLOGG, VERNON LYMAN. Evolution: The Way of Man. American Language 3: 255, Oct., 1924. Brief Notices.

KELLY, HOWARD ATWOOD.

A Scientific Man and the Bible. American Mercury 7: 251-253, Feb., 1926. Fides Ante Intellectum.

Walter Reed and Yellow Fever. [Baltimore] Evening Sun, Sept. 8, 1923. Mencken Dissects Dr. Kelly's Book.

KEMP, HARRY.

More Miles: An Autobiographical Novel. Amercian Mercury 10: 382-383, March, 1927. Literary Confidences.

Tramping on Life. Smart Set 70: 140-142, Jan., 1923. Confidences—II.

KENNEDY, CHARLES RANN.

The Idol Breaker. Smart Set 43: 157, July, 1914. Galsworthy and Others.

The Necessary Evil, a One Act Stage Play. Smart Set 40: 153-155, May, 1913. Weep for the White Slave!

The Winterfeast. Smart Set 27: 157-158, March, 1909. The Literary Clinic.

KENNEDY, MARGARET. The Constant Nymph. American Mercury 5: 382-383, July, 1925. New Fiction.

KENNEDY, WILLIAM SLOANE. The Real John Burroughs. American Mercury 3: 255, Oct., 1924. Brief Notices.

KENT, FRANK RICHARDSON.

The Great Game of Politics. American Mercury 1: 248-249, Feb., 1924. How We Are Governed.

Political Behavior. American Mercury 15: 383, Nov., 1928. The Technique of the Politician.

KENT, OLIVER. Her Right Divine. Smart Set 40: 150, June, 1913. A Nietzschean, a Swedenborgian and Other Queer Fowl.

KERR, ALFRED. New York und London. American Mercury 1: 507-508, April, 1924. God's Country: Exterior View.

KESTER, PAUL. His Own Country. Smart Set 53: 138-142, Sept., 1917. Si Mutare Potest Aethiops Pellum Suam.

KESTER, VAUGHAN. The Prodigal Judge. [Baltimore] Evening Sun, p. 6, March 14, 1911; Smart Set 34: 166, May, 1911. Novels—The Spring Crop. See "Contributions to Books and Pamphlets," 1911.

KEY, ELLEN KAROLINA SOFIA. Love and Marriage, translated from the Swedish by Arthur J. Chater with a critical and biographical introduction by Havelock Ellis. Smart Set 35: 155, Sept., 1911. A 1911 Model Dream Book.

KEYNES, JOHN MAYNARD. Monetary Reform. American Mercury 1: 510, April, 1924. Brief Notices.

KILMER, JOYCE. Joyce Kilmer, edited with a memoir by Robert Cortes Holliday. Smart Set 58: 138-139, April, 1919. Notes of a Poetry-Hater.

KING, MARY RAYNOR HYMAN. The Judgment. Smart Set 35: 154-155, Dec., 1911. An Overdose of Novels.

KING, VERONICA and PAUL KING. The Raven on the Skyscraper. Nation 122: 152-153, Feb. 10, 1926. Admonitions from the Motherland.

KINGSMILL, HUGH, *pseud. See* Lunn, Hugh Kingsmill.

KIPLING, RUDYARD.
Abaft the Funnel. Smart Set 30: 157, Jan., 1910. George Bernard Shaw As A Hero.
Actions and Reactions. *See* above, Abaft the Funnel.
With the Night Mail. Smart Set 28: 158, June, 1909. Books for the Hammock and Deck Chair.

KITTREDGE, GEORGE LYMAN. Witchcraft in Old & New England. American Mercury 17: 123-124, May, 1929. The Gods and Their Agents.

KLEIN, CHARLES. The Gamblers. Smart Set 35: 156, Sept., 1911. A 1911 Model Dream Book.

KNOWLES, MABEL WINIFRED. The Gipsy Count, by May Wynne [pseud.]. Smart Set 28: 154, Aug., 1909. Novels and Other Books—Chiefly Bad.

KNOX, JOHN. The Great Mistake. American Mercury 22: 122-126, Jan., 1931. Mr. Hoover under the Muckrake.

KOMROFF, MANUEL. The Grace of Lambs. American Mercury 6: 381, Nov., 1925. Fiction Good and Bad.

KOPALD, SYLVIA BEATRICE. *See* Selekman, Sylvia (Kopald).

KORNILOV, ALEXANDER ALEXSANDROVICH. Modern Russian History . . . translated and extended by Alexander Kaun. American Mercury 4: 127, Jan., 1925. The Land of Lunacy.

KRAPP, GEORGE PHILIP. The English Language in America. Nation 121: 599, Nov. 25, 1925. The Vulgate.

KRASNER, DAVID. Horace Traubel: His Life and Work. Smart Set 62: 142, May, 1920. More Notes from a Diary—II.

KREHBIEL, HENRY EDWARD.
Afro-American Folk-Songs. Smart Set 43: 160, July, 1914. Galsworthy and Others.
A Book of Operas. Smart Set 30: 157, March, 1910. The Literary Heavyweight Champion.
The Pianoforte and Its Music. Smart Set 34: 157, July, 1911. Novels for Hot Afternoons.

KREYMBORG, ALFRED. Troubadour. [Baltimore] Evening Sun, April 4, 1925. "As HLM Sees It."

KRUTCH, JOSEPH WOOD.
Edgar Allan Poe: A Study in Genius. Nation 122: 289-290, March 17, 1926. The Mystery of Poe.

The Modern Temper. American Mercury 17: 251-253, June, 1929. What Is It All About?

KUMMER, FREDERIC ARNOLD.

The Brute. Smart Set 38: 157-158, Sept., 1912. Prose Fiction Ad Infinitum.

A Song of Sixpence. Smart Set 40: 158, May, 1913. Weep for the White Slave!

KUPRIN, ALEXANDER IVANOVICH. The River of Life. Smart Set 49: 153, June, 1916. A Soul's Adventures—3.

KURATH, HANS and GEORGE O. CURME. A Grammar of the English Language, v. 3 Syntax. American Mercury 23: 508-509, Aug., 1931. The Growth of English.

LADD, FREDERIC PIERPONT. One Fair Daughter. Smart Set 28: 157, July, 1909. The Best Novels of the Year.

LA FOLLETTE, ROBERT MARION. Personal Narrative of Political Experiences. Smart Set 40: 154-155, Aug., 1913. A Counterblast to Buncombe.

LAGERLOF, SELMA OTTILIANA LOVISA. The Girl from the Marsh Croft. Smart Set 31: 154, Aug., 1910. A Hot Weather Novelist.

LAING, GRAHAM ALLAN. Towards Technocracy. American Mercury 28: 505-507, April, 1933. Old Dr. Scott's Bile Beans.

LAMB, FRANK H. Rotary: A Business Man's Interpretation. American Mercury 11: 379-381, July, 1927. The Philosophy of Rotary.

LA MOTTE, ELLEN N. Civilization, Tales of the Orient. Smart Set 59: 141, Aug., 1919. Novels, Chiefly Bad—II.

LANDOR, ARNOLD HENRY SAVAGE. Everywhere: The Memoirs of an Explorer. American Mercury 4: 383, March, 1925. Brief Notices.

LANDOWSKA, WANDA. Music of the Past. American Mercury 6: 506, Dec., 1925. Books About Music.

LARDNER, RING WILMER.

How To Write Short Stories [with Samples] American Mercury 2: 376-377, July, 1924. Ring W. Lardner.

Lose with a Smile. American Mercury 29: 254-255, June, 1933. Pongo Americanus.

The Love Nest, and Other Stories. American Mercury 8: 254-255, June, 1926. A Humorist Shows His Teeth.

You Know Me, Al. Chicago Sunday Tribune, May 31, 1925. Ring W. Lardner.

LATIMER, LOUISE PAYSON. Your Washington and Mine. American Mercury 2: 255, June, 1924. Brief Notices.

LAVINE, EMANUEL HENRY.

"Gimme," or, How Public Officials Get Rich. American Mercury 23: 509-510, Aug., 1931. Law Enforcement.

The Third Degree. American Mercury 22: 121-122, Jan., 1931. Cops and Their Ways.

WORKS BY H. L. M.

LAWES, LEWIS EDWARD.

Life and Death in Sing Sing. American Mercury 16: 124-127, Jan., 1929. Men in Cages.

20,000 Years in Sing Sing. American Mercury 26: 379-382, July, 1932. Notes on an Insoluble Problem.

LAWRENCE, DAVID HERBERT.

The Lost Girl. [Baltimore] Evening Sun, Feb. 26, 1921. Shoddy and Silly Piece of Work; Smart Set 65: 143-144, May, 1921. The Land of the Free—IV.

Pornography & Obscenity. American Mercury 20: 253-254, June, 1930. The Smut-Snufflers.

Psychology and the Unconscious. Smart Set 66: 144, Sept., 1921. From the Diary of a Reviewer—VII; 68: 142-143, July, 1922. Saving the World—III.

Women in Love. Smart Set 70: 139-140, Feb., 1923. Specimens of Current Fiction—III.

LAY, WILFRID. A Plea for Monogamy. American Mercury 1: 251, Feb., 1924. Pseudo-Science.

LEACOCK, STEPHEN BUTLER. Sunshine Sketches. Smart Set 39: 158, Jan., 1913. Again the Busy Fictioneers.

LEARY, LEWIS GASTON. Problems of Protestantism. American Mercury 29: 126-127, May, 1933. Sacerdotal Agonies.

LEDOUX, LOUIS VERNON. Yzdra, a Tragedy. Smart Set 29: 157, Dec., 1909. "A Doll's House"—With a Fourth Act.

LEE, GERALD STANLEY.

Crowds, a Moving Picture of Democracy. Smart Set 41: 159-160, Nov., 1913. Marie Corelli's Sparring Partner.

We. Smart Set 49: 295-296, July, 1916. Savonarolas A-Sweat—II.

LEE, IVY LEDBETTER. Present-Day Russia. American Mercury 14: 126, May, 1928. A 100% American in Muscovy.

LE FEVRE, LOUIS. Liberty and Restraint. American Mercury 25: 379-383, March, 1932. The Case for Democracy.

LE GALLIENNE, RICHARD.

Attitudes and Avowals. Smart Set 33: 168, March, 1911. A Stack of Novels.

New Poems. Smart Set 30: 155, Jan., 1910. George Bernard Shaw As A Hero.

October Vagabonds. See above, Attitudes and Avowals.

Orestes. Smart Set 31: 158-159, June, 1910. The Greatest of American Writers.

LEGENDRE, AIMÉ FRANÇOIS. Modern Chinese Civilization. American Mercury 18: 510, Dec., 1929. The Chinese As They Really Are.

LEONARD, JONATHAN NORTON. Men of Maracaibo. American Mercury 29: 379-381, July, 1933. Life Below the Isthmus.

LEONARD, MARY FINLEY. The Little Red Chimney. Town Topics 72: 16, Nov. 12, 1914. Novels of Small Importance.

LEROUX, GASTON. The Phantom of the Opera. Smart Set 33: 164, April, 1911. The Meredith of Tomorrow.

BOOK REVIEWS

LEVINE, ISAAC DON.

The Man Lenin. American Mercury 3: 382-383, Nov., 1924. Barbary in Europe. Stalin. American Mercury 23: 506-508, Aug., 1931. The Asiatic Tammany.

LEWIS, ALFRED HENRY. The Apaches of New York. Smart Set 38: 158, Nov., 1912. Novels Bad, Half Bad and Very Bad.

LEWIS, LLOYD.

Myths After Lincoln. American Mercury 17: 380-382, July, 1929. The Making of a God.

Sherman: Fighting Prophet. American Mercury 28: 379-381, March, 1933. The Attila of the West.

LEWIS, SINCLAIR.

Ann Vickers. American Mercury 28: 382-383, March, 1933. A Lady of Vision.

Arrowsmith. [Baltimore] Evening Sun, March 7, 1925. As H.L.M. Sees It; Chicago Sunday Tribune, March 8, 1925. Sinclair Lewis' "Arrowsmith"; American Mercury 4: 507-509, April, 1925. "Arrowsmith."

Babbitt. Smart Set 69: 138-140, Oct., 1922. Portrait of an American Citizen; Now and Then [London] Oct. 22, 1922.

Dodsworth. American Mercury 16: 506-508, April, 1929. Escape and Return.

Elmer Gantry. American Mercury 10: 506-508, April, 1927. Man of God: American Style.

Main Street. Smart Set 64: 138-140, Jan., 1921. Consolation—I—An American Novel; 64: 141-142, March, 1921. A Soul's Adventures—II—American Novels.

Mantrap. American Mercury 8: 509-510, Aug., 1926. Fiction.

The Man Who Knew Coolidge. American Mercury 14: 253-254, June, 1928. Babbitt Redivivus.

LEWISOHN, LUDWIG.

The Case of Mr. Crump. American Mercury 10: 379-380, March, 1927. Portrait of a Lady.

Mid-Channel: An American Chronicle. American Mercury 17: 379-380, July, 1929. Man and the Universe.

The Modern Drama. Smart Set 46: 447-448, July, 1915. The Prometheus of the Western World.

The Spirit of Modern German Literature. Smart Set 52: 140-141, June, 1917. The Plague of Books.

Up Stream: An American Chronicle. Nation 114: 434, 436, April 12, 1922. Dream and Awakening.

LINCOLN, ABRAHAM. [Comments on Style] Smart Set 62: 140-142, May, 1920. More Notes from a Diary—II.

LINDLEY, ERNEST KIDDER. Franklin D. Roosevelt, a Career in Progressive Democracy. American Mercury 25: 250-253, Feb., 1932. Nine American Statesmen.

LINDSEY, BENJAMIN BARR and WAINWRIGHT EVANS. The Companionate Marriage. American Mercury 13: 126-127, Jan., 1928. The Holy State of Bliss.

LIPPMANN, WALTER.

American Inquisitors. American Mercury 15: 123-125, Sept., 1928. The Curse of Government.

Drift and Mastery. Smart Set 45: 434-436, April, 1915. The Grandstand Flirts with the Bleachers.

The Phantom Public. American Mercury 7: 125-126, Jan., 1926. Katzenjammer.

A Preface to Morals. American Mercury 17: 379-380, July, 1929. Man and the Universe.

A Preface to Politics. Smart Set 40: 154, Aug., 1913. A Counterblast to Buncombe.

Public Opinion. Smart Set 68: 138-144, June, 1922. Demagoguery as Art and Science.

LITTLE, FRANCES, *pseud. See* Macaulay, Fannie Caldwell.

LITTLE, SHELBY. George Washington. American Mercury 12: 122-125, Jan., 1930. American Worthies.

LLOYD, HENRY DEMAREST. Men, the Workers. Smart Set 29: 158, Dec., 1909. "A Doll's House"—With a Fourth Act.

LOCKE, ALAIN LE ROY, *ed.* The New Negro: An Interpretation. American Mercury 7: 254-255, Feb., 1926. The Aframerican: New Style.

LOCKE, WILLIAM JAMES. The Fortunate Youth. Town Topics 71: 18, June 18, 1914. Lesser Novels.

LOCKE, WILLIAM JOHN.

A Christmas Mystery. Smart Set 33: 164-165, Jan., 1911. The Leading American Novelist.

The Fortunate Youth. Smart Set 43: 159, Aug., 1914. Adventures Among the New Novels.

The Glory of Clementina. Smart Set 35: 155, 156, Oct., 1911. Brieux and Others.

The Joyous Adventures of Aristide Pujol. Smart Set 39: 157-158, Jan., 1913. Again the Busy Fictioneers.

Septimus. Smart Set 27: 154-155, April, 1909. The Novels That Bloom in the Spring, Tra-La!; 28: 153-154, July, 1909.

Simon the Jester. Smart Set 31: 153-154, Aug., 1910. A Hot Weather Novelist.

Stella Maris. Smart Set 40: 149, June, 1913. A Nietzschean, a Swedenborgian and Other Queer Fowl.

The William T. Locke Calendar, compiled by Emma M. Pope. Smart Set 45: 464, Jan., 1915. A Gamey Old Gaul.

LOEB, HAROLD. Life in a Technocracy. American Mercury 28: 505-507, April, 1933. Old Dr. Scott's Bile Beans.

LONDON, JACK.

Burning Daylight. Smart Set 33: 164, Jan., 1911. The Leading American Novelist.

John Barleycorn. Smart Set 41: 160, Nov., 1913. Marie Corelli's Sparring Partner.

Lost Face. Smart Set 31: 154, June, 1910. The Greatest of American Writers.

Martin Eden. Smart Set 29: 154-155, Dec., 1909. "A Doll's House"—With a Fourth Act.

BOOK REVIEWS

Michael, Brother of Jerry. Smart Set 54: 144, March, 1918. Literae Humaniores —II.

The Mutiny of the Elsinore. Smart Set 14: 310, Dec., 1914. Mush for the Multitude.

The Scarlet Plague. Smart Set 46: 450, July, 1915. The Prometheus of the Western World.

A Son of the Sun. Smart Set 38: 158, Nov., 1912. Novels Bad, Half Bad and Very Bad.

The Star Rover. Smart Set 48: 309, Jan., 1916. Partly About Books—9—A Sound Workman.

The Strength of the Strong. Town Topics 72: 14, July 16, 1914. The Two Jack Londons; Smart Set 44: 160, Oct., 1914. A Review of Reviewers.

Long, John Luther. War, or What Happens When One Loves One's Enemy. Smart Set 40: 150-151, June, 1913. A Nietzschean, a Swedenborgian, and Other Queer Fowl.

Loos, Anita. Gentlemen Prefer Blondes. American Mercury 7: 127, Jan., 1926. Brief Notices.

Loosmore, W. Charles. Nerves and the Man. New York Evening Post Literary Review, p. 4, Feb. 26, 1921. That "Nervous Breakdown."

Lounsbery, Alice. Gardens Near the Sea. Smart Set 34: 157, June, 1911. The Horse Power of Realism.

Lovejoy, Arthur Oncken. The Revolt Against Dualism. American Mercury 24: 123-124, Sept., 1931. In the Grove of Athene.

Loveman, Robert.

April Rain. Smart Set 39: 147-148, April, 1913. The Burbling of the Bards.

The Blushful South and Hippocrene. Smart Set 29: 157, Oct., 1909. The Last of the Victorians.

Lovette, Leland P. Naval Customs, Traditions and Usage. [Baltimore] Evening Sun, Sept. 15, 1934. Amenities of the Sea.

Lowes, John Livingston. Convention and Revolt in Poetry. Smart Set 59: 138, 140-141, July, 1919. The Coroner's Inquest.

Lowie, Robert Harry.

The Origin of the State. American Mercury 12: 383, Nov., 1927. What Constitutes a State?

Primitive Religion. American Mercury 3: 510, Dec., 1924. Brief Notices.

Primitive Society. Smart Set 63: 144, Aug., 1920. Books More or Less Amusing.

Lowndes, Marie Adelaide (Belloc).

Studies in Wives. Smart Set 31: 158, July, 1910. A Fictioneer of the Laboratory.

The Uttermost Farthing. Smart Set 29: 157-158, Dec., 1909. "A Doll's House" —With a Fourth Act.

Lowrie, Donald. My Life out of Prison. Smart Set 46: 293, June, 1915. Here are Novels!

WORKS BY H. L. M.

LUBBOCK, ALFRED BASIL. Deep Sea Warriors. Smart Set 30: 158-159, April, 1910. A Glance at the Spring Fiction.

LUCATELLI, LUIGI. Teodoro, the Sage . . . translated by Morris Bishop. Smart Set 71: 141, July, 1923. Some New Books—III.

LUDOVICI, ANTHONY MARIO.
Man: An Indictment. American Mercury 11: 253-254, June, 1927. The Decline of Man.
Nietzsche and Art. Smart Set 40: 156, Aug., 1913. A Counterblast to Buncombe.

LUNN, HUGH KINGSMILL. An Anthology of Invective and Abuse, compiled by Hugh Kingsmill [pseud.] Nation 130: 549, May 7, 1930. Harsh Words.

LUTHER, MARK LEE. The Sovereign Power. Smart Set 34: 156-157, Aug., 1911. The New Dramatic Literature.

LUTZ, ALMA. Emma Willard: Daughter of Democracy. American Mercury 19: 122-125, Jan., 1930. American Worthies.

LYNCH, HARRIET POWE, comp. Year Book of Southern Poets. Smart Set 29: 159-160, Sept., 1909. The Books of the Dog Days.

LYND, ROBERT STAUGHTON and HELEN MERRELL LYND. Middletown: A Study in Contemporary American Culture [Baltimore] Evening Sun, editorial page, Jan. 14, 1929. A Treatise on the Americano; American Mercury 16: 379-381, March, 1929. A City in Moronia.

LYONS, ALBERT MICHAEL NEIL. Sixpenny Pieces. Smart Set 29: 156-157, Oct., 1909. The Last of the Victorians.

LYTTON, EDWARD ROBERT BULWER-LYTTON, 1st earl of. The Life of Bulwer-Lytton, by his grandson. Smart Set 42: 143, 149, April, 1914. Roosevelt, Bulwer-Lytton and Anthony Comstock.

MCADOO, WILLIAM GIBBS. Crowded Years, Reminiscences. American Mercury 25: 250-253, Feb., 1932. Nine American Statesmen.

MCALISTER, FRANK A. The Last Mile. Smart Set 69: 139, Dec., 1922. The Monthly Feuilleton—II—More Katzenjammer.

MACAULEY, FANNIE (CALDWELL). Little Sister Snow, by Frances Little [pseud.] Smart Set 30: 157, Jan., 1910. George Bernard Shaw As A Hero.

MACAULEY, WARD. Reclaiming the Ballot. Smart Set 50: 284-285, Sept., 1916. Portrait of a Tragic Comedian—II.

MACBETH, MADGE. The Winning Game. Smart Set 31: 155, Aug., 1910. A Hot Weather Novelist.

MCBRIDE, ROBERT EKIN, tr. The Revellers. Smart Set 29: 159, Sept., 1909. The Books of the Dog Days.

MACCALLUM, WILLIAM GEORGE. William Stewart Halsted, Surgeon. American Mercury 22: 383, March, 1931. A Great American Surgeon.

MCCARTHY, JUSTIN HUNTLY. The God of Love. Smart Set 30: 155, March, 1910. The Literary Heavyweight Champion.

BOOK REVIEWS

McClure, James Gore King. The Supreme Book of Mankind. American Mercury 20: 254-255, June, 1930. The Ghostly Realm.

McClure, John Peebles. Airs and Ballads. Smart Set 55: 138-139, June, 1918. Hark, Hark, the Lark.

MacCulloch, John Arnott and George Foot Moore, eds. The Mythology of All Races, v. 5. American Mercury 28: 121-123, Jan., 1933. The Genesis of a Deity.

McCurdy, George Grant. Human Origins: A Manual of Prehistory. American Mercury 5: 126-127, May, 1925. The Infancy of the Race; Chicago Sunday Tribune, Aug. 29, 1926. Man as a Mammal.

McCutcheon, George Barr.

The Rose in the Ring. Smart Set 33: 161-162, March, 1911. A Stack of Novels.

What's-His Name. Smart Set 34: 153, June, 1911. The Horse Power of Realism.

McCutcheon, John Tinney. In Africa. Smart Set 33: 167, March, 1911. A Stack of Novels.

MacDonagh, Thomas. Literature in Ireland. Smart Set 51: 138-141, March, 1917. The Books of the Irish.

McFee, William.

Captain Macedoine's Daughter. Smart Set 66: 140-142, Oct., 1921. Notes on Books—III.

Casuals of the Sea. Smart Set 50: 144, Oct., 1916. The Creed of a Novelist—5.

Command. Smart Set 70: 138-139, Feb., 1923. Specimens of Current Fiction.

An Ocean Tramp. Smart Set 65: 142-143, July, 1921. Literary Notes.

Race. American Mercury 2: 380, July, 1924. Rambles in Fiction.

Macfie, Ronald Campbell. Science Rediscovers God. American Mercury 23: 306-310, April, 1932. Quod Est Veritas?

MacGrath, Harold.

The Carpet from Bagdad. Smart Set 35: 155, Oct., 1911. Brieux and Others.

The Goose Girl. Smart Set 29: 156, Oct., 1909. The Last of the Victorians.

Parrot & Company. Smart Set 40: 154-155, July, 1913. Various Bad Novels.

A Splendid Hazard. Smart Set 31: 159-160, July, 1910. A Fictioneer of the Laboratory.

McGraw, John J. My Thirty Years in Baseball. Nation 117: 40, July 11, 1923. An Eminent; Smart Set 71: 138-139, Aug., 1923. Biography and Other Fiction.

Machen, Arthur.

The Hill of Dreams. Smart Set 71: 141-143, Aug., 1923. Biography and Other Fiction—III.

The House of Souls. See above.

The Shining Pyramid. See above.

Things Near and Far. See above.

McInnes, Tom. Lonesome Bar. Smart Set 29: 157-158, Oct., 1909. The Last of the Victorians.

MacIver, Robert Morrison. The Modern State. American Mercury 11: 507-510, Aug., 1927. What Constitutes a State?

Mackay, Helen Gansevoort (Edwards).

Half-Loaves. Smart Set 35: 156, Sept., 1911. A 1911 Model Dream Book.

Houses of Glass. Smart Set 28: 156, June, 1909. Books for the Hammock and Deck Chair.

MacKaye, Percy.

Anti-Matrimony. Smart Set 33: 166-167, Feb., 1911. The Revival of the Printed Play.

The Canterbury Pilgrims. Smart Set 37: 155, June, 1912. The Terrible Swede.

A Garland to Sylvia. Smart Set 32: 161-163, Sept., 1910. The MacKaye Mystery.

The Immigrants. Smart Set 48: 156, Feb., 1916. A Massacre in a Mausoleum.

The Playhouse and the Play. Smart Set 28: 155, 157, Aug., 1909. Novels and Other Books—Chiefly Bad.

Tomorrow. Smart Set 37: 155-157, June, 1912. The Terrible Swede.

Yankee Fantasies. *See* above, Tomorrow.

Mackenzie, Compton. Youth's Encounter. Smart Set 42: 158, Jan., 1914. A Pestilence of Novels.

McKinsey, Folger. Songs of the Daily Life. Smart Set 37: 155-156, May, 1912. The Bards in Battle Royal.

McKnight, George H. English Words and Their Background. [Baltimore] Evening Sun, Feb. 3, 1923. Patois and the Professor.

MacLane, Mary.

I, Mary MacLane. Smart Set 52: 138-142, July, 1917. The Cult of Dunsany—II.

The Story of Mary MacLane. New edition. Smart Set 35: 157, Dec., 1911. An Overdose of Novels.

MacLaurin, Charles. Post-Mortem, Essays Historical and Medical. Smart Set 72: 138, 140, Nov., 1923. Notices of Books.

MacLean, Charles Agnew. The Mainspring. Smart Set 38: 158, Sept., 1912. Prose Fiction Ad Infinitum.

McMurtrie, Douglas Crawford. Modern Typography & Layout. American Mercury 19: 252-253, Feb., 1930. The Art of the Printer.

McPherson, Aimée Semple. In the Service of the King. American Mercury 13: 506-508, April, 1928. Two Enterprising Ladies.

McRae, Milton Alexander. Forty Years in Newspaperdom. American Mercury 4: 123-124, Jan., 1925. A Wholesaler in Journalism.

Macvane, Edith.

Her Word of Honor. Smart Set 38: 155, Sept., 1912. Prose Fiction Ad Infinitum.

Tarantella. *See* above p. 154-155.

McWilliams, Carey. Ambrose Bierce: A Biography. American Mercury 19: 251-252, Feb., 1930. Bierce Emerges from the Shadows.

BOOK REVIEWS

McWILLIAMS, HELEN HILL. A Bit o' Silence. Smart Set 39: 158, Jan., 1913. Again the Busy Fictioneers.

MACY, JOHN ALBERT.

The Critical Game. Smart Set 70: 141, March, 1923. Adventures Among Books.

The Spirit of American Literature. Smart Set 52: 140, June, 1917. The Plague of Books.

MAETERLINCK, MAURICE. The Great Secret. Smart Set 68: 139-140, Aug., 1922. The Intellectual Squirrel-Cage—II—Camille at the Bat Again.

MAJOR, CHARLES. The Touchstone of Fortune. Smart Set 38: 155-156, Sept., 1912. Prose Fiction Ad Infinitum.

MALET, LUCAS, pseud. See Harrison, Mary St. Leger (Kingsley).

MANSFIELD, KATHERINE. The Doves' Nest and Other Stories. Smart Set 72: 142-143, Nov., 1923. Notices of Books—II.

MANSFIELD, MILBURG FRANCISCO. Italian Highways and Byways from a Motor Car, by Francis Miltoun [pseud.] Smart Set 28: 158, Aug., 1909. Novels and Other Books—Chiefly Bad.

MARCY, MARY EDNA (TOBIAS). Out of the Dump. Smart Set 28: 158, May, 1909. Some Novels—and a Good One.

MARDEN, ORISON SWETT. The Miracle of Right Thought. Smart Set 33: 165-166, April, 1911. The Meredith of Tomorrow.

MARK TWAIN. See Twain, Mark, pseud.

MARKS, HENRY KINGDON. Peter Middleton. Smart Set 60: 144, Nov., 1919. Notes for Indian Summer—IV.

MARLOWE, CHRISTOPHER. [Comments] Smart Set 58: 143, March, 1919.

MARRIOTT, CHARLES.

The Catfish. Smart Set 40: 158, July, 1913. Various Bad Novels.

The Kiss of Helen. Smart Set 27: 156-157, April, 1909. The Novels That Bloom in the Spring, Tra-La!

"Now!" Smart Set 32: 163-164, Dec., 1910. Mainly About Novels.

MARSH, Sir EDWARD HOWARD. Rupert Brooke: A Memoir. Smart Set 58: 140, Jan., 1919. Nothing Much Is Here, Alas!

MARSHALL, ROBERT. Arctic Village. American Mercury 29: 124-126, May, 1933. Utopia in Little.

MARTIN, EVERETT DEAN.

The Behavior of Crowds; a Psychological Study. Smart Set 64: 138-141, Feb., 1921. The Anatomy of Ochlocracy.

Liberty. American Mercury 21: 379-380, Nov., 1930. The Twilight of Freedom.

Psychology: What It Has To Teach You About Yourself and the World You Live In. American Mercury 2: 506-507, Aug., 1924. Mankind in the Mass.

MARTIN, FREDERICK TOWNSEND. Things I Remember. Smart Set 42: 159-160, Feb., 1914. Anything But Novels!

WORKS BY H. L. M.

MARTIN, HELEN (REIMENSNYDER). The Crossways. Smart Set 31: 157, May, 1910. In Praise of a Poet.

MARTIN, TOBA. Is Mankind Advancing? [Baltimore] Evening Sun, p. 6, Jan. 13, 1911. Do We Go Ahead?

MARTYN, WYNDHAM. The Man Outside. Smart Set 30: 159, April, 1910. A Glance at the Spring Fiction.

MARX, MAGDELEINE, *pseud. See* Paz, Magdeleine (Legendre).

MASEFIELD, JOHN.
Multitude and Solitude. Smart Set 38: 155, Nov., 1912. Novels Bad, Half Bad and Very Bad.
The Tragedy of Nan. Smart Set 33: 167, Feb., 1911. The Revival of the Printed Play.
The Tragedy of Pompey the Great. Smart Set 43: 156-157, July, 1914. Galsworthy and Others.

MASON, ALFRED EDWARD WOODLY. The Turnstile. Smart Set 38: 156, Nov., 1912. Novels Bad, Half Bad and Very Bad.

MASON, CAROLINE (ATWATER). The Spell of Italy. Smart Set 28: 158, Aug., 1909. Novels and Other Books—Chiefly Bad.

MASON, DANIEL GREGORY. The Orchestral Instruments and What They Do. Smart Set 29: 158, Oct., 1909. The Last of the Victorians.

MASON, DEXTER. The Art of Drinking. American Mercury 21: 253-254, Oct., 1930. Books About Boozing.

MASON, GRACE SARTWELL. The Godparents. Smart Set 31: 155, June, 1910. The Greatest of American Writers.

MASSON, ROSALINE ORME. The Life of Robert Louis Stevenson. American Mercury 3: 378-380, Nov., 1924. Tusitala; Chicago Tribune, Dec. 14, 1924. Robert Louis Stevenson.

MASSON, THOMAS LANSING. Within; a Guide to the Spiritual Life. American Mercury 25: 506-510, April, 1932. Quod Est Veritas?

MASTERS, EDGAR LEE.
Lincoln, The Man. New York Herald Tribune Books, p. 1, Feb. 8, 1931. The Birth of Order.
Mirage. American Mercury 2: 250-252, June, 1924. Edgar Lee Masters.
The New Spoon River. American Mercury 6: 251-254, Oct., 1925. Poetry.

MATHEWS, MITFORD McLEOD, *ed.* The Beginnings of American English. New York Herald Tribune Books, p. 3, Aug. 30, 1931. Yankee Way of Speech.

MATHEWS, SHAILER. The Growth of the Idea of God. American Mercury 25: 506-510, April, 1932. Quod Est Veritas?

MATTHEWS, BRANDER. A Study of the Drama. Smart Set 31: 158-159, Aug., 1910. A Hot Weather Novelist.

BOOK REVIEWS

MAUGHAM, WILLIAM SOMERSET.

The Explorer. Smart Set 27: 157, April, 1909. The Novels That Bloom in the Spring, Tra-La!

The Land of the Blessed Virgin. Smart Set 63: 144, Oct., 1920. Gropings in Literary Darkness.

The Magician. *See* above, The Explorer.

The Moon and Sixpence. Smart Set 60: 138-140, Nov., 1919. Novels for Indian Summer.

Of Human Bondage. *See* above, The Moon and Sixpence.

The Trembling of a Leaf. Smart Set 67: 140, Jan., 1922. Book Article No. 158—II.

MAXIM, HUDSON. The Science of Poetry and the Philosophy of Language. Smart Set 33: 166, Jan., 1911. The Leading American Novelist.

MAXWELL, WILLIAM BABINGTON. The Devil's Garden. Smart Set 43: 159-160, June, 1914. The Anatomy of the Novel.

MAY, FLORENCE LAND. The Broken Wheel. Smart Set 31: 157, July, 1910. A Fictioneer of the Laboratory.

MAYO, KATHERINE. Slaves of the Gods. American Mercury 17: 123, 125, May, 1929. The Gods and Their Agents.

MAZUR, PAUL MYER. American Prosperity: Its Causes and Consequences. American Mercury 14: 255, June, 1928. The Golden Age.

MEAD, MARGARET. Coming of Age in Samoa. American Mercury 15: 379-380, Nov., 1928. Adolescence.

MECKLIN, JOHN MOFFATT. The Ku Klux Klan: A Study of the American Mind. American Mercury 2: 120-122, May, 1924. Bravos in Bed-Sheets.

MENCKEN, HENRY LOUIS.

A Book of Prefaces (Opus 13). Smart Set 54: 143, Jan., 1918. Seven Pages About Books—IV.

Europe after 8:15, by H. L. Mencken, George Jean Nathan and Willard H. Wright. Smart Set 44: 153-155, Oct., 1914. A Review of Reviewers.

Ventures into Verse. Smart Set 51: 397-399, Feb., 1917. The Rough-House on Parnassus.

[Reminiscences and Future Prospects]. Smart Set 51: 141-144, March, 1917. The Books of the Irish—II.

["Sentimental Interlude," HLM reminisces about the Ellicott City *Times*] Smart Set 45: 434, April, 1915. The Grandstand Flirts with the Bleachers.

MEREDITH, GEORGE. Celt and Saxon. Smart Set 32: 165-167, Oct., 1910. Meredith's Swan Song.

MERRIAM, CHARLES EDWARD. Chicago: A More Intimate View of Urban Politics. American Mercury 17: 506-508, Aug., 1929. The Modern Gomorrah.

MERRICK, LEONARD.

The Actor-Manager. Smart Set 38: 156-157, Nov., 1912. Novels Bad, Half Bad and Very Bad.

WORKS BY H. L. M.

Conrad in Quest of his Youth. Smart Set 34: 157, Aug., 1911. The New Dramatic Literature.

The Man Who Understood Women. Smart Set 36: 158, Feb., 1912. Rounding Up the Novels.

The Position of Peggy. Smart Set 37: 157-158, July, 1912. A Dip into the Novels.

The Stage of Fools. Smart Set 39: 156, Feb., 1913. The Burden of Humor.

Whispers About Women. Smart Set 38: 157, Nov., 1912. Novels Bad, Half Bad and Very Bad.

MERWIN, SAMUEL. The Citadel. Smart Set 38: 154, Sept., 1912. Prose Fiction Ad Infinitum.

MESSENGER, ERNEST C. Evolution & Theology. American Mercury 25: 506-510, April, 1932. Quod Est Veritas?

MEYER, AGNES E. Chinese Painting As Reflected in the Thought and Art of Li Lung-Mien. American Mercury 1: 379-380, March, 1924. Art Criticism.

MEYER, MAX. The Fundamental Laws of Human Behavior. Smart Set 37: 158, Aug., 1912. Zola.

MICHAÉLIS, KARIN. The Dangerous Age. Smart Set 35: 156-157, Dec., 1911. An Overdose of Novels.

MICHAUD, RÉGIS. Emerson, the Enraptured Yankee, translated from the French by George Boas. American Mercury 21: 251-252, Oct., 1930. A Moonstruck Pastor.

MICHELSON, MIRIAM. Michael Thwaite's Wife. Smart Set 29: 156, Oct., 1909. The Last of the Victorians.

MIDDLETON, GEORGE.
Criminals, a One Act Play About Marriage. Smart Set 48: 155-156, Feb., 1916. A Massacre in a Mausoleum.

Possession. Smart Set 45: 436, April, 1915. The Grandstand Flirts with the Bleachers.

The Road Together. Smart Set 52: 400, May, 1917. Shocking Stuff.

MILLER, HENRY RUSSELL. The Man Higher Up. Smart Set 31: 155, Aug., 1910. A Hot Weather Novelist.

MILLIN, SARAH GERTRUDE (LIEBSON).
An Artist in the Family. American Mercury 14: 127, May, 1928. Fiction.

God's Stepchildren. American Mercury 5: 507-508, Aug., 1925. Novels Good and Bad.

Mary Glenn. American Mercury 7: 507-508, April, 1926. Fiction Good and Bad.

MILTOUN, FRANCIS, *pseud. See* Mansfield, Milburg Francisco.

MIMS, EDWIN. The Advancing South. American Mercury 8: 506-509, Aug., 1926. The South Looks Ahead.

BOOK REVIEWS

Minnigerode, Meade. The Fabulous Forties, 1840-1850. American Mercury 2: 377-380, July, 1924. The Bradford Formula.

Mr. Justice Holmes; contributions by Benjamin N. Cardozo, Morris Cohen, John Dewey [and others] . . . edited by Felix Frankfurter. American Mercury 26: 123-126, May, 1932. The Great Holmes Mystery.

Mitchell, Edward Bedinger. The Shadow of the Crescent. Smart Set 29: 159, Sept., 1909. The Books of the Dog Days.

Mitchell, Edward Page. Memoirs of an Editor. American Mercury 5: 505-507, Dec., 1924. Two Journalists.

Mitchell, Edwin Valentine. Concerning Beards. American Mercury 22: 509-510, April, 1931. The Foliage of Man.

Mitchell, John Ames. Dr. Thorne's Idea. Smart Set 32: 168, Nov., 1910. A Guide to Intelligent Eating.

Mitchell, Langdon Elwyn. Understanding America. American Mercury 12: 123-126, Sept., 1927. Autopsy.

Mitchell, Silas Weir.
The Red City, a Novel of the Second Administration of President Washington. Smart Set 27: 159, Jan., 1909. A Road Map of the New Books.
Westways. Smart Set 41: 160, Dec., 1913. The Russians.

Modjeska, Helena. Memories and Impressions. [Baltimore] Evening Sun, p. 6, Nov. 22, 1910. Modjeska's Book; Smart Set 33: 167, Feb., 1911. The Revival of the Printed Play.

Moley, Raymond. Our Criminal Courts. American Mercury 21: 380-383, Nov., 1930. The Criminal.

Molineux, Roland Burnham. The Molineux Case; edited by Samuel Klaus. American Mercury 18: 382-383, Nov., 1929. Poison through the Mails.

Monahan, Michael.
At the Sign of the Van. Smart Set 44: 155-156, Nov., 1914. Critics of More or Less Badness.
Nova Hibernia. *See* above, At the Sign of the Van.

Monkhouse, Allan Noble. Mary Broome. Smart Set 41: 155, Sept., 1913. Getting Rid of the Actor.

Montague, Charles Edward.
Dramatic Values. Smart Set 34: 155, Aug., 1911. The New Dramatic Literature.
A Hind Let Loose. American Mercury 2: 381-382, July, 1924. Rambles in Fiction.

Montagu-Nathan, Montagu. Contemporary Russian Composers. Smart Set 54: 143-144, Feb., 1918. The National Letters—IV.

Montgomery, Lucy Maud. Kilmeny of the Orchard. Smart Set 31: 155, July, 1910. A Fictioneer of the Laboratory.

MOODY, WILLIAM REVELL. D. L. Moody. American Mercury 21: 124-126, Sept., 1930. The Scourge of Satan.

MOODY, WILLIAM VAUGHN.

The Faith Healer. Smart Set 28: 157-158, July, 1909. The Best Novels of the Year; 31: 160, May, 1910. In Praise of a Poet.

The Great Divide, a Play in Three Acts. Smart Set 29: 156, Dec., 1909. "A Doll's House"—With a Fourth Act.

MOON, ROBERT OSWALD. Hippocrates and His Successors in Relation to the Philosophy of Their Time. Nation 118: 117, Jan. 30, 1924. Greek Fundamentalism.

MOORE, GEORGE.

An Anthology of Pure Poetry. American Mercury 6: 251-254, Oct., 1925. Poetry.

Hail and Farewell: I—Ave. Smart Set 36: 155-156, March, 1912. The Prophet of the Superman; II—Salve. Smart Set 39: 156-157, Feb., 1913. The Burden of Humor; III—Vale. Smart Set 44: 155, 159-160, Oct., 1914. A Review of Reviewers; Town Topics 71: 19, June 25, 1914. Moore Finishes His Story.

A Story-Teller's Holiday. Smart Set 57: 142-144, Dec., 1918. The Late Mr. Wells—III.

MOORE, HARRY HASCALL. Public Health in the United States. American Mercury 1: 376-377, March, 1924. Cheating the Mortician.

MOORS, HARRY JAY. With Stevenson in Samoa. Smart Set 34: 167-168, May, 1911. Novels—The Spring Crop.

MORDELL, ALBERT. Dante and Other Waning Classics. Smart Set 48: 151-153, Feb., 1916. A Massacre in a Mausoleum.

MORE, PAUL ELMER.

The Catholic Faith. American Mercury 25: 506-510, April, 1932. Quod Est Veritas?

A New England Group and Others. Smart Set 65: 141-143, June, 1921. Books About Books—II—III.

Shelburne Essays, v. 1. [Baltimore] Evening Sun, editorial page, April 9, 1921. "Strangely Polite" to Nietzsche.

With the Wits. Smart Set 61: 139-140, Feb., 1920. From the Diary of a Reviewer—Dec. 4.

MORF, GUSTAV. The Polish Heritage of Joseph Conrad. American Mercury 23: 251-253, June, 1931. Freudian Autopsy upon a Genius.

MORGAN, JACQUES JEAN MARIE DE. Prehistoric Man: A General Outline of Pre-History. American Mercury 5: 126-127, May, 1925. The Infancy of the Race.

MORRIS, GOUVERNEUR.

It, and Other Stories. Smart Set 38: 157-158, Nov., 1912. Novels Bad, Half Bad and Very Bad.

Yellow Men and Gold. Smart Set 34: 153, June, 1911. The Horse Power of Realism.

MORRISON, ARTHUR. Green Ginger. Smart Set 29: 157, Dec., 1909. "A Doll's House"—With a Fourth Act.

MORSE, NORTHROP. Peach Bloom. Smart Set 42: 151, April, 1914. Roosevelt, Bulwer-Lytton and Anthony Comstock.

MOSES, BARR, *i.e.* WILLIAM JOHN BARR. Dreaming River. Smart Set 27: 159, April, 1909. The Novels That Bloom in the Spring, Tra-La!

MOSES, MONTROSE JONAS.

The American Dramatist. Smart Set 36: 156, April, 1912. An Antidote to "Yankee Doodle."

Henrik Ibsen; the Man and His Plays. Smart Set 27: 158, March, 1909. The Literary Clinic.

MOULT, THOMAS, *comp.* The Best Poems of 1924. American Mercury 6: 251-254, Oct., 1924. Poetry.

MUILENBURG, WALTER J. Prairie. American Mercury 6: 379, 381, Nov., 1925. Fiction Good and Bad.

MÜLLER-FREIENFELS, RICHARD. Mysteries of the Soul. American Mercury 18: 253-254, Oct., 1929. Ghostly Matters.

MURFREE, MARY NOAILLES. The Fair Mississippian, by Charles Egbert Craddock [pseud.] Smart Set 28: 154-155, June, 1909. Books for the Hammock and Deck Chair.

MURRY, JOHN MIDDLETON.

The Evolution of an Intellectual. Smart Set 63: 144, Nov., 1920. Notes in the Margin—V.

God. American Mercury 19: 255, Feb., 1930. Confessional.

MUSGROVE, CHARLES DAVID. Nervous Breakdowns and How To Avoid Them. Smart Set 41: 158, Dec., 1913. The Russians.

MYERS, GUSTAVUS.

The History of the Great American Fortunes. Smart Set 30: 158, March, 1910. The Literary Heavyweight Champion; 32: 164-165, Sept., 1910. The MacKaye Mystery.

The History of Tammany Hall. Smart Set 54: 139, March, 1918. Literae Humaniores.

NATHAN, GEORGE JEAN.

Another Book of the Theatre. Smart Set 47: 304-308, Nov., 1915. After All, Why Not?

Bottoms Up. Chicago News, p. 11, June 6, 1927. For Cynics and Sinners Only; Smart Set 52: 140-141, Aug., 1917. Criticism of Criticism of Criticism.

Mr. George Jean Nathan Presents. Smart Set 53: 140-141, Dec., 1917. Critics Wild and Tame—II.

NATHAN, ROBERT. Autumn. Smart Set 67: 142, April, 1922. The Niagara of Novels—II.

NATIONAL HEALTH COUNCIL. The National Health Series. American Mercury 3: 125-126, Sept., 1924. The Art of Keeping Well.

NEALE, WALTER. Life of Ambrose Bierce. American Mercury 18: 124-126, Sept., 1929. The Ambrose Bierce Mystery.

NEARING, SCOTT. Where Is Civilization Going? American Mercury 16: 122-124, Jan., 1929. What Is Civilization?

NEEDHAM, HENRY BEECH. Divorcing Lady Nicotine, Smart Set 40: 155-156, Aug., 1913. A Counterblast to Buncombe.

NEEDHAM, JOSEPH.

The Great Amphibium. American Mercury 25: 506-510, April, 1932. Quod Est Veritas?

Man a Machine. American Mercury 16: 509-510, April, 1929. The Riddle of the Universe.

NEIHARDT, JOHN GNEISENAU.

Man Song. Smart Set 30: 155, Jan., 1910. George Bernard Shaw As A Hero.

The Stranger at the Gate. Smart Set 39: 151-152, April, 1913. The Burbling of the Bards.

NESBIT, E. *See* Bland, Edith (Nesbit).

NEVINS, ALLAN. Grover Cleveland: A Study in Courage. American Mercury 27: 125-127, Jan., 1933. A Good Man in a Bad Trade.

THE NEW DEAL: Technochracy Illustrated. American Mercury 28: 505-507, April, 1933. Old Dr. Scott's Bile Beans.

NEW INTERNATIONAL ENCYCLOPAEDIA, rev. ed. Smart Set 54: 137-139, Jan., 1918. Seven Pages About Books.

NEW INTERNATIONAL ENCYCLOPAEDIA WITH "WISDOM UP TO DATE." American Mercury 26: 254-255, June, 1932. (Compared to Americana.)

NEWELL, PETER. The Hole Book. Smart Set 27: 156, Feb., 1909. The Literary Olio.

NEWMAN, ERNEST.

The Life of Richard Wagner; Vol. I (1813-1848). American Mercury 30: 381-383, Nov., 1933. Notes on Wagner.

A Musical Critic's Holiday. American Mercury 6: 506-507, Dec., 1925. Books About Music.

A Musical Motley. *See* above, A Musical Critic's Holiday.

The Unconscious Beethoven; an Essay in Musical Psychology. American Mercury 11: 251-253, June, 1927. Old Ludwig and His Ways.

Wagner As Man & Artist. American Mercury 4: 127, Jan., 1925. Brief Notices.

NEWMAN, FRANCES. Frances Newman's Letters, edited by Hansell Baugh with a prefatory note by James Branch Cabell. American Mercury 19: 382-383, March, 1930. The Lady from Georgia.

NEWTE, HORACE W. C.

The Lonely Lovers. Smart Set 32: 164, Dec., 1910. Mainly About Novels.

Pansy Mears. Smart Set 38: 155, Dec., 1912. A Visit to a Short Story Factory.

NEWTON, JOSEPH FORT, *ed.* The Best Sermons of 1924. American Mercury 3: 509, Dec., 1924. Anthologies.

NICHOLS, ROY FRANKLIN. Franklin Pierce; Young Hickory of the Granite Hills. American Mercury 25: 250-253, Feb., 1932. Nine American Statesmen.

BOOK REVIEWS

Nicholson, Meredith.

The Lords of High Decision. Smart Set 30: 154, Feb., 1910. Books To Read and Books To Avoid.

Otherwise Phyllis. Smart Set 41: 155, Nov., 1913. Marie Corelli's Sparring Partner.

Nicolson, Harold George. Tennyson; Aspects of His Life, Character, and Poetry. American Mercury 1: 510, April, 1924. Brief Notices.

Niebuhr, Reinhold. Leaves from the Notebook of a Tamed Cynic. American Mercury 18: 253-254, Oct., 1929. Ghostly Matters.

Nietzsche, Friedrich Wilhelm.

Also Sprach Zarathustra, edited by Thomas Common; introduction by Frau Förster-Nietzsche. Smart Set 30: 155-157, March, 1910. The Literary Heavyweight Champion.

Anti-Christ. Chicago Sunday Tribune, Aug. 23, 1925. Nietzsche—.

The Complete Works edited by Dr. Oscar Levy. Smart Set 36: 153-155, March, 1912. The Prophet of the Superman; 40: 156-157, Aug., 1913. A Counterblast to Buncombe: [Baltimore] Evening Sun, Feb. 18, 1913.

The Future of Education, edited by Thomas Common; introduction by Frau Förster-Nietzsche. See Also Sprach Zarathustra.

Human All-Too-Human, edited by Thomas Common; introduction by Frau Förster-Nietzsche. See Also Sprach Zarathustra.

Life of Nietzsche, by Elizabeth Förster-Nietzsche. Smart Set 46: 155-156, Aug., 1915. The Saw Dust Trail.

The Nietzsche-Wagner Correspondence, edited by Elizabeth Förster-Nietzsche. Atlantic 129: 14, Feb., 1922.

The Will to Power, edited by Thomas Common, introduction by Elizabeth Förster-Nietzsche. Smart Set 30: 155-157, March, 1910. The Literary Heavyweight Champion.

[Comments] Smart Set 29: 153-157, Nov., 1909; 30: 155-157, March, 1910; 36: 153-155, March, 1912; 56: 143-144, Sept., 1918; 67: 142-143, Feb., 1922.

Nock, Albert Jay. Jefferson. American Mercury 9: 123-124, Sept., 1926. The Immortal Democrat.

Noel, Jean. The Courage of Paula. Smart Set 41: 160, Oct., 1913. "With Your Kind Permission—"

Norris, Charles Gilman.

Brass; a Novel of Marriage. Smart Set 66: 140-141, Oct., 1921. Notes on Books —III.

Pig Iron. American Mercury 7: 507, April, 1926. Fiction Good and Bad.

Salt, or The Education of Griffith Adams. Smart Set 57: 141-142, Nov., 1918. Dithyrambs Against Learning—II.

Norris, Frank.

McTeague, a Story of San Francisco. Smart Set 40: 158-159, July, 1913. Various Bad Novels.

Vandover and the Brute. Town Topics 71: 18, June 18, 1914. The Primrose Path; Smart Set 43: 157-158, Aug., 1914. Adventures Among the New Novels.

WORKS BY H. L. M.

NORRIS, KATHLEEN (THOMPSON). Saturday's Child. Smart Set 44: 310, Dec., 1914. Mush for the Multitude.

NORTON, MARY DOWE HERTER. *See* Herter Norton, Mary Dowe.

NORTON, THOMAS JAMES. Loving Liberty Judicially, Prohibitory and Kindred Laws Examined. American Mercury 16: 127, Jan., 1929. The Nine Against Liberty.

NOYES, ALFRED.
The Book of Earth. American Mercury 6: 251-254, Oct., 1925. Poetry.

The Enchanted Island, and Other Poems. Smart Set 31: 159-160, Aug., 1910. A Hot Weather Novelist.

Sherwood, or Robin Hood and the Three Kings, a Play in Five Acts. Smart Set 37: 158, June, 1912. The Terrible Swede.

NOYES, ANNA BOGERT (GAUSMANN). How I Kept My Baby Well. Smart Set 41: 156-157, Oct., 1913. "With Your Kind Permission—"

NYBURG, SIDNEY LAUER. The Final Verdict. Smart Set 45: 433, April, 1915. The Grandstand Flirts with the Bleachers.

O. HENRY, *pseud.*
Cabbages and Kings. [Baltimore] Sunday Herald, Dec. 18, 1904. Notes in the Margin.

Roads of Destiny. Smart Set 28: 156-157, July, 1909. The Best Novels of the Year.

Strictly Business. Smart Set 31: 159, May, 1910. In Praise of a Poet.

[Comments.] Smart Set 35: 152, Dec., 1911. An Overdose of Novels.

O'BRIEN, EDWARD JOSEPH HARRINGTON, *ed.*
The Grim Thirteen. Smart Set 55: 141-143, May, 1918. The Stream of Fiction—III.

Short Story Anthology. Smart Set 59: 143-144, July, 1919. The Coroner's Inquest—III.

O'BRIEN, FLORENCE ROMA MUIR WILSON. Martin Schüler, by Romer Wilson [pseud.] Smart Set 59: 144, Aug., 1919. Novels, Chiefly Bad—V.

O'BRIEN, FREDERICK. White Shadows in the South Seas. Smart Set 60: 144, Dec., 1919. Exeunt Omnes.

ODEGARD, PETER H. Pressure Politics; the Story of the Anti-Saloon League. American Mercury 15: 252-254, Oct., 1928. Shock Troops of Zion.

ODUM, HOWARD WASHINGTON. Rainbow Round My Shoulder. American Mercury 15: 126, Sept., 1928. Black Boy.

ODUM, HOWARD WASHINGTON and GUY BENTON JOHNSON.
The Negro and His Songs . . . American Mercury 6: 507, Dec., 1925. Books About Music.

Negro Workaday Songs. American Mercury 9: 251-253, Oct., 1926. The Southern Negro.

O'HARA, BARRATT. From Figg to Johnson. Smart Set 30: 157-158, March, 1910. The Literary Heavyweight Champion.

BOOK REVIEWS

O'HENRY, *pseud. See* O. Henry, *pseud.*

O'HIGGINS, HARVEY JERROLD and EDWARD HIRAM REEDE. The American Mind in Action. American Mercury 2: 377-380, July, 1924. The Bradford Formula.

O'MARA, PATRICK. The Autobiography of a Liverpool Irish Slummy. American Mercury 30: 126-127, Sept., 1933. Zola cum Gorky.

OPDYCKE, JOHN BAKER. News, Ads and Sales. Town Topics 72: 17, Sept. 24, 1914. How To Become a Journalist.

OPPENHEIM, EDWARD PHILLIPS.

The Illustrious Prince. Smart Set 32: 168, Sept., 1910. The MacKaye Mystery.

The Mischief Maker. Smart Set 40: 157, May, 1913. Weep for the White Slave!

Mr. Grex of Monte Carlo. Smart Set 45: 294, March, 1915. The Bugaboo of the Sunday Schools.

The Moving Finger. Smart Set 34: 154-155, July, 1911. Novels for Hot Afternoons.

Passers-By, by Anthony Partridge [pseud.]. Smart Set 30: 158-159, April, 1910. A Glance at the Spring Fiction.

A People's Man. Smart Set 42: 157, March, 1914. The Raw Material of Fiction.

OPPENHEIM, JAMES.

The Book of Self. Smart Set 53: 138-140, Nov., 1917. Whoopers and Twitterers.

War and Laughter. *See* above, The Book of Self.

ORANGE, A. R. Nietzsche in Outline and Aphorism. [Baltimore] Evening Sun, p. 6, July 2, 1910. A Wild German.

ORTEGA Y GASSET, JOSÉ. The Revolt of the Masses. Nation 135: 260, Sept. 21, 1932. Spanish Katzenjammer.

OSBORN, HENRY FAIRFIELD. The Earth Speaks to Bryan. American Mercury 6: 381-383, Nov., 1925. Genesis vs. Sense.

OSBORNE, WILLIAM HAMILTON.

The Red Mouse, a Mystery Romance. Smart Set 27: 156, April, 1909. The Novels That Bloom in the Spring, Tra-La!

The Running Fight. Smart Set 31: 158, July, 1910. A Fictioneer of the Laboratory.

OSBOURNE, LLOYD.

Infatuation. Smart Set 28: 156-157, June, 1909. Books for the Hammock and Deck Chair.

An Intimate Portrait of R.L.S. American Mercury 3: 378-380, Nov., 1924. Tusitala.

A Person of Some Importance. Smart Set 35: 154, Dec., 1911. An Overdose of Novels.

O'SULLIVAN, VINCENT.

The Good Girl. Smart Set 52: 142-143, Aug., 1917. Criticism of Criticism of Criticism.

Sentiment. Smart Set 54: 143, March, 1918. Literae Humaniores.

THE OTHER KIND OF GIRL. Smart Set 45: 296, March, 1915. The Bugaboo of the Sunday Schools.

OURSLER, FULTON. The True Story of Bernarr Macfadden. American Mercury 20: 124-125, May, 1930. The American Idealist.

OURSLER, GRACE (PERKINS). Chats with the Macfadden Family, by Grace Perkins. American Mercury 20: 124-125, May, 1930. An American Idealist.

OVINGTON, MARY WHITE. The Shadow. Smart Set 68: 140-141, Oct., 1920. Gropings in Literary Darkness—II.

OWSLEY, FRANK LAWRENCE. State Rights in the Confederacy. American Mercury 7: 126-127, Jan., 1926. The Confederate Collapse.

OXENHAM, JOHN. Maid of the Mist. Town Topics 72: 16, Oct. 29, 1914. Novels of No Importance.

OXFORD AND ASQUITH, MARGOT ASQUITH, *countess* of. Autobiography. Smart Set 64: 144, March, 1921. A Soul's Adventures—III.

OXFORD ENGLISH DICTIONARY. *See* Shorter Oxford English Dictionary.

PACH, WALTER. Georges Seurat. American Mercury 1: 379, March, 1924. Art Criticism.

PACKARD, WINTHROP. Florida Trails, as Seen from Jacksonville to Key West . . . Smart Set 33: 167-168, March, 1911. A Stack of Novels.

PAGE, ROSEWELL. Thomas Nelson Page; a Memoir of a Virginia Gentleman. Smart Set 71: 139, 141, Aug., 1923. Biography and Other Fiction—II.

PAGE, THOMAS NELSON. The Land of the Spirit. Smart Set 40: 155-157, July, 1913.

PAGE, WALTER HINES. The Southerner, a Novel, Being the Autobiography of Nicholas Worth [pseud.]. Smart Set 29: 155-156, Dec., 1909. "A Doll's House" —With a Fourth Act.

PAINE, ALBERT BIGELOW. Mark Twain, a Biography. Smart Set 39: 152-153, Feb., 1913. The Burden of Humor.

PALMER, HAROLD E., JAMES VICTOR MARTIN and FRANCIS GEORGE BLANDFORD. A Dictionary of English Pronunciation with American Variants [in Phonetic Transcription]. American Mercury 11: 125-126, May, 1927. American Speech.

PALMER, JOHN LESLIE. George Bernard Shaw; Harlequin or Patriot? Smart Set 46: 447, July, 1915. The Prometheus of the Western World.

PANKHURST, ESTELLE SYLVIA. The Suffragette, the History of the Women's Militant Suffrage Movement 1905-1910. Smart Set 35: 155, Sept., 1911. A 1911 Model Dream Book.

PAPINI, GIOVANNI. Life of Christ, translated freely from the Italian by Dorothy Canfield Fisher. Smart Set 71: 136-137, May, 1923. Notices of Books—I—On the Mourners' Bench.

PARÉ, AMBROISE. Life and Times of Ambroise Paré (1510-1590) . . . by Francis Randolph Packard. Smart Set 66: 139-140, Nov., 1921. More Notes on Books.

PARKER, GEORGE HOWARD. What Evolution Is. American Mercury 7: 127, Jan., 1927. Brief Notices.

PARKER, *Sir* GILBERT, *bart.* Northern Lights. Smart Set 29: 155, Dec., 1909. "A Doll's House"—With a Fourth Act.

PARKER, LOUIS NAPOLEON. Disraeli, a Play. Smart Set 36: 156, April, 1912. An Antidote to "Yankee Doodle."

PARKS, LEIGHTON. What Is Modernism? American Mercury 2: 124-125, May, 1924. Christian vs. Christian.

PARRISH, ANNE. The Perennial Bachelor. American Mercury 6: 381, 510, Nov., 1925. Fiction Good and Bad.

PARRISH, HERBERT. What Is There Left To Believe? American Mercury 25: 506-510, April, 1932. Quod Est Veritas?

PARSHLEY, HOWARD MADISON. Science and Good Behavior. American Mercury 17: 251-253, June, 1929. What Is It All About?

PARSON, ELSIE WORTHINGTON CLEWS. Fear and Conventionality. Smart Set 47: 304-310, Sept., 1915. The Genealogy of Etiquette.

PARTRIDGE, ANTHONY, *pseud. See* Oppenheim, Edward Phillips.

PARTRIDGE, ERIC. A Dictionary of Slang and Unconventional English. Saturday Review of Literature 15: 6, April 10, 1937. Loose Language.

PASSFIELD, SIDNEY JAMES WEBB, *baron.* The Decay of Capitalist Civilization, by Sidney and Beatrice Webb. Smart Set 71: 142-144, July, 1923. Some New Books —V.

PATERSON, WILLIAM ROMAINE. The Old Dance Master. Smart Set 35: 138, Oct., 1911. Brieux and Others.

PATTEE, FRED LEWIS.
The First Century of American Literature, 1770-1870. Pennsylvania Magazine of History and Biography 60: 79-80, Jan., 1936.
A History of American Literature Since 1870. Smart Set 50: 142, Oct., 1916; 50: 281-282, Nov., 1916. Professors at the Bat.
Sidelights on American Literature. Smart Set 70: 141-143, March, 1923. Adventures Among Books—II.

PATTERSON, JOSEPH MEDILL.
A Little Brother of the Rich. Smart Set 26: 156-157, Dec., 1908. Oyez! Oyez! All Ye Who Read Books.
Rebellion. Smart Set 35: 153-154, Dec., 1911. An Overdose of Novels.

PATTERSON, MARJORIE.
The Dust of the Road. Smart Set 41: 155-157, Nov., 1913. Marie Corelli's Sparring Partner.
Fortunata. Smart Set 34: 153-154, June, 1911. The Horse Power of Realism.

PAUL, ELLIOT HAROLD. Indelible, a Story of Life, Love, and Music, in Five Movements. Smart Set 68: 142-143, Aug., 1922. The Intellectual Squirrel-Cage —IV.

WORKS BY H. L. M.

PAYNE, WILL. The Automatic Capitalists. Smart Set 30: 156, Feb., 1910. Books To Read and Books To Avoid.

PAZ, MAGDELEINE (LEGENDRE).

The Romance of New Russia, by Magdeleine Marx [pseud.] translated by Anita Grannis. American Mercury 4: 127, Jan., 1925. The Land of Lunacy.

Woman, by Magdeleine Marx [pseud.] translated from the French by Adele Szold Seltzer. Smart Set 68: 142-143, Oct., 1920. Gropings in Literary Darkness —V.

PEARL, RAYMOND.

Alcohol and Longevity. [Baltimore] Evening Sun, Oct. 18, 1926. Alcohol; American Mercury 9: 508-509, Dec., 1926. The Effects of Alcohol.

The Biology of Death. Smart Set 72: 138-139, Nov., 1923. Notices of Books.

The Biology of Population Growth. American Mercury 7: 121-122, Jan., 1926. The Growth of Population.

The Natural History of Population. [Baltimore] Sun, p. 10, Feb. 19, 1929. Man's Breeding.

Studies in Human Biology. American Mercury 4: 252-253, Feb., 1925. Homo Sapiens.

[PEARSON, DREW and ROBERT SHARON ALLEN.] Washington Merry-Go-Round. American Mercury 24: 251-253, Oct., 1931. The Men Who Govern Us.

PEATTIE, ELICE (WILKINSON). The Precipice. Smart Set 43: 156-157, June, 1914. The Anatomy of the Novel.

PENDLETON, CHARLES SUTPHIN. The Social Objectives of School English. American Mercury 4: 380-381, March, 1925. The Schoolmarm's Goal.

PERKINS, GRACE. See Oursler, Grace (Perkins).

PERRIER, EDMOND. The Earth before History; Man's Origin and the Origin of Life. American Mercury 5: 126-127, May, 1925. The Infancy of the Race.

PERRY, BLISS. The American Spirit in Literature. Smart Set 59: 138, 141-142, July, 1919. The Coroner's Inquest.

PERSKY, SERGE M. Contemporary Russian Novelists, translated by Frederick Eisenmann. Smart Set 41: 153-155, Dec., 1913. The Russians.

PERTWEE, ROLAND. The Old Card. Smart Set 60: 141-143, Nov., 1919. Novels for Indian Summer—III.

PETERSON, HOUSTON.

Havelock Ellis, Philosopher of Love. American Mercury 15: 127, Sept., 1928. A Gentle Revolutionist.

Huxley, Prophet of Science. Nation 134: 374, March 30, 1932. Darwin's Bulldog.

PETROVA, NATALIA, pseud. Twice Born in Russia, translated by Baroness Mary Budberg, introduction by Dorothy Thompson. American Mercury 22: 506-508, April, 1931. Life in the Marxian Utopia.

PHELPS, WILLIAM LYON.

The Advance of the English Novel. Smart Set 52: 138-140, June, 1917. The Plague of Books.

BOOK REVIEWS

The Advance of English Poetry. Smart Set 58: 140-141, Jan., 1919. Nothing Much Is Here, Alas!—II.

Archibald Marshall. *See* above, The Advance of English Poetry.

Browning: How to Know Him. Smart Set 47: 156, Dec., 1915. A Literary Behemoth.

Essays on Modern Dramatists. [Baltimore] Evening Sun, April 23, 1921.

Essays of Modern Novelists. Smart Set 31: 153-154, June, 1910. The Greatest of American Writers; 65: 141-142, June, 1921. Books About Books—II.

Essays on Russian Novelists. Smart Set 34: 156-157, June, 1911. The Horse Power of Realism; 41: 154-155, Dec., 1913.

The Twentieth Century Theatre. Smart Set 58: 142, Feb., 1919. Sunrise on the Prairie—IV.

PHILLIPS, DAVID GRAHAM.

Degarmo's Wife, and Other Stories. Smart Set 41: 159, Oct., 1913. "With Your Kind Permission—"

The Fashionable Adventures of Joshua Craig. Smart Set 27: 158, April, 1909. The Novels That Bloom in the Spring, Tra-La!

The Grain of Dust. Smart Set 34: 153-154, July, 1911. Novels for Hot Afternoons.

The Hungry Heart. Smart Set 29: 153-154, Dec., 1909. "A Doll's House"— With a Fourth Act; 33: 163-164, Jan., 1911. The Leading American Novelist.

The Husband's Story. Smart Set 33: 163-164, Jan., 1911. The Leading American Novelist.

PHILLIPS, HENRY ALBERT.

Art in Short Story Narration. Smart Set 41: 157, Nov., 1913. Marie Corelli's Sparring Partner.

The Plot of the Short Story. Smart Set 38: 151-153, Dec., 1912. A Visit to a Short Story Factory.

PHILLPOTTS, EDEN.

Demeter's Daughter. Smart Set 34: 158, Aug., 1911. The New Dramatic Literature.

The Haven. Smart Set 30: 155-156, Feb., 1910. Books To Read and Books To Avoid.

The Thief of Virtue. Smart Set 31: 155-156, June, 1910. The Greatest of American Writers.

The Three Brothers. Smart Set 27: 158, April, 1909. The Novels That Bloom in the Spring, Tra-La!

Widecombe Fair. Smart Set 40: 157, July, 1913. Various Bad Novels.

PINK, LOUIS HEATON. Gaynor, the Tammany Mayor Who Swallowed the Tiger. American Mercury 25: 250-253, Feb., 1932. Nine American Statesmen.

PINSKY, DAVID. Three Plays, authorized translated from the Yiddish by Isaac Goldberg. Smart Set 55: 144, Aug., 1918. A Sub-Potomac Phenomenon—IV.

PLANCK, MAX KARL ERNST LUDWIG. Where Is Science Going? . . . prologue by Albert Einstein. American Mercury 30: 379-380, Nov., 1933. Science vs. Religion.

POE, EDGAR ALLAN. [Memorial Monument] Smart Set 32: 168, Dec., 1910. Mainly About Novels.

POLLARD, PERCIVAL.
Masks and Minstrels of New Germany. [Baltimore] Evening Sun, p. 6, April 29, 1911. The Ueberbrettl; Smart Set 34: 154-155, Aug., 1911. The New Dramatic Literature.
Their Day in Court. Smart Set 30: 157-158, Feb., 1910. Books To Read and Books To Avoid.

POLLOCK, CHANNING. The Footlights, Fore and Aft. Smart Set 36: 155-156, April, 1912. An Antidote to "Yankee Doodle."

POOLE, ERNEST.
The Harbor. Smart Set 46: 295-296, June, 1915. Here Are Novels!
His Second Wife. Smart Set 55: 141, Aug., 1918. The Sub-Potomac Phenomenon.

POOLEY, ROBERT CECIL. Teaching English Usage. English Journal 37: 440, Oct., 1948. Mencken on Pooley on Usage.

POPHAM, WILLIAM LEE. Poems of Truth, Love and Power. Smart Set 32: 168, Dec., 1910. Mainly About Novels.

PORTE, JOHN FIELDER. Sir Edward Elgar. Smart Set 66: 140-141, Nov., 1921. More Notes on Books.

PORTER, ELEANOR (HODGMAN). Just David. Smart Set 49: 150-151, July, 1916. A Soul's Adventures.

PORTER, GENE STRATTON. Laddie, a True Blue Story. Smart Set 41: 155, Nov., 1913. Marie Corelli's Sparring Partner.

PORTER, WILLIAM SYDNEY. See O. Henry, pseud.

POST, EMILY (PRICE).
The Eagle's Feather. Smart Set 33: 163, March, 1911. A Stack of Novels.
Etiquette: The Blue Book of Social Usage. American Mercury 13: 255, Feb., 1928. Refinement Made Easy.
The Title Market. Smart Set 30: 157, Feb., 1910. Books To Read and Books To Avoid.

POTEAT, WILLIAM LOUIS. Can a Man Be a Christian Today? American Mercury 6: 381-383, Nov., 1925. Genesis vs. Sense.

POUND, EZRA LOOMIS.
Antheil and the Treatise on Harmony. American Mercury 14: 506-508, Aug., 1928. Musical Explorers.
Instigations. Smart Set 62: 143-144, Aug., 1920. Books More or Less Amusing —IV.
Provença. Smart Set 33: 166-167, April, 1911. The Meredith of Tomorrow.

POUND, LOUISE. Poetic Origins and the Ballad. Smart Set 65: 143-144, June, 1921. Books About Books—IV.

BOOK REVIEWS

POWDERMAKER, HORTENSE. Life in Lesu. American Mercury 29: 506-508, Aug., 1933. How People Live.

POWELL, LYMAN PIERSON. The Art of Natural Sleep. Smart Set 27: 154-155, March, 1909. The Literary Clinic.

PRATT, AMBROSE. The Living Mummy. Smart Set 30: 157-158, April, 1910. A Glance at the Spring Fiction.

PRATZ, CLAIRE DE. Elisabeth Davenay. Smart Set 32: 167-168, Sept., 1910. The MacKaye Mystery.

PRESCOTT, FREDERICK CLARKE. Poetry and Dreams. Smart Set 50: 139, Oct., 1916. The Creed of a Novelist—2.

PREUSS, ARTHUR. A Dictionary of Secret and Other Societies. Nation 119: 290-291, Sept. 17, 1924. Wizards and High Priests.

PRICE, MAURICE THOMAS. Christian Missions and Oriental Civilizations, a Study in Cultural Contact. American Mercury 5: 250-251, June, 1925. Spreading the Kingdom.

PRICE, WILLIAM THOMPSON. The Analysis of Play Construction and Dramatic Principle. Smart Set 28: 157, July, 1909. The Best Novels of the Year.

PRINCE, LEON CUSHING. The Sense and Nonsense of Christian Science. Smart Set 35: 154-155, Sept., 1911. A 1911 Model Dream Book.

PRINGLE, HENRY FOWLES. Theodore Roosevelt, a Biography. Amercian Mercury 25: 250-253, Feb., 1932. Nine American Statesmen.

PRUETTE, LORINE. Women and Leisure, a Study of Social Waste. American Mercury 4: 383, March, 1925. Brief Notices.

PUCKETT, NEWBELL NILES. Folk Beliefs of the Southern Negro. American Mercury 9: 251-253, Oct., 1926. The Southern Negro.

PULVER, MARY BRECHT. The Spring Lady. Town Topics 72: 16, Oct. 29, 1914. Rita and Laurence.

PUTNAM, EMILY JAMES (SMITH). The Lady, Studies of Certain Significant Phases of Her History. Smart Set 33: 167, April, 1911. The Meredith of Tomorrow.

PYCRAFT, WILLIAM PLANE, ed. The Standard Natural History from Amoeba to Man. America Mercury 27: 127, Sept., 1932. The World of Creatures.

QUILLER-COUCH, Sir ARTHUR THOMAS.
Brother Copas. Smart Set 34: 158, Aug., 1911. The New Dramatic Literature.
On the Art of Writing. Smart Set 50: 280-281, Nov., 1916. Professors at the Bat.

RALEIGH, CECIL, pseud. and HENRY HAMILTON. The Sins of Society. Smart Set 30: 158, April, 1910. A Glance at the Spring Fiction.

RAMSAYE, TERRY. A Million and One Nights: A History of the Motion Picture. American Mercury 10: 252-254, Feb., 1927. The Movies.

RANDALL, JOHN HERMAN. Religion & The Modern World. American Mercury 18: 253-254, Oct., 1929. Ghostly Matters.

WORKS BY H. L. M

RANKIN, THOMAS ERNEST. American Writers of the Present Day, 1890 to 1920. Smart Set 65: 140-142, May, 1921. The Land of the Free—II.

RANSOM, JOHN CROWE. God without Thunder: An Unorthodox Defense of Orthodoxy. American Mercury 22: 126-127, Jan., 1931. The Old Religion vs. the New.

RANSOME, ARTHUR.
Edgar Allan Poe: A Critical Study. Smart Set 36: 156, March, 1912. The Prophet of the Superman.
Oscar Wilde: A Critical Study. Smart Set 38: 151, Oct., 1912. Synge and Others.

RAO, K. SREENVASCE. The Dramatic History of the World. [Baltimore] Evening Sun, p. 6, April 12, 1911. The Indian Drama.

RAYMOND, ALLEN. What Is Technocracy? American Mercury 28: 505-507, April, 1933. Old Dr. Scott's Bile Beans.

READ, ALFRED BAKER. Social Chaos and the Way Out. Smart Set 66: 142-143, Dec., 1921. Variations on a Familiar Theme—4.

READ, HARLAN EUGENE. The Abolition of Inheritance. Smart Set 57: 143, Oct., 1918. Suite Élégiaque—II.

THE RECOLLECTIONS OF A SOCIETY CLAIRVOYANT. Smart Set 34: 157, June, 1911. The Horse Power of Realism.

REDFIELD, JOHN. Music: A Science and an Art. American Mercury 14: 506-508, Aug., 1928. Musical Explorers.

REDFORD, ELIZABETH ADAMSON. Neither Do I. Smart Set 32: 167-168, Oct., 1910. Meredith's Swan Song; 32: 168, Nov., 1910.

REESE, LIZETTE WOODWORTH.
A Branch of May. Smart Set 29: 157, Oct., 1909. The Last of the Victorians.
A Wayside Lute. Smart Set 31: 153-155, May, 1910. In Praise of a Poet.

REEVES, JEREMIAH BASCOM. The Hymn as Literature. American Mercury 2: 255, June, 1924. Brief Notices.

REID, Sir GEORGE ARCHDALL O'BRIEN. The Laws of Heredity. [Baltimore] Evening Sun, July 8, 1910. editorial page. On Heredity.

REINACH, SALOMON. Apollo. American Mercury 2: 510, Aug., 1924. Brief Notices.

REMARQUE, ERICH MARIA. All Quiet on the Western Front. American Mercury 17: 510, Aug., 1929. Im Westen Nichts Neues.

RENIER, GUSTAAF JOHANNES. The English: Are They Human? American Mercury 24: 509-510, Dec., 1931. Two Views of the English.

REPPLIER, AGNES. A Happy Half-Century. Smart Set 26: 156, Dec., 1908. Oyez! Oyez! All Ye Who Read Books.

RICE, ALICE CALDWELL (HEGAN). Mr. Opp. Smart Set 28: 154, Aug., 1909. Novels and Other Books—Chiefly Bad.

BOOK REVIEWS

RICE, CALE YOUNG.

The Immortal Lure. Smart Set 34: 157-158, July, 1911. Novels for Hot Afternoons.

Many Gods. Smart Set 31: 158, June, 1910. The Greatest of American Writers.

RICE, EDWARD LEROY. Monarchs of Minstrelsy, from "Daddy" Rice to Date. [Baltimore] Evening Sun, p. 6, May 2, 1911. The Minstrel Men.

RICE, GEORGE GRAHAM. My Adventures with Your Money. Smart Set 41: 158, Oct., 1913. "With Your Kind Permission—"

RICHARDS, CHARLES RUSSELL. Art in Industry. American Mercury 19: 380-381, March, 1930. The Anatomy of Philistinism.

RICHARDSON, DOROTHY M. Pilgrimage, with an introduction by May Sinclair. Smart Set 61: 138-139, Feb., 1920. From the Diary of a Reviewer.

[RICHARDSON, HENRIETTA.] Maurice Guest, by Henry Handel Richardson [pseud.]. Smart Set 27: 159, April, 1909. The Novels That Bloom in the Spring, Tra-La!

RICHARDSON, NORVAL. The Lead of Honour. Smart Set 32: 165-166, Dec., 1910. Mainly About Novels.

RICHMOND, MARY ELLEN and FRED SMITH HALL. Marriage & The State. American Mercury 17: 125-127, May, 1929. The Holy Estate.

RIDEOUT, HENRY MILNER.

Dragon's Blood. Smart Set 28: 153-155, July, 1909. The Best Novels of the Year.

The Twisted Foot. Smart Set 31: 155, July, 1910. A Fictioneer of the Laboratory.

RIDER, FREMONT.

Are the Dead Alive? Smart Set 28: 155-156, Aug., 1909. Novels and Other Books—Chiefly Bad.

Rider's New York City; a Guide to Travelers. Smart Set 72: 138-143, Sept., 1923. New York.

RIEGEL, OSCAR WETHERHOLD. Mobilizing for Chaos. Yale Review 24: 386-388, Dec., 1934. Tainted News.

RIESENBERG, FELIX. Under Sail. American Mercury 4: 127, Jan., 1925. Brief Notices.

RIIS, JACOB AUGUST. The Old Town. Smart Set 30: 159, Jan., 1910. George Bernard Shaw As A Hero.

RIMSKY-KORSAKOFF, NIKOLAI ANDREEVICH. My Musical Life, translated by Judah A. Joffe, with an introduction by Carl Van Vechten. American Mercury 1: 120-121, Jan., 1924. Russian Music.

RINEHART, MARY ROBERTS.

The Amazing Adventures of Letitia Carberry. Smart Set 36: 152, Feb., 1912. Rounding Up the Novels.

The Case of Jennie Brice. Smart Set 40: 157, May, 1913. Weep for the White Slave!

The Circular Staircase. Smart Set 26: 157-158, Nov., 1908. The Good, the Bad and the Best Sellers.

The Man in Lower Ten. Smart Set 28: 153, June, 1909. Books for the Hammock and Deck Chair.

When a Man Marries. Smart Set 30: 155, Feb., 1910. Books To Read and Books To Avoid.

The Window at the White Cat. Smart Set 32: 168, Nov., 1910. A Guide to Intelligent Eating.

RITCHIE, ANNE ISABELLA (THACKERAY) *lady*. The Blackstick Papers. Smart Set 27: 159, Feb., 1909. The Literary Olio.

RITTER, WILLIAM EMERSON. The Natural History of Our Conduct. American Mercury 10: 510, April, 1927. Man and His Instincts.

RIVES, AMÉLIE. *See* Troubetzkoy, Amélie (Rives) Chanier.

ROBACK, A. A. The Psychology of Character. American Mercury 13: 510, April, 1928. The Nature of Man.

ROBERTS, CARL ERIC BECHHOFER. The Mysterious Madame, Helena Petrovna Blavatsky. American Mercury 24: 379-380, Nov., 1931. Hooey from the Orient.

ROBERTS, MORLEY.
David Bran. Smart Set 29: 156, Oct., 1909. The Last of the Victorians.

Malignancy and Evolution: A Biological Inquiry into the Nature and Causes of Cancer. American Mercury 8: 379-381, July, 1926. The Origin of Variations.

Thorpe's Way. Smart Set 35: 156-157, Oct., 1911. Brieux and Others.

ROBERTSON, JOHN WOOSTER. Edgar A. Poe: A Study. Smart Set 60: 144, Sept., 1921. From the Diary of a Reviewer—VI—Friday.

ROBINS, ELIZABETH. My Little Sister. Smart Set 40: 155-156, May, 1913. Weep for the White Slave!

ROBINSON, EDGAR EUGENE. The Evolution of American Political Parties. American Mercury 4: 383, March, 1925. Brief Notices.

ROBINSON, LUTHER EMERSON. Abraham Lincoln as a Man of Letters. Nation 116: 574, May 16, 1923. The Style of Lincoln.

ROBINSON, WILLIAM JOSEPHUS. Soviet Russia as I Saw It: Its Accomplishments, Its Crimes & Stupidities. American Mercury 28: 253-255, Feb., 1933. The Russian Imposture.

ROCKEFELLER, JOHN DAVISON. Random Reminiscences of Men and Events. Smart Set 29: 154-155, Sept., 1909. The Books of the Dog Days.

ROCKEFELLER, JOHN DAVISON, JR. The Personal Relation in Industry. American Mercury 2: 382-383, July, 1924. The Slave and His Ways.

RODA RODA, ALEXANDER FRIEDRICH LADISLAUS. Ein Fruehling in Amerika. American Mercury 1: 507-508, April, 1924. God's Country: Exterior View.

BOOK REVIEWS

ROE, GILBERT ERNSTEIN. Our Judicial Oligarchy. Smart Set 37: 157, Aug., 1912. Zola.

ROGERS, ANNA (ALEXANDER). Why American Marriages Fail. Smart Set 30: 159, Feb., 1910. Books To Read and Books To Avoid.

ROGERS, CAMERON. Colonel Bob Ingersoll. American Mercury 11: 254-255, June, 1927. The Hound of Hell.

ROHLFS, ANNA KATHARINE (GREEN). Three Thousand Dollars, by Anna Katharine Green. Smart Set 30: 154-155, Feb., 1910. Books To Read and Books To Avoid.

ROLFE, AMY LUCILE. Interior Decoration for the Small Home. American Mercury 2: 255, June, 1924. Brief Notices.

ROLLAND, ROMAIN. Beethoven the Creator. Smart Set 52: 141-142, Aug., 1917. Criticism of Criticism of Criticism; American Mercury 18: 505-507, Dec., 1929. Beethoveniana.

ROMAINS, JULES. The Death of a Nobody. Smart Set 45: 152-153, Feb., 1915. Lachrymose Love.

ROOSEVELT, NICHOLAS. America and England. Now and Then [London]. p. 11, Spring, 1930.

ROOSEVELT, THEODORE.

Autobiography. Smart Set 42: 143-149, April, 1914. Roosevelt, Bulwer-Lytton and Anthony Comstock.

[Comments] Smart Set 61: 140-141, Feb., 1920. From the Diary of a Reviewer; 61: 138-144, March, 1920. Roosevelt and Others; 63: 141-142, Nov., 1920. Notes in the Margin—III—A Give-Away.

ROSE, HOWARD N., *comp.* A Thesaurus of Slang. Nation 139: 331-332, Sept. 19, 1934. Aids to Verisimilitude.

ROSENFELD, SYDNEY. Children of Destiny, a Play in Four Acts. Smart Set 31: 159, Aug., 1910. A Hot Weather Novelist.

ROSETT, JOSHUA.

The Middle Class, a Play in Four Acts. Smart Set 39: 157, March, 1913. Gerhart Hauptmann.

The Quandary, a Play in Three Acts. Smart Set 41: 158-159, Nov., 1913. Marie Corelli's Sparring Partner.

ROTHERT, OTTO ARTHUR.

The Outlaws of Cave-In-Rock. American Mercury 1: 505-507, April, 1924. Provincial Literature.

The Story of a Poet: Madison Cawein. Smart Set 67: 142-143, Jan., 1922. Book Article No. 158—IV.

ROYAL SOCIETY OF LITERATURE OF THE UNITED KINGDOM, *London*. The Eighteen-Seventies, edited by Harley Granville-Barker. Nation 129: 440, Oct. 16, 1929. Fifty Years Ago.

RUDWIN, MAXIMILIAN JOSEF. The Devil in Legend & Literature. American Mercury 25: 506-510, April, 1932. Quod Est Veritas?

RUHRÄH, JOHN, *ed.* Pediatrics of the Past, an Anthology. [Baltimore] Evening Sun, Aug. 8, 1925.

RUMSEY, FRANCES. Leonora. Smart Set 32: 164-165, Dec., 1910. Mainly About Novels.

[RUSSELL, MARY ANNETTE (BEAUCHAMP) RUSSELL, *countess.*] The Pastor's Wife. Smart Set 45: 461, Jan., 1915. A Gamey Old Gaul.

RYAN, P. F. WILLIAM. Queen Anne and Her Court. Smart Set 28: 158-159, June, 1909. Books for the Hammock and Deck Chair.

SACKVILLE-WEST, VICTORIA MARY. Heritage. Smart Set 60: 140, Nov., 1919. Novels for Indian Summer—II.

SADLEIR, MICHAEL. Privilege. Smart Set 67: 138-139, Jan., 1922. Book Article No. 158—I—On Log-Rolling.

SAINT HUBERT, R. LA MONTAGNE. The Art of Fresco Painting. American Mercury 4: 127, Jan., 1925. Brief Notices.

SAINTSBURY, GEORGE EDWARD BATEMAN. Notes on a Cellar-Book. Nation 138: 193, Feb. 14, 1934. For Thy Stomach's Sake.

SALISBURY, WILLIAM. The Career of a Journalist. Smart Set 26: 157, Nov., 1908. The Good, the Bad and the Best Sellers.

SALTUS, EDGAR. Imperial Purple. Chicago Sunday Tribune, Oct. 11, 1925. Edgar Saltus.

SANBORN, MARY FARLEY. The Canvas Door. Smart Set 30: 155, March, 1910. The Literary Heavyweight Champion.

SANDBURG, CARL.
Abraham Lincoln: The Prairie Years. American Mercury 8: 381-382, July, 1926. Sandburg's "Lincoln."
The American Songbag. American Mercury 13: 383, March, 1928. American Folk-Song.
Rootabaga. Smart Set 70: 138, 140, March, 1923. Adventures Among Books.
[Talk About National Literature.] Smart Set 63: 138-144, Sept., 1920. Notes and Queries.

SANGER, MARGARET (HIGGINS). The Pivot of Civilization. Smart Set 70: 141-143, Feb., 1923. Specimens of Current Fiction—IV.

SAPIR, EDWARD. Language: An Introduction to the Study of Speech. Smart Set 68: 143-144, May, 1922. Reflections on Prose Fiction—III—Philological.

SAVAGE-LANDOR, A. H. *See* Landor, Arnold Henry Savage.

SCHAUFFLER, ROBERT HAVEN. Beethoven, The Man Who Freed Music. American Mercury 18: 505-507, Dec., 1929. Beethoveniana.

SCHEFFAUER, HERMAN GEORGE. Das Land Gottes. American Mercury 1: 507-509, April, 1924. God's Country: Exterior View.

SCHEM, LIDA CLARA. The Voice of the Heart, by Margaret Blake, [pseud.] Smart Set 40: 153-154, July, 1913. Various Bad Novels.

BOOK REVIEWS

SCHLAPP, MAX GUSTAV and EDWARD HENRY SMITH. The New Criminology:
A Consideration of the Chemical Causation of Abnormal Behavior. American
Mercury 14: 381-383, July, 1928. Pseudo-Science.

SCHMIDT, ANNALISE. Der Amerikanische Mensch. American Mercury 1: 507-508,
April, 1924. God's Country: Exterior View.

SCHNITZLER, ARTHUR. Professor Bernhardi . . . an adaptation in English by
Mrs. Emil Pohli. Smart Set 41: 157, Dec., 1913. The Russians.

SCHÖNEMANN, FRIEDRICH. Die Kunst der Massenbeeinflussung in den Vereinigten
Staaten von Amerika. American Mercury 3: 252-253, Oct., 1924. Hornswoggling
the Rabble.

SCHOENRICH, OTTO. Santo Domingo, a Country with a Future. Smart Set 57: 142-
143, Oct., 1918. Suite Élégiaque—II.

SCOTT, C. KAY. Siren. American Mercury 7: 508, April, 1926. Fiction Good and
Bad.

SCOTT, ERNEST FINDLAY.
  The Gospel & Its Tributaries. American Mercury 20: 254-255, June, 1930. The
Ghostly Realm.
  The Kingdom of God in the New Testament. American Mercury 25: 506-510,
April, 1932. Quod Est Veritas?

SCOTT, EVELYN.
  Escapade. Smart Set 72: 142-143, Oct., 1923. Holy Writ—III.
  Narcissus. Smart Set 69: 143-144, Nov., 1922. Chiefly Pathological—III.
  The Narrow House. Smart Set 16: 142-143, Nov., 1921. More Notes on Books
—3.

SCOTT, FRED NEWTON. The Standards of American Speech and Other Papers.
American Mercury 9: 255, Oct., 1926. Professors of English.

SCOTT, HOWARD. Introduction to Technocracy. American Mercury 28: 505-507,
April, 1933. Old Dr. Scott's Bile Beans.

SCOTT, JOHN REED. The Duke of Oblivion. Town Topics 72: 16, Nov. 12, 1914.
Novels of Small Importance.

SEDGWICK, ANNE DOUGLAS.
  The Encounter. Smart Set 45: 461-462, Jan., 1915. A Gamey Old Gaul.
  Franklin Winslow Kane. Smart Set 31: 156, Aug., 1910. A Hot Weather
Novelist.

SEIBERT, VENITA. The Gossamer Thread. Smart Set 32: 168, Oct., 1910. Meredith's
Swan Song.

SEITZ, DON CARLOS. Joseph Pulitzer; His Life & Letters. American Mercury 4:
250-252, Feb., 1925. Joseph Pulitzer.

SELDES, GILBERT VIVIAN. The Future of Drinking. American Mercury 21: 252-
254, Oct., 1930. Books About Boozing.

SELEKMAN, SYLVIA (KOPALD). Rebellion in Labor Unions, by Sylvia Beatrice
Kopald. American Mercury 3: 383, July, 1924. The Slave and His Ways.

WORKS BY H. L. M.

SELIGMAN, HERBERT JACOB. The Negro Faces America. Smart Set 68: 141, Oct., 1920. Gropings in Literary Darkness—II.

SERGEL, ROGER L. Arlie Gelston. American Mercury 1: 509-510, April, 1924. The Husk of Dreiser.

SERVICE, ROBERT WILLIAM. The Trail of '98. Smart Set 34: 154, June, 1911. The Horse Power of Realism.

SHAKESPEARE, WILLIAM. Chronicle History of King Leir. Introduction and notes by Sidney Lee. Smart Set 29: 158-159, Dec., 1909. "A Doll's House"—With a Fourth Act.

SHAND, PHILIP MORTON.
A Book of Other Wines Than French. American Mercury 21: 253-254, Oct., 1930. Books About Boozing.
A Book on Wine. Nation 123: 177, Aug. 25, 1926. A Bible for Bibuli.

SHANE, PEGGY (SMITH). The Love Legend, by Woodward Boyd [pseud.]. Smart Set 70: 138-140, March, 1923. Adventures Among Books.

SHARBER, KATE TRIMBLE. Annals of How Old Was Ann? Smart Set 36: 152, Feb., 1912. Rounding Up the Novels.

SHARP, EVELYN. Here We Go Round; The Story of the Dance. American Mercury 16: 122-124, Jan., 1929. What Is Civilization?

SHARPE, MAY CHURCHILL. Chicago May: Her Story. American Mercury 16: 124-127, Jan., 1929. Men in Cages.

SHASTRI, PRABHU DUTT. The Essentials of Eastern Philosophy. American Mercury 15: 254-255, Oct., 1928. Blather from the East.

SHAW, GEORGE BERNARD.
Androcles and the Lion. Smart Set 49: 138-140, Aug., 1916. The Ulster Polonius.
Back to Methuselah. Smart Set 66: 144, Sept., 1921. From the Diary of a Reviewer—V—Thursday.
The Doctor's Dilemma. Smart Set 34: 153, Aug., 1911. The New Dramatic Literature.
The Fabian Essays in Socialism, by George Bernard Shaw, Mrs. Annie Besant, Sir Sydney Olivier. Smart Set 28: 155, 157-158, Aug., 1909. Novels and Other Books —Chiefly Bad.
Getting Married. See The Doctor's Dilemma.
Man and Superman. [Baltimore] Sunday Herald, Oct. 30, 1904. Notes in the Margin.
Misalliance; The Dark Lady of the Sonnets; Fanny's First Play, with a Treatise on Parents and Children. Town Topics 72: 13-14, July 16, 1914. Shaw Is At It Again.
Saint Joan. American Mercury 3: 255, Oct., 1924. Brief Notices.
The Showing-Up of Blanco Posnet. See The Doctor's Dilemma.
[Comment]. Smart Set 44: 153-157, 160, Sept., 1914. Thirty-Five Printed Plays.

BOOK REVIEWS

SHEEHAN, PERLEY POORE and ROBERT HOBART DAVIS. "We Are French!" Smart Set 45: 152-153, Feb., 1915. Lachrymose Love.

SHELDON, EDWARD BREWSTER. "The Nigger," an American Play in Three Acts. Smart Set 33: 165, Feb., 1911. The Revival of the Printed Play.

SHELLEY, HENRY CHARLES.

Inns and Taverns of Old England. Smart Set 30: 158-159, March, 1910. The Literary Heavyweight Champion.

The Tragedy of Mary Stuart. Smart Set 42: 149-150, April, 1914. Roosevelt, Bulwer-Lytton and Anthony Comstock.

SHERMAN, LUCIUS ADELNO. How To Describe and Narrate Visually. American Mercury 9: 255, Oct., 1926. Professors of English.

SHERMAN, STUART PRATT.

Americans. Smart Set 70: 141-143, March, 1923. Adventures Among Books—II.

Roosevelt and the National Psychology, article in *Nation* 109: 599-605, Nov. 8, 1919. Smart Set 61: 138, 144, March, 1920. Roosevelt and Others.

SHIEL, ROGER R. Twenty Years in Hell with the Beef Trust. Smart Set 29: 155-156, Sept., 1909. The Books of the Dog Days.

SHORE, MRS. TEIGNMOUTH. Circe's Daughter, by Priscilla Craven [pseud.] Smart Set 42: 155, Jan., 1914. A Pestilence of Novels.

THE SHORTER OXFORD ENGLISH DICTIONARY ON HISTORICAL PRINCIPLES. American Mercury 29: 251-252, June, 1933. The Oxford in Two Volumes.

SIDGWICK, ETHEL. Le Gentleman. Smart Set 38: 157-158, Dec., 1912. A Visit to a Short Story Factory.

SIEGFRIED, ANDRÉ.

America Comes of Age; a French Analysis. Nation 124: 533, May 11, 1927. A Frenchman Takes a Look.

England's Crisis . . . translated from the French by Henry Harold Hemming and Doris Hemming. American Mercury 23: 380-382. July, 1931. The Panting Motherland.

Impressions of South America, translated from the French by Henry Harold Hemming and Doris Hemming. American Mercury 29: 379-381, July, 1933. Life below the Isthmus.

SIENKIEWICZ, HENRYK.

In Desert and Wilderness . . . translated from the Polish by Max A. Drezmal. Smart Set 37: 155, Aug., 1912. Zola.

Whirlpools . . . translated from the Polish by Max A. Drezmal. Smart Set 31: 155-156, Aug., 1910. A Hot Weather Novelist.

SINCLAIR, BERTHA (MUZZY).

The Happy Family, by B. M. Bower [pseud.]. Smart Set 31: 157, July, 1910. A Fictioneer of the Laboratory.

The Uphill Climb, by B. M. Bower [pseud.]. Smart Set 40: 154-155, July, 1913. Various Bad Novels.

247

SINCLAIR, BERTRAND WILLIAM. The Land of Frozen Suns. Smart Set 31: 157, July, 1910. A Fictioneer of the Laboratory.

SINCLAIR, MAY.

The Creators. Smart Set 32: 165, Dec., 1910. Mainly About Novels.

The Immortal Moment, the Story of Kitty Tailleur. Smart Set 27: 156-157, Jan., 1909. A Road Map of the New Books.

The New Idealism. Smart Set 68: 138-139, Aug., 1922. The Intellectual Squirrel-Cage.

SINCLAIR, UPTON BEALL.

The Book of Life, Mind and Body. Smart Set 68: 138-144, July, 1922. Saving the World.

The Brass Check, a Study of American Journalism. Smart Set 61: 138-144, April, 1920. On Journalism.

Good Health and How We Won It, an Account of the New Hygiene by Upton Sinclair and Michael Williams. Smart Set 27: 154, March, 1909. The Literary Clinic.

The Goose-Step, a Study of American Education. Smart Set 71: 141-144, May, 1923. Nordic Blond Art—IV.

The Goslings: A Study of the American Schools. [Baltimore] Evening Sun, Feb. 23, 1924; American Mercury 1: 504-505, April, 1924. The Little Red Schoolhouse.

Love's Pilgrimage. Smart Set 34: 156, Aug., 1911. The New Dramatic Literature.

Mammonart. American Mercury 5: 252-253, June, 1925. Four Critics of Letters.

Money Writes! American Mercury 13: 253-254, Feb., 1928. Inside Stuff.

The Moneychangers. Smart Set 26: 155-157, Nov., 1908. The Good, the Bad and the Best Sellers.

100%: The Story of a Patriot. Smart Set 64: 143-144, Feb., 1921. The Anatomy of Ochlocracy—III.

Sylvia. Smart Set 40: 160, Aug., 1913. A Counterblast to Buncombe.

Upton Sinclair Presents William Fox. American Mercury 29: 252-254, June, 1933. A Hollywood Martyr.

The Wet Parade. Nation 133: 310, Sept. 23, 1931. A Moral Tale.

[Comments] Smart Set 58: 143-144, Jan., 1919.

SMALL, ALBION WOODBURY. Origins of Sociology. American Mercury 3: 383, Nov., 1924. Brief Notices.

SMALLEY, GEORGE WASHBURN. Anglo-American Memories. Smart Set 34: 152, June, 1911. The Horse Power of Realism.

SMITH, ALFRED EMANUEL. Up to Now: An Autobiography. Saturday Review of Literature 6: 229-230, Oct. 12, 1929. The Boy from Oliver Street; American Mercury 19: 122-125, Jan., 1930. American Worthies.

SMITH, ARTHUR DOUGLAS HOWDEN. Fighting the Turk in the Balkans. Smart Set 27: 158, March, 1909. The Literary Clinic.

SMITH, CHARLES ALPHONSO. New Words Self-Defined. Smart Set 61: 140, Feb., 1920. From the Diary of a Reviewer—Dec. 7.

BOOK REVIEWS

SMITH, FRANCIS HOPKINSON.

Forty Minutes Late. Smart Set 30: 157, Jan., 1910. George Bernard Shaw As A Hero.

Kennedy Square. Smart Set 35: 155-156, Nov., 1911. A Novel of the First Rank.

Peter. Smart Set 26: 158-159, Nov., 1908. The Good, the Bad and the Best Sellers.

SMITH, Sir GRAFTON ELLIOT. In the Beginning; the Origin of Civilization. American Mercury 16: 122-124, Jan., 1929. What Is Civilization?

SMITH, HARRY JAMES. Enchanted Ground. Smart Set 32: 163, Dec., 1910. Mainly About Novels.

SMITH, HENRY JUSTIN. Deadlines. Smart Set 70: 138-139, March, 1923. Adventures Among Books.

SMITH, LOGAN PEARSALL.

Stories from the Old Testament. Smart Set 65: 143, July, 1921. Literary Notes —III.

Words and Idioms: Studies in the English Language. American Mercury 6: 126-127, Sept., 1925. The English Language.

SMITH, SAMUEL CALVIN. How Is Your Heart? American Mercury 3: 125-126, Sept., 1924. The Art of Keeping Well.

SMITH, WEBSTER. The Kingfish: A Biography of Huey P. Long. Nation 136: 507, May 3, 1933. The Glory of Louisiana.

SMITS, LEE J. The Spring Flight. American Mercury 5: 124-126, May, 1925. Fiction.

SNAITH, JOHN COLLIS. Broke of Covenden. Smart Set 45: 433, April, 1915. The Grandstand Flirts with the Bleachers.

SOMER, H. M. Amazing America. American Mercury 1: 507-508, April, 1924. God's Country: Exterior View.

SOMERVELL, DAVID CHURCHILL. Critical Epochs in History. American Mercury 3: 383, Nov., 1924. Brief Notices.

SONNTAG, CHARLES F. The Morphology and Evolution of the Apes and Man. Chicago Sunday Tribune, Nov. 8, 1925. Cousin Jocko.

SOROKIN, PITIRIM ALEKSANDROVICH. Leaves from a Russian Diary. American Mercury 4: 127, Jan., 1925. The Land of Lunacy.

SPAETH, SIGMUND GOTTFRIED. The Common Sense of Music. American Mercury 2: 507-508, Aug., 1924. Apostle to the Philistines.

SPARGO, JOHN.

Applied Socialism. Smart Set 37: 157-158, Aug., 1912. Zola.

Marxian Socialism and Religion. Smart Set 48: 151-152, April, 1916. The Publishers Begin Their Spring Drive—2—The Red Cross.

SPENCER, HENRY PERCIVAL. The Lilies. Smart Set 27: 155, March 1909. The Literary Clinic.

WORKS BY H. L. M.

SPINGARN, JOEL ELIAS. Creative Criticism. Smart Set 52: 138-140, Aug., 1917. Criticism of Crtiicism of Criticism.

SPRADING, CHARLES T. Liberty and the Great Libertarians. Smart Set 41: 158-159, Dec., 1913. The Russians.

SQUIRE, JOHN COLLINGS. Life and Letters. Smart Set 65: 141-142, June, 1921. Books About Books—II.

STALEY, JOHN EDGCUMBE. Tragedies of the Medici. American Mercury 4: 383, March, 1925. Brief Notices.

STARNES, DEWITT T. and GERTRUDE S. NOYES. The English Dictionary from Cawdrey to Johnson, 1604-1755. William and Mary Quarterly 3 (3d ser.): 597-599, Oct., 1946.

STARR, FREDERICK. Confucianism; Ethics, Philosophy, Religion. American Mercury 20: 254-255, June, 1930. The Ghostly Realm.

STARRETT, VINCENT. Arthur Machen: A Novelist of Ecstasy and Sin. Smart Set 59: 142-143, July, 1919. The Coroner's Inquest—II.

STARRETT, WILLIAM AIKEN. Skyscrapers and the Men Who Build Them. American Mercury 16: 382-383, March, 1929. An American Saga.

STAWELL, MAUD MARGARET (KEY). "Mrs. Rodolph Stawell." Motor Tours in Wales and the Border Counties. Smart Set 28: 158, Aug., 1909. Novels and Other Books—Chiefly Bad.

STEARNS, HAROLD EDMUND. Liberalism in America. Smart Set 62: 144, May, 1920. More Notes from a Diary—V.

STEELE, ROBERT. One Man. Smart Set 46: 290-293, June, 1915. Here Are Novels!; American Mercury 13: 380, March, 1928. The Ways of the Wicked.

STEFFENS, JOSEPH LINCOLN. The Autobiography of Lincoln Steffens. American Mercury 23: 382-383, July, 1931. Footprints on the Sands of Time.

STEIN, GERTRUDE.
Geography and Plays. Smart Set 72: 144, Oct., 1923. Holy Writ—III.
Tender Buttons. Smart Set 44: 158-159, Oct., 1914. A Review of Reviewers.

STEINBECK, JOHN. Grapes of Wrath. [Baltimore] Sun, editorial page, May 28, 1939. Disaster in Moronia.

STELZLE, CHARLES. Why Prohibition? Smart Set 57: 138-142, Oct., 1918. Suite Élégiaque.

STEPHENS, HENRY.
Journeys and Experiences in Argentina, Paraguay and Chile . . . Smart Set 67: 143, Aug., 1920. Books More or Less Amusing—IV.
South American Travels. Smart Set 58: 144, March, 1919. Mainly Fiction.

STEUART, JOHN ALEXANDER. Robert Louis Stevenson. Chicago Tribune, Dec. 14, 1924. Robert Louis Stevenson; American Mercury 4: 125-127, Jan., 1925. Stevenson Again.

STEUART, JUSTIN. Wayne Wheeler: Dry Boss. American Mercury 15: 252-254, Oct., 1928. Shock Troops of Zion.

250

BOOK REVIEWS

STEVENS, DORIS. Jailed for Freedom. Smart Set 63: 144, Dec., 1920. Chiefly Americans—IV.

STEVENS, JAMES.

Brawny-man. American Mercury 9: 380-381, Nov., 1926. Three Lively Lives.

Paul Bunyan. American Mercury 5: 254-255, June, 1925. An American Saga.

STEVENSON, ROBERT LOUIS.

Familiar Studies of Men and Books. American Mercury 3: 378-380, Nov., 1924. Tusitala.

Virginibus Puerisque and Other Papers. See above, Familiar Studies.

STEWART, GEORGE RYPEY. Names on the Land; A Historical Account of Place-naming in the United States. New York Herald Tribune Book Review, p. 5, April 22, 1945. Our Place-Names Drip with Human Juices.

STIDGER, WILLIAM LEROY, ed. The Pew Preaches. American Mercury 20: 254-255, June, 1930. The Ghostly Realm.

STILES, GEORGE KEAN. The Dragoman. Smart Set 40: 157-158, May, 1913. Weep for the White Slave!

STILLWELL, LEANDER. The Story of a Common Soldier of Army Life in the Civil War. New York Evening Mail, Feb. 9, 1918. The Story of a Common Soldier; Smart Set 54: 142-143, April, 1918. Business—III.

STINDE, JULIUS ERNST WILHELM. The Hausfrau Rampant, by E. V. Lucas, from the German. Smart Set 50: 283-284, Nov., 1916. Professors at the Bat.

STODDARD, THEODORE LOTHROP.

Racial Realities in Europe. American Mercury 4: 252-253, Feb., 1925. Homo Sapiens.

Re-Forging America. American Mercury 12: 123-126, Sept., 1927. Autopsy.

STOPES, MARIA CHARLOTTE CARMICHAEL. Contraception: Theory, History and Practice. American Mercury 1: 251-252, Feb., 1924. Pseudo-Science.

STRATTON-PORTER, GENE. See Porter, Gene Stratton.

STREET, JULIAN LEONARD. Wines: Their Selection, Care and Service. Nation 138: 193, Feb. 14, 1934. For Thy Stomach's Sake.

STRIBLING, THOMAS SIGISMUND. Teeftallow. American Mercury 8: 509-510, Aug., 1926. Fiction.

STRINDBERG, AUGUST.

The Confession of a Fool. Smart Set 40: 157-160, Aug., 1913. A Counterblast to Buncombe.

The Creditor . . . translated from the Swedish by Francis J. Zeigler. Smart Set 33: 166, Feb., 1911. The Revival of the Printed Play.

Easter, a Play in Three Acts . . . translated by Velma Swanston Howard. Smart Set 39: 156, March, 1913. Gerhart Hauptmann.

The Father. Smart Set 66: 141-142, Nov., 1921. More Notes on Books—2.

The Inferno . . . translated by Claud Field. Smart Set 40: 157-160, Aug., 1913. A Counterblast to Buncombe.

Lucky Pehr, a Drama in Five Acts . . . translated by Velma Swanston Howard. *See* above, Easter.

Married. *See* above, The Inferno.

Mother Love (Moderskärlek), an Act . . . English version by Francis Joseph Ziegler. *See* The Creditor.

On the Seaboard, translated by Elizabeth Clarke Westergren. Smart Set 42: 155-156, Feb., 1914. Anything But Novels!

Plays, translated from the Swedish with an introduction by Edwin Björkman. Smart Set 37: 153-155, June, 1912. The Terrible Swede.

Swanwhite, a Fairy Drama, translated by Francis Joseph Ziegler. Smart Set 28: 158, July, 1909. The Best Novels of the Year.

Zones of the Spirit . . . translated by Claud Field. *See* above, The Inferno.

STRINGER, ARTHUR JOHN ARBUTHNOTT.

The Gun Runner. Smart Set 28: 157, June, 1909. Books for the Hammock and Deck Chair.

The Shadow. Smart Set 40: 157, May, 1913. Weep for the White Slave!

STRONG, ANNA LOUISE. The First Time in History: Two Years of Russia's New Life . . . with a preface by Leon Trotsky. American Mercury 2: 122-123, May, 1924. Two Views of Russia.

STRUNSKY, SIMEON. The Rediscovery of Jones, Studies in the Obvious. American Mercury 25: 379-383, March, 1932. The Case for Democracy.

STUART, HENRY LOGAN. Fenella. Smart Set 35: 155-156, Oct., 1911. Brieux and Others.

STURGEON, R. McCORMICK. A Bundle of Kisses. Smart Set 49: 143-144, Aug., 1916. The Ulster Polonius—III—The Labial Infamy.

SUCKOW, RUTH.

The Bonney Family. American Mercury 14: 127, May, 1928. Fiction.

Cora. American Mercury 19: 126-127, Jan., 1930. Fiction by Adept Hands.

Country People. American Mercury 2: 382, July, 1924. Rambles in Fiction.

Iowa Interiors. American Mercury 9: 382-383, Nov., 1926. Certain Works of Fiction.

The Odyssey of a Nice Girl. American Mercury 7: 506-507, April, 1926. Fiction Good and Bad.

SUDERMANN, HERMANN.

The Book of My Youth, translated by Wyndham Harding. [Baltimore] Evening Sun, June 30, 1923. Sudermann's Story of His Youth in a Bad Translation; Smart Set 72: 143-144, Sept., 1923. New York—II.

The Indian Lily. Smart Set 36: 152-155, Feb., 1912. Rounding Up the Novels.

Morituri. Smart Set 33: 166, Feb., 1911. The Revival of the Printed Play.

The Purpose. *See* The Indian Lily.

The Song of Songs (Das Hohe Lied) . . . translated by Thomas Seltzer. Smart Set 30: 153-155, April, 1910. A Glance at the Spring Fiction.

[Comments] Smart Set 39: 153-155, March, 1913. Gerhart Hauptmann.

SULLIVAN, JOHN WILLIAM NAVIN. Beethoven; His Spiritual Development. American Mercury 13: 381-382, March, 1928. Colossus.

SUMMERS, MONTAGUE.
The History of Witchcraft and Demonology. American Mercury 11: 123-125, May, 1927. The Powers of the Air.
The Vampire: His Kith and Kin. American Mercury 17: 123-124, May, 1929. The Gods and Their Agents.

SUMNER, WILLIAM GRAHAM. Reminiscences (Mainly Personal) . . . [comp.] by Albert Galloway Keller. Yale Review 23: 389-390, Winter, 1934. The Discoverer of the Forgotten Man.

SUTCLIFFE, HALLIWELL. Priscilla of the Good Intent. Smart Set 30: 156, Feb., 1910. Books To Read and Books To Avoid.

THE SWAN DRAMATISTS [Series Reprints]. Smart Set 39: 158-159, Oct., 1909. The Last of the Victorians.

SWEDISH SOCIETY FOR ANTHROPOLOGY AND GEOGRAPHY, Stockholm. Andrée's Story: The Complete Record of His Polar Flight, 1897, from the Diaries and Journals of Salomon August Andrée, Nils Strindberg and K. Fraenkel, translated from Swedish by Edward Adams-Ray. American Mercury 22: 254-255, Feb., 1931. Martyrs to Service.

SWINBURNE, ALGERNON CHARLES. Posthumous Poems, edited by Edmund Gosse and T. J. Wise. Smart Set 58: 140, April, 1919. Notes of a Poetry-Hater—III.

SWINNERTON, FRANK ARTHUR. Nocturne. Smart Set 55: 141, July, 1918. The Public Prints—III.

SYNGE, JOHN MILLINGTON.
Riders to the Sea. Smart Set 34: 152-153, Aug., 1911. The New Dramatic Literature.
The Tinker's Wedding. See above, Riders to the Sea.
The Works of John Synge. Smart Set 38: 147-149, Oct., 1912. Synge and Others.

TAGORE, Sir RABINDRANATH.
Sadhana: The Realization of Life. Town Topics 71: 18-19, June 4, 1914. Buncombe from the Orient.
Thought Relics. Smart Set 65: 143, July, 1921. Literary Notes—III.

TANNER, JUANITA, pseud. The Intelligent Man's Guide to Marriage & Celibacy. American Mercury 18: 126-127, Sept., 1929. The Fruits of Emancipation.

TARKINGTON, BOOTH.
Alice Adams. Smart Set 66: 140-142, Oct., 1921. Notes on Books—III.
Penrod. Town Topics 71: 19, June 25, 1914. Best-Sellers and Others; Smart Set 43: 159, Aug., 1914. Adventures Among the New Novels.
Ramsay Milholland. Smart Set 60: 143, Oct., 1919. Mark Twain—IV.

TASSIN, ALGERNON DE VIVIER. The Magazine in America. Smart Set 50: 138-140, Dec., 1916. The Literary Shambles.

TATE, ALLEN. Jefferson Davis: His Rise and Fall. American Mercury 19: 122-125, Jan., 1930. American Worthies.

TAYLOR, ALRUTHEUS AMBUSH. The Negro in South Carolina During the Reconstruction. American Mercury 4: 383, March, 1925. Brief Notices.

TAYLOR, MARY IMLAY. Caleb Trench. Smart Set 31: 155, June, 1910. The Greatest of American Writers.

TAYLOR, THOMAS GRIFFITH. Environment and Race. American Mercury 12: 507-508, Dec., 1927. The Races of Man.

TEASDALE, SARA.
Helen of Troy and Other Poems. Smart Set 37: 154-155, May, 1912. The Bards in Battle Royal.
Rivers to the Sea. Smart Set 49: 309, 310, May, 1916. Tra-La! Tra-La La! Tra-La La La!

TECHNOCRACY: The Magazine of the New Deal. American Mercury 28: 505-507, April, 1933. Old Dr. Scott's Bile Beans.

TERHUNE, ALBERT PAYSON. The Fighter. Smart Set 30: 154, March, 1910. The Literary Heavyweight Champion.

TERPENNING, WALTER ABRAM. Village and Open-Country Neighborhoods. American Mercury 25: 123-125, Jan., 1932. How Americans Live.

TERRETT, COURTNAY. Only Saps Work. American Mercury 21: 255, Oct., 1930. The Land of Rackets.

TERRY, Dame ELLEN. The Story of My Life. Smart Set 28: 159, May, 1909. Some Novels—and a Good One.

THANET, OCTAVE, pseud. See French, Alice.

THAYER, JOHN ADAMS. Astir, a Publisher's Life-Story. Smart Set 32: 168, Oct., 1910. Meredith's Swan Song; 34: 151-152, June, 1911. The Horse Power of Realism.

THAYER, WILLIAM ROSCOE. Theodore Roosevelt, an Intimate Biography. Smart Set 61: 140-141, Feb., 1920; 61: 138-144, March, 1920.

THOM, HELEN (HOPKINS). Johns Hopkins; a Silhouette. American Mercury 19: 122-125, Jan., 1930. American Worthies.

THOMA, LUDWIG. "Moral," a Comedy in Three Acts. Smart Set 52: 398-399, May, 1917. Shocking Stuff—3.

THOMAS, ALBERT ELLSWORTH. Her Husband's Wife, a Comedy in Three Acts. Smart Set 44: 159, Sept., 1914. Thirty-Five Printed Plays.

THOMAS, AUGUSTUS. As a Man Thinks, a Play in Four Acts. Smart Set 35: 154, Oct., 1911. Brieux and Others.

THOMAS, EDWARD. Maurice Maeterlinck, a Biography. Smart Set 36: 156, April, 1912. An Antidote to "Yankee Doodle."

THOMAS, HENRY WILLIAM. Life and Letters of Henry William Thomas, Mixologist. American Mercury 10: 254-255, Feb., 1927. In Honor of an Artist. This review is reprinted in the second edition of the book, 1929. p. 12–14.

THOMAS, ROWLAND. The Little Gods, a Masque of the Far East. Smart Set 28: 159, June, 1909. Books for the Hammock and Deck Chair.

THOMPSON, FRANCIS. A Renegade Poet, and Other Essays, with an introduction by Edward J. O'Brien. Smart Set 33: 166-167, March, 1911. A Stack of Novels.

THOMPSON, VANCE. Woman. Smart Set 53: 138-144, Oct., 1917. Woman, Lovely Woman.

THOMSON, *Sir* JOHN ARTHUR. What Is Man? American Mercury 4: 252-253, Feb., 1925. Homo Sapiens.

THOMSON, *Sir* JOHN ARTHUR, *ed.* The Outline of Science. Smart Set 69: 142-144, Oct., 1922. Portrait of an American Citizen.

THORNDIKE, ASHLEY HORACE. The Outlook for Literature. American Mercury 24: 507-508, Dec., 1931. The American as Literatus.

THOROLD, ALGAR LABOUCHERE. Six Masters of Disillusion. Smart Set 29: 159, Oct., 1909. The Last of the Victorians.

THURSTON, ERNEST TEMPLE. The Greatest Wish in the World. Smart Set 33: 162, March, 1911. A Stack of Novels.

THURSTON, KATHERINE CECIL. Max. Smart Set 33: 165, March, 1911. A Stack of Novels.

THYSIA, an Elegy. Smart Set 31: 160, Aug., 1910. A Hot Weather Novelist.

TILNEY, FREDERICK. The Brain from Ape to Man. American Mercury 14: 508-510, Aug., 1928. Cousin Jocko.

TOLSTOI, LEV NIKOLAEVICH, *Graf.*

The Death of Ivan Ilyitch. Smart Set 47: 309, Nov., 1915. After All, Why Not?

The Forged Coupon. Smart Set 37: 155-156, Aug., 1912. Zola.

Hadji Murád. *See* above, The Forged Coupon.

The Pathway of Life, translated by Archibald J. Wolfe. Smart Set 61: 142-143, May, 1920. More Notes from a Diary—III.

TOWNER, RUTHERFORD HAMILTON. The Philosophy of Civilization. American Mercury 1: 251, Feb., 1924. Pseudo-Science.

TOWNSEND, EDWARD WATERMAN. The Climbing Courvatels. Smart Set 28: 157, May, 1909. Some Novels—And a Good One.

TOWNSEND, WILLIAM HENRY. Lincoln and His Wife's Home Town. American Mercury 19: 122-125, Jan., 1930. American Worthies.

TRAIN, ARTHUR CHENEY.

The Goldfish. Town Topics 72: 14, Aug. 13, 1914. Adventures in Babylon.

The Man Who Rocked the Earth, by Arthur Train and Robert Williams Wood. Smart Set 46: 449-450, July, 1915. The Prometheus of the Western World.

TRASK, KATE (NICHOLS). In the Vanguard, by Katrina Trask. Smart Set 41: 155, 156, Sept., 1913. Getting Rid of the Actor.

TRATTNER, ERNEST ROBERT.

As a Jew Sees Jesus. American Mercury 23: 506-510, April, 1932. Quod Est Veritas?

The Autobiography of God. American Mercury 20: 254-255, June, 1930. The Ghostly Realm.

TRAUBEL, HORACE. Optimos. Smart Set 34: 158, July, 1911. Novels for Hot Afternoons.

TREPOFF, IVAN, *pseud. See* Gossip, George Hatfield Dingley.

TRIDON, ANDRÉ.

The New Unionism. Smart Set 41: 157, Oct., 1913. "With Your Kind Permission—"

Psychoanalysis and Behavior. Smart Set 64: 144, Jan., 1921. Consolation—IV— Psychoanalyzing the Uplift.

TRITES, WILLIAM BUDD. John Cave. Smart Set 40: 160, Aug., 1913. A Counter-blast to Buncombe.

TROTSKII, LEV. My Life. American Mercury 20: 381-383, July, 1930. The Russian Phantasmagoria.

TROUBETZKOY, AMÉLIE (RIVES) CHANIER. Shadows of Flames. Smart Set 67: 309, Nov., 1915. After All, Why Not?

TRUDEAU, EDWARD LIVINGSTON. An Autobiography. Smart Set 49: 155-156, June, 1916. A Soul's Adventures—3—Americans.

TRUMBULL, C. G. Anthony Comstock, Fighter. Smart Set 42: 145-148, April, 1914. Roosevelt, Bulwer-Lytton and Anthony Comstock.

TUCKER, GILBERT MILLIGAN. American English. Smart Set 65: 144, July, 1921. Literary Notes—IV—Americanese; Bookman 53: 353-355, June, 1921. The American Language.

[TUCKER, RAY THOMAS.] The Mirrors of 1932. American Mercury 24: 251-253, Oct., 1931. The Men Who Govern Us.

TULLY, JIM.

Beggars of Life. American Mercury 3: 510, Dec., 1924. Brief Notices.

Jarnegan. American Mercury 9: 382, Nov., 1926. Certain Works of Fiction.

TURNBULL, ARCHIBALD DOUGLAS. Commodore David Porter, 1780-1843. American Mercury 19: 122-125, Jan., 1930. American Worthies.

TURNER, JOHN KENNETH.

Barbarous Mexico. Smart Set 33: 167-168, April, 1911. The Meredith of Tomorrow.

Shall It Be Again? Smart Set 69: 138-144, Sept., 1922. The Coroner's Inquest.

TURNER, WALTER JAMES. Wagner. American Mercury 30: 381-383, Nov., 1933. Notes on Wagner.

TWAIN, MARK, *pseud.*

The Curious Republic of Gondour. Smart Set 60: 138-143, Oct., 1919. Discussion of Twain.

BOOK REVIEWS

Huckleberry Finn. Smart Set 31: 153-154, June, 1910. The Greatest of American Writers; 48: 308-309, Jan., 1916. Partly About Books; 66: 142, Sept., 1921; Chicago Tribune, Feb. 8, 1925. H. L. Mencken on Mark Twain.

The Innocents Abroad. Smart Set 47: 152, Oct., 1915. The Literature of a Moral Republic.

Is Shakespeare Dead? Smart Set 28: 155, 156-157, Aug., 1909. Novels and Other Books—Chiefly Bad.

Mark Twain's Autobiography, with an introduction by Albert Bigelow Paine. Smart Set 39: 152-153, Feb., 1913; [Baltimore] Evening Sun, Oct. 18, 1924; American Mercury 3: 507-508, Dec., 1924. Mark Twain on Himself.

Mark Twain's Letters, edited by Albert Bigelow Paine. Smart Set 54: 139-140, March, 1918. Literae Humaniores.

The Mysterious Stranger. Smart Set 52: 394-396, May, 1917. Shocking Stuff.

What Is Man? Smart Set 53: 142-143, Sept., 1917. Si Mutare Potest Aethiops Pellum Suam—II; 60: 141-143, Oct., 1919. Mark Twain.

[Comments.] Smart Set 39: 151-154, Feb., 1913. The Burden of Humor.

TWEEDIE, ETHEL BRILLIANA (HARLEY). America as I Saw It, by Mrs. Alec Tweedie. Smart Set 42: 159, Feb., 1914. Anything But Novels!

TYDINGS, MILLARD EVELYN. Before and After Prohibition. American Mercury 24: 381-382, Nov., 1931. Coroner's Inquest.

UDDGREN, CARL GUSTAF. Strindberg the Man, Translated from the Swedish by Axel Johan Uppval. Smart Set 66: 141-142, Nov., 1921. More Notes on Books —2.

ULMAN, JOSEPH NATHAN. A Judge Takes the Stand. American Mercury 29: 381-383, July, 1933. The Job of the Judge.

UNDERWOOD, OSCAR WILDER. Drifting Sands of Party Politics. American Mercury 17: 123-125, Sept., 1928. The Curse of Government.

UNTERMEYER, LOUIS.

Challenge. Town Topics 72: 16, July, 30, 1914. Poetry Fit To Read.

First Love, a Lyric Sequence. Smart Set 39: 150, April, 1913. The Burbling of the Bards.

The New Era in American Poetry. Smart Set 59: 138-140, July, 1919. The Coroner's Inquest.

UNWIN, STANLEY. The Truth About Publishing. American Mercury 11: 126-127, May, 1927. The Art of Barabbas.

UPTON, GEORGE PUTNAM. The Standard Concert Repertory and Other Concert Pieces. Smart Set 30: 159, Jan., 1910. George Bernard Shaw As A Hero.

UPWARD, ALLEN.

Lord Alistair's Rebellion. Smart Set 33: 165-166, Jan., 1911. The Leading American Novelist.

The New Word. Smart Set 31: 159, July, 1910. A Fictioneer of the Laboratory.

URNER, MABEL HERBERT. The Journal of a Neglected Wife. Smart Set 28: 156-157, May, 1909. Some Novels—and a Good One; 28: 153-154, July, 1909.

VAIHINGER, HANS. The Philosophy of "As If," translated by C. K. Ogden. American Mercury 3: 253-255, Oct., 1924. Philosophers as Liars.

VANCE, LOUIS JOSEPH.

The Fortune Hunter. Smart Set 30: 158, April, 1910. A Glance at the Spring Fiction.

Joan Thursday. Smart Set 41: 159, Dec., 1913. The Russians.

VAN DOREN, CARL CLINTON.

The American Novel. Smart Set 66: 142, Sept., 1921. From the Diary of a Reviewer—III—Tuesday.

Modern American Prose. Nation 139: 165, Aug. 8, 1934. The Slough of Words.

Swift: A Biography. New York Herald Tribune Books, p. 1, Oct. 19, 1930. A Fascinating Biography.

Three Worlds. Nation 143: 337, Sept. 19, 1936. The Life of a Critic.

VAN DYKE, HENRY.

Six Days of the Week: A Book of Thoughts About Life and Religion. American Mercury 4: 382-383, March, 1925. Sweet Stuff.

The Unknown Quantity. Smart Set 39: 158, Feb., 1913. The Burden of Humor.

VAN DYKE, JOHN CHARLES.

American Painting and Its Tradition. Smart Set 61: 141-142, Feb., 1920. From the Diary of a Reviewer—Dec. 12.

The New New York. Smart Set 29: 158, Dec., 1909. "A Doll's House"—With a Fourth Act.

VAN LOON, HENDRIK WILLEM. The Fall of the Dutch Republic. Smart Set 64: 140, Jan., 1921. Consolation—II—The Incomparable Bok.

VAN VECHTEN, CARL.

The Blind Bow-Boy. American Mercury 1: 381, March, 1924. Three Gay Stories.

Fire-Crackers. American Mercury 6: 380-381, Nov., 1925. Fiction Good and Bad.

In the Garret. Smart Set 62: 140, May, 1920. More Notes from a Diary.

Interpreters and Interpretations. Smart Set 54: 143-144, Feb., 1918. The National Letters.

The Merry-Go-Round. Smart Set 58: 138-139, Jan., 1919. Nothing Much Is Here, Alas!

Music after the Great War. Smart Set 49: 296-298, July, 1916. Savonarolas A-Sweat—III—The Tone Art.

Music and Bad Manners. Smart Set 52: 396-398, May, 1917. Shocking Stuff.

The Music of Spain. Smart Set 58: 143-144, March, 1919. Mainly Fiction.

Nigger Heaven. American Mercury 9: 127, Sept., 1926. Three Novels.

The Tiger in the House. Smart Set 64: 144, March, 1921. A Soul's Adventures —III.

VEBLEN, THORSTEIN.

[Discussion.] Smart Set 59: 138-144, May, 1919. Prof. Veblen and the Cow.

BOOK REVIEWS

VILLARD, OSWALD GARRISON.

Fighting Years, Memoirs of a Liberal Editor. [Baltimore] Sun, p. 10, April 16, 1939. Mr. Villard's Recollections.

Prophets True and False. Nation 127: 90, July 25, 1928. Americans All.

Some Newspapers and Newspaper Men. [Baltimore] Evening Sun, editorial page, Oct. 26, 1923. Dr. Villard, the Sunpapers and Newspapers in General.

VITTE, SERGIĔI ĬUL'EVICH, Graf. The Memoirs of Count Witte, translated from the original manuscript and edited by Abraham Yarmolinsky. Smart Set 65: 139-140, July, 1921. Literary notes.

VON GRUBER, MAX. Hygiene of Sex. American Mercury 8: 127, May, 1926. The Literature of Sex.

WADE, JOHN DONALD. Augustus Baldwin Longstreet. American Mercury 5: 510, Aug., 1925. Other Biographies.

WAGNER, PHILIP MARSHALL. American Wines and How To Make Them. Nation 138: 193, Feb. 14, 1934. For Thy Stomach's Sake.

WAGNER, RICHARD. Tristan and Isolde, translated into English verse by Richard Le Gallienne. Smart Set 30: 155, Jan., 1910. George Bernard Shaw As A Hero.

WAGSTAFF, BLANCHE (SHOEMAKER). Eris: A Dramatic Allegory. Town Topics 72: 16, July 30, 1914. Poetry Fit To Read.

WALKER, STANLEY. The Night Club Era. New York Herald Tribune Books, p. 3, Nov. 12, 1933. How New York Survived the Prohibition Era.

WALLAS, GRAHAM. The Life of Francis Place, 1771-1854. Smart Set 68: 144, Oct., 1920. Gropings in Literary Darkness—VI.

WALLER, MARY ELLA. A Year out of Life. Smart Set 28: 156, July, 1909. The Best Novels of the Year.

WALLIN, IVAN EMMANUEL. On Symbiotism and the Origin of Species. American Mercury 10: 508-510, April, 1927. The Origin of Species.

WALPOLE, HUGH.

The Cathedral. Smart Set 70: 143-144, March, 1923. Adventures Among Books —III.

The Duchess of Wrexe. Smart Set 44: 310, Dec., 1914. Mush for the Multitude.

The Gods and Mr. Perrin. Smart Set 36: 156, Feb., 1912. Rounding Up the Novels.

The Green Mirror. Smart Set 54: 140-141, March, 1918. Literae Humaniores —II.

Joseph Conrad. Smart Set 50: 138-140, Oct., 1916. The Creed of a Novelist.

WALSH, JAMES JOSEPH. Cures, the Story of the Cures that Fail. Smart Set 72: 138, 140-141, Nov., 1923. Notices of Books.

WALTER, EUGENE. Homeward Bound. [Baltimore] Evening Sun, Feb. 23, 1911. Eugene Walter.

WALTER, EUGENE and ARTHUR HORNBLOW. The Easiest Way. Smart Set 34: 167, May, 1911. Novels—The Spring Crop.

WORKS BY H. L. M.

WAND, JOHN WILLIAM CHARLES. A History of the Modern Church from 1500 to the Present Day. American Mercury 20: 254-255, June, 1930. The Ghostly Realm.

WAPLES, DOUGLAS and RALPH WINFRED TYLER. What People Want To Read About. American Mercury 24: 253-254, Oct., 1931. The Progress of Science.

WARD, MARY AUGUSTA (ARNOLD) "Mrs. Humphrey Ward."
Lady Merton, Colonist. Smart Set 31: 155-156, July, 1910. A Fictioneer of the Laboratory.
Marriage à la Mode. Smart Set 28: 152-153, Aug., 1909. Novels and Other Books—Chiefly Bad.
The Mating of Lydia. Smart Set 40: 157-158, July, 1913. Various Bad Novels.

WARNER, ANNE. See French, Anne (Warner).

WARNER, HENRY EDWARD. That House I Bought. Smart Set 37: 158-159, July, 1912. A Dip into the Novels.

WARREN, ROBERT PENN. John Brown; The Making of a Martyr. American Mercury 19: 122-125, Jan., 1930. American Worthies.

WARWICK, ANNE, pseud. See Cranston, Mrs. Ruth.

WASSERMANN, JAKOB. The World's Illusion, translated by Ludwig Lewisohn. Nation 111: 668, 670, Dec. 8, 1920. A Pathological Movie; Smart Set 64: 142-143, Feb., 1921. The Anatomy of Ochlocracy—III.

WATERMAN, PHILIP F. The Story of Superstition. American Mercury 17: 123, 125, May, 1929. The Gods and Their Agents.

WATSON, E. L. GRANT. See Grant Watson, Elliot Lovegood.

WATSON, FORBES. William Glacksens. American Mercury 1: 379, March, 1924. Art Criticism.

WATSON, Sir WILLIAM. Sable and Purple, with Other Poems. Smart Set 32: 168, Nov., 1910. A Guide to Intelligent Eating.

WATTERSON, HENRY.
The Editorials of Henry Watterson, compiled . . . by Arthur Krock [Baltimore] Evening Sun, Aug. 11, 1923. Reveal "Vacuity of Journalism."
"Marse Henry," an Autobiography. Smart Set 62: 144, May, 1920. More Notes from a Diary—V—March, 24.

WATTS, MARY (STANBERY).
The Rise of Jennie Cushing. Smart Set 45: 461-462, Jan., 1915. A Gamey Old Gaul.
Van Cleve. Smart Set 42: 155-156, Jan., 1914. A Pestilence of Novels.

WAY, L. N. The Call of the Heart. Smart Set 30: 155, Feb., 1910. Books To Read and Books To Avoid.

WAY, NORMAN. Mary Jane's Pa, from a play of the same name by Edith Ellis. Smart Set 30: 154-155, March, 1910. The Literary Heavyweight Champion.

BOOK REVIEWS

WEAVER, GERTRUDE (RENTON). Priests of Progress, by G. Colmore [pseud.]. Smart Set 28: 157-158, May, 1909. Some Novels—And a Good One.

WEAVER, RAYMOND MELBOURNE. Herman Melville, Mariner and Mystic. Smart Set 67: 141-142, Feb., 1922. Frank Harris and Others—II.

WEBB, SIDNEY. *See* Passfield, Sidney James Webb, *baron*.

WEBER, FREDERICK PARKES. Aspects of Death and Correlated Aspects of Life in Art, Epigram and Poetry. Smart Set 60: 138-143, Dec., 1919. Exeunt Omnes.

WEBSTER, HENRY KITCHELL. The Sky-Man. Smart Set 31: 157, July, 1910. A Fictioneer of the Laboratory.

WEBSTER'S NEW INTERNATIONAL DICTIONARY OF THE ENGLISH LANGUAGE, edited by William Allan Neilson [and others]. Nation 139: 450, Oct. 17, 1934. The New Webster.

WEDEKIND, FRANK.

The Awakening of Spring, a Tragedy of Childhood, translated from the German by Francis Joseph Ziegler. Smart Set 30: 158, March, 1910. The Literary Heavyweight Champion.

Such Is Life, a Play in Five Acts, English version by Francis Joseph Ziegler. Smart Set 38: 152, Oct., 1912. Synge and others.

WEEKLEY, ERNEST. An Etymological Dictionary of Modern English. Smart Set 66: 141-142, Dec., 1921. Variations on a Familiar Theme—3.

WELLS, HERBERT GEORGE.

Ann Veronica. Smart Set 30: 153-154, Feb., 1910. Books To Read and Books To Avoid; 33: 161, April, 1911.

Bealby, a Holiday. Smart Set 46: 295, June, 1915. Here Are Novels!

Boon. Smart Set 47: 156, Oct., 1915. The Literature of a Moral Republic.

Christina Alberta's Father. American Mercury 6: 509-510, Dec., 1925. The English Novel.

The Diary of a Disappointed Man. Smart Set 59: 144, Sept., 1919.

The Discovery of the Future. Smart Set 40: 152, June, 1913. A Nietzschean, a Swedenborgian, and Other Queer Fowl.

Experiment in Autobiography; Discoveries and Conclusions of a Very Ordinary Brain (since 1860). Nation 139: 567, Nov. 14, 1934. Wells Nearing Three Score.

First and Last Things. Smart Set 26: 155-156, Dec., 1908. Oyez! Oyez! All Ye Who Read Books.

History of Mr. Polly. Smart Set 31: 153-155, July, 1910. A Fictioneer of the Laboratory.

Joan and Peter. Smart Set 57: 138-140, Dec., 1918. The Late Mr. Wells.

Little Wars. Smart Set 42: 153, 155, Feb., 1914. Anything But Novels!

Marriage. Smart Set 39: 153-155, Jan., 1913. Again the Busy Fictioneers.

Mr. Britling Sees It Through. Smart Set 50: 143-144, Dec., 1916. The Literary Shambles—4.

The New Machiavelli. Smart Set 33: 161-163, April, 1911. The Meredith of Tomorrow.

The Open Conspiracy: Blue Prints for a World Revolution. American Mercury 15: 380-382, Nov., 1928. A Glance Ahead.

The Outline of History. Smart Set 64: 138-141, March, 1921. A Soul's Adventures [Baltimore] Evening Sun, Jan. 10, 1921. Mr. Wells' History; American Mercury 22: 382, March, 1931.

The Passionate Friends. Smart Set 42: 152, April, 1914. Roosevelt, Bulwer-Lytton and Anthony Comstock.

The Research Magnificient. Smart Set 47: 310, Nov., 1915. After All, Why Not?

The Science of Life, by H. G. Wells, Julian Huxley and G. P. Wells. American Mercury 22: 381–383, March, 1931. Wells At His Best.

Tono-Bungay. Smart Set 27: 154-155, April, 1909. The Novels That Bloom in the Spring, Tra-La! 28: 153-154, July, 1909.

The War in the Air. Smart Set 27: 158, Jan., 1909. A Road Map of the New Books.

The Wife of Sir Isaac Harman. Smart Set 45: 459-461, Jan., 1915. A Gamey Old Gaul.

The Work, Wealth & Happiness of Mankind. American Mercury 25: 505-506, April, 1932. Wells Completes His Magnum Opus.

The World of William Clissold: A Novel at a New Angle. American Mercury 9: 506-508, Dec., 1926. Wells Redivivus.

WELLS, MORRIS BENJAMIN. Five Gallons of Gasoline. Smart Set 34: 155-156, July, 1911. Novels for a Hot Afternoon.

WENDELL, BARRETT. The Privileged Classes. Smart Set 27: 156, March, 1909. The Literary Clinic.

WERNER, MORRIS ROBERT.

Brigham Young. Chicago Sunday Tribune, July 12, 1925. Biography—; American Mercury 5: 510, Aug., 1925. Other Biographies.

Bryan. American Mercury 17: 255, June, 1929. American Worthies.

Tammany Hall. American Mercury 14: 383, July, 1928. Chronicles of Sin.

WESEEN, MAURICE HARLEY. A Dictionary of American Slang. Nation 139: 628, Nov. 28, 1934. The Treasures of the Vernacular.

WEST, VICTORIA MARY SACKVILLE. See Sackville-West, Victoria Mary.

WEYL, MAURICE. The Choice. Smart Set 60: 144, Oct., 1919. Mark Twain.

WEYMAN, STANLEY JOHN. The Wild Geese. Smart Set 28: 158-159, May, 1909. Some Novels—And a Good One.

WHARTON, EDITH NEWBOLD (JONES).

The Age of Innocence. Smart Set 64: 143, Feb., 1921. The Anatomy of Ochlocracy—III.

Ethan Frome. Smart Set 35: 151, Dec., 1911. An Overdose of Novels; 42: 159, Jan., 1914.

The Hermit and the Wild Woman. Smart Set 27: 157-158, Jan., 1909. A Road Map of the New Books.

The Reef. Smart Set 39: 157, Feb., 1913. The Burden of Humor.

BOOK REVIEWS

WHELESS, JOSEPH. Is It God's Word? American Mercury 8: 123-125, May, 1926. Counter-Offensive.

WHIPPLE, LEON. The Story of Civil Liberty in the United States. American Mercury 12: 123-126, Sept., 1927. Autopsy.

WHITAKER, ALMA (FULLFORD). Bacchus Behave! The Lost Age of Polite Drinking. Nation 138: 193, Feb. 14, 1934. For Thy Stomach's Sake.

WHITAKER, HERMAN, *ed.* West Winds. Smart Set 45: 153-154, Feb., 1915. Lachrymose Love.

WHITE, BOUCK. The Book of Daniel Drew. Smart Set 58: 144, Jan., 1919. Nothing Much Is Here, Alas!—IV.

WHITE, OWEN. Out of the Desert. American Mercury 1: 505-507, April, 1924. Provincial Literature.

WHITE, WALTER FRANCIS. Rope & Faggot: A Biography of Judge Lynch. American Mercury 17: 382-383, July, 1929. Sport in the Bible Country.

WHITE, WILLIAM ALLEN.

A Certain Rich Man. Smart Set 29: 153-155, Oct., 1909. The Last of the Victorians.

In the Heart of a Fool. Smart Set 58: 143-144, Feb., 1919. Sunrise on the Prairie.

WHITE, WILLIAM CHAPMAN. These Russians. American Mercury 22: 506-508, April, 1931. Life in the Marxian Utopia.

WHITEHEAD, ALFRED NORTH. The Aims of Education & Other Essays. American Mercury 17: 251-253, June, 1929. What Is It All About?

WHITING, LILIAN. The Brownings; Their Life and Art. Smart Set 38: 150, Oct. 1912. Synge and Others.

WHITLOCK, BRAND.

The Little Green Shutter. American Mercury 24: 381-382, Nov., 1931. Coroner's Inquest.

On the Enforcement of Law in Cities. Smart Set 40: 153-154, Aug., 1913. A Counterblast to Buncombe.

WHITMAN, STEPHEN FRENCH.

The Isle of Life. Smart Set 40: 145, 147-149, June, 1913. A Nietzschean, a Swedenborgian and Other Queer Fowl.

Predestined. Smart Set 31: 158-159, June, 1910. The Greatest of American Writers.

WHITMAN, WALT.

Song of the Broad-Axe. American Mercury 6: 251-254, Oct., 1925. Poetry.

Uncollected Poetry and Prose . . . collected and edited by Emory Holloway. Smart Set 67: 141-142, Jan., 1922. Book Article No. 158—III.

WHITMORE, CLARA HELEN. Woman's Work in Fiction. Smart Set 30: 157, March, 1910. The Literary Heavyweight Champion.

WORKS BY H. L. M.

WHITNEY, HARRY. Hunting with the Eskimos. Smart Set 33: 167, March, 1911. A Stack of Novels.

WHO'S WHO IN AMERICA 1926-1927 (14th ed.) American Mercury 9: 509-510, Dec., 1926. Notables.

WHO'S WHO IN AMERICA 1928-1929 (15th ed.) American Mercury 15: 509-510, Dec., 1928. American Worthies.

WHO'S WHO IN AMERICA 1936-1937 (19th ed.) Saturday Review of Literature 14: 3-4, Oct. 24, 1936. Tap-Day in America; abridged in Review of Reviews 94: 86-87, Dec., 1936.

WIETH-KNUDSEN, K. A. Understanding Women. American Mercury 18: 126-127, Sept., 1929. The Fruits of Emancipation.

WILDE, OSCAR. The Poems of Oscar Wilde, edited by Robert Ross. Smart Set 30: 154-155, Jan., 1910. George Bernard Shaw As A Hero.

WILDER, ELIZABETH and EDITH MENDALL TAYLOR. Self Help and Self Cure. Smart Set 31: 157-158, Aug., 1910. A Hot Weather Novelist.

WILDER, THORNTON NIVEN. The Bridge of San Luis Rey. American Mercury 14: 127, May, 1928. Fiction.

WILKINSON, LOUIS UMFREVILLE. Brute Gods. Smart Set 61: 140-141, Jan., 1920. The Flood of Fiction—II.

WILLIAMS, EGERTON RYERSON. Plain-Towns of Italy. Smart Set 36: 158, March, 1912. The Prophet of the Superman.

WILLIAMS, HENRY SMITH. Alcohol: How it Affects the Individual, the Community, and the Race. Smart Set 29: 158-159, Sept., 1909. The Books of the Dog Days.

WILLIAMS, JESSE LYNCH. The Married Life of the Frederic Carrolls. Smart Set 33: 165-166, March, 1911. A Stack of Novels.

WILLIAMSON, CHARLES NORRIS and MRS. ALICE MURIEL (LIVINGSTON) WILLIAMSON. Lord Loveland Discovers America. Smart Set 30: 156, April, 1910. A Glance at the Spring Fiction.

WILLIS, JOHN. Roosevelt in the Rough, by Jack Willis. American Mercury 25: 250-253, Feb., 1932. Nine American Statesmen.

WILSON, HARRY LEON.
Bunker Bean. Smart Set 40: 156, May, 1913. Weep for the White Slave!
Ruggles of Red Gap. Smart Set 46: 294-295, June, 1915. Here Are Novels!
Somewhere in Red Gap. Smart Set 50: 143, Dec., 1916. The Literary Shambles —4.

WILSON, MARGARET. The Crime of Punishment. American Mercury 24: 124-127, Sept., 1931. What Is To Be Done About It?

WILSON, ROMER, pseud. See O'Brien, Florence Roma Muir Wilson.

BOOK REVIEWS

WILSON, WOOD LOVETTE. The End of Dreams. Smart Set 33: 164-165, March, 1911. A Stack of Novels.

WILSTACH, FRANK JENNERS. Dictionary of Similes. Smart Set 50: 142-143, Dec., 1916. The Literary Shambles.

WILSTACH, PAUL.

Jefferson and Monticello. American Mercury 7: 381-383, March, 1926. The Heroic Age.

Mount Vernon, Washington's Home and the Nation's Shrine. Smart Set 52: 141-144, June, 1917. The Plague of Books.

Richard Mansfield, the Man and the Actor. Smart Set 27: 157, Feb., 1909. The Literary Olio.

WILSTACH, PAUL, ed. Correspondence of John Adams and Thomas Jefferson, 1812-1826. American Mercury 7: 381-383, March, 1926. The Heroic Age.

WINCHESTER, PAUL. Men of Maryland Since the Civil War. American Mercury 1: 505-507, April, 1924. Provincial Literature.

WINKLER, JOHN KENNEDY. W. R. Hearst, an American Phenomenon. American Mercury 14: 379-381, July, 1928. The Case of Hearst.

WINSLOW, THYRA (SAMTER).

Picture Frames. Smart Set 71: 141, July, 1923. Some New Books—IV.

Show Business. American Mercury 8: 509-510, Aug., 1926. Fiction.

WITTE, SERGIĔI ĬUL'EVICH, Graf. See Vitte, Sergiĕi Ĭul'evich, Graf.

WITTELS, FRITZ. Sigmund Freud, His Personality, His Teaching & His School, translated by Eden and Cedar Paul. American Mercury 3: 380, Nov., 1924. Marvels from Vienna.

WOOD, CASEY ALBERT and FIELDING HUDSON GARRISON, comps. Physician's Anthology of English and American Poetry. Smart Set 66: 138-139, Nov., 1921. More Notes on Books.

WOOD, CLEMENT.

Bernarr Macfadden, a Study in Success. American Mercury 20: 124-125, May, 1930. An American Idealist.

Don't Tread On Me: A Study of Aggressive Legal Tactics for Labor, by Clement Wood, McAlister Coleman and Arthur Garfield Hays. American Mercury 17: 123-125, Sept., 1928. The Curse of Government.

WOODS, HENRY F. American Sayings: Famous Phrases, Slogans and Aphorisms. California Folklore Quarterly 5: 319-320, July, 1946.

WOODWARD, HELEN (ROSEN). Through Many Windows. American Mercury 4: 380-381, Nov., 1926. Three Lively Lives.

WOODWARD, WILLIAM E. Meet General Grant. American Mercury 16: 251-253, Feb., 1929. Portrait of an Immortal.

WOOLF, LEONARD SIDNEY. After the Deluge; a Study of Communal Psychology. American Mercury 25: 379-383, March, 1932. The Case for Democracy.

WORKS BY H. L. M.

WORLD COMMITTEE FOR THE VICTIMS OF GERMAN FASCISM. The Brown Book of the Hitler Terror and the Burning of the Reichstag. American Mercury 30: 506-510, Dec., 1933. Hitlerismus.

WORTH, NICHOLAS, *pseud. See* Page, Walter Hines.

WRIGHT, HAROLD BELL. The Calling of Dan Matthews. Smart Set 29: 158-160, Nov., 1909. What About Nietzsche?

WRIGHT, WILLARD HUNTINGTON.

The Creative Will. Smart Set 50: 140-142, Dec., 1916. The Literary Shambles.

The Man of Promise. Forum 55: 490-496, April, 1916. America Produces a Novelist; Smart Set 48: 151-154, April, 1916. The Publishers Begin Their Spring Drive—3.

Misinforming a Nation. Smart Set 52: 142-143, July, 1917. The Cult of Dunsany —III.

Modern Painting, Its Tendency and Meaning. Smart Set 47: 153-156, Oct., 1915. The Literature of a Moral Republic.

What Nietzsche Taught. Smart Set 45: 290-293, March, 1915. The Bugaboo of the Sunday Schools.

WUORINEN, JOHN HENRY. The Prohibition Experiment in Finland. American Mercury 24: 382, Nov., 1931. Coroner's Inquest.

WYLIE, IDA ALEXA ROSS.

The Germans. Smart Set 36: 156-158, March, 1912. The Prophet of the Superman.

The Native Born, or The Rajah's People. Smart Set 32: 167-168, Nov., 1910. A Guide to Intelligent Eating.

WYNNE, MAY, *pseud. See* Knowles, Mabel Winifred.

YEATS, WILLIAM BUTLER. Later Poems. American Mercury 6: 251-254, Oct., 1925. Poetry.

YERKES, ROBERT M. Almost Human. Chicago Sunday Tribune, Aug. 29, 1926. Man as a Mammal.

YOST, CASPER SALATHIEL. The Principles of Journalism. American Mercury 2: 248-250, June, 1924. The Newspaper Man.

YOUNG, ARTHUR MORGAN. Japan in Recent Times, 1912-1926. American Mercury 18: 254-255, Oct., 1929. The Yankee of the East.

YOUNG, FRANCIS BRETT. Sea Horses. Chicago Sunday Tribune, May 24, 1925. The Heirs of Conrad; American Mercury 5: 383, July, 1925. New Fiction.

ZANGWILL, ISRAEL.

Italian Fantasies. Smart Set 33: 168, April, 1911. The Meredith of Tomorrow.

The Melting Pot, a Drama in Four Acts. Smart Set 29: 156, Dec., 1909. "A Doll's House"—With a Fourth Act.

The War God. Smart Set 37: 157-158, June, 1912. The Terrible Swede.

ZEITLIN, JACOB and HOMER EDWARDS WOODBRIDGE. Life and Letters of Stuart P. Sherman. American Mercury 18: 507-509, Dec., 1929. Stuart P. Sherman.

ZOLA, EMILE. For a Night, translated by Alison M. Lederer, Smart Set 37: 153-155, Aug., 1912. Zola.

ZUCKERMAN, SOLLY. The Social Life of Monkeys and Apes. American Mercury 26: 126-127, May, 1932. Cousin Jocko.

ZURCHER, ARNOLD JOHN. The Experiment with Democracy in Central Europe. American Mercury 30: 506, Dec., 1933. Hitlerismus.

PLAYS AND THE THEATRE

Occasionally HLM reviewed printed plays and books dealing with the theatre in one collective review. These are listed below by the title of the month's book review section.

After All, Why Not? Smart Set 47: 304-310, Nov., 1915.
Getting Rid of the Actor. Smart Set 41: 153-156, Sept., 1913.
A Hot Weather Novelist. Smart Set. 31: 158-159, Aug., 1910.
New Dramatic Literature. Smart Set 34: 151-155, Aug., 1911.
The Revival of the Printed Play. Smart Set 33: 163-168, Feb., 1911.
Thirty-Five Printed Plays. Smart Set 44: 153-160, Sept., 1914.

POETRY

HLM would let volumes of poetry accumulate until he had a sufficient number for an entire month's column or a large section;

then they appeared in a collective review. These group reviews have been entered below under the title of the monthly book feature.

Ambitious Bards. [Baltimore] Evening Sun p. 6, March 13, 1911.

The Bards in Battle Royal. Smart Set 37: 151-156, May, 1912.

Books of Verse. American Mercury 8: 251-254, June, 1926.

The Burbling of the Bards. Smart Set 39: 145-152, April, 1913.

Exeunt Omnes. Smart Set 60: 138-143, Dec., 1919.

The Coroner's Inquest. Smart Set 59: 138-144, July, 1919.

Hark, Hark, the Lark! Smart Set 55: 138-144, June, 1918.

The Harp, the Sackbut and the Psaltry. Smart Set 43: 153-160, May, 1914.

In Praise of a Poet. Smart Set 31: 153-156, May, 1910.

More Poetry. [Baltimore] Evening Sun p. 6, March 23, 1911.

Notes of a Poetry-Hater. Smart Set 58: 138-144, April, 1921.

Notes on Poetry. Smart Set 64: 138-144, April, 1921.

Poetry. American Mercury. 6:251-254, Oct., 1925.

The Poets (IV of Taking Stock) Smart Set 67: 138-144, March, 1922.

Reflections on Poetry. Smart Set 62: 138-144, June, 1920.

The Rough-House on Parnassus. Smart Set. 51: 394-400, Feb., 1917.

Tra-La! Tra-La-La! Tra-La-La-La! Smart Set 49: 304-311, May, 1916.

The Troubadours A-Twitter. Smart Set 46: 150-156, May, 1915.

The Vernal Bards. [Baltimore] Evening Sun April 14, 1911.

Whoopers and Twitterers. Smart Set 53: 138-144, Nov., 1917.

SPEECHES, TALKS AND
RADIO ADDRESSES

Here are listed public addresses for which the texts are available. No attempt has been made to present a calendar of HLM's speeches or radio interviews. For example, we have omitted listing the Tenth Annual Radio Dinner of the New York Academy of Medicine, May 31, 1939, at which HLM was the principal speaker. The talk was not printed because of the Academy's policy of keeping the proceedings strictly off the record.

The only available recording of HLM's voice is a phonograph disc made at the Recording Laboratory of the Library of Congress on June 30, 1948, during an interview conducted by Donald Howe Kirkley, Sr. (*See* Books and Pamphlets by HLM, 1948)

1933

BEER, Radio Interview with William Lundell. NBC Oct. 18, 1933. mimeo. text.

Excerpts reprinted with comments in John Crosby's syndicated "Radio and Television" column, New York *Herald Tribune* and Baltmiore *Evening Sun,* Sept. 30, 1955.

1934

THIS YEAR OF PROMISE. NBC Jan. 14, 1934, 8-9 P.M. mimeo. text.

Three-minute speech by HLM ending with his introduction of Frank R. Kent. In this national hook-up, HLM spoke from Baltimore.

WHAT IS AHEAD, a Bed Time Story. [Baltimore] Sun, April 28, 1934.

Text of broadcast over NBC (WBAL, Baltimore) on April 27, 1934, 7:15-7:30 P.M. Fable of an ill friend made sicker by bad advice of doctors, likened to Uncle Sam ruined by specialists of the New Deal Brain Trust.

1935

TWO YEARS OF THE BRAIN TRUST. NBC Feb. 26, 1935, 6:30-6:45 P.M. mimeo. text.

1936

PRESS ONLY VITAL CRITIC REMAINING. Editor & Publisher 69: 10, 126, April 25, 1936.

Text of speech at Associated Press luncheon, broadcast over NBC and CBS chains. Brief interview following address is blast "against gangster atmosphere of comic strips," p. 8.

1937

AMERICAN SCHOOL OF THE AIR. Interview with H. L. Mencken. CBS Nov. 16, 1937, 2-3 P.M.

Third of series. HLM interviewed on the American language by Prof. William Cabell Greet. Excerpt titled "Our Literary Independence" reprinted in *Literary Digest* 125: 15, Jan. 15, 1938.

ARE EDITORIALS EFFECTIVE? [Speech made at] American Society of Newspaper Editors. 15th Annual Convention, April 15–17, 1937, National Press Club, Washington, D. C. Proceedings. p. 45–54.

HLM spoke at the Friday morning session, April 16. Text of speech was reprinted in *Editor & Publisher*, "Mencken Dissects the Editorial Page," 70: 23, 34, April 24, 1937.

1938

THE FUTURE OF AMERICAN MEDICINE, *In* Duke University Centennial Addresses, Dec. 11, 1937—April 23, 1939. Durham, N. C., Duke University Library. Typescripts.

Speech delivered at Duke University Centennial Symposium on Medical Problems, Oct. 13, 1938. Other speakers were Dr. Morris Fishbein, editor of the *Journal of the American Medical Association,* and Dr. John P. Peters of the Yale Medical School.

MAX BRÖDEL AS A PIANIST. Some Comments At the Dinner in Honor of Max Brödel At Philadelphia, March 4. Journal of the American Medical Association 110: 52, 54, March 26, 1938. Tonics and Sedatives.

1940

INTERVIEW BY VESTA EALES, Director of the Roving Library. Washington Inquirer March 3, 1940.

Broadcast over station WJSV-CBS, in which HLM reminisced about his childhood, in conjunction with the publication of *Happy Days.*

1945

PROCEEDINGS AT TESTIMONIAL DINNER ON THE RETIREMENT OF HON. EUGENE O'DUNNE AS MEMBER OF THE SUPREME BENCH. Held at the

Emerson Hotel on June 25, 1945 . . . Baltimore, Daily Record 115: 2-3, Nov. 5, 1945.

Issued as pamphlet. HLM's speech p. 7-9, port. on cover.

1946

CAREY-THOMAS AWARD PRESENTED TO A. A. KNOPF. Publishers' Weekly 149: 859-861, Feb. 2, 1946. port.

HLM describes his relations with his publisher at presentation of award on Jan. 24. It was given for "handling and publishing *Supplement I*" of the *American Language*.

1947

NATIONAL CONFERENCE OF EDITORIAL WRITERS. First Annual Meeting. Washington, D.C., Statler Hotel, Oct. 16-18, 1947. Stenographic transcript.

HLM's remarks p. 51-60.

CORRESPONDENCE

There has only been one published volume of HLM's vast correspondence (*see* below). The bulk was bequeathed to the New York Public Library. His letters to and from Marylanders were left to the Enoch Pratt Free Library. Other collections are at Dartmouth College (extensive; over 150 to Herbert F. West); Goucher College (to and from Sara Haardt); Harvard University (among others, 43 to Gamaliel Bradford, 17 to Howard Mumford Jones, 23 to Oswald Garrison Villard); Princeton University (among others, 288 to Ernest A. Boyd, many to Carl Van Vechten and Theodore Dreiser); Yale University (550 letters, including those to James Weldon Johnson, Bradford F. Swan and Carl Van Vechten).

The Guide to Archives and Manuscripts in the United States, edited by Philip M. Hamer (New Haven, Yale University Press, 1961) lists the following collections: Henry E. Huntington Library (139 pieces); Smith College (67 letters in the Sophea Smith Collection); Brooklyn Public Library (138 to Benjamin DeCasseres, 1933-1942); Yivo Institute for Jewish Research; University to North Carolina, Chapel Hill (restricted until 1978); Penn State University (59 in Fred Lewis Pattee Collection); University of Virginia (73 letters, 1935-1951, mainly to James Branch Cabell).

This listing is by no means inclusive, as many libraries possess small collections; and a great many letters are still in the possession of the recipients or other individual owners.

The listing below of printed letters does not include letters specifically written for printing in magazines (for those *see* Magazine Articles by HLM section), nor does it include letters intended to form an integral part of a book, e.g. Will Durant *On the Meaning of Life* or Jacob Helder *Greatest Thoughts on Immortality.* Some letters were used by the recipients as integral parts of the text, e.g. Emily Clark *Innocence Abroad,* and have therefor not been noted in this section.

CORRESPONDENCE

CASE, FRANK. Tales of a Wayward Inn. New York, Stokes, 1938. p. 348-351.

HLM letter reminisces about the Algonquin Hotel, Oct. 24 [1933?].

DREISER, THEODORE. Letters of Theodore Dreiser; a Selection. Edited with a preface and notes by Robert H. Elias. Philadelphia, University of Pennsylvania, 1959. 3v.

Numerous letters from 1911 to 1945 given either full, in part, or summarized to elucidate Dreiser's answers.

DURHAM, FRANK. Mencken as Missionary. American Literature 29: 478-483, Jan., 1958.

Two letters to Henry Sydnor Harrison in 1916, attempting to obtain his signature on a petition protesting the suppression of Dreiser's The "Genius."

GRENANDER, M. E., Comp. H. L. Mencken to Ambrose Bierce. Quarterly Newsletter of the Book Club of California. 22: 5-10, Winter, 1956.

Four letters to "My dear Major Bierce," April 22—May 18, 1913. Bierce's answers, compiled by Joseph Vincent Ridgely, 26: 27-33, Fall, 1961.

MENCKEN, HENRY LOUIS. Letters of H. L. Mencken, selected and annotated by Guy J. Forgue with a personal note by Hamilton Owens. New York, Knopf, 1961. xxxix, 506 xxiii p. front.

A selection from HLM's prodigious correspondence, dating from 1900 to 1956.

NEWMAN, FRANCES. Frances Newman's Letters, edited by Hansell Baugh, with a prefatory note by James Branch Cabell. New York, Liverwright, 1929. p. 64, 65, 82, 84.

Four brief notes from Sept. 12, 1921—Dec. 7, 1922.

SINCLAIR, UPTON. My Lifetime in Letters. Columbia, University of Missouri Press, 1960. p. 228-241, 249-253, 314-328.

Twenty-seven of 186 letters written to Sinclair, Feb. 26, 1918—Oct. 27, 1939. Continuation of their discussion of Sinclair's campaign to "End Poverty in California" in letters in the "Open Forum" of the American Mercury 38: iv-vii, June, 1936.

UNIVERSITY OF TEXAS. HUMANITIES RESEARCH CENTER. Joseph Hergesheimer, American Man of Letters, 1880-1954. [Catalog of] an Exhibition at the Humanities Research Center. Jan. 1961. p. 27-30. ports., facsim.

Annotated listing of sixteen exhibited letters, 1917-1948, from the vast correspondence between HLM and Hergesheimer. Also inscriptions from books HLM gave J.H.; facsimile of p. 27 from Ventures into Verse with HLM's marginal comment, p. 31.

WORKS ABOUT
H. L. MENCKEN

BOOKS AND PAMPHLETS

1920

H. L. MENCKEN: Fanfare, by Burton Rascoe; The American Critic, by Vincent O'Sullivan; Bibliography, by F. C. Henderson [pseud.]. New York, Knopf, 1920. 32 p. front., ports., facsims.

> Rascoe's article, a review of *A Book of Prefaces* in answer to the "critic's battle," was first published in his column in the *Chicago Sunday Tribune*, Nov. 11, 1917. O'Sullivan's article first appeared in the *New Witness* [London] Nov. 28, 1919. *See also* sections "Bibliographies" and "Portraits and Caricatures." This pamphlet was issued by Knopf as publicity, and is frequently referred to as *Fanfare*.

1924

GOLDBERG, ISAAC. H. L. Mencken. Girard, Kan., Haldeman-Julius, 1920. 64 p. ports. (Little Blue Books, no. 611)

1925

BOYD, ERNEST AUGUSTUS. H. L. Mencken. New York, McBride, 1925. 89 p. (Modern American Writers Ser., no. 4)

GOLDBERG, ISAAC. The Man Mencken, a Biographical and Critical Survey, illustrated and documented. New York, Simon, 1925. xiv, 388 p. front., ports, illus., facsims. (incl. music)

VAN ROOSBROECK, GUSTAVE LEOPOLD. The Reincarnation of H. L.

Mencken. New York, The Institute of French Studies, 1925. 22 p.

HLM described as the reincarnation of his ancestor Johann Burkhard Mencke.

1926

LOGAN, JOHN DANIEL. A Literary Chameleon, a New Estimate of Mr. Mencken, with a foreword by J. L. O'Sullivan. Milwaukee, Priv. print., 1926. 22 p. front. (port.)

1927

HARRISON, JOSEPH E. A Short View of Menckenism in Menckenese. Seattle, University of Washington Book Store, 1927. 26 p. (University of Washington Chapbooks, no. 1)

1929

BARNETT, ESTHER FRANCES. The Creative Destructiveness of Pío Baroja and H. L. Mencken. Urbana, University of Illinois, 1929. 70 *l.* Master's thesis; unpublished.

SCHMIDT, W. E. F. Mencken, Monkeys and Men. Des Moines, Pearl Pub. Co., 1929. 32 p.

1930

DECASSERES, BENJAMIN. Mencken and Shaw, the Anatomy of America's Voltaire and England's Other John Bull. New York, Silas Newton [1930]. x, 146 p.

MENCKEN AT FIFTY. New York, The American Mercury [1930]. [4 p.]

A birthday tribute of friendly quotations; issued also as advertisement for *Treatise on the Gods.*

1931

DALY, J. A. Mencken and Einstein Look At Religion. New York, Paulist Press [1931]. 24 p.

1935

ORSZÁGH, LÁSZLÓ. Az Amerikai Irodalömtorténtírás Fejlödése. Budapest [G. Buzárovits] 1935. 60 p. Doctoral dissertation; English summary p. 58–60.

1937

STONE, EDWARD. Henry Louis Mencken's Debt to Friedrich Wilhelm Nietzsche. Austin, University of Texas, 1937. 123 *l.* Master's thesis; unpublished.

1938

KRAMORIS, IVAN J. The Principles of Literary Criticism of H. L. Mencken. Milwaukee, Marquette University, 1938. 215 *l*. Master's thesis; unpublished.

1947

MANCHESTER, WILLIAM RAYMOND. A Critical Study of the Work of H. L. Mencken as Literary Critic for the Smart Set Magazine, 1908-1914. Columbia, University of Missouri, 1947. 225 *l*. Master's thesis; unpublished.

1950

KEMLER, EDGAR. The Irreverent Mr. Mencken. Boston, Little, 1950. 317 p. front., illus., ports.

MANCHESTER, WILLIAM RAYMOND. Disturber of the Peace. The Life of H. L. Mencken, with an introduction by Gerald W. Johnson. New York, Harper [1950]. xiv, 336 p.

> In 1952, with the title changed to *The Sage of Baltimore, the Life and Riotous Times of H. L. Mencken*, it was issued in London by Melrose (272 p.).

SWAN, BRADFORD F. Making a Mencken Collection. *See* Bibliographies, 1950.

1956

ANGOFF, CHARLES. H. L. Mencken, a Portrait from Memory. New York, Yoseloff [1956]. 240 p.

BIOGRAPHIES IN SOUND. H. L. Mencken, the Bitter By-Line. New York, National Broadcasting Company, July 10, 1956. 1 reel (7 in.), 3¾ in. per second.

> Narrator Chet Huntley, written and edited by William Hill and Jerome Jacobs of NBC News. The tape consists of interviews.

MARYLAND. GENERAL ASSEMBLY. SENATE RESOLUTION 9. SENATE JOINT RESOLUTION 22. Senate Joint Resolution Expressing the Sorrow of the General Assembly of Maryland over the Passing of Henry Louis Mencken. [Annapolis] By the Senate, Feb. 20, 1956. 8 p.

OPEN[ING] OF THE H. L. MENCKEN ROOM. Baltimore, Monumental Recording, April 17, 1956. 6 sides, 12 in. 33⅓ rpm.

> Ceremonies at the Enoch Pratt Free Library; includes Alistair Cooke's "Funeral Oration for H. L. Mencken." In connection with this event the

BOOKS AND PAMPHLETS

Enoch Pratt Free Library issued a biographical pamphlet of *H. L. Mencken,* compiled by Jane Wilhelm (4 p. port. by Nikol Schattenstein tipped in).

1957

DOLMETSCH, CARL RICHARD. A History of the Smart Set Magazine, 1914-1923. Chicago, University of Chicago, 1957. 157 *l.* Doctoral dissertation; microfilm and Xerox.

A supplement "An Index to the Smart Set Magazine, 1914-1923" is also available on microfilm. This author index is the only extant key, as the magazine was not indexed in the standard tools.

1958

PETERS, OTTO. Henry Louis Mencken's Attitude towards Germany. Berlin-Steglich, Freie Universität, 1958? 92 p. Doctoral dissertation; unpublished.

THOMA, GEORGE NICHOLAS. A Study of the Rhetoric of H. L. Mencken's Essays, 1917-1927. Chicago, University of Chicago, 1958. Doctoral dissertation; Photoduplication Dept. of the University.

1959

BELL, DAVID L. Mencken At Large, a Television Program. Baltimore, John Hopkins University, 1959. 23 p.

Script of program no. 467 of "Johns Hopkins File 7" for ABC-TV network, first given over station WJZ-TV Dec. 15, 1959. Dr. Carl Bode gave a biographical sketch, Dr. Kemp Malone commented on *The American Language.*

KLOEFKORN, JOHNNY L. A Critical Study of the Work of H. L. Menchen [sic.] as Literary Editor and Critic of the American Mercury. Emporia, Graduate Division of the Kansas State Teachers College, 1959. 48 p. (The Emporia State Research Studies, v. 7, no. 4)

1960

PICKETT, ROY GLENWOOD. H. L. Mencken's Rhetorical Battle. Iowa City, State University of Iowa, 1960. 180 p. Doctoral dissertation; microfilm and Xerox.

1961

STENERSON, DOUGLAS C. A. Genetic History of the Prejudices of H. L. Mencken, 1880-1926. Minneapolis, University of Minnesota [in preparation June 1961] 520, 55 *l.?* Doctoral dissertation; microfilm.

"The Literary Apprenticeship of H. L. Mencken," chapter 4 in slightly revised form, received the 1960 Humanities Award given by the McKnight Foundation of St. Paul, Minn.

SECTIONS OF BOOKS
DEVOTED TO H. L. MENCKEN

Length of treatment as well as significance of the material and the author's personal knowledge of HLM, were taken into consideration in compiling this selective list of books devoting part of their text to HLM. A complete, inclusive listing is beyond the scope of this work, for most books dealing with the literary, social or political history of the U.S.A. for the first half of the twentieth century mention HLM. In fiction his name is used in such diverse items as Anita Loos's *Gentlemen Prefer Blondes* to Ernest Hemingway's *The Sun Also Rises*.

Chapters that first appeared as magazine articles are so indicated, but only annotated in the section "Magazine and Newspaper Articles About HLM." Annotations have been supplied as a help for the student who wishes to investigate a specific phase of HLM's work or to gain a better understanding of his many-sided personality.

1905

WINCHESTER, PAUL and FRANK D. WEBB, *eds.* Newspapers and Newspaper Men of Maryland Past and Present. Published for the benefit of the Journalists' Club of Baltimore. Baltimore, Frank L. Sibley & Co., 1905. p. 73.

Biographical sketch as assistant manager of the *Herald*. Poem from *Ventures into Verse* quoted on p. 46.

1909

COURTNEY, WILLIAM LEONARD. Rosemary's Letter Book; the Record of a Year. London, Melrose, 1909. p. 159.

"This is the first book of criticism, so far as I know, in which my name appeared." HLM, written on flyleaf (EPFL—G379).

SECTIONS OF BOOKS

1917

PISTOLS FOR TWO. *See* "Contributions to Books and Pamphlets," 1917.

1918

VAN VECHTEN, CARL. The Merry-Go-Round. New York, Knopf, 1918.

HLM on Puritanism, Huneker and American composers. *See* index for various references.

1920

NATHAN, GEORGE JEAN. On H. L. Mencken. *In* The Borzoi, 1920. New York, Knopf, 1920. p. 34-36.

A "snapshot" of HLM by his partner.

1921

STEWART, DONALD OGDEN. A Parody Outline of History, Wherein May Be Found a Curiously Irreverent Treatment of American Historical Events. New York, Doran, 1921. p. 66-67, 75, 76-77.

"Smart Set Medicine Show," "Priscilla, Drank Mencken Medicine . . . ," and "H. L. Mencken Causes Rumpus Among Puritans."

1922

BLEI, FRANZ. Das Grosse Bestiarium der Modernen Literatur. Berlin, Rowohlt, 1922. p. 49-50.

In the bestiary of current literature, HLM ranks as foremost American zoologist.

PATTEE, FRED LEWIS. Side-Lights on American Literature. New York, Century, 1922. p. 57-97.

"A Critic in C Major" can be understood as poet and journalist, but the "bloody angles" of his literary criticisms are puzzling.

SHERMAN, STUART PRATT. Americans. New York, Scribner, 1922. p. 1-12.

This literary critic, who bitterly fought HLM, expresses his dislikes in "Mr. Mencken, the Jeune Fille, and the New Spirit in Letters," a review of *Prejudices: First Series,* reprinted from the New York *Times Book Review,* Dec. 7, 1919, p. 718. Reprinted in *Men and Books,* edited by Malcolm S. MacLean (New York, Smith, 1930. p. 272-280).

UNTERMEYER, LOUIS. Heavens. New York, Harcourt, 1922. p. 75-80, 85-86.

Parody of how "the wild Webster of the American Language" might report the heavenly scene; and how he reviews the best unwritten books. Reprinted in his *Collected Parodies* (New York, Harcourt, 1926. p. 270-274, 291).

1923

HARRIS, FRANK. Contemporary Portraits, Fourth Series. New York, Brentano [1923]. p. 143-154.

"H. L. Mencken, Critic" discusses his work in this art form, which has become one of the most creative in our literature.

ROBERTS, CARL ERIC BECHHOFER. The Literary Renaissance in America, by C. E. Bechhofer [pseud.] London, Heinemann [1923]. *See* index for various paging.

First published in the *Times* [London] *Literary Supplement* May 26-June 30, 1921.

SCHEFFAUER, HERMAN GEORGE. Das Land Gottes, das Gesicht des Neuen Amerika. Hannover, Steegemann [1923]. p. 119-125.

HLM discussed as the fearless exponent of American political life.

SINCLAIR, UPTON. The Goose-Step, a Study of American Education. Pasadena, Cal., By the Author [1923]. p. 303-305.

HLM expounds the process of "Fordization," assembly line education now prevalent at the Johns Hopkins University.

1924

BOYD, ERNEST AUGUSTUS. Portraits: Real and Imaginary, Being Memories and Impressions of Friends and Contemporaries. New York, Doran [1924]. p. 165-167.

Impressions of HLM, the "transatlantic exotic."

BOYNTON, PERCY HOLMES. Some Contemporary Americans; a Personal Equation in Literature. Chicago, University of Chicago Press, 1924. p. 231-241.

"The Younger Set and the Puritan Bogey" features HLM as leader of this discredited set.

FARRAR, JOHN, ed. The Literary Spotlight. With Portrait Caricatures by William Gropper. New York, Doran [1924]. p. 108-115. port.

"H. L. Mencken" reprinted from the series of profiles in the *Bookman*.

STARK, HAROLD. People You Know, by Young Boswell [pseud.] New York, Boni, 1924. p. 101-103.

"The Ignorant Man" is an imaginary interview based on quotations from HLM's writings.

VAN DOREN, CARL CLINTON. Many Minds. New York, Knopf, 1924. p. 120-135; bibliog. p. 226-228.

"Smartness and Light" treats HLM as critic of the democratic dogma, reprinted from *Century*.

1925

CALVERTON, VICTOR FRANCIS. The Newer Spirit, a Sociological Criticism of Literature. Introduction by Ernest Boyd. New York, Boni, 1925. p. 165-179.

"The Vaudeville Critic, H. L. Mencken" is only the "prophet of the tawdry run of anti-bourgeois liberals."

HERGESHEIMER, JOSEPH. Mr. Henry L. Mencken. *In* The Borzoi, 1925. New York, Knopf, 1925, p. 102-106. port. facing p. 143.

Intimate portrait by a close friend.

SPIES, HEINRICH. Kultur und Sprache im Neuen England. Leipzig, Teubner, 1925; 2. Aufl. 1928.

Much of the material is taken from *The American Language*, which Prof. Spies had translated into German.

UNIVERSITY DEBATERS' ANNUAL, 1924/25. Edited by Edith M. Phelps. New York, Wilson, 1925. p. 277-319.

Stenographic report of debate held April 7, 1925, in which it was "Resolved: That the school of thought typified by Mencken is a harmful element in American life."

VAN DOREN, CARL CLINTON and MARK VAN DOREN. American and British Literature Since 1890. New York & London, Century [1925]. p. 124-128.

HLM is essentially a satirist and journalist; admire his impudence and vitality.

1926

BEACH, JOSEPH WARREN. The Outlook for American Prose. Chicago, University of Chicago Press, 1926.

HLM as author, stylist and critic. *See* index for various references.

CROTHERS, SAMUEL McCHORD. The Modern Essay. Chicago, American Library Association, 1926. (Reading with a Purpose. 24) p. 17-18.

"H. L. Mencken; Stuart Sherman" presented as the two outstanding critics.

GOLDBERG, ISAAC. The Theatre of George Jean Nathan. New York, Simon, 1926.

HLM's relation to Nathan, especially during their magazine partnership. Outline of three scenarios they considered writing after *Heliogabalus*, p. 211-219.

MICHAUD, RÉGIS. Panorama de la Littérature Américaine Contemporaine. Paris, Kra, 1926. p. 232-234, and others.

HLM is the inspirer and leader of the new intellectual revolt.

NICHOLS, BEVERLY. 25, Being a Young Man's Candid Recollections of His Elders and Betters. New York, Doran [1926]. p. 174-177.

Interview with "a most amusing man" who describes how he would rebuild London.

SHERMAN, STUART PRATT. Critical Woodcuts. New York, London, Scribner, 1926. p. 235-243.

"My animadversions against Mr. Mencken as critic and historian of American letters."

STRACHEY, JOHN ST. LOE. American Soundings. London, Hodder: New York, Appleton [1926]. p. 209-219.

HLM as satirist, based mainly on "Americana" department in the *American Mercury*.

1927

ELGSTRÖM, ANNA LENAH and GUSTAF COLLIJN. U.S.A. Liv och Teater. Stockholm, Bonniers [1927]. p. 114-126. port. p. 95

HLM's personality and his interests in politics and Baltimore.

SERGEANT, ELIZABETH SHEPLEY. Fire Under the Andes. New York, Knopf, 1927. p. 239-257. port. (by E. O. Hoppé)

The chapter on HLM entitled "He Must and Will Be Titan," reprinted from the *Nation*.

SINCLAIR, UPTON. Money Writes! New York, Boni, 1927. p. 34-38, 129-135, 162-165.

"Artificial Selection" and "Boobus Americanus" deal with HLM's editorial policies at the *American Mercury*; "Adonais" with his attitude towards George Sterling's drinking.

TAKAGAKI, MATSUO. Amerika Bungaku. Tokyo, Kenkyu-sha, 1927.

Chapter in Japanese on HLM's place in American literature. Index, p. 21-22, and bibliography, p. 31-32, in English.

1928

BENCHLEY, ROBERT. 20,000 Leagues under the Sea, or David Copperfield. New York, Holt [1928] p. 95-100.

Parody of HLM reviewing Nathan and vice versa.

FINDAHL, THEODOR. Manhattan Babylon, en Bok om New York Idag. Oslo, Gyldendahl Norsk, 1928. p. 72-79. port. p. 66.

Personal impression of the most famous American literary critic.

HAYS, ARTHUR GARFIELD. Let Freedom Ring. New York, Boni, 1928. p. 157-192.

The "American Mercury" Case retold by the lawyer who fought for freedom of the press.

MORE, PAUL ELMER. The Demon of the Absolute. *In* New Shelburne Essays. v.1. Princeton, Princeton University Press, 1928. p. 2-11.

Champion of the New Humanism attacks HLM as "leader of malignity" of the new field of criticism. Partially reprinted from his "The Modern Currents in American Literature" *Forum* 79: 127-136, Jan., 1928.

OPPENHEIM, JAMES. Behind Your Front. New York and London, Harper, 1928. p. 49-53.

HLM and Woodrow Wilson contrasted as typical extroverted thinkers, one guided by sensation, the other by intuition.

SHAW, CHARLES GREEN. The Low-Down. New York, Holt [1928]. p. 51-61, and others.

"Three Literary Radicals" reprinted from *Vanity Fair*.

WILLIAMS, MICHAEL. Catholics and the Modern Mind. New York, Dial; Toronto, Longmans, 1928. p. 223-238.

"A Prayer for Mr. Mencken" reprinted from *Commonweal* with slight variation of title.

1929

DeCASSERES, BENJAMIN. The Superman in America. Seattle, University of Washington, 1929. p. 15, 17-18.

HLM's influence "has the furious onesidedness of Nietzsche."

LEVINSON, ANDRÉ. Figures Américaines. Paris, Attinger, 1929. (Occident 9) p. 95-109.

"L'Ironie de H. L. Mencken," also his humor shines forth from his burlesques and "Americana" department in the *American Mercury*.

NICOLIS DI ROBILANT, IRENE. Vita Americana (Stati Uniti del Nord-America). Torino, Bocca [1929]. p. 222-225, 399.

Literary influence exerted by the *American Mercury*.

RASCOE, BURTON. A Bookman's Daybook, edited with an introduction by C. Hartley Grattan. New York, Liverwright, 1929. *See* note for pagination.

Reprints from Rascoe's literary column in the New York *Herald Tribune*: p. 25-26 "A Psychograph of Mencken," July 15, 1922; p. 81-84, 119 "How

Mencken and Nathan Play" Jan. 16 and July 5, 1923; p. 161-162 "Pulling Mencken's Leg" Nov. 18, 1923; p. 195-196 "Mencken: Shirtsleeve Autocrat" Jan. 25, 1924; p. 240-241 "Mencken on Eating and Yodelers" May 21, 1924.

SCHMALHAUSEN, SAMUEL D. Our Changing Human Nature. New York, Macauley, 1929. p. 214-230.

"H. L. Mencken: Idol of the Booboisie" attempts to be Nietzsche Junior, and "suffers from intellectual enuresis."

WICKHAM, HARVEY. The Impuritans. New York, MacVeigh; Toronto, Longmans, 1929. p. 229-234; front. (caricature by Scheel.)

"The Meaning of Mencken" describes his burning passion for personal liberty, for HLM "is really a super-Puritan rather than an Impuritan."

1930

CABELL, JAMES BRANCH. Some of Us, an Essay in Epitaphs. New York, McBride, 1930. p. 105-118.

"Dreams of Cosmogony. A Note as to Henry L. Mencken." HLM is less a human being than a "force which has reshaped all the present world of American letters."

CHESTERTON, GILBERT KEITH. The Thing; Why I Am a Catholic. New York, Dodd, 1930. p. 1-11.

"The Sceptic as Critic," discusses effects of HLM's weakening influence on America, for his scepticism invariably leads to loss of faith.

PATTEE, FRED LEWIS. The New American Literature 1890-1930. New York, London, Century, 1930. p. 415-432.

"Mencken" as author and critic; Pattee's estimate has not changed basically since 1922.

SCHMIDT, W. E. F. "In the Name of God." 2nd edition. Des Moines, Pearl Pub. Co., 1930. p. 20-23.

HLM as foremost wrecker of frauds.

1931

ALLEN, FREDERICK LEWIS. Only Yesterday, an Informal History of the Nineteen-Twenties. New York and London, Harper, 1931. p. 230-244.

Discusses the "highbrow credo" influenced by HLM through the *American Mercury*.

BLANKENSHIP, RUSSELL. American Literature as an Expression of the National Mind. New York, Holt, 1931.

HLM as critic and champion of writers. *See* index for various references.

BOYNTON, PERCY HOLMES. The Challenge of Modern Criticism. Chicago, Rockwell, 1931. p. 29-46, 52-69.

HLM compared to Edgar Allan Poe, Beelzebub and Shaw, one of a series of lectures on "Tradition, Criticism and Humanism."

CLARK, EMILY. Innocence Abroad. New York and London, Knopf, 1931. p. 109-126.

HLM's influence and personality by the editor of the *Reviewer*, Richmond, Va. Long quotations from his letters are used as part of the text.

SMITH, SAMUEL STEPHENSON. The Craft of the Critic. New York, Crowell [1931].

HLM as critic and catalytic agent; p. 33-37 "His own Chief Jester" consists of conversations in Berlin "with the greatest reviewer of his time." *See* index for other references.

STRUNSKY, SIMEON. The Rediscovery of Jones, Studies in the Obvious. Boston, Little, 1931. p. 60-66.

HLM's "school of anti-democratic thought" interprets man either as the wolf or puppet.

TOBIN, A. I. and ELMER GERTZ. Frank Harris, a Study in Black and White. [Chicago] Madelaine Mendelsohn, 1931.

HLM's expressed opinions about Frank Harris. *See* index for various references.

WOOLF, LEONARD. After the Deluge, a Study of Communal Psychology. v. 1. London, By the Author, 1931. p. 258-268.

Discussion of HLM's intellectual aristocrat, based on *Notes on Democracy*.

1932

BABBITT, IRVING. On Being Creative and Other Essays. Boston, Houghton, 1932. p. 203-212, and others. *See* index.

Reprint of "The Critic and American Life" first published in the *Forum*.

BROOKS, VAN WYCK. Sketches in Criticism. New York, Dutton, [1932]. p. 26-33.

"H. L. Mencken and the Prophets" of the spiritual awakening of America.

CHESTERTON, GILBERT KEITH. All Is Grist, a Book of Essays. New York, Dodd, 1932. p. 58-64.

Discussion of HLM and Fundamentalism.

DUDLEY, DOROTHY. Forgotten Frontiers; Dreiser and the Land of the Free. New York, H. Smith, 1932; London, Wishart, 1933. p. 233, 258, 327-371, 395-404.

HLM's relations to Dreiser. Portrait of HLM, p. 259-266; letters p. 309-311.

KNOX, RONALD. Broadcast Minds. London, Sheed & Ward, 1932. p. 121-153.

An English clergyman attacks *Treatise on the Gods.*

LEWISOHN, LUDWIG. Expression in America. New York and London, Harper, 1932. p. 415-461.

HLM's part in the "Great Critical Debate."

NATHAN, GEORGE JEAN. The Intimate Notebooks of George Jean Nathan. New York, Knopf, 1932. p. 94-121.

Impressions and reminiscences of a long association; several undated letters. Reprinted in *The World of George Jean Nathan,* edited by Charles Angoff (New York, Knopf, 1952. p. 43-66).

ROGERS, CAMERON. Oh Splendid Appetite! New York, Day [1932]. p. 85-97.

"H. L. Mencken: The Maverick Turned Bell Mare" reprinted from *Outlook.* Book chapter reprinted in *Essay Annual* 1933, p. 182-191.

SEMPER, ISIDORE J. The Return of the Prodigal and Other Essays. New York, Edward O'Toole, 1932. p. 63-85, 86-111.

Both articles reprinted from the *Catholic World*: "H. L. Mencken and Catholicism" and "H. L. Mencken: Doctor Rhetoricus."

1933

COMBS, GEORGE HAMILTON. Three American Moderns. St. Louis, Bethany Press [1933] p. 31-52.

"H. L. Mencken, the Celebrant of Cynicism" evinces bludgeoning prejudices and narrowness.

HAZLITT, HENRY. Anatomy of Criticism, a Trialogue. New York, Simon, 1933, p. 45-49, 151-152.

HLM's place as critic, and the creative function critics exert.

HICKS, GRANVILLE. The Great Tradition, an Interpretation of American Literature Since the Civil War. New York, Macmillan, 1933. p. 210-215, and others. *See* index.

HLM's place in the literary picture of 1912-1925, when the impressionists were battling the conservatives.

PARTRIDGE, ERIC. Slang Today and Yesterday. London, Routledge, 1933.

In this and subsequent editions, the *American Language* is used as base for Part IV "American Slang" and is quoted throughout the work.

VAN DOREN, CARL CLINTON. American Literature, an Introduction. Los Angeles, U. S. Library Association [1933]. p. 76-78.

Capsule appraisal of HLM's influence; he "educated a generation to be alert against flat truisms and swollen postures." The chapter is contained in his *What is American Literature?* (London, Routledge, 1935. p. 102-104.)

VAN DOREN, CARL CLINTON. Sinclair Lewis, a Biographical Sketch. Garden City, N.Y., Doubleday, 1933.

HLM's influence on Lewis. "*Elmer Gantry* is Mr. Mencken's criticism rendered flesh and blood." *See* index for various references.

1934

CRANDALL, ALLEN. ISAAC GOLDBERG, an Appreciation. Sterling Col., By the Author, 1934. p. 53-58.

Background material for the writing of his first biography, *The Man Mencken.*

RASCOE, BURTON, and GROFF CONKLIN, *eds.* The Smart Set Anthology. New York, Reynal [1934]. p. xxxi-xliv.

The history of HLM's connection with the *Smart Set* and his attitude toward the publication of this anthology. This introduction was published separately in advance of publication of the entire book (p. 11-34).

SCHWARTZ, HARRY W. This Book-Collecting Racket. Part 2. Milwaukee, Casanova Press, 1934. p. 16-17, 25, 27, 33.

HLM's books that have become collector's items, also many quotations from his book reviews as evidence of other modern books.

1935

FORSYTHE, ROBERT. Redder Than the Rose. New York, Covici Friede, 1935. p. 1-12.

"In Defense of Mencken" is a sarcastic defense by accusation, pointing out the weaknesses of his literary attitudes.

SHAFER, ROBERT. Paul Elmer More and American Criticism. New Haven, Yale University Press; London, Oxford University Press, 1935.

The controversy between these two critics, More claiming that HLM "vulgarized more than one good cause," and attacking HLM's ideas and vocabulary. *See* index for various references.

SPOTSWOOD, CLAIRE MYERS. The Unpredictable Adventure, a Comedy of Woman's Independence. Garden City, N.Y., Doubleday, 1935. p. 332-345.

"The Search for Mt. Certitude Continued; How Mencken Showed Tellectina his View of the Land of Err; And Rascoe Acted as Official Guide to the Great Mountain."

STEARNS, HAROLD EDMUND. The Street I Know. New York, Furman [1935]. p. 193-204.

Compiler of *Civilization in the United States* tells of HLM's role in securing writers for the various parts of this first symposium on national culture.

SULLIVAN, MARK. Our Times. The United States, 1900-1925. VI. The Twenties. New York and London, Scribner, 1935. p. 413-421.

"Mencken of Baltimore" was more than just a literary figure, "he was a national character . . . a national institution."

1936

GILLIS, ADOLPH and ROLAND KETCHUM. Our America. Boston, Little, 1936. p. 234-250. port.

"Henry Louis Mencken, Watchdog of Liberty," one of twenty-four inspirational biographies for high school study. Study questions, p. 404-405.

STEFANSSON, VILHJALMUR. Adventures in Error. New York, McBride [1936]. p. 280-286.

"A Neglected Anniversary" reprinted, accompanied by a history of the bathtub hoax's exposure by journalists, leaders of thought and government agencies.

TAYLOR, WALTER FULTON. A History of American Letters. Boston, American Book Co., 1936.

HLM's influence on an entire epoch. A partially revised edition *The Story of American Letters* (Chicago, Regnery, 1956) calls HLM's influence "Rebellion with Hilarity" p. 347-350, and deals specifically with his influence on Sinclair Lewis.

VAN DOREN, CARL CLINTON. Three Worlds. New York, Harper, 1936.

HLM as the idol of the young rebels. *See* index for various references.

1937

CLEATON, IRENE and ALLEN. Books & Battles: American Literature, 1920-1930. Boston, Houghton, 1937. p. 112-122, 128-132, 183-187. port.

"A Bad Writer Has No Rights"; "Declaration of Independence"; "A Professor Recants" Sherman on HLM; and "The Lively Mercury."

FRANK, WALDO. In the American Jungle (1925-1936). New York, Toronto, Farrar [1937]. p. 135-139.

"H. L. Mencken, King of the Philistines," first appeared as "Philosophy Hunting" in the New *Republic* 48: 300-301, Nov. 3, 1926.

LOGGINS, VERNON. I Hear America . . . New York, Crowell, 1937. p. 228-238.

> An essay entitled "Iconoclasm: H. L. Mencken." "He will go down in history as a reformer."

RASCOE, BURTON. Before I Forget. Garden City, N.Y., Doubleday, 1937. p. 438-442, and others.

> "Unconventional portrait" of HLM as he was at the beginning of the 1920s. Correspondence about *Fanfare*, p. 354; the critical battle with Sherman, p. 355-357.

1938

FORSYTHE, ROBERT. Reading from Left to Right. New York, Covici Friede [1938]. p. 74-80.

> "Winken, Blinken and Nod" reprinted from *New Masses*.

KAGAN, SOLOMON R. Life and Letters of Fielding H. Garrison. Boston, Medico–Historical Press, 1938.

> HLM's relations to and influence on Dr. Garrison. *See* index for various references.

PARTRIDGE, ERIC. The World of Words. [London] Routledge [1938].

> *The American Language* used as guide and extensively quoted. *See* index for various references.

PEGLER, WESTBROOK. The Dissenting Opinions of Mr. Westbrook Pegler. New York, Scribner, 1938. p. 312-315.

> "Farewell to Mencken (1936)" reprinted from his column in the New York *World Telegram*. Berates HLM for supporting Landon in presidential campaign.

WHITE, ELWYN BROOKS. The Fox of Peapack & Other Poems. New York, London, Harper, 1938. p. 39-44.

> "H. L. Mencken Meets a Poet in the West Side Y.M.C.A." reprinted from the *Saturday Review of Literature*.

1939

ANDERSON, GEORGE KUMLER and EDA LOU WALTON, *eds.* This Generation; a Selection of British and American Literature from 1914 to the Present, with Historical and Critical Essays. Chicago, Scott, Foresman [1939]. p. 36-40, 100-127.

> Influence of Puritanism and the frontier on American literature; biographical sketch of HLM preceding reprint of his "Puritanism as a Literary Force," from *A Book of Prefaces*.

SMITH, BERNARD. Forces in American Criticism, a Study in the History of American Literary Thought. New York, Harcourt [1939]. p. 303-313.

"The Urban Tory: Mencken," the foremost critic in the war of traditions.

UNTERMEYER, LOUIS. From Another World, the Autobiography of Louis Untermeyer. New York, Harcourt [1939]. p. 184-205.

"The Bad Boy of Baltimore" with whom the author established "a friendship that lasted the rest of my life." Many quotations from HLM's letters.

1940

MacDOUGALL, CURTIS DANIEL. Hoaxes. New York, Macmillan, 1940. p. 302-309.

History of the bathtub hoax, the "grand finale of all such deceptions."

1941

CARGILL, OSCAR. Intellectual America, Ideas on the March. New York, Macmillan, 1941. p. 481-495.

Critical and unsympathic appraisal.

GOLD, MICHAEL. The Hollow Men. New York, International Publishers, 1941. p. 11-25.

"At King Mencken's Court," one of a series in the *Daily Worker* called "The Great Tradition. Can the Literary Renegades Destroy It?"

1942

BIRD, GEORGE L. and FREDERIC E. MERWIN, *eds.* The Newspaper and Society. New York, Prentice-Hall,1942. p. 307, 334-340.

HLM as editorial writer and crusading journalist, including excerpt from his magazine article "Newspaper Morals."

FOOTNER, HULBERT. Maryland Main and the Eastern Shore. New York, London, Appleton-Century, 1942. p. 62-71.

"Leaving his philosophy to others, I would speak of him as a figure of Baltimore life."

KAZIN, ALFRED. On Native Ground, an Interpretation of Modern American Prose Literature. New York, Reynal [1942]. p. 198-204, and others.

HLM's influence on American letters; he was "civilization incarnate . . . gaiety the secret of his charm."

RALBAG, J. HOWARD. Hope for Humanity. [New York, Victory Publishing Co., 1942] p. 57-65.

A rabbi writes on faith and immortality as "An Answer to H. L. Mencken."

1943

SMITH, HARRY ALLEN. Life in a Putty Knife Factory. Garden City, N.Y., Doubleday, 1943. p. 170-177.

During an interview, HLM reveals his tastes and habits. Abridged in *Omnibook* 5: 179-180, May, 1943.

TULLY, JIM. A Dozen and One. Hollywood, Murray & Gee, 1943. p. 229-242.

Biographical portrait by a friend whom HLM encouraged and inspired to write.

WILSON, EDMUND, *ed.* The Shock of Recognition. Garden City, N.Y., Doubleday, 1943, p. 1115-1159.

Evaluation of HLM as literary critic and editor, used as introduction to the HLM section that reprints five of his pieces from *Prejudices* and the *Nation*, p. 1160-1245.

WOLGAMOT, JOHN BARTON. In Sara Haardt Were Men and Women. [New York] By the Author [1943]. 1 v. unpaged.

"Wolgamot began writing this balderdash before Sara's death in 1935 . . . He talked very plausibly by telephone. I said to him: "What is the matter with you, Wolgamot: Are you insane?" He replied unpreturbed: "Not at all. I am quite sane. I simply like to write that way." HLM on verso of front cover (EPFL—G1891). In 1944 he published *In Sara, Mencken, Christ and Beethoven There Were Men and Women.*

1945

WRIGHT, RICHARD. Black Boy, a Record of Childhood and Youth. New York and London, Harper [1945]. p. 214-222.

Vicious attacks of HLM in the Memphis *Commercial Appeal* aroused Wright's interest. HLM's works became a revelation. Abridged in *Omnibook* 7: 38-39, Aug., 1945.

1946

EVANS, BERGEN. The Natural History of Nonsense. New York, Knopf, 1946. p. 258-262.

The bathtub hoax as an example of the paleontology of delusion.

HOLBROOK, STEWART H. Lost Men of American History. New York, Macmillan, 1946. p. 340-344.

HLM's protests, mainly against Prohibition, during the Harding era.

VAN GELDER, ROBERT. Writers and Writing. New York, Scribner, 1946. p. 20-22.

Interview with HLM on politics and writing reprinted from the New York *Times*, Feb. 11, 1940.

WILSON, EARL. Pikes Peek or Bust. Garden City, Doubleday, 1946. p. 54-55.

"Mencken, Ickes, and God," envies HLM's "guts to blast people." Reprinted in *Omnibook*.

1947

GEISMAR, MAXWELL DAVID. The Last of the Provincials, the American Novel, 1915-1925. Boston, Houghton, 1947. p. 3-66, 355-377 bibliog. p. 391.

"H. L. Mencken: On the Dock" for his artistic withdrawal and negation. Attempt to explain the key American writer, a curious rebel "captive of his own aesthetics, and led to the void by his own antics."

GUNTHER, JOHN. Inside U.S.A. New York, Harper, 1947.

HLM's place in the American scene. *See* index for various references.

WITHAM, W. TASKER. Panorama of American Literature. New York, Stephen Day Press [1947]. p. 262-263, 275.

Superficial summary of HLM's role as critical force during decade after World War I.

1948

CUNZ, DIETER. The Maryland Germans: A History. Princeton, Princeton University Press, 1948. p. 410-414.

HLM's ancestry and pro-German bias.

GREENE, WARD. Star Reporters and 34 of Their Stories. New York, Random House [1948]. p. 226-228, 229-255.

"The Baltimore Nonpareil" as reporter, specifically of the Scopes trial; followed by excerpts of the trial from the Baltimore *Evening Sun*, July 9-27, 1925.

PATTERSON, GROVE. I Like People. New York, Random House, 1948. p. 276-278.

HLM as reporter, and quotations from his humorous correspondence with the editor-in-chief of the Toledo *Blade*.

1949

ELIAS, ROBERT HENRY. Theodore Dreiser, Apostle of Nature. New York, Knopf; Toronto, McClelland, 1949.

HLM's relations with Dreiser. *See* index for various references.

HOGUE, RICHARD WALLACE. Spindrift. Asheville, N.C., By the Author [1949]. p. 63-64.

"This Fellow Mencken," poem in a volume of original verse.

SECTIONS OF BOOKS

KNOPF, ALFRED A. Some Random Recollections. New York, The Typophiles, 1949. (Typophiles Chapbooks. XXII) p. 33-34.

Recollections about design and typeface of the *American Mercury,* made at "an informal talk . . . at the Grolier Club, New York, 21 October, 1948."

1951

DREISER, HELEN. My Life with Dreiser. Cleveland, World, 1951. p. 114-118.

Describes the Dreisers' visit to HLM at his Hollins Street home.

1952

BEWLEY, MARIUS. The Complex Fate. London, Chatto, 1952. p. 193-210.

HLM as critic, philosopher and philologist. (*The American Language*).

BROOKS, VAN WYCK. The Confident Years: 1885-1915. [New York] Dutton, 1952. p. 455-474.

"Mencken of Baltimore" analyses influence on HLM, and how he in turn, influenced his era. Slightly expanded from pre-publication chapter in the *American Scholar.*

GOLDMAN, ERIC F. Rendezvous with Destiny, a History of Modern American Reform. New York, Knopf, 1952. p. 315-317, 329, 343.

HLM's place among the "Liberals of the Twenties."

WILSON, EDMUND. The Shores of Light, a Literary Chronicle of the Twenties and Thirties. New York, Farrar [1952]. p. 229-247, 293-297, 367-372, 630-639.

Reprints from the *New Republic* of "The All Star Literary Vaudeville"; "Mencken's Democratic Man"; "The Critic Who Does Not Exist." And excerpts from "Talking United States," a review of *The American Language,* 4th edition, 87: 299, July 15, 1936.

1953

HOWE, QUINCY. The World between the Wars. New York, Simon, 1953. (A World History of Our Own Times, v. 2) p. 128-130, caricature p. 131.

HLM's influence during the Wilson-Bryan era.

1954

FARRELL, JAMES T. Reflections at Fifty, and Other Essays. New York, Vanguard, 1954. p. 42-57.

"H. L. Mencken: Criticus Americanus" reprinted from *New World Writing.*

HECHT, BEN. A Child of the Century. [New York] Simon, 1954. p. 175-180.

Personal reminiscences about "one of my two heroes."

1955

HOFFMAN, FREDERICK J. The Twenties, American Writing in the Postwar Decade. New York, Viking, 1955. p. 304-314, and others.

"Critiques of the Middle Class: I. The Booboisie" evaluates HLM's role and influence.

KRONENBERGER, LOUIS. The Republic of Letters. New York, Knopf, 1955. p. 236-243.

"H. L. Mencken" is reprint of "An Ill-Will Tour of the American Mind" from the *Saturday Review of Literature.*

1956

WILSON, EDMUND. A Literary Chronicle: 1920-1950. Garden City, N.Y., Doubleday Anchor Books, 1956. p. 76-92.

"The All Star Literary Vaudeville" reprinted from the *Saturday Review of Literature.*

1957

MARYLAND HISTORICAL Society. Baltimore;a Pictorial History 1858-1958 . . . Commentary by Francis F. Beirne. New York, Random House, 1957. p. 128-129. ports.

Sketch of the State's most prominent citizen.

SCHLESINGER, ARTHUR MEIER. The Age of Roosevelt: v.1 The Crisis of the Old Order; v.2 The Coming of the New Deal: v.3 The Politics of Upheaval. Boston, Houghton, 1957-1960.

HLM's political orientation and opinions. *See* indexes for various references.

1959

LEARY, LEWIS. H. L. Mencken: Changeless Critic in Changing Times. *In* The Young Rebel in American Literature, edited by Carl Bode. London, Heineman, 1959; New York, Praeger, 1960. p. 97-117.

Admires "the spark which Mencken gave off," but maintains that HLM was "destroyed by his pretensions." One of a series of seven lectures sponsored by the U.S. Information Service, delivered at the American Embassy in London, 1957.

MAY, HENRY FARNHAM. The End of Innocence, a Study of the First

SECTIONS OF BOOKS

Years of Our Own Time 1912-1917. New York, Knopf, 1959. p. 205-216, 389-391.

Committed to uncompromising naturalism, HLM "raised the standard of battle against all three of the main elements of the dominant American culture."

THURBER, JAMES. The Years with Ross. Boston, Little [1959]. p. 70-85, and others.

"Mencken, Nathan and Ross" describes an evening spent at the apartment of the editor of the *New Yorker*; mentions of HLM's contributions to the magazine.

1960

BOORSTIN, DANIEL JOSEPH. America and the Image of Europe. New York, Meridian Books [1960]. p. 27-28, 30-31.

HLM believed that America could profit by a stronger infusion of European culture.

1961

JOHNSON, GERALD WHITE. The Man Who Feels Left Behind. New York, Morrow, 1961. p. 118-120.

Laments the absence of the most accurate bowman of the twentieth century who substantially reduced the sum total of imbecility in American life and letters.

MAGAZINES AND
NEWSPAPER ARTICLES

This is a selective list of articles about HLM's work and personality. A complete file of both magazine and newspaper articles, started by HLM in 1903 and kept up to date, is available in his Clipping Books (108 v.) in the Mencken Room of the Enoch Pratt Free Library. The extent of this material has precluded the inclusion of brief mentions, thumb-nail biographies and reviews of his books. However, when a book review is used as a springboard for a critical appraisal of the range and extent of HLM's work, it has been included, with the title of the book or name of biographer given in parenthesis. To assist the student, entries have been annotated to indicate the content and tone of the article, preferably using the writer's own words. Articles subsequently reprinted as book chapters are so indicated, although complete citation of the book is given only in "Section of Books Devoted to HLM."

1908

THE RINGMASTER, *pseud.* Making a Mad Philosopher Appeal to the Mob. Town Topics 59: 18, April 2, 1908.

Popularizing Nietzsche is a literary tour de force.

1910

HITCH, MARCUS. Marxian vs. Nietzschean. International Socialist Review 10: 1021-1027, May, 1910.

HLM's "false view of socialism" (*Men vs. the Man*).

THE RINGMASTER, *pseud.* Thoughtful Letters by Hewlett and Mencken. Town Topics 63: 16, June 2, 1910.

Aristocratic anarchy may reveal the "Art of Life" (*Men vs. the Man*).

1913

PROMINENT CRITICS. Dramatic Review Jan. 1, 1913.

Biographical sketch of dramatic critic of the Baltimore *Evening Sun*.

ARTICLES

1916

OUR MOST SUPPRESSED NOVELIST. Current Opinion 61: 338-339, Nov. 6, 1916.

Suppression of Dreiser's books and HLM's part in the struggle for the publication of *Sister Carrie*.

UNTERMEYER, LOUIS. The Review's the Thing. Bellman 21: 149, July 15, 1916.

"As HLM Might Review Him" is first of series of parodies on how prominent critics would review Shakespeare were he a current author.

1917

BOURNE, RANDOLPH. H. L. Mencken. New Republic 13: 102-103, Nov. 24, 1917.

A critic with "an able mind so harried and irritated by philistinism of American life, that it has not been able to attain its full power" (*A Book of Prefaces*).

COOLING, H. LOWREY. Pertinent Pictures, Mencken—Highbrow and Free Lance. [Baltimore] Evening Sun, Feb. 2, 1917, editorial page.

MENCKEN BEATS THE DRUM. Living Men p. 9-16, 1917.

Of all critics the most readable and the one who "contains most ideas" (*A Book of Prefaces*).

RASCOE, BURTON. Fanfare. Chicago Sunday Tribune, Nov. 11, 1917, Part 8, p. 7.

Answer to Sherman's attack, *see* below. *A Book of Prefaces* is used as a mere pretext to review the entire range of HLM's work. Reprinted in *H. L. Mencken: Fanfare*.

SHERMAN, STUART PRATT. Beautifying American Literature. Nation 105: 593-594, Nov. 29, 1917.

A noted salvo in critic's battle. Uses HLM's dissatisfaction with the beauty of American literature as culture-propaganda for German standards (*A Book of Prefaces*). Reprinted in *Chicago Tribune* under the title "What H. L. Mencken's 'Kultur' is Doing to American Literature."

1918

JOHNSON, JAMES WELDON. American Genius and Its Local. New York Age, July 20, 1918, editorial page, "Views and Reviews."

"The chief charm of Mencken is that he always has a fresh point of view on even the oldest subject . . . , the best part of Mencken is truth."

THREE VIEWS OF H.L.M. The Little Review p. 10-14, Jan., 1918.

Opinions by Raoul Root, j h (Jane Heap), and Margaret Anderson (*A Book of Prefaces*).

UNTERMEYER, LOUIS. A Preface to —. Liberator 1: 43-45, May, 1918.

Applauds HLM's attack on the veneration of the past (*A Book of Prefaces*).

1919

GILMAN, LAWRENCE. The American Language. North American Review 209: 697-703, May, 1919.

Review of 1st edition from the English point of view. "It is deplorably engrossing."

HACKETT, FRANCIS. The Living Speech. New Republic 19: 155-156, May 31, 1919.

"Sagacious thoroughness" of *The American Language* is its great value; a review.

HARRIS, FRANK. American Values: Howe and Mencken. Pearson's Magazine 40: 112-113, Jan., 1919.

Comparison of their points of view, especially as regards the businessman.

JONES, L. L. The Hope of American English. Vanity Fair 13: 67, 106, Dec., 1919.

The American Language assessed for "its criticism, expressed or implied, of American literary standards."

O'SULLIVAN, VINCENT. The American Critic. New Witness [London] p. 30-32, Nov. 28, 1919.

Appraisal as critic. Included in *H. L. Mencken: Fanfare*. Reprinted as "El Crítico Norte Americano" in *El Porvenir* [Cartagena, Col.] Jan. 29, 1921. Slightly augumented in *Living Age* 303: 798-802, Dec. 27, 1919.

O'SULLIVAN, VINCENT. La Littérature Américaine. Mercure de France 13: 246-257 Jan. 16, 1919.

The best American critic since Poe.

THE PRUDERY OF THE PRESS. Journal of the American Medical Association 72: 1547, May 24, 1919.

HLM's assistance, through his *American Language,* in educating the public is a factor in campaign to overcome venereal disease.

1920

BEARD, CHARLES AUSTIN. On Puritans. New Republic 25: 15-17, Dec. 1, 1920.

HLM's reactions to the Pilgrims upon their tercentenary celebration.

BENNETT, JESSE LEE. Mencken Again Shows Contempt for Democracy. [Baltimore] Evening Sun, May 8, 1920, editorial page.

ARTICLES

HLM's Preface to his translation of Nietzsche's *Antichrist* voices vitriolic disdain for the "botched."

BOYD, ERNEST AUGUSTUS. American Literature or Colonial? Freeman 1: 13-15, March 17, 1920.

"Clashes become more frequent between these original personalities and the professional guardians of colonial precedents and traditions."

BOYD, ERNEST AUGUSTUS. A Modern Reactionary. Athenaeum [London] no. 4698, p. 637 May 14, 1920.

HLM's impact as "the most original . . . rapidly becoming the most important critic in America."

BOYNTON, PERCY HOLMES. American Literature and the Tart Set. Freeman 1: 88-89, April 7, 1920.

HLM is high priest of the tart set, who claim that "American literature ought to be national, and American writers and critics ought to be independent of old world standards." Answer to Boyd, *see* above. Rebuttal of Boynton in "Literary Notes" department of the *New Republic*, 22: 289, April 28, 1920.

BRALEY, BERTON. Three—Minus One. New York *Sun*, Dec. 3, 1920.

Most famous poem about HLM, whose meter and refrain "Mencken/Nathan/ and God" are often parodied. Reprinted in "Brick versus Brick" by George Jean Nathan, *Vanity Fair* 29: 60, 120, Nov., 1927; and *Readers Digest* 6: 489-490, Dec., 1927. The most recent parody is "Mencken, Lincoln and God" by Steve Allen (*Wry on the Rocks*. New York, Holt, 1956. p. 145-146).

THE CRITIC AND THE ORDINARY MAN. Freeman 2: 199-200, Nov. 10, 1920.

HLM as critic, advocates idea of the leadership of the aristocracy, but "he expects too much of forces that are fettered."

HUXLEY, ALDOUS LEONARD. American Criticism. Athenaeum [London] no. 4679, p. 10 Jan. 2, 1920.

HLM as critic of contemporary American life (*Prejudices: First Series*).

THE IVORY TOWER. Nation 111: 263, Sept. 4, 1920.

Editors' reply to HLM's accusation that they exist in an ivory tower, unduly conservative and academic in their criticism.

JOHNSON, JAMES WELDON. H. L. Mencken on Lynching. New York Age, Feb. 21, 1920, editorial page, "Views and Reviews."

LITERATURE AND ARISTOCRACY. Boston Evening Transcript, June 19, 1920, editorial page.

WORKS ABOUT H. L. M.

A LITERARY CRITIC. The Christian Register 99: 615, June 24, 1920;

HLM's value outweighs his "Nietzschean excesses." Issued as two-page pamphlet.

MR. MENCKEN AND THE PROPHETS. Freeman 2: 103-104, Oct. 13, 1920.

HLM discomforts prophets who predict a spiritual awakening of American letters.

MR. MENCKEN'S "CHICAGOIAD." Literary Digest 66: 29-30, July 24, 1920.

Comments and long quote from HLM's "A Literary Capital."

ON READING MENCKEN. The Step Ladder 1: 93-94, Aug., 1920.

Three cardinal delusions of the Mencken style.

A REVIEWER'S NOTE-BOOK. Freeman 2: 262-263, Nov. 24, 1920.

HLM claims that good writers are neither appreciated nor wanted, and thus become victims of the environment that fails to nourish them. Critics should be concerned with good writing and not its effects. Answer to this dictum by Burton Rascoe, "Reviewing the Reviewer," p. 473-474, Jan. 26, 1921.

SPINGARN, JOEL ELIAS. American Criticism Today. Nation and Athenaeum [London] 27: 62-64, April 17, 1920.

HLM as "the most raucous" critic using his own vernacular.

THAT LITERARY CAPITAL. Nation 110: 844, June 26, 1920.

Comments on HLM's choice of Chicago; the writer prefers New York.

VIATOR, *pseud.* Engländer v. Amerikaner, der Unterschied zwischen Diesen, für Deutsche Dargestellt. Der Arbeiter, Spring, 1920.

HLM as best interpreter of American soul, humor and language.

WILSON, EDMUND. Some Reviews of Job. Dial 68: 469-470, April, 1920.

The Biblical book of Job as HLM might have written it.

1921

BOYD, ERNEST AUGUSTUS. Mencken, or Virtue Rewarded. Freeman 2: 491-492, Feb. 2, 1921.

HLM "has made himself famous in this country by means of unpopular ideas." Compared with those who have done the same in England and France.

FITZGERALD, FRANCIS SCOTT KEY. Baltimore Anti-Christ. Bookman 52: 79-81, March, 1921.

Appraisal of "the incomparable Mencken" (*Prejudices: Second Series*).

ARTICLES

GALSWORTHY, JOHN. Comments on Fiction. Publishers Weekly 99: 1359-1360, May 7, 1921.

Agrees with HLM's diagnosis of American handicaps, but believes Washington should be our literary center. Further remarks in "Browsing" in The Literary Review of the New York *Evening Post,* April 23, 1921.

H. L. MENCKEN—DEMOCRAT. The [New York] Globe and Commercial Advertiser, August 25, 1921, editorial page.

HARRIS, FRANK. H. L. Mencken: Critic. Pearson's 46: 405-408, May, 1921.

Criticism is the true art of the twentieth century, and HLM its chief exponent.

HAVE WE NO CRITICS? New Republic 28: 174-175, Oct. 12, 1921.

HLM's disparaging remarks concerning Henry James arouses English critics, especially Conrad Aiken.

KRUTCH, JOSEPH WOOD. Antichrist and the Five Apostles. Nation 113: 733-734, Dec. 21, 1921.

HLM's "real genius is for denunciation."

McFEE, WILLIAM. Mencken and Mencken, or the Gift of Tongues. Bookman 54: 361-363, Dec., 1921.

English is far superior to HLM's pet folly, the American language.

NEW MUTTERINGS IN SOUTHERN LITERATURE. Current Opinion 71: 360-362, Sept., 1921.

Answer and amplification of HLM's article "The South Begins to Mutter" in *Smart Set* 65: 138-144, Aug., 1921.

R.Q. *pseud.* The Omnivorous Mencken. [Baltimore] Evening Sun, July 18, 1921, editorial page.

RATCLIFFE, S. K. Mencken: An English Plaint. New Republic 26: 191-192, April 13, 1921.

Critical methods versus power of criticism *(Prejudices: Second Series).*

ROBERTS, CARL ERIC BECHHOFER. Impressions of Recent American Literature, by C. E. Bechhofer [pseud.]. Times [London] Literary Supplement, May 26, June 9-30, 1921.

A series of five articles on the American literary scene, stressing HLM's influence and points of view. Reprinted as *The Literary Renaissance in America.*

SCHÖNEMANN, FRIEDRICH. Ein Amerikanischer Kritiker und Satiriker. Grenzboten p. 179-182, Aug. 17, 1921.

HLM analyzed as author and critic of American mores.

SCHÖNEMANN, FRIEDRICH. Henry Louis Mencken, ein Moderner Amerikanischer Kritiker. Die Neue Zeit, p. 8-10, Jan. 22, 1921.

Detailed description of HLM's ancestry and works.

SLATER, ETHEL SPALDING. Here's the Real Mencken Gleaned from His Photos by a Character Engineer. [Baltimore] Sun, Nov. 6, 1921, Part 8, p. 4.

THE SOUTH AND MR. MENCKEN. The Arkansas Democrat, Aug. 5, 1921, editorial page.

TO MY FRIEND, H. L. Mencken. Medical Critic and Guide, p. 325-326, Sept., 1921.

HLM's opposition to democracy believed to be a pose by the cleverest and most fearless critic.

WILSON, EDMUND. H. L. Mencken. New Republic 27: 10-13, June 1, 1921.

Extensive analysis of "a not ungenial materialist . . . . Behind the comic mask, a critic and evangelist, an artist . . . a mind of extraordinary vigor." Reprinted in the Baltimore *Evening Sun*, May 30, 1921.

1922

ARVIN, NEWTON. The Role of Mr. Mencken. Freeman 6: 381-382, Dec. 27, 1922.

Rebuttal of Burton Rascoe's "Notes for an Epitaph," in the New York *Evening Post*, March 4, 1922. HLM neither sceptic nor idealist, falls short as literary critic. "It is as a humorist . . . that he may be most justly considered."

COBB, ELIZABETH. The Infallible Three, or Finding America. Bookman 54: 603, Feb., 1922.

Poem set as pageant by humorist Irving Cobb's daughter. Uses refrain made popular by Berton Braley's poem "Three—Minus One." *See* above, Braley, 1920.

COMPOSER AS SCIENTIST. Musical America 36: 20, June 3, 1922.

Editorial on HLM's article "The Tone Art" in "Répétition Générale" column, *Smart Set* 68: 46, June, 1922.

GROOME, MOSES. The Great American Critic. [Baltimore] Evening Sun, May 26, 1922, editorial page.

HILTON, JOSEPH KENNICOTT. More About the Mencken Menace. Des Moines Sunday Register, April 9, 1922, Section E, p. 5.

JONES, VERA MACBETH. Mr. Mencken and the Movies. Screenland, p. 44, June, 1922.

ARTICLES

Her impressions of HLM while he expressed his opinions in an interview. She wrote of his kindness during this interview as an obituary letter to *Gardens, Houses and People* 31: 5, Feb., 1956.

LIPPMANN, WALTER. Near Machiavelli. New Republic 30: 12-14, May 31, 1922.

"The author of the American Dunciad and the prophet of the new aristocracy . . . wants to recreate the world by words in the image of his dreams."

THE LITERARY SPOTLIGHT, V: H. L. Mencken. Bookman 54: 551-554, Feb., 1922 port. (caricature by William Gropper)

Humorous personality sketch in the style of *Pistols for Two*. Reprinted in *The Literary Spotlight*, p. 108-115.

LOGAN, MALCOLM R. Vale Mencken Imperator. [Baltimore] Evening Sun, July 10, 1922, editorial page.

Concerning the style and content of the "Monday Articles" in *The Evening Sun*.

McCULLOUGH, ARTHUR F. A Precursor of Mencken. [Baltimore] Evening Sun, September 29, 1922, editorial page.

Comparison of HLM and William Cowper Brann, "two strange American writers who within two decades of one another essayed the thankless task of patching together Truth's broken mirror, each using the same means, almost the identical language."

MR. MENCKEN, WAR AND THE EDITOR. Critic and Guide, p. 284-287, Aug., 1922.

Two letters from William J. Robinson and two replies by HLM on *his* "Fragment on War" in "Répétition Générale," *Smart Set* 68: 34-37, May, 1922.

NEW ORDER OF CRITICAL VALUES. Vanity Fair 18: 40-41, April, 1922.

Logarithm table charts "transvaluation of values" of ten modern critics.

A PSYCHOANALYST, *pseud*. What's the Matter with Mencken? [Baltimore] Evening Sun, August 7, 1922, editorial page.

"The writer of this article, a prominent New York authority on Freudian psychology, attempts to explain Mr. Mencken's attitude to society, conventional morality, etc., on the basis of Mr. Mencken's essay on marriage, entitled 'For Better, For Worse,' and published on this page on July 17." Editor's note.

RASCOE, BURTON. Notes for an Epitaph. [New York] Evening Post, March 4, 1922, Literary Review, p. 1.

HLM has become respectable.

SMITH, LEWIS WORTHINGTON. H. L. Mencken, the Billy Sunday of Current Criticism. Des Moines Sunday Register, Feb. 26, 1922, Section E, p. 7.

WORKS ABOUT H. L. M.

VISIT OF MR. MENCKEN. English Review 35: 142-143, Aug., 1922.
The London visit of "the man with the hammer" may improve the flabbiness of English criticism. Condensed as "Mencken in London" in *Literary Review* Sept. 2, 1922.

1923

DeCASSERES, BENJAMIN. Mencken: Candidate of Booze or Bust Party. [New York] Morning Telegraph, June 17, 1923, Section 2, p. 1.

EVANS, DELIGHT. "With the Horses Running Around," Said Mr. Mencken; "And the Band Playing," Said Mr. Nathan. [New York] Morning Telegraph, Dec. 2, 1923, Sunday Magazine, p. 3.
On the launching of the *American Mercury*.

HOFFENSTEIN, SAMUEL. Mr. Menckenathan: An Imaginary Interview. New York Tribune, Feb. 4, 1923, Part 6, p. 21.

JOHNSON, GERALD WHITE. The Congo, Mr. Mencken. Reviewer 3: 887-893, July, 1923.
Reply to HLM's "outrageous" remarks about the South in "The Sahara of the Bozart."

MIMS, EDWARD. American Idealism is Defended by Dr. Mims, Sounds Call to Battle Against Spirit of Cynicism and Destructive Criticism. Greensboro Daily News, Sept. 20, 1923, p. 2.
The Sherman vs. Mencken controversy joined by Head of English Department of Vanderbilt University.

RASCOE, BURTON. A Cantrip of Critics. Shadowland 7: 35-36, 78, Feb., 1923. port. (sketch by Djuna Barnes)
HLM as a force in American literature and popular culture. Contrasted with Huneker, Percival Pollard and S. P. Sherman.

RAYNOR, HENRY C. Mencken a False Prophet, Says Convict. [Baltimore] Sun, June 3, 1923, Part 2, Section 1, p. 1.
A convict critic discusses and dismisses HLM and others.

RENNELS, MARY. So Clever That They Can't Be Free! The Strange Paradox of the Two "Free" Men—Nathan and Mencken—Who Are Slaves to Their Prejudices—How Mary Rennels Ran the Battery of Their Sarcasm and Satire. [Cleveland] Sunday News-Leader, June 10, 1923, Magazine Section, p. 1.

ARTICLES

THE SOUTH AND A MALIGNER. [Memphis] Commercial Appeal, May 27, 1923, editorial page.

A long editorial, typical of the type of article that appeared in Southern newspapers.

SPINGARN, JOEL ELIAS. The Growth of the Literary Myth. Freeman 7: 181-183, May 2, 1923.

HLM responsible for creating "Croce-Spingarn-Carlyle-Goethe theory."

VAN DOREN, CARL. Smartness and Light, H. L. Mencken, a Gadfly for Democracy. Century 105: 791-796, March, 1923.

HLM's quarrels are a service to the country, his stream of humor an enrichment. Compared to Whitman, Poe and Mark Twain.

VAN DYKE, HENRY. Middle-Western Professor Sneers at H. L. Mencken: Ridicules "Sterile Vulgarity" of His "American Language"—Van Dyke Calls Idea an Enormity. [Baltimore] Evening Sun, June 14, 1923, p. 3.

1924

BEARDSLEY, WILFRED ATTWOOD. A Spanish Mencken Revealed in Person of de Unamuno. [Baltimore] Evening Sun, Sept. 5, 1924, editorial page.

A comparison of HLM and Miguel de Unamuno.

HUSSEY, L. M. Note upon an Artist. Saturday Review of Literature 1: 297-298, Nov. 22, 1924.

"Like most artists, he shys away from tight, coherent systems" yet provokes more vehement discussion of his ideas and purposes by a wider audience (*Prejudices: Fourth Series*).

KALTEN, HORACE MEYER. What Is an Elephant? A Fable for Critics. New Republic 41: suppl., 1-4, Dec. 10, 1924.

Viewpoints of contemporary critics, players in a dangerous game.

WILLIAMS, MICHAEL. Bishop and Brains. Commonweal 1: 209-211, Dec. 31, 1924.

Catholic answer to HLM's article on the Ku Klux Klan in "Clinical Notes" of the *American Mercury* 3: 447-448, Dec., 1924.

1925

BODENHEIM, MAXWELL. Criticism in America. Saturday Review of Literature 1: 801-802, June 6, 1925.

HLM compared to Stuart P. Sherman.

CHANTICLEER, *pseud.* Contemporaries: This Man Mencken. Independent 114: 45-47, Jan. 10, 1925.

Objects to HLM's views on art and poetry, for "he has stood stock-still as a progressive thinker" (*Prejudices: Fourth Series*).

FEDERALIST: 1925 MODEL. Saturday Review of Literature 2: 401, 409, Dec. 12, 1925.

HLM "has become a Federalist in mind if not in manner" (*Americana 1925*).

GENZMER, GEORGE. Mr. Mencken Triumphant. Nation 121: 664-665, Dec. 9, 1925.

HLM has reached a turning point of his career, emerging as "a writer of unmistakeable distinction and importance."

GOLDBERG, ISAAC. Musician and Critic of Musicians: H. L. Mencken Disclosed in New Virtue, Composer on the Staves: Pianist at the Keys: Justicier in Opera House and Concert-Hall. Boston Evening Transcript, May 23, 1925. Part 3, p. 10. facsim. (music)

Includes letter from HLM on his musical taste, also score for an "Unnamed Salon Piece," a waltz composed about 1900. Reprinted in his *The Man Mencken* (p. 175-186).

HALL, GROVER CLEVELAND. E. W. Howe and H. L. Mencken. [Baltimore] Evening Sun, June 24, 1925, editoral page.

Compared as philosophers, scholars and critics. Reprinted in *Haldeman-Julius Monthly* p. 163-167, July, 1925; and Montgomery, Ala., *Advertiser* Dec. 26, 1959, editorial page as "Essay Assay of the Sages of Potato Hill and of Baltimore."

KELLEY, WILLIAM VALENTINE. At the Sign of Basilisk. Methodist Review 108: 518-527, July, 1925.

Denunciation of the "boss basilisk" who is poisoning the nation, by the editor of the magazine.

McCLURE, JOHN. Literature—and Less. [New Orleans] Times-Picayune, Sept. 13, 1925, Sunday Magazine, p. 5.

McWILLIAMS, CAREY. Notes on H. L. Mencken. The Wooden Horse [Univ. of S. Calif.] p. 23-27, Winter, 1925.

HLM as critic and idol-smasher.

MANCHESTER, H. F. On First Seeing a Cut of H. L. Mencken. [Baltimore] Evening Sun, Aug. 24, 1925, editorial page.

Poem reprinted from the Boston *Globe*.

MILLARD, BAILEY. H. L. Mencken, a Lesser G.B.S. The Los Angeles Times, July 12, 1925, Part 3, p. 28.

ARTICLES

NEWSPAPERS AND NEWSPAPER MEN: H. L. Mencken. The Marylander 1: 6, April 18, 1925.

Marylanders should recognize HLM's talents, for he is more appreciated abroad than at home. Planned as a series, this was first and only article.

PARSHLEY, H. M. H. L. Mencken: An Appreciation. American Review 3: 72-84, Jan.—Feb., 1925.

Exposition of HLM's iconoclastic influence as journalist and editor, philologist and philosopher, critical observer of life and letters, and creative writer. Reprinted as pamphlet, 13 p.

ROSSER, JOHN E. Turning the Spotlight on Mr. Mencken. Literary Digest, International Book Review 3: 773-774, Nov., 1925. port. (by Covarrubias)

Examines HLM's opinions and work, which by "sheer bulk, heft and horsepower . . . compels remark," (Boyd biog.).

SHERMAN, STUART PRATT. Mr. Brownell and Mr. Mencken. Bookman 60: 632-634, Jan., 1925.

Comparison of *Prejudices: Fourth Series* with William Crary Brownell's *The Genius of Style,* as confrontation of literary proletariat with the literary aristocracy.

1926

BEACH, JOSEPH WARREN. Pedantic Study of Two Critics. American Speech 1: 299-306, March, 1926.

HLM's prose style and use of words compared to Cabell and Sherman.

BLUNDEN, EDMUND. Counter Attack on Mencken: England Replies To Indictment. Trans-Pacific 13: 5, July 3, 1926.

Caustic rejoinder to HLM's "boyish and horseplay" articles on the present state of England and the British attitude towards America.

BOYD, ERNEST AUGUSTUS. Readers and Writers. Independent 117: 505, Oct. 30, 1926.

Comparison of views on socialism as expressed in *Notes on Democracy* with George Bernard Shaw's contemporary writings.

BROWN, IVOR. What Is America? [Baltimore] Sun, Feb. 25, 1926, p. 13.

London writer cannot match Mencken's America with the America he meets.

GOLDBERG, ISAAC. Critical Playwrights: Nathan, Mencken, and the Fringes of the Theatre. Boston Evening Transcript, Jan. 16, 1926, Part 3, p. 4.

WORKS ABOUT H. L. M.

[THE HATRACK CASE]. [Baltimore] Sun and Evening Sun, March 30—June 10, 1926.

Boston Bans April "American Mercury." Evening, March 30, p. 1.

Mencken to Defy Arrest in Boston. Morning, April 5, p. 1.

Mencken Defies Ban; Will See Magazine. Evening, April 5, p. 1.

Mencken Freed on $1,000 Bond in Boston Court. Morning, April 6, p. 1.

Mencken Defies His Accusers on Witness Stand. Evening, April 6, p. 1.

Mencken Case to be Decided This Morning. Morning, April 7, p. 1.

Mencken Found "Not Guilty" on Morals Charge. Evening, April 7, p. 1.

Mencken Honored At Harvard Following Victory in Court. Morning, April 8, p. 1.

Case of Mencken Finds Parallel in German Blasphemy Trial. Evening, April 8, p. 1.

Resolution to New Asks Mercury Ban. Evening, April 8, p. 1.

U. S. Mails Bar April Mercury; Issue Sold Out. Morning, April 9, p. 1.

Mencken Precocious Youngster in Eyes of Boston Transcript. Morning, April 9, p. 2.

Mencken Returns, Rejoicing in Victory Over Reformers. Morning, April 10, p. 24.

Mencken Damage Suit to Open Today. Morning, April 12, p. 1.

Mencken Renews Magazine Fight. Evening, April 12, p. 1.

Decision in Mercury Suit Reserved by Federal Judge. Morning, April 13, p. 1.

Diverse Opinions of Mencken's Sally Into Puritan Land. Morning, April 13, p. 14. Reprinted from other newspapers.

Johnson, Gerald W. Donnelly, "Hatrack" and Jefferson. Evening, April 13, editorial page.

Federal Court Enjoins Chase in Mencken Suit. Morning, April 15, p. 1.

Refuses to Reopen Mail to Mercury. Evening, April 15, p. 1.

Ban on April Issue of Mercury Stands. Morning, April 16, p. 1.

Boston Police Head Puts Curb on Chase. Morning, April 22, p. 5.

Postmaster-General Sued by Mencken's Lawyer. Morning, April 29, p. 2.

U.S. Judge Enjoins Postmaster-General on Plea of Mencken. Evening, May 11, p. 1.

U.S. Court Rescinds Ban on Mercury. Morning, May 12, p. 1.

News Dealer Fined in Mercury Case. Morning, June 10, p. 1.

HILL, ALFRED G. What Kansas Thinks of H.L.M. [Baltimore] Evening Sun, Feb. 10, 1926, editorial page.

Comments on HLM's syndicated articles in the *Chicago Sunday Tribune*.

JOHNSON, BURGES. Mencken and the Boston Massacre. The Writer 38: 296-297, June, 1926.

The "Hatrack" censorship battle.

LIPPMANN, WALTER. H. L. Mencken. Saturday Review of Literature 3: 413-414, Dec. 11, 1926.

ARTICLES

"I have not written this as a eulogy but as an explanation" of HLM's political philosophy and personal influence on the national scene (*Notes on Democracy*). Reprinted as pamphlet by Knopf, 1926. 8 p.

LORD, DANIEL A. Mencken Among the Metaphysicians. America 35: 587-589, Oct. 2, 1926.

A Jesuit priest writes of HLM as a strange combination of seeker and cynic.

MENCKEN AS SMOKE-EATER, A Sentimental Journey—American Style. [Baltimore] Evening Sun, Oct. 25, 1926, editorial page.

Excerpts from Southern newspapers about HLM as he tours the South.

MR. MENCKEN JOUSTS AT HIS VERY OWN WINDMILLS. San Francisco Chronicle, Nov. 16, 1926, p. 17.

HLM on U.S. tour arrives in San Francisco.

MONROE, HARRIET. Mephistopheles and the Poet. Poetry 28: 210-215, July, 1926.

Agrees with HLM's "cry of despair" over the "standardization of the American mind" and editors who want only what is saleable rather than "genuinely novel."

MUSTARD PLASTER MENCKEN. Bookman 64: 388, Dec., 1926.

Wants HLM to stop "being an irritant and turn to more useful pursuits."

RASCOE, BURTON. Contemporary Reminiscences. Arts & Decoration 24: 49, 73, 77, 95, Jan., 1926. port.

Differences between HLM and Nathan, both having become popular through denunciation (Goldberg biog.).

SALISBURY, WILLIAM. Mencken, the Foe of Beauty. American Parade 1: 34-49, July, 1926.

Appraisal as critic, artist and poet. Reprinted as "*The Baltimore Phenomenon*" New Rochelle, Independent Pub. Co., 1926. 19 p.

SPARRING DISPLAYS OF LITERARY MOGULS ARE JUDGED LIGHTLY. [Baltimore] Sun, Nov. 12, 1926, p. 10.

The Swinnerton-Mencken verbal duel. *See* below, Swinnerton.

STRUNSKY, SIMEON. About Books. New York Times Book Review, Nov. 28, 1926, p. 4.

HLM on democracy and popular government (*Notes on Democracy*).

SWINNERTON, FRANK. The Great Mencken Fight. Bookman 64: 463-467, Dec., 1926.

Championship match between Swinnerton and HLM for the glory of English or American letters, with Knopf acting as referee.

WIGGINS, DUBOIS K. Mountebanks Amuse Mencken. Brooklyn Eagle Aug. 22, 1926, Sunday Eagle Magazine, p. 3.

WILCOX, HELEN J. H. L. Mencken. The Triad [Sydney, N.S.W.] March 1, 1926, port.

Portrait and description of a busy day at the *American Mercury* office, by one of HLM's former secretaries.

WILLIAMS, MICHAEL. Men, the Mob, and Mr. Mencken. Commonweal 3: 488-489, March 10, 1926.

Reply to Mencken's criticism of a series of articles published in the *Survey* upon the decay of liberals and radicalism.

[WILSON, EDMUND] The All-Star Literary Vaudeville. New Republic 47: 159-160, June 30, 1926.

HLM's place as critic in the contemporary panorama of American literature. Reprinted in his *The Shores of Light*, p. 229-247.

WILSON, EDMUND. Mencken's Democratic Man. New Republic 49: 110-111, Dec. 15, 1926.

Discussion of HLM's political philosophy (*Notes on Democracy*). Reprinted in his *The Shores of Light*, p. 292-297.

1927

ALLEN, FREDERICK LEWIS. These Disillusioned Highbrows. Indepependent 118: 378-379, April 9, 1927.

Against the "new school of hard knockers" as exemplified by HLM on Coolidge. Condensed in *Readers Digest* 6: 13-14, May, 1927.

AMERICA'S SEVEREST CRITIC—H. L. MENCKEN. Vanity Fair 27: 69, Feb., 1927. port.

Steichen's photo accompanied by brief biography of Editor-in-Chief of the *American Mercury*.

ARMSTRONG, EVERHARDT. Mencken and America. Nineteenth Century 101: 117-125, Jan., 1927.

HLM as "critic of literature . . . tends to evolve into critic of civilization."

BACON, LEONARD. From a New Dunciad [poem]. Saturday Review of Literature 4: 87, Sept. 3, 1927.

HLM and Orage in combat.

BRIDGES, HORACE JAMES. Presenting Mr. H. L. Mencken. Standard 16: 237-248, April, 1927.

HLM's views on democracy and ethics. Paper read before the Chicago Literary Club, on Jan. 17, 1927.

ARTICLES

BURNS, GEORGE V. "Democracy Is Inferior Man's Envy of His Superiors," Proclaims Henry Louis Mencken. [Denver] Rocky Mountain News, June 12, 1927, Drama Section, p. 7.

CONRAD, JOSEPH. Joseph Conrad's American Notes and Thoughts on Life. A final installment from the author's private letters. World's Work 53: 452-454, Feb., 1927.

Letter to Keating, Dec. 14, 1922, expressing his opinion of HLM. Translated by Leo Klein in *Neue Rundschau,* p. 636-637, June, 1927.

"DR." MENCKEN, WIT, TURNING POLITICAL EXHORTER, HIS FEAR. Washington Correspondent Points to Baltimorean's "Impassioned" Crusade for [Sen. James A.] Reed [D. Mo.] and Thinks Man of Letters May End as Candidate Himself. [Baltimore] Sun, Jan. 16, 1927, p. 20.

FITCH, W. T. Portrait in Sand. Overland, n.s. 85: 54, Feb., 1927.

The Mencken lance has "thrown a scare into the ranks of the pious peddlers of popular platitudes."

GOLDBERG, ISAAC. Music and Mencken, Pardonable Prejudices of a Critic. Dance 8: 18-19, 58-59, Aug., 1927. port. (drawing by Willem Wirtz of HLM and Max Broedel at piano), illus. (facsim. of waltz c. 1893)

HLM's appreciation and knowledge of music. Description of Saturday Night Club.

GOOCH, R. K. H. L. Mencken: Notes on Democracy. Political and Social Science Quarterly 7: 442-444, March, 1927.

Evaluation of HLM's political influence.

H.L.M. IS THE ACID TEST OF RELIGION, Says Church Paper, Reaction of Christians to Critic's Assaults Will Prove Reality of Faith They Profess or Demonstrate Its Hollowness. [Baltimore] Evening Sun, Jan. 10, 1927, editorial page.

HALDEMAN-JULIUS, EMANUEL. A Good Man. Reflex 1: 82-84, Dec., 1927; same in Haldeman-Julius Weekly Jan. 7, 1928.

Summary and comments on HLM's "Testament" in *Review of Reviews.* See "Works by H. L. Mencken—Magazine Articles," 1927.

KUMMER, FREDERIC ARNOLD. Something Must Have Happened to Henry. Bookman 65: 408-410, June, 1927.

HLM's contempt for the South, further proved by his attacks on Bryan, Poe and O. Henry.

311

LEWIS, WYNDHAM. Paleface. The Enemy no. 2, p. 5-24, Sept., 1927.

Discussion of religious and racial prejudices in the U.S.A. "The Nature of Mencken's Responsibility" p. 11-12; "Mencken's America" p. 17-23.

MEAD, EDWIN D. A Vigorous Answer to the Defamers of Henry Ward Beecher. Boston Evening Transcript, Oct. 22, 1927, Part Two-A, p. 3.

PATTEE, FRED LEWIS. The New Muck-Rake School of Literature. Christian Advocate 102: 523-524, April 28, 1927.

HLM's "cult of the sneer" widespread; Sinclair Lewis has become a "Menckenette."

PEW, MARLEN. Shop Talk at Thirty. Editor & Publisher 60: 46, July 9, 1927.

Answer to HLM's article on need for alert and competent criticism.

RASCOE, BURTON. Contemporary Reminiscences: People and Books in the New York Literary World. Arts & Decoration 26: 50, Jan., 1927.

HLM charms Southerners on personal tour.

SCHÖNEMANN, FRIEDRICH. Der Amerikanische Anti-Demokrat. Deutsche Rundschau 213: 216-218, Dec., 1927.

HLM as "Kultur Kritiker."

SERGEANT, ELIZABETH SHEPLEY. H. L. Mencken. Nation 124: 174-176, Feb. 16, 1927.

Appraisal of his many-faceted character. Reprinted in her *Fire under the Andes*, p. 239-257.

SHAW, ALBERT. Mencken and His Aims. Review of Reviews 76: 412, Oct., 1927.

Discussion of HLM's basic convictions, as stated in "Testament."

SHAW, CHARLES G. Three Literary Radicals, Wherein F. Scott Fitzgerald, Anita Loos, and H. L. Mencken are Completely Vivisected. Vanity Fair 29: 134-138, Dec., 1927.

Biographical sketch parodying style of *Pistols for Two*. Reprinted in his *Low-Down*, p. 51-61.

SIMRELL, VIVIAN EARL. H. L. Mencken, the Rhetorician. Quarterly Journal of Speech Education 13: 399-412, Nov., 1927.

Detailed study of HLM's rhetoric.

ARTICLES

SINCLAIR, UPTON. Mr. Mencken Calls on Me. Bookman 66: 254-265, Nov., 1927. port. (caricature with text by William H. Cotton)

Needles HLM's prejudice against the "libertarian crusader."

STEIN, HANNAH. H. L. Mencken (Bachelor) Says: "Most Men Marry When Women Make Up Their Minds That They Shall Marry— and Then There Is No Escape!" [Philadelphia] Public Ledger Dec. 18, 1927, Magazine Section, p. 5.

STOLBERG, BENJAMIN. Walter Lippmann, Connoisseur of Public Life. Nation 125: 640, Dec. 7, 1927.

Lippmann's views on HLM, and their political concepts contrasted (*Notes on Democracy*).

SYRKIN, MARIE. The Whimsical Mr. Mencken. Reflex 1: 85-88, Dec., 1927.

HLM's many facets as presented in his own works and by his biographers.

1928

AMERICAN BOOKS AND BINDINGS ARE SUPERIOR, SAYS H. L. MENCKEN. Bookbinding Magazine June, 1928.

BABBITT, IRVING. The Critic and American Life. Forum 79: 161-176, Feb., 1928.

Chief opponent of HLM and his school. His "criticism as self expression, reduces it to temperamental urge, uttering of gustos and disgustos." Reprinted in his *On Being Creative and Other Essays*, chapter 7; *American Poetry and Prose* edited by Norman Foerster (New York, Houghton, 1934. p. 1401-1409); *American Life in Literature* edited by Jay Broadus Hubbell (New York, Harper, 1936. p. 508-516); which volume also appeared as War Department Education Manual EM 114.

BOYD, ERNEST AUGUSTUS. Readers and Writers: Menckeniana, a Schimpflexicon. Independent 120: 91, Jan. 28, 1928.

Abusive criticism aimed at HLM actually earned him royalties.

CARNEAL, GEORGETTE. In Defense of Marriage, an authorized interview with H. L. Mencken. Smart Set 82: 30-31, 102, Aug., 1928. ports. (by Carlo Leonetti, Schattenstein and Covarrubias)

"He scoffs at custom, pokes fun at convention . . . " (Subtitle).

CASEY, LEE TAYLOR. An American Cato. [Denver] Rocky Mountain News, Feb. 12, 1928, Magazine Section, p. 12.

ELY, CATHERINE BEACH. The Sorrows of Mencken. North American Review 225: 23-26, Jan., 1928.

"On his peak of scorn he noisily bewails America; but he enjoys his sorrows." Abridged in *Readers Digest* 6: 637-638, Feb., 1928.

ERVINE, ST. JOHN. America and the Nobel Prize. Philadelphia Inquirer, Dec. 16, 1928, Theatre Section, p. 5.

Suggests HLM as recipient of world's greatest literary award.

FRANK, WALDO. Our Arts. The Re-Discovery of America: XII. New Republic 54: 343-347, May 9, 1928.

Rhetorical art of HLM, p. 345.

HARROLD, CHARLES FREDERICK. Two Critics of Democracy. South Atlantic Quarterly 27: 130-141, April, 1928.

Comparison of Carlyle and HLM as critics of democracy and the popular will.

JONES, HOWARD MUMFORD. Professor Babbitt Cross-Examined. New Republic 54: 158-160, March 21, 1928.

In defense of HLM, against attacks by Babbitt in *Forum. See* above.

KESSINGER'S MID-WEST REVIEW. [Chicago] v. 10, no. 3, p. 3–6 (entire issue) March, 1928.

HLM as leading exponent of "whateveris, is wrong."

MAGILL, DAN H. What Should Be Done with Mencken? Georgia Alumni Record 8: 141-143, 146, March, 1928.

"Put him and his writings into a text-book and seriously study what he has to say," is the answer by a reporter on the Athens *Banner Herald*.

MICHAUD, RÉGIS. Henry Mencken ou le Collectionneur de Préjugés. Nouvelles Littéraires 7: 8+, June 9, 1928.

RASCOE, BURTON. Those Who Can, Criticize. Bookman 66: 674-676, Feb., 1928.

Prejudices: Sixth Series reveals HLM's compassion, tenderness and his views on hollowness of fame.

ROGERS, CAMERON. Mencken. Outlook 150: 1187-1189, 1224 port. (by Nathaniel Yonteff)

HLM's widespread popularity has led to his "decline as critical power in the land." Reprinted in his *Oh Splendid Appetite*, p. 85–97.

WILLIAMS, MICHAEL. Prayer for a Man Writing a Book. Commonweal 7: 1058-1059, Feb. 15, 1928.

Reply to HLM's "Hiring a Hall" in the New York *World* Jan. 29, 1928, in which he requests mass prayers be said for him while he writes *Treatise on the Gods.* Reprinted in his *Catholicism and the Modern Mind,* p. 223-238.

WILSON, EDMUND. Literary Politics. New Republic 53: 289-290, Feb. 1, 1928.

We now have powerful parties, acting more or less on a set of principles. In first place is HLM with his satellites and disciples.

1929

BUCKNER, R.H.A. H. L. Mencken. Landmark 11: 29-32, Jan., 1929. port. (by Carlo Leonetti)

English viewpoint, explaining "the bomb shell critic of genus Americanus."

CHESTERTON, GILBERT KEITH. The Sceptic as Critic. Forum 81: 65-69, Feb., 1929. port.

"Umpire with Catholic bias, in debate about America and the puritans." Fails to see how iconoclasts, though very able, will serve the country.

GILMAN, LAWRENCE. Orchestral Master Works. Musical America 48: 8, 30, Jan. 5, 1929.

Discusses HLM's opinions on Beethoven's Eroica.

MR. MENCKEN CONVERT. Commonweal 10: 145, June 12, 1929.

Reply to HLM book review of Krutch *The Modern Temper. See* Book Reviews. Has HLM "succumbed to the blandishments of Prof. Charles Beard, dispenser of machine-age optimism?"

THE PASSING OF H. L. MENCKEN. Bookman 70: 186-188, Oct., 1929.

"Evidence of weariness in writing, which has lost its force."

SARAYON, WILLIAM. The American Clowns of Criticism. Overland Monthly, n.s. 87: 77-78, 92-93, March, 1929.

HLM, Nathan and Haldeman-Julius accused of being intolerant, prejudiced, and failing to understand the younger generation.

SEMPER, ISIDORE J. H. L. Mencken, Doctor Rhetoricus. Catholic World 130: 30-41, Oct., 1929.

Discussion of vocabulary and philosophy of this "bane of professors." Reprinted in his *The Return of the Prodigal and Other Essays,* p. 86-111.

1930

BRAININ, JOSEPH. Is H. L. Mencken an Anti-Semite? Jewish Criterion [Pittsburgh] April 11, 1930. port.

"This is the first interview that HLM has ever given any newspaper on matters of Jewish interest." This Seven Arts Feature syndicated column appeared in the Toronto *Jewish Standard,* April 30, 1930, and *The Ivri* (Johannesburg, South Africa) p. 16-20, June 1, 1930.

COLLINS, SEWARD B. Criticism in America. Bookman 71: 241-256, 353-364, 400-415, June-July, 1930.

Battle of the critics; espouses Babbitt and More against HLM.

MELAMED, S. M. H. L. Mencken's Encyclopedia of Platitudes. Reflex 6: 3-17, May, 1930.

Attacks alleged anti-Semitic sentiments in *Treatise on the Gods.*

MENCKEN AND LEWISOHN IN PARIS. Living Age 338: 27-28, 61-62, March 1, 1930.

Report of an informal debate in Paris, "a combined assault on American culture."

MENCKEN LOOKS AT BOOKSELLING. Publishers' Weekly 118: 2072-2073, Nov. 1, 1930.

Editorial reply to HLM's editorial in the *American Mercury* 21: 151-155, Oct., 1930. Reissued as *Lo, the Poor Bookseller.*

PHELPS, WILLIAM LYON. As I Like It. Scribner 88: 205-208, Aug., 1930.

Defines his attitude toward religion, what he likes and dislikes in HLM (*Treatise on the Gods*).

ROIG DE LEUCHSENRING, EMILIO. El Caso Mencken. Social [Habana] p. 42, 83, Nov., 1930. ports.

When the heretic weds, it becomes a world event.

SEMPER, ISIDORE J. H. L. Mencken and Catholicism. Catholic World 131: 641-650, Sept., 1930.

On HLM's religious views (*Treatise on the Gods*). Reprinted in his *The Return of the Prodigal and Other Essays,* p. 63-85.

TACKE, C. A. H. L. Mencken. New World Monthly 1: 124-132, Feb., 1930.

HLM as critic of esthetics and morals.

TAYLOR, DEEMS. Words and Music. McCall's 58: 3, 46, Dec., 1930.

Imaginary concert with "orchestra under the direction of H. L. Mencken."

WEISGAL, MEYER. Jews down on Mencken for Turning His Lance Against Them in Book, Editor Had Been an Idol among a Great Many of Them but He Has Been Removed from His Pedestal

ARTICLES

and All because of a Single Paragraph in 300-Page Publication. Brooklyn Daily Eagle, April 20, 1930, p. 8.

Cited as an example of the uproar caused by *A Treatise on the Gods* in the Jewish press in America.

WILLIAMS, MICHAEL. Mr. Mencken's Bible for Boobs. Commonweal 11: 607-610, April 2, 1930.

"Upholder of Darwinism ·produces a Bible for village atheism," says spokesman for Catholic point of view on *Treatise on the Gods*.

1931

BRADISH, C. R. Mencken and Nathan. Stead's Review 68: 34-35, April 1, 1931.

Interview at the *American Mercury* office, second in series of "Personalities with a Tang."

BROOKE, BISSELL. Household—What Mencken Thinks of American Cuisine. [Baltimore] Sun, Dec. 6, 1931, Section 2, p. 10.

BUNKER, JOHN. The Failure of Mencken as Artist. The Sign 10: 597-598, May, 1931.

Has drive and gusto, but lacks love.

MURET, M. La Philosophie à Coups de Matraque: Mencken contre l'Amérique. Journal des Débats 37, pt. 2: 681-683, Oct. 24, 1931.

1932

BOYD, ERNEST AUGUSTUS. H. L. Mencken, Homo Americanus. Vanity Fair 38: 23, March, 1932. port. (by Steichen)

Steichen portrait features "the American citizen quitessential."

GREGORY, HORACE. Our Writers and the Democratic Myth. Bookman 75: 377-382, Aug., 1932.

Embarassing dilemma of democracy that can "face toward aristocratic libertarianism on one side, and toward plain-man-of-the-people on the other." HLM's influence waning, for his "original disciples are beyond middle age and the new recruits are mere Menckenoids."

THE NATION'S HONOR ROLL FOR 1931. Nation 134: 7, Jan. 6, 1932.

HLM for journalism; reports denouncing Salisbury, Md., lynching.

1933

CUSHING, EDWARD. Love of Art is Bunk, Says Mencken. Brooklyn Eagle, June 18, 1933, The Eagle Magazine, p. 1.

GRATTAN, CLINTON HARTLEY. A Good Word for Mr. Mencken. Brooklyn Eagle, Dec. 10, 1933, The Sunday Review, p. 7.

MENCKEN TIRED OF EDITING, Will Quit "Mercury," Acid-Tongue Critic of Men and Morals to Desert Mouthpiece of Decade. Turning Point in Life, Now He'll Do Those Books He's Always Had in Mind. New York Herald Tribune, Oct. 6, 1933, p. 19.

MENCKEN v. GOGUES. Time 21: 30, 32, Feb. 20, 1933. port. (with wife)

> Comments on high cost of public education, editorial in *American Mercury* 28: 129-135, Feb., 1933.

MR. MENCKEN LEAVES THE MERCURY. Christian Century 50: 1292, Oct. 18, 1933.

> Editorial pointing out significance of HLM's retirement; symptomatic of the passing of a type of criticism and the change in American mood.

ROSSER, JOHN E. H. L. Mencken, the Bad Boy of Baltimore, an X-ray photograph of the Maryland terror. Real America 2: 22-27, Sept., 1933. ports.

> Biographical sketch and evaluation of career.

1934

COWLEY, MALCOLM. Former Fugelman. New Republic 81: 50-51, Nov. 21, 1934.

> Fugelman of new fiction on proletarian writers.

GILLIS, JAMES M. Mencken, Moralist! Catholic World 139: 257-266, June, 1934.

> Editorial attack on HLM in field of ethics and religion, especially in answer to H. M. Parshley's favorable review of *Treatise on Right and Wrong* in New York *Herald Tribune Books,* April 8.

MAYNARD, THEODORE. Mencken Leaves "The American Mercury." Catholic World 139: 10-20, April, 1934.

> HLM's contributions as personality and editor.

ROSENE, M. R. The Five Best American Books Published since 1900. The Writer 46: 371, Oct., 1934.

> *A Book of Prefaces* ranked among top five; others by Anderson, Dreiser, Hemingway and Eliot.

1935

HESSLER, L. B. On "Bad Boy" Criticism. North American Review 240: 215-216, Sept., 1935.

> Of all types of literary criticism, HLM's is "the most insiduously misleading."

ARTICLES

MENCKEN BACKS TEST OF LYNCH LAW PROPOSAL: Baltimorean Testifies at Senate Hearing on Wagner-Costigan Bill. [Baltimore] Evening Sun, Feb. 14, 1935, p. 1.

MONKEY BUSINESS. Nation 141: 118, July 31, 1935.

Tenth anniversary of the "monkey trial" at Dayton, where "over the entire proceedings brooded the spirit of Mencken."

1936

CALVERTON, VICTOR FRANCIS. H. L. Mencken: A Devaluation. Modern Monthly 10: 7-10, Nov., 1936.

HLM's retrogression as a social philosopher and literary critic.

CLARK, JOHN ABBOT. H. L. Mencken: An Obituary. American Spectator 4: 11-12, Dec., 1936—Jan., 1937.

HLM the master debunker, who portrays "the American circus" in the light of a confused and changing social and cultural climate.

FORSYTHE, ROBERT. Mencken, Nathan and Boyd (Winken, Blinken and Nod) New Masses 19: 29-30, April 21, 1936.

"Anguished cries of senile writers who do not want to be forgotten." Reprinted in his *From Left to Right*, p. 74-80. Poetic paraphrase by William J. Shultz. *New Masses* 19: 22, May 19, 1936.

KRONENBERGER, LOUIS. H. L. Mencken. New Republic 88: 243-245, Oct. 7, 1936.

Analysis of HLM's many aspects as revolutionary, diagnostician, stylist and popularizer. Fifth in series of Revaluations. Reprinted in *After the Genteel Tradition*, edited by Malcom Cowley (New York, Norton, 1937. p. 100-111).

SELLERS, CHARLES W. Henry L. Mencken, a Skeleton Sketch. Genesis, a Magazine for Creative Youth [Detroit]. p. 3-4, 14-15, Feb., 1936.

Biography and evaluation.

TODAYS PROFILE—H. L. Mencken: He Likes To Stir up the Animals, Journalist of First Rank, Who Shuns Praise and Whose Home is a Literary Shrine. Boston Evening Transcript, Sept. 28, 1936, p. 11.

WHITE, ELWYN BROOKS. H. L. Mencken Meets a Poet in the West Side Y.M.C.A. Saturday Review of Literature 14: 10-11, May 9, 1936.

Imaginary interview on HLM's three abominations: poetry, religion and Franklin D. Roosevelt. Reprinted in his *The Fox of Peapack & Other Poems*, p. 39-44.

WILLIAMS, WILLIAM CARLOS. The American Language, 4th edition North American Review 242: 181-184, Autumn, 1936.

HLM's use of words appraised by a noted poet. Reprinted in his *Selected Essays* (New York, Random House, 1954. p. 170-174).

1937

HIS MARYLAND: Mencken, Clown-Turned-Lawyer, Offers New State Constitution. Literary Digest 123: 8-9, May 1, 1937. port.

Resumé and remarks on "A Proposed New Constitution." *See,* Baltimore *Sun,* April 12, 1937, Newspaper Work section.

ROOT, E. MERRILL. Aesthetic Puritans. Christian Century 54: 1043-1045, Aug. 25, 1937.

HLM and aesthetic puritanism; always was "one of the most consistent and naive" puritans.

SHIGEMI, H. The American Language, 4th edition. Studies in English Literature [Tokyo] p. 631-633, Oct., 1937.

Significance of work from Japanese point of view.

1938

ANGOFF, CHARLES. Mencken Twilight: Another Forgotten Man— That Enfant Terrible of Our Era of Nonsense. North American Review 246: 216-232, Winter, 1938-39.

Only the ghost of a former immortal remains.

ANTIC DOTS. Time 31: 44, Feb. 21, 1938. port.

Comments on odd editorial page of the Baltimore *Evening Sun,* Feb. 10, that was made up of 1,000,075 dots. *See* "Object Lesson," in Newspaper Work.

GLICKSBERG, CHARLES I. H. L. Mencken: The Dean of Iconoclasts. Calcutta Review April, 1938. 28 p. reprint.

Detailed evaluation of his work and influence.

HERZBERG, MAX J. A Gallery of Philologists. Word Study 14: 1-4, Nov., 1938.

"Passage of arms" with Prof. Cabell Greet.

MONCHAK, STEPHEN J. H. L. Mencken Rides Again, Rowelling U.S. Newspapers. Editor & Publisher 71: 9, 14, Sept. 10, 1938. port.

Interview "voicing same objections . . . but there are some soft words among the hard . . . news covered better . . . advises beginners to work hard and learn."— (Subtitle) The article caused an outburst of replies: "U.S. Editorial Page Appraised by Leaders of Journalism. Mencken Broadside at Weakest Page Answered" p. 3, 20, Sept. 17, and p. 38, Oct. 1, 1938.

ARTICLES

1939

ESPEY, WILLARD H. The Baltimore "Sun" Goes Down. Nation 148: 143-146, Feb. 4, 1939.

Historical review of Sunpapers political policy and HLM's influence (anti-liberal).

MINTON, ARTHUR and EMANUEL BLOOM. Are We Like This? English Journal (College edition) 28: 383-393, May, 1939.

"Undertakes to defend both college and high school teachers of English against the attacks of a well known critic" voiced in *The American Language,* 4th edition.

WAR CORRESPONDENCE—1939. Editor & Publisher 72: 24, Sept. 23, 1939.

Editorial remarks on HLM's editorial "False News" in the Sunday *Sun,* Sept. 17, p. 12.

1940

DANIELS, JONATHAN. Nonage of an Iconoclast. Saturday Review of Literature 21: 6, Jan. 27, 1940. ports.

Nostalgic recall by a contemporary, evoked by *Happy Days.*

KRETZMAN, O. P. Bach, Mencken, and Beer. Cresset 3: 13-14, April 1940.

Disagrees with "the most unusual essay in musical criticism," HLM's article on the Bethlehem Bach Choir in the Baltimore *Evening Sun,* May 21, 1928. The magazine's regular music critic, Walter A. Hansen answered Kretzman: "Music and Music Makers, Some Reactions to Henry L. Mencken's Divagations on Bach and Beer," p. 25-28, June, 1940.

OWENS, HAMILTON. Happy Days. Maryland Historical Magazine 35: 81-82, March, 1940.

This book review, and the succeeding one on *Newspaper Days* (36: 444-445, Dec., 1941) are the only published articles written about HLM by the editor-in-chief of the Sunpapers and one of HLM's closest friends.

RASCOE, BURTON. Mencken, Nathan and Cabell. American Mercury 49: 362-368, March, 1940.

Evaluation of their styles, natures and goals, and compared to younger writers.

1941

MENCKEN AT 61. Time 38: 106-108, Oct. 20, 1941. port.

Reviews past career and tells of current activities (*Newspaper Days*).

SALPETER, HARRY. The Human Touch: Menckenian Memories. American Hebrew 148: 7, 11 April 18, 1941. port.

Jewish boys at Knapp's School as recalled in *Happy Days.*

WILLS, ROSS B. John Fante. Common Ground 1: 84-90, Spring, 1941.

HLM's great influence on the career and thinking of Fante.

1942

EASTMAN, MAX. About H. L. Mencken. American Mercury 55: 242-247, Aug., 1942.

Appraisal of his prejudices, humor and brain power (*New Dictionary of Quotations*).

JOHNSON, GERALD WHITE. Mencken as Collector of the Telling Phrase. [Baltimore] Sun, April 19, 1942, Section 1, p. 1, Full page.

McMANUS, GEORGE WILLIAM, JR. H. L. Mencken Reviews Literary Experiences. Greyhound [Loyola College, Balto.] 15: 3, Feb. 13, 1942. port.

Interview with school paper editor, tells of his own working methods and gives advice to would-be writers.

1943

COWLEY, MALCOLM. Mencken and Mark Twain. New Republic 108: 321-322, March 8, 1943.

Comparison of their content and concepts, and the influence of Twain on forming HLM's "style and literary picture of himself."

KRUTCH, JOSEPH WOOD. Mr. Mencken and the Good Old Days. Nation 156: 456-457, March 27, 1943.

Mainly a discussion of HLM's political philosophy (*Heathen Days*).

1944

HONCE, CHARLES. Mencken Discusses War Slang Output. [Baltimore] Sun, June 11, 1944, Section A, p. 12.

1946

BARZUN, JACQUES. Mencken's America Speaking. Atlantic Monthly 177: 62-65, Jan., 1946.

Wide implications of *The American Language,* revealing the national psyche.

BUTTERFIELD, ROGER. Mr. Mencken Sounds Off. Life 21: 45-46, 48, 51-52, Aug. 5, 1946. port.

In interview at Stork Club, HLM voices opinions on public questions and politics.

CROSS, LESLIE. H. L. Mencken, Vitriolic Sage of Baltimore. Milwaukee Journal, Feb. 1, 1946, editorial page.

ARTICLES

DEYO, FELIX. Sage of Baltimore Really a Frustrated Musician. Musical America 66: 19, 292, Feb., 1946. port. (by Carl Van Vechten)

"H. L. Mencken, enthusiastic amateur who has been playing chamber music for 40 years, ventures some views (his own) on the tonal art."— (Subtitle)

GILLIS, JAMES M. American GBS? Catholic World 163: 486-489, Sept., 1946.

Section of article "What Shaw Really Taught." Comparisons of HLM and Shaw as iconoclasts, atheists and literary ruffians.

MOREHOUSE, WARD. Quiet Chat. New York Sun Digest p. 13-14, July, 1946.

Luncheon interview at the Maryland Club, during which HLM airs his views on current politics. Reprint of "H. L. Mencken Speaks a Piece," New York *Sun*, June 5, 1946.

SORRY LOT. Time 47: 68, Jan. 14, 1946. port.

HLM criticizes the poor reporting of World War II war correspondents.

1947

BATHTUB HOAX PAYS OFF IN BEER FOR MENCKEN, Case a Month Is Dividend on Gag Story. [Toronto] Globe and Mail, Jan. 4, 1947, p. 3.

BOYLE, HAL. Profile of a Gray-Haired Man. [Philadelphia] Evening Bulletin, July 30, 1947, p. 19.

HONCE, CHARLES. Few Have All of Mencken's Works, Prolific Writer Has Turned Out Huge Amount of Material—First Book, in Verse, Rarest. Boston Sunday Post, Aug. 24, 1947, p. 25.

INTERESTING PEOPLE: FIRST. American 144: 101, Sept., 1947. port. (by Jack Manning)

Thumbnail sketch of HLM as spoofer, and note acknowledging his launching of the oldest and most popular feature of this magazine.

SHOCK TREATMENT. Time 50: 76, Oct. 27, 1947. port.

Opinion on "what is wrong with the editorial page," as stated at First National Conference of Editorial Writers. *See* Speeches . . . 1947.

1948

BOYLE, HAROLD V. Mencken Is Neutral; He's 'Against 'Em All.' [Baltimore] Evening Sun, June 21, 1948, p. 3.

DANIEL, JAMES. Whatever Happened to—H. L. Mencken? Revival

of Interest Reported in Work of "Sage of Baltimore." Pittsburgh Press, March 14, 1948, p. 13.

DAVIDSON, SPENCER L. The "'Free Lance," Mencken vs. Puritanism. Evergreen [Loyola College, Balto.] 4: 4-11, Spring, 1948.

Review of ideas contained in the column.

HELLMAN, GEOFFREY T. Alfred A. Knopf. New Yorker 24: 44-48, 50-56; 36-40, 42, 48; 40-42, 44-47, Nov. 20, 27, Dec. 4, 1948.

New Yorker profile contains many references to HLM's personality and work. Reprinted in book form and privately issued.

KEMLER, EDGAR. Lion of the Twenties, H. L. Mencken as Editor. Gardens, Houses and People [Balto.] 23: 13-15, 56, Feb., 1948.

Portrait of HLM as author-editor just emerging as a national character. This article was incorporated into his *The Irreverent Mr. Mencken.*

MR. MENCKEN AGAIN. Newsweek 31: 89-91, April 5, 1948. ports. (one as cover)

Personal sketch, upon appearance of Supplement II of *The American Language.*

"WE WANT MENCKEN." New York Times Book Review, July 4, 1948, p. 10.

Draft Mencken for Supplement III of *The American Language.*

1949

THE "AMERICAN SCENE" OWES MUCH TO MENCKEN'S LABORS. Saturday Evening Post 222: 10, 12, Dec. 17, 1949.

The *Chrestomathy* is a further reminder of HLM's great educational service.

BENDINER, ROBERT. From Mencken to Pegler. Nation 169: 206-207, Aug. 27, 1949.

Sad to note "how far we have slipped into nervous conformity since the 20s."

HARRISS, ROBERT PRESTON. Life with Mencken. Gardens, Houses and People [Balto.] 24: 21-23, May, 1949. port. (by Bodine)

Reminiscences of the days when HLM was in charge of the editorial page of the Baltimore Evening *Sun.*

JOHNSON, GERALD WHITE. Mencken, Scholar, Wit, One Man Tornado. New York Herald Tribune Books, p. 1, 10-11, June 26, 1949. port.

ARTICLES

"Best assesses HLM's place in American culture," Goldman, *Rendezvous with Destiny* p. 314. (*A Mencken Chrestomathy*).

KRONENBERGER, LOUIS. An Ill-Will Tour of the American Mind. Saturday Review of Literature 32: 38, 40, 42, Aug. 6, 1949.

Evaluation of the career and influence of "this once fiercest of dragons . . . slain by his own crusade." Reprinted in his *The Republic of Letters,* p. 236-243.

LARDNER, JOHN. Chrestomathy à la Maryland. New Yorker 25: 53-54, 57, July 9, 1949.

HLM's influence and work as a serious writer and literary entertainer (*A Mencken Chrestomathy*).

WHO *WAS* MENCKEN? Colliers 124: 8, Nov. 19, 1949. port. (col. cartoon by Al Hirschfeld)

This Armistice Day editorial based on gist of war articles of "the once unquestioned spokesman of American intellectual life."

1950

BREADY, JAMES HALL. Mencken Has a Birthday. [Baltimore] Sun, Sept. 10, 1950, Section A, p. 3.

BREADY, JAMES HALL. Mencken Observes 70th Birthday; Peale [Museum] Plans Menckeniana Display. [Baltimore] Evening Sun, Sept. 12, 1950, editorial page.

FRANCIS, RAYMOND L. Mark Twain and H. L. Mencken. Prairie Schooner 24: 31-40, Spring, 1950.

Comparison of their similarities and "identity of views and things satirized."

H. L. MENCKEN TO BE HONORED BY ARTS AND LETTERS ACADEMY. [Baltimore] Sun, Feb. 17, 1950, p. 32.

The only medal HLM ever willingly accepted was the Gold Medal upon graduating from the Polytechnic Institute. This one was foisted upon him before he had the opportunity to reject it. "Presentation of the Gold Medal for Essays and Criticism" in absentia by Mark Van Doren (*Proceedings of the American Academy of Arts and Letters and the National Institute of Arts and Letters,* II. ser., no. 1. New York, Spiral Press, 1951. p. 13-14). "Mencken Given Gold Medal for Essays and Criticism" Baltimore *Sun,* May 26, 1950, p. 40.

IN THE MERCURY'S OPINION. American Mercury 71: 665-667, Dec., 1950.

Efforts to recreate the *New Mercury* in the Mencken image.

LERNER, MAX. Mencken. New York Post, Oct. 19, 1950, p. 30.

MANCHESTER, WILLIAM. Mencken and the Mercury. Harper's 201: 65-73, Aug., 1950.

Account of HLM's editorship of the *Smart Set* and the founding of the *American Mercury*.

MANCHESTER, WILLIAM. Mencken and the Twenties; with decorations characteristic of the era by John Held, Jr. Harper's 201: 62-72, July, 1950. illus.

Impact of HLM on the national scene; description of his personality.

MANCHESTER, WILLIAM. Private Life of a Literary Fireball: 1. His Ailments. II. His Automobile. Garden, Houses and People [Balto.] 25: 17, Nov., 1950.

Two vignettes from the manuscript of the forthcoming biography *Disturber of the Peace*.

MONFREID, WALTER. When Mencken Berated the "Boobs," with Death of Bernard Shaw, 70 Year Old Baltimore Writer and Editor, Who Recently Won a Bout with Serious Illness, Survives as Outstanding Iconoclast of the Old School. Milwaukee Journal, Nov. 14, 1950, p. 24.

PRINGLE, HENRY F. The Irreverent Mr. Mencken. New Republic 123: 17-18, July 3, 1950.

Personal recollections of HLM's personality, his kindness and innate courtesy (Kemler biog.).

1951

ASBURY, HERBERT. The Day Mencken Broke the Law. American Mercury 73: 62-69, Oct., 1951.

Author of "Hatrack" tells story of its publication and ensuing excitement.

BROOKS, VAN WYCK. Mencken in Baltimore. American Scholar 20: 409-421, Autumn, 1951.

Assessment of influences upon HLM, and those he influenced in turn. Slightly expanded as chapter of his forthcoming *The Confident Years*, p. 455-474.

NATHAN, ADELE. Mr. Mencken and the Vagabond Players. Theatre Arts 35: 30, 90, June, 1951.

How HLM helped start Baltimore's little theatre and read one act plays for possible performance. For their opening, Nov. 2, 1916, the Vagabonds gave HLM's *The Artist*.

ARTICLES

1952

CARGILL, OSCAR. Mencken and the South. Georgia Review 6: 369-376, Winter, 1952.

HLM's attitudes toward the South; speculation on his role as their awakener.

SMITH, BEVERLY. The Curious Case of the President's Bathtub. Saturday Evening Post 225: 25, 91-94, Aug. 23, 1952. illus.

Investigation of legend started by HLM's hoax, and all its ramifications.

1953

BOUQUETS FOR MENCKEN; Symposium. Nation 177: 210-214, Sept. 12, 1953.

As birthday tribute the editor requested the following to state their recollections of HLM as editor and encourager of new talent: William Manchester, Harvey Fergusson, Stewart Holbrook, H. L. Davis, George Milburn, Gerald W. Johnson, James Branch Cabell, Ruth Suckow, Michael Gold, Thyra Sampter Winslow, and Idwal Jones.

GREET, WILLIAM CABELL. George Philip Krapp and Henry L. Mencken. Word Study 29: 1-4, Oct., 1953.

Compared as influential linguists.

1954

ANGOFF, CHARLES. The Inside View of Mencken's Mercury. New Republic 131: 18-22, Sept. 13, 1954. port.

HLM's assistant wants to "set the record straight," writes of HLM's strong points and foibles "that dominated the magazine in its days of great influence"; his innovations and features, and above all his personality.

COUSINS, NORMAN. Our Times and the Mercury. Saturday Review of Literature 37: 22, June 12, 1954.

Evaluation of the "brilliant, cold" magazine on its thirtieth birthday.

FARRELL, JAMES T. Dr. Mencken: Criticus Americanus. New World Writing #6. p. 64-76, Fall, 1954.

HLM as political and literary critic. Reprinted in his *Reflection at Fifty,* p. 42-57.

KLOSS, GERALD. When Mencken Was Our No. 1 Firebrand, Babbitts, Legionnaires, Bible Belt, Stuffed Shirts Were Favorite Targets for His Vituperation, but His Long Range Reputation as a Scholar Rests on His Book "The American Language." Milwaukee Journal, Jan. 27, 1954, p. 24.

STONE, EDWARD. Baltimore's Friendly Dragon. Georgia Review 8: 347-353, Fall, 1954.

> Visit to HLM while writing his graduate thesis on Nietzsche. *See* Works about H. L. Mencken, Books and Pamphlets, 1937.

1955

ADAMS, J. DONALD. Speaking of Books. New York Times Book Review, Sept. 11, 1955, p. 2.

> HLM considered as irritant and tonic. In his column of March 6, 1955, HLM's *New Dictionary of Quotations* is compared to Stevenson and Bartlett.

BONE, JAMES. The Sage of Baltimore. Manchester Guardian, Sept. 10, 1955, p. 5.

BREADY, JAMES HALL. The Man in the Back Yard, by Jim Bready. New York Post, Sept. 18, 1955, Week-End Magazine Section, p. 2.

CHAMBERLAIN, JOHN. A Reviewer's Notebook. Freeman 5: 749-750, Nov., 1955.

> Analyses HLM's "Olympian attitude" as humorist and craftsman (*Vintage Mencken*).

COOKE, ALISTAIR. The Baltimore Fox. Saturday Review 38: 13, 63-64, Sept. 10, 1955. port. (by H. George Aschaffenburg)

> A seventy-fifth birthday tribute. "This essay is drawn from the introduction to 'The Vintage Mencken' . . . to be published September 12, 1955." *See* also Manchester below.

HARRISS, ROBERT PRESTON. H. L. Mencken at Seventy-Five. Gardens, Houses and People [Balto.] 30: 12-13, Aug., 1955.

> The Harriss family pays a visit to HLM at 1524 Hollins Street. Further "Birthday Observations" (p. 13, Sept., 1955) point out that the characteristic smile is missing from the Bodine portrait.

HARRISS, ROBERT PRESTON. Summer in the Country. Gardens, Houses and People [Balto.] 30: 11, July, 1955.

> Although the Maryland countryside has changed, some rural areas remain just as described in *Happy Days*; long quote.

HUTCHENS, JOHN K. A Birthday Salute to Henry L. Mencken. New York Herald Tribune Book Review, Sept. 11, 1955, p. 2.

JOHNSON, GERALD WHITE. Mencken—His Laughter Cleared the Air [Baltimore Sunday] Sun, Sept. 11, 1955, Section A, p. 1. port. (by Bodine)

> Portrait and evaluation by a close friend of many years.

ARTICLES

Kemler, Edgar. The Bright Twilight of H. L. Mencken. New York Times Magazine, Sept. 11, 1955, p. 14, 44, 47, 49 port.

"The acerb Baltimore author and editor, 75 tomorrow, has made a comeback from his illness and finds once again that life can be enjoyed."— (Subtitle) A List of "Menckenisms," p. 44. Reply in letter by Ed Schindler, Oct. 2, 1955, p. 6.

McKelway, St. Clair. Thorns without Roses. New Yorker 31: 217-221, Nov. 19, 1955.

Review of *Vintage Mencken*, contains numerous quotes, and emphasizes his timeliness and humor.

Manchester, William. H. L. Mencken at Seventy-Five; America's Sam Johnson. Saturday Review 38: 11-13, 64-65, Sept. 10, 1955. port. (as cover)

Salute on seventy-fifth birthday. Compared to eighteenth-century critic, essayist and lexicographer.

Rayford, J. L. Fourteen Years to H. L. Mencken. Amateur Book Collector 6: 1-2, Dec., 1955.

Brief reminiscences of a visit with HLM.

... Remember me? Newsweek 46: 68-69, Sept. 12, 1955. port.

Brief biography on seventy-fifth birthday.

Sinclair, Upton. A Letter. New World Writing #8. p. 280-281, 1955.

Letter to James T. Farrell about HLM.

1956

Bode, Carl. Henry Louis Mencken. *In* Memoriam. Society for the History of the Germans in Maryland [Balto.] Report 29: 70-73, 1956.

Summation of his career and influence. Also contains "A Mencken Reminiscence," by Adolf Eduard Zucker (who does not claim to have known HLM personally) p. 68-69; a concise bibliography, p. 69; and "On First Seeing a Cut of H. L. Mencken," poem, by H. F. Manchester, reprinted from the Boston *Globe*.

Brogan, D. W. H. L. Mencken. Spectator 196: 212, Feb. 17, 1956.

Appreciation of his contribution to American culture, as obituary.

Brooke, Bissell. America's New Literary Cradle. Hobbies 61: 106-107, 124, Nov., 1956. illus.

Mostly description of Mencken Room at Enoch Pratt Free Library.

WORKS ABOUT H. L. M.

CHAMBERLIN, WILLIAM HENRY. Mencken, Scourge of Boobs. New Leader 39: 29, March 19, 1956.

Considered as "supreme prose caricaturist"; many quotations.

CHESLOCK, LOUIS. Mencken—The Musician. [Baltimore] Sun, Sept., 9, 1956, Section A, p. 6.

First violinist of the Saturday Night Club and professor of the Peabody Conservatory of Music, discusses HLM's music appreciation and performance. Reprinted in *Peabody Notes* 12: 1-4. Autumn, 1957.

CONNOLLY, FRANCIS X. H. L. Mencken, 1880-1956. America, National Catholic Weekly Review 94: 532, Feb. 11, 1956.

Review of career and ideas, for he was the "sum of all qualities he attacked."

COOKE, ALISTAIR. Last Happy Days of H. L. Mencken. Atlantic 197: 33-38, May, 1956. port. (as cover)

Account of HLM's coverage of the Wallace convention, 1948. Discussion by H. M. Truby 198: 23, Aug., 1956.

FARRELL, JAMES T. Personal Memories of H. L. Mencken. New Leader 39: 7, Feb. 13, 1956.

Account of a visit to HLM after 1948.

GORDON, DOUGLAS HUNTLY. A Last Glimpse of Mencken. Maryland Historical Magazine 51: 337-340, Dec., 1956.

A last visit paid to HLM, accompanied by André Siegfried.

H. L. MENCKEN. Commonweal 63: 474, Feb. 10, 1956.

Confirming a 1928 editorial by Williams (*See* above, 1928) that Mencken's attacks on religion "cannot but help the unending work of the Church."

HACKETT, FRANCIS. Chicago's Opportunity. New Republic 134: 21-22, June 25, 1956.

Chicago failed to live up to HLM's hopes of 1920.

HARRISS, ROBERT PRESTON. Mencken: A Home Town Review. Gardens, Houses and People [Balto.] 31: 10-11, July, 1956.

Angoff biography better than rumored; voices objection to emendations and updating of *Minority Report*. Letter of clarification by August Mencken (p. 10, Aug.) explaining how notes were found and HLM personally corrected and amended them. Further discussion by Harriss (p. 10–11, Aug.). Theme of social inequality runs through book (p. 12–13, June).

HARRISS, ROBERT PRESTON. Mencken Memoranda. Gardens, Houses and People [Balto.] 31: 10-11, Feb., 1956. port.

Rough notes on name, dress, food, habits, etc., by "one who saw him often, knew him well, and enjoyed him hugely." Presentation of Schattenstein portrait, p. 26. Letter from Alfred A. Knopf, p. 5, March.

HAZLITT, HENRY. Mencken: A Retrospect. Newsweek 47: 90, Feb. 20, 1956.

Review of HLM's political and economic opinions by his successor as editor of the *American Mercury*.

HORCHLER, R. T. Beleaguered Reputation of a Great Iconoclast. Commonweal 64: 422-423, July 27, 1956.

Evaluation of polemicist of the past (Angoff biography and *Minority Report*).

HOWE, IRVING. A Comedian Playing Hamlet. New Republic, 134: 17-18, May 21, 1956.

HLM never veered from his original role and "really believed everything he said." (*Minority Report*)

JOHNSON, GERALD WHITE. H. L. Mencken, 1880-1956. New Republic 134: 18, Feb. 6, 1956.

Capsule appraisal. "Something was subtracted from American freedom when Mencken died." A longer intimate portrait "of a close friend as known to a relatively small circle in Baltimore" in *Saturday Review* 39: 12-13, Feb. 11, 1956. port.

KRUTCH, JOSEPH WOOD. This Was Mencken, An Appreciation. Nation 182: 109-110, Feb. 11, 1956.

HLM's work will live on as the best prose of the twentieth century.

McHUGH, ROBERT P. Last Days of Mencken. American Mercury 83: 17-20, July, 1956.

"Brave warrier of rock-ribbed resistance determined to wring dry from life every promise it can conceivably contain."

MATHIS, MARJORIE. With Rites "Rich in Irony," Pratt Opens Mencken Room. [Baltimore] Sun, April 18, 1956, p. 42.

MENCKEN IS STILL A STORM CENTER. [Baltimore] Sun, Feb. 29, 1956, p. 38.

Maryland Senate Resolution on death of HLM brings old feuds to light as one Southern Maryland and four Eastern Shore Senators vote against the Joint Resolution of the General Assembly.

MORGENSTERN, GEORGE. Mencken's Zoo. Chicago Sunday Tribune, April 22, 1956, Section 1, p. 20.

"Mencken could survey the whole passing show—politics, social phenomena, literature—and what he saw never failed to please [amuse] him."

MORRIS, JOE ALEX. Nimble Axeman. Saturday Review 39: 21, May 26, 1956.

"A most pursuant giant-killer leaves a fascinating encephalograph." (*Minority Report*)

MUST WE BE SAVED BY THE GOP? New Republic 134: 7, Feb. 6, 1956.

Editorial expressing HLM's probable reactions to the *Nation's* editorial of Jan. 28, advising liberals to refrain from supporting Adlai Stevenson.

NEW TRIBUTE TO MENCKEN: Boston and Chicago Papers Eulogize Noted Author. [Baltimore] Sun, Jan. 31, 1956, p. 4.

NOCK, SAMUEL ALBERT. H.L.M. College and University 31: 354–355, Spring, 1956.

Editor expresses his tribute of HLM as teacher.

[OBITUARIES IN NEWSPAPERS.] Jan. 30, 1956.

Associated Press. Henry L. Mencken Succumbs; was 75. [Lynchburg] News p. 1.

Cooke, Alistair. Death of H. L. Mencken, Newspaperman and Philologist. Manchester Guardian p. 1.

Greene, Lawrence. Mr. Mencken of The Sun. Washington Daily News p. 25.

H. L. Mencken, 75, Dies in Baltimore. New York Times p. 1.

Hutchinson, Anne W. H. L. Mencken, Author, Dies At 75. [Baltimore] Sun p. 1.

Literary Output Had Wide Range. New York Times p. 20.

McHugh, Robert. Mencken a Genial Host to End; Looked Forward to Next Book. New York Times p. 20.

McManus, John. Mencken the Witty Ran Gamut from "Bad Boy" to "The Sage." Detroit News p. 30.

Mayor and Governor Express Regret of City and State. [Baltimore] Sun p. 4.

Mencken to British a Strange U.S. Species. [Baltimore] Sun p. 4.

Owens, Hamilton. H. L. Mencken's Pungent Pen a Challenge to Orthodoxy. [Baltimore] Sun p. 1.

United Press. Forgive Some Sinner and Wink Your Eye, The Sage of Baltimore Is Dead. Washington Daily News p. 4.

O'HARA, JOHN. Appointment with O'Hara. Colliers 137: 6, 8, April 13, 1956. port. (by Al Hirschfeld)

HLM compared to Will Rogers; although HLM operated on a higher level, their "acts were essentially similar."

PICKREL, PAUL. Captive Critics. Harper 231: 91-92, July, 1956.

HLM compared to Ring Lardner; they "thought of themselves as most at odds with their environment, seem aftertimes most representative of it, or even its victims." (*Minority Report*)

ARTICLES

POUDER, GEORGE HARRY. Mencken. Baltimore 49: 14, Feb., 1956.

Executive Vice-President of the Baltimore Association of Commerce, and editor of its magazine, considers HLM as one of the city's "most effective promotional devices."

PREZZOLINI, GUISEPPE. Mencken l'Iconoclasta. L'Illustrazione Italiana 83: 37, 74, March, 1956. port.

Considered as critic of American life and mores by the noted editor, who once considered issuing *Prejudices* in Italian translation.

RUBIN, PHILIP. H. L. Mencken and the Jews. Congress Weekly 23: 6–8, Feb. 20, 1956.

HLM's attitudes, which at times were misunderstood, for his goal was extreme individualism.

SCHMIDT, JOHN C. The [Enoch Pratt Free] Library's Mencken Room. [Baltimore] Sun, April 15, 1956, Section A, p. 3.

UNCOMMON SCOLD. Time 67: 38, Feb. 6, 1956. port.

Salient achievements and personal traits.

YARLING, BASS. Mencken and Politics. New Republic 135: 20–21, Oct. 22, 1956.

Carnival of Buncombe adds to legend, if not to lustre.

1957

ANGOFF, CHARLES. From Mencken to Maguire, the Tragedy of the American Mercury. Anti-Defamation League Bull. 3 p. May, 1957. ports.

The magazine has gone from progress and liberalism to complete reactionary extremes.

BENDINER, ROBERT. Mencken Blunderbuss. Reporter 16: 42–43, Jan. 24, 1957.

HLM compared to other political writers (*Carnival of Buncombe*).

CHESLOCK, LOUIS. At Home with Henry Mencken. Gardens, Houses and People [Balto.] 32: 12–13, Aug. 1957.

An old friend presents an intimate vignette of HLM's later years, spent in the company of his brother August.

COVINGTON, ROY. The Art of Christian Winking. Charlotte [North Carolina] Observer, February 4, 1957, Section B, p. 1.

"But one reader, Dr. Raymond Adams, saw in the epitaph a sermon and put it down on paper."

WORKS ABOUT H. L. M.

JOHNSON, GERALD WHITE. Oh, For Mencken Now. New Republic 137: 11, Sept. 30, 1957.

How sad "the Old Defender of freedom and intelligence" would be by the removal of *Huckleberry Finn* from high school reading lists by New York City's Board of Education. Charles Angoff wrote a rebuttal, pointing out HLM's Nazi sympathies, "Mencken and the Wrong Side" (p. 3, 23, Nov. 18). Arthur Schlesinger, "Mencken and Prejudice" (p. 23, Dec. 16) denies crypto-racial charges, presenting as evidence HLM's support of the Wagner-Costigan Anti-Lynch Bill. Angoff further upholds HLM's pro-German leanings in "Was Mencken Anti-Semitic?" (138: 3, 23, Jan. 13, 1958), Guy Forgue joins "The Mencken Debate" showing that HLM's "entire life was devoted to defending the freedom of thought and writing." (p. 3, 22-23, Feb. 17, 1958)

NATHAN, GEORGE JEAN. The Happiest Days of H. L. Mencken. Esquire 48: 146–150, Oct. 25, 1957.

The gala years of the *Smart Set,* when all was fun, even the grousing. Reprinted in *The Armchair Esquire,* edited by Arnold Gingrich and L. Rust Hills (New York, Putnam, 1958. p. 340-349).

1958

CHESLOCK, LOUIS. Mencken as a Talker. Gardens, Houses and People [Balto.] 34: 13–14, Sept. 1958. port. (NBC broadcast, 1934)

HLM as witty and brilliant conversationalist and impromptu speechmaker.

DURR, ROBERT ALLEN. The Last Days of H. L. Mencken. Yale Review 48: 58–77, Autumn, 1958.

Intimate description of HLM and his brother August, by a Johns Hopkins graduate student who saw them almost daily. Reprinted in *Best Articles and Stories Magazine* 3: 40-48, May, 1959.

HARRISS, ROBERT PRESTON. Mencken on Babies. Gardens, Houses and People [Balto.] 34: 9, Aug., 1958.

HLM once confessed to have written text of *What You Ought to Know About Your Baby.*

HARRISS, ROBERT PRESTON. Mencken's Poetry Plagued Him Plenty. Baltimore American, Oct. 5, 1958, Section HL, p. 11.

SMITH, HARRY ALLEN. The Most Unforgettable Character I've Met. Reader's Digest 73:93–97, Dec. 1958. port.

Profile sketch of HLM's personality.

1959

COWING, CEDRIC B. H. L. Mencken the Case of the "Curdled" Progressive. Ethics 69: 255–267, July, 1959. bibliog.

ARTICLES

HLM analyzed as the "epitome of waning progressivism," a study undertaken to affirm David Riesman's thesis expounded in *The Lonely Crowd.*

FORGUE, GUY. La Carrière de H. L. Mencken et les Critiques. Études Anglaises 12: 112–123, Avril-Juin, 1959.

How critics have viewed HLM through the decades.

HARRISS, ROBERT PRESTON. Was H. L. Mencken Anti-Semitic?—No. Baltimore American, June 7, 1959, Section AL, p. 7, "Man About Town."

This article as well as two later ones ("He Derided Life and Made it Gay" *Baltimore American,* June 21, 1959, Sec. AL, p. 5; "Letters to the Editor, H. L. Mencken," London *Times Literary Supplement,* July 3, 1959, p. 399) were written in response to the controversy raised by the review of the Angoff biography in the *Times Literary Supplement* on March 13, 1959.

KNOPF, ALFRED A. For Henry, with Love: My Friendship with Mencken. Atlantic 203: 50–54, May, 1959. port.

A personality profile by his publisher and dear friend.

1960

BABCOCK, C. MERTON. Profiles of Noted Linguists: Henry Louis Mencken. Word Study 36: 1–4, Dec., 1960.

HLM's contribution to philology.

FITZGERALD, STEPHEN E. The Mencken Myth. Saturday Review 43: 13–15, 71, Dec. 17, 1960. ports. (by M. Kuhn and Covarrubias)

An attempt to search beyond the myth for the real man, by a former co-worker on the Baltimore *Evening Sun.*

GARDNER, RUFUS HALLETTE. The Reel vs. the Real Mencken. [Baltimore] Sun, Oct. 23, 1960, Section A, p. 2.

How different the actual man was from his supposititious portrayal in "Inherit the Wind." *See* Miscellany, Lawrence.

PINDELL, WATSON F. and ALBERT W. DOWLING. The First Mencken Work the Public Ever Saw. [Baltimore] Sunday Sun Magazine, Jan. 24, 1960. illus., ports. (front. by Bodine) facsims.

School essays and prize won at Baltimore Polytechnic Institute. Further elucidation in letter by August Mencken (Feb. 21, p. 27); reply by Dowling (March 20, p. 21).

WALT, JAMES. Morning, Noon and Night. Michigan Quarterly Review 66: 138–145, Feb. 27, 1960.

"Preview of a biography." Second installment "Shadows at Noon: Mencken in the Twenties" p. 220-229, May 21, 1960.

WEINTRAUB, STANLEY. Apostate Apostle: H. L. Mencken as Shavophile and Shavophobe. Educational Theatre Journal 12: 184–190, Oct., 1960.

HLM's changing attitudes toward George Bernard Shaw, traced by the editor of the *Shaw Bulletin*.

1961

ADAMS, J. DONALD. Speaking of Books. New York Times Book Review, Aug. 6, 1961, p. 2.

Tribute to the "indefatigable scholar" of the American language.

GINGRICH, ARNOLD. How To Become the Second-Best Authority on Almost Anything. Esquire 55: 6, April, 1961.

Recollections of an evening spent with HLM and Dreiser.

PORTRAITS AND CARICATURES

Nikol Schattenstein painted the best known portrait of HLM, which was also his favorite. It shows him in a pensive mood, informally dressed in the red suspenders Rudolph Valentino gave him and a pair of red slacks. The latter was an artistic invention, as HLM never owned such a garment. The portrait now hangs in the Mencken Room of the Enoch Pratt Free Library. The Library also owns photographic studies by Aldine Aubrey Bodine, Robert Francis Kniesche, Jack Engeman, and several albums collected and assembled by HLM. The best known bust is a small caricature sculptured by Annette Rosenshine, and formerly sold by E. Weyhe, New York art dealers.

Below are listed portraits and caricatures in books, but there has been no attempt to make a complete iconography of HLM. In other sections of this bibliography, portraits are always indicated, and the name of the artist given when known. For a list of portraits in some of the popular magazines, *see* successive issues of *Readers Guide to Periodical Literature,* under "Mencken."

AUERBACH-LEVY, WILLIAM. Is That Me? A Book About Caricature . . . assisted by Florence von Wien. [New York] Watson-Guptill [1947] Caricatures p. 104, 126.

The latter caricature was to be used as column head for the New York *World*; the other was drawn for an article for *Colliers,* March 16, 1929, showing HLM with Babe Ruth.

COVARRUBIAS, MIGUEL. The Prince of Wales, and Other Famous Americans. With a preface by Carl Van Vechten. New York, Knopf, 1925. Caricature [no. 8.]

THE DAVART COMPANY. Davart Collection of Photographic Portraits for Publication. [n.p., n.d.] 6 p. HLM listed on p. 4.

DAVIS, ROBERT E. Man Makes His Own Mask. Foreword by Benjamin DeCasseres. New York, Huntington Press, 1932. Photo port. p. 160.

H. L. MENCKEN: FANFARE . . . *See* "Books and Pamphlets About HLM," 1920.

Portrait photo by Meredith Janvier used as frontispiece, and opposite p. 20 a pencil drawing by William Wirtz, a Baltimore artist. Opposite p. 24 is a half-tone reproduction of McKee Barclay's caricature "An Inductive Synthesis," entitled "The Subconscious Mencken," which was locally rumored to be an exact likeness of the acerb author of the *Sun's* "Free Lance" column. Oddly enough, it never appeared as a device on this column, although it had been used in the Sunday *Sun*, pt. 3, p. 1, Nov. 3, 1913, and again on Oct. 18, 25, and Nov. 22, 1914. On its initial appearance it was noted as "Photograph by Bachrach."

HOUSE, JAMES. Fifty Drawings. Philadelphia, Centaur Press, 1930. Caricature, p. 16.

LYNCH, JOHN GILBERT BOHUN. A History of Caricature. Boston, Little, 1927. Caricature p. 96.

MARKEY, GENE. Literary Lights, a Book of Caricature. New York, Knopf, 1923. Caricatures p. 18, 40.

POSSELT, ERICH, *ed.* On Parade, Contributions by Prominent Authors, Caricatures by Eva Herrmann. New York, Coward-McCann, 1929. Caricature p. 107.

SANDBURG, CARL. Steichen, the Photographer. New York, Harcourt [1929] Photo. taken for Vanity Fair, untitled, unpaged.

SCHEEL, TED. The Face Is Familiar. New York, Beechhurst Press, 1951. Caricature p. 43.

SCHREIBER, GEORGES. Portraits and Self-Portraits. Boston, Houghton, 1936. Pen and ink sketch p. 106.

THE SUN, Baltimore. Program of the Tenth Anniversary Dinner, Nov. 9, 1929. Caricature by Bertha Kelley, p. 16.

TAYLOR, HELEN. H. L. Mencken. New York Herald Tribune Books, p. 6, May 24, 1942.

The page consists solely of four portraits.

ULMANN, DORIS, *comp.* A Portrait Gallery of American Editors, Being a Group of XLIII Likenesses. New York, Rudge, 1925. Photo port. p. 111.

MISCELLANEOUS

MUSICAL SETTINGS OF
H. L. MENCKEN'S WORKS

1900

THAT IS BUSINESS. Words by Henry Louis Mencken, music by Julian K. Schaefer. Baltimore, George Willig & Co., 1900.

Song in the popular vein.

1904

THE END OF IT ALL. Words by Henry Louis Mencken, music by Joseph M. Callahan. Baltimore   pyright by Mencken and Callahan, 1904. 5 p.

Song in the popular vein.

1919

ARABESQUE. Part Song for Men's Voices. Words by Henry L. Mencken from Ventures into Verse, music by Franz Carl Bornschein. Boston, Ditson, 1919. 10 p.

1923

SHIPS IN HARBOR; Ballad for Men's Voices. Words by H. L. Mencken, music by Franz Carl Bornschein. New York, J. Fisher, 1923. 12 p.

From an unsigned poem in *Smart Set* 45: 226, March 1915, though originally in *Ventures into Verse*.

1932

THOMPSON, RANDALL. Americana, a Sequence of Five Choruses for Mixed Voices. Text from The American Mercury. New York, E. C. Schirmer, 1932. 61 p.

Scored for four voices and piano.

BOOKS AND MUSIC
DEDICATED TO H. L. MENCKEN

BOOKS

BROWN, ROBERT CARLTON. Let There Be Beer! New York, Smith, 1932. 321 p.

COLBY, ELBRIDGE. Army Talk, a Familiar Dictionary of Soldier Speech, illustrated by Richard Hurd. Princeton, Princeton University Press, 1942. 332 p. illus.

DECASSERES, BENJAMIN. The Superman in America. Seattle, University of Washington, 1929. 30 p. (University of Washington Chapbooks, no. 30)

FANTE, JOHN. Full of Life. Boston, Little, 1952. 177 p.

HONCE, CHARLES. Tales from a Beekman Hill Library, and Other News Stories on Tunes, Travels, Tribulations and Trenchering; drawings by Joe Cunningham and Milt Morris. Mt. Vernon, N. Y. The Golden Eagle Press, 1952. 125 p. front., illus., ports.

JANVIER, MEREDITH. Baltimore in the Eighties and Nineties. Baltimore, Roebuck, 1933. 312 p. illus., ports.

JEROME, HELEN. The Secret of Women. New York, Boni, 1923. 144 p.; also London, Chapman & Bell, 1923. 240 p.

JOHNSON, BURGES. The Lost Art of Profanity; foreword by H. L. Mencken, drawings by Orson Lowell. Indianapolis, Bobbs-Merrill, 1948. 223 p. illus.

LEWIS, SINCLAIR. Elmer Gantry. New York, Harcourt, 1927. 432 p.; also London, Cape, 1927. 479 p.; and Berlin, Rowohlt, 1928. 638 p.

McCLURE, JOHN, *ed.* The Stag's Hornbook. New York, Knopf, 1918. 444 p.

MASTERS, EDGAR LEE. Poems of People. New York, Appleton-Century, 1936. 198 p.

NATHAN, GEORGE JEAN. The New American Credo, a Contribution Toward the Interpretation of the National Mind. Completely rev., and enl. ed. New York, Knopf, 1927. 223 p.

PEARL, RAYMOND. To Begin With, Being Prophylaxis Against Pedantry. New York, Knopf, 1927. 96 p. Reissued in 1930, 123 p.

PRINGLE, HENRY FOWLES. Big Frogs . . . ports. by Bry. New York, Vanguard, 1928. 276 p. ports.

RANDOLPH, VANCE. Down in the Holler: A Gallery of Ozark Folk Speech. Norman, University of Oklahoma Press, 1953. 320 p.

RHOIDES, EMMANUEL D. Papissa Joanna; translated from the original Greek by T. D. Kriton [pseud.] Athens, Govostis, 1935. 179 p. front. (port.)

SMITH, HARRY ALLEN. Rhubarb; drawings by Leo Hershfield. Garden City, N. Y., Doubleday, 1946. 301 p. illus.

SMITH, THOMAS ROBERT, *ed.* Poetic Erotica, a Collection of Rare and Curios Amatory Verse. New York, Pub. for subscribers only by Boni, 1921-22. 3v.

UNTERMEYER, LOUIS. Heavens; with a cover design and frontispiece by C. Bertram Hartman. New York, Harcourt, 1922. 153 p. front.

UNTERMEYER, LOUIS. Including Horace. New York, Harcourt, 1919. 158 p.

WALDMAN, MILTON. America Conquers Death. New York, Rudge, 1928. 30 p.

MISCELLANEOUS

MUSIC

CHESLOCK, LOUIS. Cinderella, ballet. Première May 11, 1946.

CHESLOCK, LOUIS. The Congo, chorus and orchestra, poem by Vachel Lindsay. Première Oct. 30, 1942. Winner in National Composers' Clinic Contest of University of Akron.

CHESLOCK, LOUIS. The Jewel Merchants, opera from play by James Branch Cabell. Première Feb. 26, 1940.

"The opera and ballet premières were given at the Peabody Conservatory of Music, Baltimore, both of which Mr. Mencken attended with me. The Congo was first given at the University of Akron, Ohio, and neither of us could attend." (Letter from Mr. Cheslock)

JANSSEN, WERNER. American Kaleidoscope, for string quartet. 1932.

Speak-easy and subway uproar used as motifs.

BOOKS, MAGAZINES AND MAGAZINE ARTICLES INSPIRED BY H. L. MENCKEN

A great number of writers were inspired and personally encouraged to continue writing by HLM's letters and by first being accepted for publication in the pages of his magazines. In this section, however, the word "inspired" has been used in a narrower sense, and only those works specifically referring to HLM in approbation or disapproval are listed.

BOOKS

BARNES, J. R. The Spirit of the Eastern Shore. Priv. print., 1933. 15 p.

> Reply to two of HLM's articles "in the Baltimore *Sun* insulting every man, woman and child of the Del-Mar-Va peninsula."

BARRY, GERALD, *comp.* This England. London, Geoffrey, 1933.

> "I hasten to salute the genius of Mr. Mencken, its editor, ['Americana' from the *American Mercury*] who first had the idea and whose idea we frankly copied in the *Week-End Review.*"

EMSLEY, CLAIRE. The True Physician. London, Stanley Paul, 1955.

> Contents inspired by HLM and title taken from an HLM quotation: "The true physician does not preach repentance; he offers absolution."

GRAHAM, JOHN E. The Way of a Skeptic. New York, MacVeagh, 1931.

> A Catholic priest from Baltimore answers *Treatise on the Gods.*

JANVIER, MEREDITH. Baltimore in the Eighties and Nineties. Baltimore, H. G. Roebuck, 1933.

> Encouraged by HLM to write this series, which first appeared in the Baltimore *Evening Sun.*

MISCELLANEOUS

JEROME, HELEN. The Secret of Women. London, Chapman & Hall; New York, Boni, 1923.

"The first woman arisen to explode or explain, or bring Mr. Mencken up to the way he should go" *In Defense of Women.*

MAURIN, GENEVIÈVE. Blue Baby. Préface du Dr. Olivier. Histoire de l'Hospital Johns Hopkins, d'après H. L. Mencken. Lisieux, Moriere, 1949.

History of Johns Hopkins Hospital based on HLM's series in the Baltimore *Evening Sun.*

MUNRO, CHARLES KIRKPATRICK. The True Woman; a Handbook for Husbands and Others. London, Howe [1932].

"This essay . . . was originally prompted by a book of Mr. Mencken's," *In Defense of Women.*

NATHAN, GEORGE JEAN. Monks Are Monks, a Diagnostic Scherzo. New York, Knopf, 129. p. 76-126.

A parody of HLM and Nathan, called H. G. Morton and John Greene Norton "the self-elected and enthusiastically self-indorsed . . . critics of everything."

OLIVIER STUART. Wine Journeys. New York, Duell [1949].

Credits HLM's insistence with the book's eventual publication.

PYLES, THOMAS. Words and Ways of American English. New York, Random House, 1952.

"My debt to Mencken is tremendous in the chapters dealing wtih the American vocabulary."

STEELE, ROBERT. One Man. New York, Kennerly, 1913.

HLM provided the title and revised the text of this autobiographical novel.

MAGAZINES

AESTHETE, 1925. no. 1. Feb., 1925.

A single issue, born of witty indignation and collective grudge against HLM.

BOZART; the Bi-Monthly Poetry Review. Sept./Oct., 1927—March/April, 1935. Atlanta, Ga.

Ernest Hartsock's reply to HLM's "The Sahara of the Bozart." Issued irregularly.

EL DELATOR [Cheltenham High School, Elkins Park, Pa.] v. 18 April, 1927.

The entire issue is a parody of the *American Mercury.*

MAIN STREET; a Magazine of American Opinion, Arts and Letters. March—July, 1929. New York, N. Y.

Opposed to HLM's destructive criticism, "we will endeavor to publish what is worthy and gallant in American arts and letters."

MERCURY [The College of the City of New York] v. 2 Dec., 1929.

The entire issue and its cover is a parody of the *American Mercury*.

THE PURPLE PARROT [Northwestern University] v. 8 March, 1928.

The entire issue and its cover is a parody of the *American Mercury*.

THE WIDOW [Cornell University] v. 33 Jan., 1927.

The entire issue and its cover is a parody of the *American Mercury*. Extremely clever.

MAGAZINE ARTICLES

CHASE, KATHERINE. On Keeping Christmas, by H. L. M*nck*n. Scrawl [Northwestern University] p. 14-16, Dec. 1927.

Parody of HLM's tone and style.

DUNNING, DECLA. In Search of Mr. Mencken. New Yorker 10: 112, Oct. 13, 1934.

Accepts a drunken date in order to meet the elusive Mencken. Not in out-of-town edition.

HALE, WILLIAM HARLAN. A Memorandum from H. L. Mencken to the President-Elect. Subject: On Entering the Millenium. Horizon 3: 70–71, Nov., 1960. port.

Political dicta written in HLM style.

HIRSHBERG, LEONARD KEENE. Artificial Sterilization by Active Immunity with Spermatozoon from the Same Species. New York Medical Journal 95: 335-336, Feb. 17, 1912.

A four-year-research program inspired by a discussion with HLM.

JOHNSON, NORMAN W. Mencken Comes to Sleepy Eye. Harvard Advocate 122: 18–21, 50–53, June, 1936.

A spoof on getting HLM to address the local Chautauqua.

KOBER, ARTHUR. The Grey Is Sittin' There, See, Hangin' with Her Tongue Out. New Yorker 22: 18–21, Aug. 17, 1946.

A spoof of *The American Language*.

LARDNER, RING. Pluck and Luck, or The Rise of a Home Run

King. Colliers 33: 13, 74, March 16, 1929. ports. (caricatures by Auerbach-Levy)

As a friendship might have been between HLM and Babe Ruth.

SMITH, HARRY ALLEN. Aftermath: A Wink at a Homely Girl. Esquire 51: 34-36, March, 1959.

Adventures that befell the writer as consequence of following the wish expressed by HLM in his "Epitaph."

MISCELLANY

BERREY, LESTER V. and MELVIN VAN DEN BARK, *comps.* The American Thesaurus of Slang. New York, Crowell, 1942; 5th print. with suppl. 1947.

Lists definitions for Menckenese, Menckenthusiasm and Menckenoclast.

KINGSLEY, ELIZABETH SEELMAN. Double-Crostics, No. 168. Saturday Review of Literature 16: 23, June 12, 1937.

The solution, which appeared the following week, page 19, read "H. L. Mencken. In Defense of Women." Doris Nash Wortman, Mrs. Kingsley's successor, used quotations from *The American Language: Supplement II* as No. 85 of her *Series 33*, and No. 22 of *Series 41* (New York, Simon, 1954 and 1958).

LAWRENCE, JEROME and ROBERT E. LEE. Inherit the Wind. New York, Random House, 1955, 162 p.

This successful play, which opened in Washington, D.C. April 21, 1955, deals with the Scopes trial, although all names have been changed. E. K. Hornbeck, the brash reporter, was assumed by reviewers and the public to represent HLM. The play was adapted for the screen by Nathan E. Douglas and Harold Jacob Smith, produced and directed by Stanley Kramer, released by United Artists, Oct. 1960. In the moving picture version Gene Kelly was cast as Hornbeck.

MACNAMARA, H. C. Is There an American Language? Hong Kong, Standard Press, 1938? 23 p.

Address on *The American Language* given to the Hong Kong branch of the English Association on Feb. 8, 1938.

MEYER, JEROME S. Mind Your P's and Q's. [New York] Simon, 1927. p. 116–118. facsim.

HLM's character analyzed through a study of his handwriting.

MITCHELL, LEONARD JAN. Lüchow's German Cookbook. New York, Doubleday, 1952. p. 95, 102.

Mentions some of HLM's favorite dishes.

OLYANOVA, NADYA. Handwriting Tells. New York, Covici Friede, 1936. p. 132–133; facsim. p. 85.

Character analysis through study of his handwriting.

PSEUDONYMS USED BY
H. L. MENCKEN

Pseudonyms shared by the office staff of the *Smart Set* are marked with an asterisk. The most famous one, Owen Hatteras, sometimes designated "Major," was shared by HLM and Nathan. In fact, the Major developed such a personality that when it was time to "eliminate" him, at the end of HLM's editorship, his obituary notice was carried by many newspapers.

Pseudonyms	Date Used	Magazine
Allison, George W.	1902	[Baltimore] Sunday Herald
Anderson, C. Farley	1919, 1920	Smart Set, Heliogabalus
Archer, Herbert Winslow	1914	Smart Set
Aubigny, Pierre d'	1914	Smart Set
Bell, W. L. D.	1915-1918, 1921	Smart Set
Bellamy, Atwood C.	1930	American Mercury
Brownell, Charles F.	1905	Leslie's Monthly Magazine
Brownell, John F.	1903, 1904	Frank Leslie's Popular Mag., Leslie's Monthly Magazine
Drayham, James	1923	Smart Set
*Drayham, William	1915-1919	Smart Set
Fink, William	1914-1915	Smart Set
Gilray, J. D.	1914	Smart Set
Hatteras, Amelia	1913	Smart Set
*Hatteras, Major Owen Arthur James, 1862-1923	1912-1923	Smart Set, Pistols for Two
Henderson, F. C.	1920	H. L. Mencken: Fanfare
Jefferson, Janet	1914	Smart Set
McLoughlin, R. B.	1914	Smart Set
Morgan, Harriet	1914	Smart Set
Peregoy, George Weems	1913-1914	Smart Set
Ratcliffe, James P., Ph.D.	1915-1916	Smart Set

PSEUDONYMS

The Ringmaster	1914	Town Topics, book reviews
Torre, Raoul della	1914	Smart Set
Thompson, Francis Clegg	1914	Smart Set
Trimball, W. H.	1915	Smart Set
Verdi, Marie de	1914	Smart Set
W. G. L.	1899	Bookman
Watson, Irving S.	1914	Smart Set
Wharton, James	1915	Smart Set
Woodruff, Robert W.	1914-1915	Smart Set

Probable pseudonyms suggested by Carl R. Dolmetsch in his *Index to the Smart Set Magazine, 1914-1923* (University of Chicago, 1957) are: *John Hamilton; *Henry Hugh Hunt; *Seumas LeChat; *John F. Lord; Harcourt Mountain; William Sanford; Lew Tennant; Helen Trask; Henry Trask; John Trask; *Patience Trask; Charles Vale; Robert D. Vale; *Dennison Varr.

INDEX

All books written by HLM are entered under title. Books or pamphlets for which he wrote a chapter, the introduction or preface are listed by title, author and/or editor. Only magazine articles that appeared serially are entered under the name of the series; all individual titles are omitted. The same system was followed in the Newspaper Section, which has its own separate table of contents. Newspaper series and reporter columns are listed, but not individual articles. The entire Book Review Section has been omitted as it is arranged alphabetically by the name of author reviewed, and thus entries are easily located.

Books, articles and newspaper stories about HLM listed by author only. However, for the greater convenience of the user, and to further illustrate the range of HLM's writings as well as the extent of his coverage, all magazines and newspapers to which he contributed or that printed articles about him, have been entered. There has been no attempt at indexing by subject.

INDEX

INDEX

INDEX

INDEX

INDEX

INDEX

INDEX

INDEX

INDEX

INDEX

INDEX

INDEX

INDEX